The Red Road *and*
Other Narratives *of*
the Dakota Sioux

Studies in the Anthropology of North American Indians Series

Editors
Raymond J. DeMallie
Douglas R. Parks

The Red Road *and* Other Narratives *of the* Dakota Sioux

Samuel Mniyo *and* Robert Goodvoice

Edited by Daniel M. Beveridge
With Jurgita Antoine
Foreword by David R. Miller

Published by the University of Nebraska Press, Lincoln and London,
in cooperation with the American Indian Studies Research Institute,
Indiana University, Bloomington

© 2020 by the Board of Regents of the University of Nebraska

Acknowledgments for the use of copyrighted material appear on page 220, which constitutes an extension of the copyright page.

Library of Congress Cataloging-in-Publication Data
LCCN: 2019015633

Set in MeropeBasic by Mikala R. Kolander.

Frontispiece: Samuel Mniyo. Photo by Leona Anderson, Wahpeton Dakota.

to Angelina

Contents

Part 2. The Narratives of Samuel Mniyo (Sam Buffalo)

Part 3. The Narratives of Robert Goodvoice

Illustrations

Photographs

Figures

Maps

Foreword

DAVID R. MILLER

An inevitable clash of cultures and histories marked the relations among the resident Eastern Dakota and the intermittently arriving fur traders and settlers in the eighteenth and nineteenth centuries. Initially the Dakota were able to teach many of the newcomers about what it meant to be relatives within the context of Dakota culture. This meant a basic disposition to be generous with everyone encountered. However, by the first decades of the nineteenth century it became a difficult time when subsequent generations and more newly arrived settlers did not want to understand the responsibilities of being kinsmen to the Dakota. A series of treaties manipulated the Dakota to the point of frustration that by mid-century, abetted by corruption and the increased failures of communication, thwarted any proper implementation of the treaties. Left with no lands within their traditional homelands, people rebelled, and the Dakota outbreak of 1862 resulted in a diaspora that scattered Dakota refugees from Minnesota to far-flung locations in present-day Montana, North Dakota, South Dakota, Nebraska, Saskatchewan, and Manitoba. The retribution against the Dakota was extensive, and finding new locations for their survival was gradually achieved by various groups.

My interest in learning about Dakota history began when I was researching the life of Charles Alexander Eastman, the Dakota intellectual born a mere four years before the outbreak. Naturally the previous scholarship about the Dakota outbreak and its impact on relocations of portions of the people and their culture became part of my quest. My relocation to Saskatchewan has furthered my interest in the northwestern direction taken by the diaspora of the Dakota peoples. I have been blessed to teach about this and have had many Dakota students from whom I have learned as much as I have taught. Conjointly, I met Dan Beveridge and have known him for almost three decades, and I became aware of his efforts to see the ideas and information he had learned from his Dakota friends in Saskatchewan being published at their behest. His commitment to this work has been unrelenting and admirable. The three contributions by these Dakota documentarians included in this volume are unique and revealing. Each has a different emphasis, and each is an important representation of cultural survival and persistence. The context for these texts demonstrates the extent of the Dakota struggles to reestablish themselves in locations where they could be safe.

The Dakota communities have a renewed interest in their culture, just as is occurring among those of the Assiniboine, Cree, Saulteaux, Dene, and Métis on the Canadian prairies. The information that Dan Beveridge has assembled and presented in the words of the three men will be available to be read by all interested generations. This is a contribution that will allow the subsequent development of educational materials for the schools so that younger generations in these Dakota communities can appreciate the contributions of their knowledge keepers.

Editor's Preface and Acknowledgments

DANIEL M. BEVERIDGE

This book is like a rope made up of strands representing several voices, voices from the past.

The first voice is that of Samuel Mniyo, the major author of this book. When we first met in 1962 he told me he wanted to write a book, a book with stories about the history of the Dakota people. Some years later he said, "I want to tell the story of the Dakota people as my elders and sponsors gave it to me. This book will be for the younger generation of Dakota to look at, to learn about who they are and where they came from, and for other people who are interested."

The second major voice is that of Robert Goodvoice, an uncle of Sam's. Their grandparents were among those who left their homes in Minnesota and the adjacent Dakota territories after the 1862 Dakota War and settled in what is now Canada. A knowledge keeper, he tape-recorded much Dakota oral history in the 1970s. Other voices are those of James Black (Sapa) who was a major mentor of Sam's, and Henry Two Bear. These four men (all now deceased) were members of the Wahpeton Dakota Nation, near Prince Albert, Saskatchewan, Canada. They represent four of the seven branches of the *Dakóta Oyáte* (Sioux Nation): Mdewakanton, Wahpeton, Sisseton, and Yanktonai. Another voice is my own: as editor, I see my main task as helping Sam's wish come to be fulfilled.

My hope, and I trust that I speak also on behalf of Sam, is that these strands come together in this book in a mutually reinforcing way. I trust that these voices will reach you and speak to you, the readers, with one voice about the Red Road as understood by these Dakota people.

These narratives of Dakota oral tradition tell one story of the Dakota people starting with the distant past and moving to the twentieth century. They take us back in time seven generations in the history of the *Isáŋti* Dakota people, most remarkably, to the time of the great-grandfather of Robert Goodvoice's grandfather! The central threads through this story are the *Ċaŋkú Dúta* (Red Road) and the *Wakáŋ Waċípi* (Holy Dance or Medicine Dance): their supernatural origin, evolution, importance in the society of the Dakota, and final days. A central feature of eastern

Dakota society was the *Wakáŋ Waćípi* ceremony. It persisted much longer in Canada than in the United States and was practiced until 1921 at the Wahpeton.

This book contains several unique features: one of the only two photographs of the *Wakáŋ Waćípi* known to exist; the actual songs used in the *Wakáŋ Waćípi* at the Wahpeton in the early 1900s, which may be the oldest known Dakota texts; a tracing of the *Wakáŋ Waćípi* song board that was used there and may have belonged to *Mazámani*, a Wahpeton chief and *Wakáŋ Waćípi* leader in Minnesota in the early 1800s; a participant's account of the last ever complete *Wakáŋ Waćípi* ceremony performed, in 1934; and pictographs (drawings) from notebooks used in the *Wakáŋ Waćípi* ceremony.

Other important features include the distinct voices of the Dakota authors, presented at length, with relevant photographs; an account of the origin of the *Ćaŋkú Dúta* (Red Road/Red Path), the path to a good and long life, from Robert's grandfather's great-grandfather; an account of how the Dakota people began the Sundance; some details of the 1862 Dakota War in Minnesota; the editor's placing these oral history narratives in the context of the relevant literature from early missionaries, anthropologists, archaeologists and others, augmenting the book's ethnographic or ethnohistorical value; a family tree chart and notes that take us back to Sam's great-great-grandfather and great-grandmother and show connections among the four Dakota "voices" of this book; and the storytellers' extensive use of over 230 original Dakota words, names, and concepts, which will support current efforts of Dakota language and culture revitalization.

Indigenous youth face more than their share of challenges. The future of the Dakota language is uncertain. Similar to biological diversity, the cultural diversity of small Indigenous groups in Saskatchewan and around the world is under threat from various forms of globalization and colonization. As Dakota communities seek treaties and rightful recognition for their traditional occupancy of territory north of the forty-ninth parallel, and Indigenous people become a major demographic feature of the population of Saskatchewan, their full participation in the life of the province is crucial. My hope is that this book may be of some value in illuminating part of the history of the Dakota people and thus assisting those, both Indigenous and non-Indigenous people, who are seeking to understand and recover that history.

Readers are reminded that the voices in this book reflect the realities of the times, the mid-1900s, not necessarily the present. Much has changed since then. One of the changes is terminology. Readers should not be surprised by terms such as Indians, Indian reserves, Sioux, half-breeds, etc. used by the narrators and in the literature. Some of the terminology used in the book may no longer be considered acceptable, but is retained for the purpose of historical accuracy. Further examples are given in the notes.[1]

It is possible that the expectation by the narrators that their stories would be shared with non-First Nations people influenced what they said, what they felt comfortable talking about.

Likewise, readers should be aware that attitudes and awareness regarding many subjects may have changed over the decades, among both Indigenous and non-Indigenous people, for example on assimilation policies, colonialism, "Indian" identity, Dakota self-government and autonomy, the Christian church, traditional Indigenous spiritual beliefs and practices, the role of schools, and relations between Indigenous and non-Indigenous people. Readers should not expect to find such changes reflected in this volume, where the intention is to present the voices of the narrators.

Acknowledgments

I wish to thank the many people who have contributed to this project and made it possible. I trust that I speak on behalf of Samuel Mniyo. In particular I wish to acknowledge the following community members: from the Wahpeton Dakota Nation, Leona Anderson and Shirley Goodvoice for use of photographs, Dr. Leo Omani for information, reading of the draft manuscript, encouragement, and suggestions, and Velma Buffalo and Cy Standing; from the Whitecap Dakota First Nation, the late Harry Buffalo for use of the Jim Sapa notebooks, Mavis Olson and Gene Buffalo, and Stephanie Danyluk; from the Sturgeon Lake First Nation, Eric Bird.

I am indebted to the late Fr. Gontran Laviolette, O.M.I., and the *Indian Record*, for early encouragement to write and publish an article on this subject; to the late Rev. Dr. Adam Cuthand, the late Rev. Dr. Stanley Cuthand, the late Rev. Dr. Ahab Spence, and the Rev. Nelson Hart for translating Cree syllabics in the Jim Sapa notebooks; and to Dr. Arok Wolvengrey for translating and interpreting the Cree syllabics.

I thank the people at University of Nebraska Press, Matt Bokovoy,

Heather Stauffer, Joeth Zucco, and particularly Sally Antrobus, the copy-editor, who was a real pleasure to work with. I am grateful to the University of Nebraska Press for enabling Dr. Jurgita Antoine to assist with matters related to Dakota language and culture.

Thanks go also to the Prince Albert Historical Museum (Bill Smillie, Jamie Benson, and Ron Smith) for assistance regarding the McKay family, Lucy Baker, and the King George III medal; to Louis Garcia for organizing the Henry Two Bear Papers, assisting in translating the Dakota songs, and other assistance; Dr. Mary C. Marino for suggestions regarding the Dakota language; Darlene Speidel for suggestions; and Donald Johnson and Tim Novak at the Provincial Archives of Saskatchewan.

I thank Dr. David R. Miller for encouragement, careful reading of the draft manuscript, attention to details, and suggestions. Dr. Raymond DeMallie provided major editing, and assistance on Dakota orthography came from him and Dr. Douglas Parks. I thank Dr. Jurgita Antoine for major assistance on Dakota orthography and the songs.

I am grateful to my family for their help: my brother John Beveridge for assistance with photographs; our son Danny Beveridge for assistance with the maps and editing; his partner Molly Seaton-Fast for assistance with the figures; our daughter Michelle Beveridge; and my wife Angelina for her support, understanding, and patience with my preoccupation with this project over four decades.

Finally, I feel humbled to have been able to play a small part in helping this project to happen.

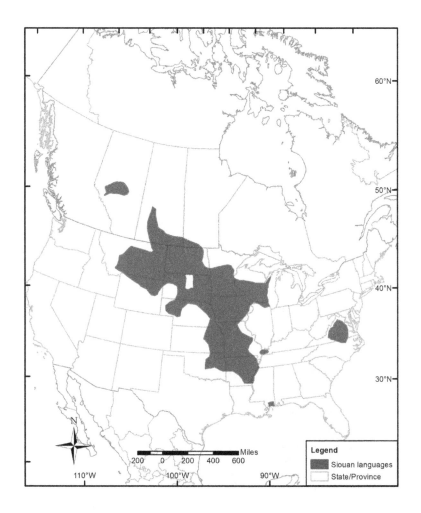

MAP 1. Pre-contact distribution of the western Siouan languages in North America. Outlier language groups shown include the Tutelo (in Virginia) and Biloxi (on the Mississippi coast), both extinct, and the Stoney (in northwestern Alberta). Linguistic and historical records indicate a possible southern origin of the Siouan people, with migrations over a thousand years ago from North Carolina and Virginia to Ohio. Some continued down the Ohio River to the Mississippi River and up to the Missouri River. Others went down the Mississippi River, settling in what are now Alabama, Mississippi, and Louisiana. Others traveled across Ohio to what are now Illinois, Wisconsin, and Minnesota, home of the Dakota. Data sources: https://en.wikipedia.org/wiki/Western_Siouan_languages (retrieved June 3, 2019); Goddard 2001, 62; Martin 2004, 69. Prepared by Danny Beveridge.

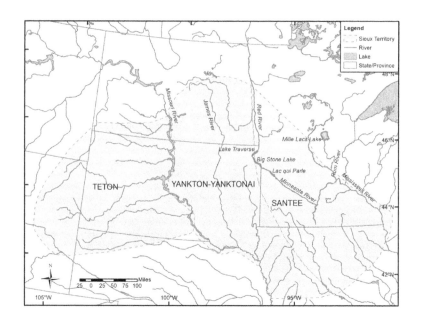

MAP 2. Sioux territory, early to mid-nineteenth century. Boundaries between the divisions suggest areas of greatest use. Neighboring tribes (not shown) include the Ojibwa (to the northeast of the Santee), the Saulteaux (north of the Yankton-Yanktonai), and the Assiniboine (northwest of the Yankton-Yanktonai). Also shown here are the lakes and rivers referred to in this book. Data source: DeMallie 2001b, 719. Used by permission of the Smithsonian Institution. Prepared by Danny Beveridge.

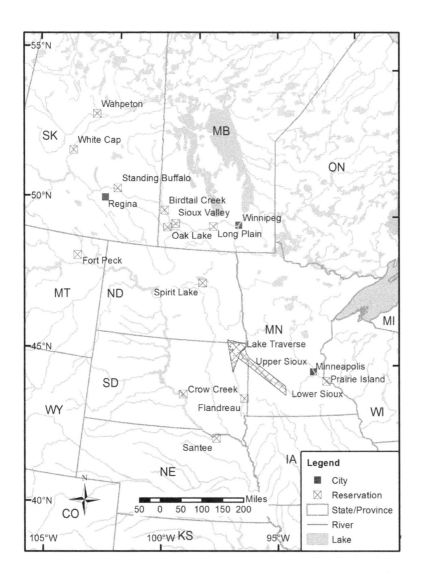

MAP 3. Santee Sioux reservations, mid-nineteenth century, and the modern reservations and reserves they occupy either alone or with other tribes. The Upper Sioux and Lower Sioux reservations were established in 1851; the portion north of the Minnesota River was ceded to the federal government in 1858 and the remainder was terminated in 1863. Data source: Albers 2001, 761. Used by permission of the Smithsonian Institution. Prepared by Danny Beveridge.

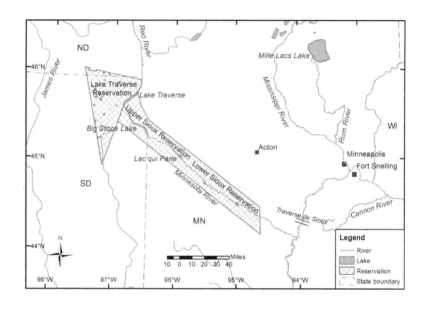

MAP 4. Santee Sioux reservations, mid-nineteenth century, in southwestern Minnesota and adjacent portions of South and North Dakota. Data source: Map 3, enlarged detail. Prepared by Danny Beveridge.

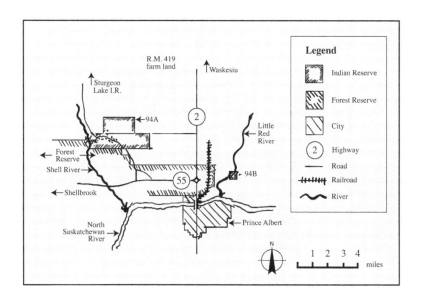

MAP 5. Wahpeton Dakota Indian Reserve 94A, formerly known as Round Plain reserve (top left); Reserve 94B, formerly known as Little Red River Sioux Camp (center right); and city of Prince Albert (lower right), about 1962. Drawn by Daniel M. Beveridge and Molly Seaton-Fast.

Abbreviations

DB	Daniel M. Beveridge
HBC	Hudson's Bay Company
PAS	Provincial Archives of Saskatchewan
RG	Robert Goodvoice
SB	Sam Buffalo/Samuel Buffalo
SM	Samuel Mniyo
WDFN	Whitecap Dakota First Nation

Part 1

Editor's Introduction

The Red Road (Ċaŋkú Dúta) and the Holy Dance (Wakáŋ Waċípi)

This book is about the Red Road (*Ċaŋkú Dúta*) and the Holy Dance (*Wakáŋ Waċípi*), two of the most important traditions of the Dakota people, as told by three Dakota men from the Wahpeton Dakota Nation near Prince Albert, Saskatchewan, Canada. These men, now all deceased, were Sam Buffalo (who later called himself Samuel Mniyo), Robert Goodvoice and James Black (Jim Sapa). They had a keen interest in passing on their knowledge and that of their grandparents and elders to present and future generations. As Sam said to me in 1997, "When I die, I don't want these stories to die with me. James Black chose me to pass on these stories." I made a promise to Sam I would keep these stories alive, and I see my main task as editor as helping to make this happen.

The Wahpeton Dakota Nation (formerly referred to as Round Plain) is one of the seven reserves in Canada obtained by Dakota Sioux coming from Minnesota and South Dakota in the United States, who sought refuge in Canada during the 1860s and 1870s. They have dwelled in Canada continuously since then but occupied the region on both sides of the 49th parallel intermittently long before that (Marino 2002, 251). The five maps in the front of this book show the border region, Sioux lands over time, and locations mentioned in the text.

The book began as an idea in Sam Buffalo's mind in the 1960s or earlier, which he mentioned when he and I first met in 1962. He presented the core of the idea in a speech at the Wahpeton Reserve cemetery on Flower Day, May 30, 1965, an occasion when Henry Two Bear, another Wahpeton resident, also spoke. After Henry Two Bear died, leaving behind a *Wakáŋ Waċípi* song stick (*Wakáŋ Dowáŋpi*) and a notebook in which he had transcribed songs used in the *Wakáŋ Waċípi* ceremony, Sam outlined the subject further, putting it to paper in a letter to me in 1966. The project was inactive for many years, and I temporarily forgot these early beginnings. The project then took on new life and developed as a narrative that Sam dictated to me in 1985, when he also made an English translation of the

Wakáŋ Waćípi songs, provided here. He added to this narrative in further sessions in the 1980s and 1990s, regarding the Red Road and the Holy Dance. I then added material from the extensive oral histories collected by Robert Goodvoice and given by Sam and Robert in 1977.[1] Sam's family tree illuminates visually the connections of the four central project participants—Sam Buffalo, Robert Goodvoice, James Black, and Henry Two Bear. Although from different generations and Dakota groups, the four were closely related (see appendix 2 for the family tree and appendix 3 for biographical sketches). After Sam's death in 1999 I added some material from books written by early missionaries, anthropologists, and others, Indigenous and non-Indigenous.

The Good Red Road means the good way of living or the path of goodness. As Robert Goodvoice says, "This is the good path of life. . . . The red path leads to life everlasting" (Howard 1984, 130). As Robert further states, the *Ćaŋkú Dúta* (Red Road or Red Path) was an important symbolic concept in the *Wakáŋ Waćípi* (Holy Dance), which has also been called the Medicine Dance or Medicine Lodge. Robert says, "One hundred and fifty different roots are used in the various medicines found in the medicine bags" (Howard 1984, 130). Sam believed that for many years the central function of the *Wakáŋ Waćípi* was to maintain and perpetuate the *Ćaŋkú Dúta* and that way of life.

The *Wakáŋ Waćípi* is an ancient Dakota ceremony of generations past. It also was widely practiced by neighboring tribes in the upper Mississippi Valley, particularly woodland peoples. Although it is no longer practiced by the Dakota, it was a central part of their tradition and probably their most important ceremonial organization, particularly for the most eastern Santee (*Isáŋti*) Dakotas, among whom this semi-secret membership society sometimes included as members more than a quarter of the population of the community. The *Wakáŋ Waćípi* society was based on a Dakota tribal origin story; its practices, following the "Red Road," were intended to lead to a long life.

For Sam, following the Red Road was not only a spiritual quest, a striving to follow the good way of living. In this book what Sam calls the Red Road Journey or the Red Road Pilgrimage and Lifestyle was also a physical journey from the Atlantic coast: it became a migration of the ancestors of the Dakota people from east to west, then a dispersal in four directions, and the eventual settling in the upper Mississippi Valley area in and around present-day Minnesota. Then it survived one final migration as some Dakota people moved north across the 49th parallel and practiced some features of this ceremony and associated way of life into the early twentieth century.

James Black (Jim Sapa) participated in what was very likely the very last complete *Wakáŋ Waćípi* ceremony of the Dakota people, in 1934. Sam gives James Black's account of that event here. Black, a relative and mentor of Sam's, was a Dakota man also from the Wahpeton Dakota Nation and, later, the Whitecap Dakota First Nation near Saskatoon, Saskatchewan (see map 3). I believe he was the artist who produced the colored drawings displayed in two notebooks (some of which are reproduced here) that were used in at least some of the *Wakáŋ Waćípi* ceremonies, either the full ceremony or the feast.

Although both Sam and Robert regretted that much knowledge had been lost and that their narratives were incomplete, we are fortunate to have their accounts of this central spiritual tradition and some other aspects of Dakota life and history. More generally, their narratives are significant in helping to illuminate the worldview of these Dakota people, including their perspective on the relationship among humans, plants, animals and the Creator—central features of Indigenous spirituality, science, and philosophy. Thus what began as Sam's narrative focused strictly on the *Wakáŋ Waćípi* and the Red Road evolved into a larger work including more context, particularly historical background, which I hope helps make it more understandable and relevant. Based primarily on oral history interviews or narration sessions, this work might be considered an ethnographic or ethnohistorical study.

Before presenting the narratives by Sam beginning in part 2, and Robert in part 3, I provide in this introduction some background on the authors whose voices form the strands running through this book; I then present an overview of the *Dakóta Oyáte* (the greater Sioux Nation) and its history, who they are and where they came from, with emphasis on what Sam called the Santee, Dakota, or eastern Sioux. I then discuss aspects of the *Ćaŋkú Dúta* (Red Road) and the *Wakáŋ Waćípi*, particularly its origin and how it was performed, as viewed by several writers. And I outline the contents of the book and discuss features of the editing and the spelling systems used here for words in the Dakota language.

Four Strands, One Rope

This book is like a rope made up of four strands, representing four voices. The first voice is that of Sam Buffalo, or, as he called himself later in his life (after about 1979), Samuel Mniyo. The second voice is my own, Dan Beveridge, based on a variety of sources. The third is that of Robert Goodvoice, and the fourth is that of an artist whose identity we don't know for certain but who I believe was Jim Sapa (James Black).

Sam Buffalo/Samuel Mniyo

The first strand, the voice of the late Samuel Mniyo, is the longest and thickest strand. Sam was a member of the Wahpeton Dakota Nation near Prince Albert, Saskatchewan. His family background is *Isáŋti*: his father was Sisseton/Wahpeton and his mother was Wahpeton. Sam was born and raised and spent most of the first fifty years of his life at the Wahpeton reserve. Robert Goodvoice, a maternal uncle of Sam's and regarded by some as the tribal historian or knowledge keeper at Wahpeton, asserts that Sam would have been chief of the reserve if the traditional hereditary system had been followed.

The first time Sam and I met was in 1962, in connection with the field work I was doing for my university graduate studies. The field work for my MA thesis in sociology (Beveridge 1964) included doing survey interviews with the residents of the four Sioux communities in Saskatchewan, which at that time were called the Round Plain, Moose Woods, Standing Buffalo, and Wood Mountain Indian Reserves.

Sam told me he wanted to write a book about some of the Dakota history and traditions passed to him by his elders. I encouraged him to do so, but I had no particular desire or expertise to be involved in that project. As the years went by, however, and I kept in contact with Sam off and on, I found myself drawn in, so that by 1987 I was working with him on this project. As Sam would talk to me of the knowledge passed to him by his elders, I would take notes or tape-record his voice, type up a draft, and give it to him to read. We would then discuss the draft and modify as needed. Sam would elaborate on the draft, and the writing process would continue intermittently over many drafts and several decades.

Although Sam refers to "the" Dakota history, "the" story of how the *Wakáŋ Waċípi* began, and "the" story of the Red Road Journey, I should point out that his is but one account of these aspects of the history of the

Dakota people. We do not claim this to be the one and only story of the Dakota people. I also should emphasize that the *Wakáŋ Waćípi*, which Sam translates as the "Holy Dance" or the "Holy Dance Society," was just one society or organization within the broader society of the Dakota peoples, not the belief system of the whole nation or tribe. It was one membership society, somewhat comparable to a fraternal lodge (e.g., Masonic Lodge, Elks Lodge, etc.) or to a denomination in the Christian Church (Presbyterian, Roman Catholic, Pentecostal, etc.). As Sam says, he is passing on to the younger generation the stories and knowledge passed to him by his elders, as faithfully as he can. He is not claiming to be a shaman, priest, prophet, or person with special powers but simply a common person wishing to pass on the traditions of his people, as he heard them, to future generations, as his elders asked him to do. The viewpoint expressed by Sam may not be the same as that held by other members of the Wahpeton and Whitecap bands.

In 1997 Sam and I had a phone conversation after one of his relatives from Moose Woods (Whitecap) came in and "asked me about our history, who was our grandmother, where did we come from, etc." Sam told me he was trying to get his tape recorder set up to record more and extend what we had started writing, "because I have other stories I haven't recorded yet. When I finish, I'll send it to you to transcribe and edit if you like that. I'll shoot for 150 pages. When I die, I don't want the stories to die with me. James Black chose me to pass on these stories" (Mniyo, March 15, 1997). Shortly after that Sam had some serious health setbacks that made self-recording impossible and interviews very difficult. He hoped that this knowledge from the past would be of value to the younger generation, not only to his own relatives and other Indigenous youth but to others who might be interested.

Sam was aware, however, that there were persons who believed one should not talk or write about *wakáŋ* subjects like the *Wakáŋ Waćípi* — that because *wakáŋ* means holy, mystery, powerful or sacred, such subjects should be left alone; that associated words, practices, and information should be allowed to die with the last believers. Several times Sam himself even doubted whether we should continue with this project, but each time he overcame his doubts and desired to continue, to pass it on. We have tried to treat the subject with proper respect, keeping in mind that this is one story of the *Isáŋti* people, about how the divine mystery was presented to them and called them to follow the Red Road, the path of goodness toward *oúŋ*, a promised land, and *odákota*, a state of peace and fellowship; about how they followed that call and that path in their physical migration or pilgrimage westward; how they searched for their destiny, and how that searching and living shaped their social organization and identity; and about how the Holy Dance as a spiritual ceremony played a key role in maintaining connection between the people and the spirit world.

Sam also was trying to understand, explain, and make sense of his own life in light of both traditional Dakota spiritual perspectives and certain Christian perspectives. Sam was perhaps attempting to combine and integrate these into his own evolving perspective. Now that he is gone, I regret that it was not possible for Sam to pass on more stories, particularly his animal stories, before his illness and pain became too severe. I am so thankful for those stories he was able to share with us.

Keeping in mind Sam's original intent to pass on the knowledge he received from elders to the younger generation, I saw the value in adding more voices to his narrative, particularly that of Robert Goodvoice, to enlarge and deepen his story of the *Isáŋti* people. I believe these voices serve to confirm and strengthen his story.

Daniel M. Beveridge

The second strand of this book is my own voice. This really involved two separate roles, that of secretary/transcriber/editor and that of researcher.

Initially I saw myself simply as a transcriber or recorder, but I soon saw this role expand into editor. As editor I was and am committed to recording Sam's material as faithfully as possible, editing it as needed, and bringing it to the public in an accessible form. In part 2 of this volume, where Samuel Mniyo/Sam Buffalo is indicated as author, the words are his, as close as possible to the words he spoke. We had "interviews" in 1985, 1986, 1987, 1988, 1996, and 1997; more correctly these were not interviews, assuming an interviewer and interviewee, but narration sessions where Sam spoke and I asked few if any questions. Most but not all narration sessions were tape-recorded. I did edit somewhat to improve readability: after the recording, transcribing, and selecting of material, this consisted, first, of rearranging content quoted from interviews, and second, of making minor grammatical changes. Since Sam sometimes discussed the same topic several times over the several interviews, I often organized the material by topic, putting together paragraphs or sentences on the same topic but from different interviews, so some duplication occurred. In cases where I felt the need to insert my own words, I indicate this in square brackets with the sign-off [DB], meaning edited by myself. I made every effort, however, to retain Sam's words, tenses, and sentences unchanged as far as possible, even though his usage of English, not his first language, appeared to me awkward at times, especially in the earlier cases, 1965 and 1977. This was partly because he was sometimes struggling to express somewhat abstract ideas in English.

I sometimes was tempted to make comments if I believed the "facts" Sam reported were inaccurate or required explanation. With a few exceptions, I decided not to interrupt, but to leave Sam's oral history narration to speak for itself to the reader.

The interviews were in English. I do not speak the Dakota language. Sam provided the Dakota words for many terms—there are probably over 230 from Sam and Robert—and spelled them for me in a simplified form (using the letters of the Roman alphabet that are used in English, without accents or diacritics). Recently, in preparation for this book, Jurgita Antoine, a linguist fluent in Lakota and Dakota, modified these words in accordance with an orthography or spelling system that is phonemically more accurate, indicating the proper sound and pronunciation (see appendix 6 for her guide to pronunciation). With the Sam Buffalo 1977 oral history transcripts, my role as editor also involved selecting material from the transcripts and rearranging it slightly according to topic. Those transcripts had been typed by Oral History Project staff from cassette tapes that Sam recorded himself in 1977 with no interviewer and passed to Robert Goodvoice (see appendix 4 for a guide to the tapes).

With Robert Goodvoice's material, my role as editor was to select material from the transcripts of the oral history cassette tapes he made in 1977 and rearrange it slightly according to topic. I often selected long quotations, not wanting to intrude on the flow of his remarkable storytelling. Because the transcripts typed by Oral History Project staff from the cassette tapes frequently did not attempt to spell out Dakota words, Jurgita Antoine made new phonemic transcriptions from the sound recordings. Although I knew Robert and had interviewed him in the 1960s, this book uses only his material from the 1977 oral history project.

As editor I provided the organization of content, including the chapters and other headings.

I also found myself in the role of researcher. On one hand, I believed that the truth value of Sam's stories as literature should stand on their own merit and not depend on whether they were "fact," fiction, or legend. It should not matter critically whether anyone else had a story similar to his. But on the other hand, because Sam made claims that certain events actually happened in Dakota history, I believed the value of his narrative would be greater if we found it was consistent with or similar to accounts reported by other sources, or at least referred to matters discussed by others. So from a starting point of knowing absolutely nothing about the *Wakáŋ Waćípi*, I began to search for more information and to research a variety of sources. This information included literature from non-Indigenous sources regarding the *Wakáŋ Waćípi* and the Dakota people who practiced it.

Particularly after Henry Two Bear died in 1966, leaving behind a *Wakáŋ Waćípi* song stick and song words written in a notebook, I felt the need to learn more about this subject. In 1967 I wrote to James Howard, an authority on Dakota culture, who was most helpful. In 1987, encouraged by Father Gontran Laviolette, editor of the *Indian Record*, I also wrote an article about the song stick, which he published.

I discovered that readers of my early drafts found it difficult to understand the *Wakáŋ Waćípi* and the Red Road and their significance without knowing something about their historical context, so I also found it necessary to research and include information on the history of the Dakota Sioux in the United States and Canada. This included the oral history of the Dakota as given by Robert Goodvoice and by Sam Buffalo in 1977 as well as a variety of other Indigenous and non-Indigenous sources. Although the central voices in this oral history book are those of Sam and Robert, I include some material from other sources to provide a context enabling better appreciation and understanding of what Sam and Robert are saying. Adding such material is not meant to analyze or discount what Sam or Robert is saying if other accounts appear different, especially on details of time and place, but rather to show that others have also discussed these subjects. Readers may not always agree with the "facts" and opinions expressed here.

As researcher, I have presented my comments in three ways. In several cases I have written a section of a chapter, clearly identifying myself as the author. In some cases I enter into the narrative with editorial comments clearly identified in square brackets. And in other cases I have used endnotes at the back of the book.

For my biographical sketch and that of Jurgita Antoine and others see appendix 3.

Robert Goodvoice

The third strand is the voice of the late Robert Goodvoice, as spoken in the Oral History Project and as recorded in 1977 in seventeen cassette audio tapes and later transcribed to paper, narrating stories that had been told to him by his grandfather and grandmother. He deserves much credit for undertaking and completing this oral history or oral tradition project. He was concerned that the history of the Wahpeton Sioux had not been recorded accurately and was distressed that the knowledge of his grandparents and their generation was being lost or had been lost already—knowledge of food preservation and hunting; of plants, herbs, medicine, and home remedies; of historical events like the war of 1812 or the uprising of 1862; of songs and games; and of Uŋktómi (spirit helper), the Red Path, the sun dance, and spiritual experiences. "Really," he said, "I would like to know and remember everything that my grandparents used to tell me and used to say. They never depended on anybody but themselves" (Robert Goodvoice 2, 1977, 14; see appendix 4 for a guide to the oral histories cited). He also was distressed that his own generation did not seem concerned about this loss, that those who had known a lot were now gone, and that he was having a hard time getting any oral history from others. Although feeling that he did not have a lot of the knowledge of his grandparents, he felt fortunate that he had learned much from them and was doing his best to get what he could on tape. It was after he was deceased that I made the decision to include material narrated by Robert; therefore I had no opportunity to discuss this book with him. I trust that he would approve.

Robert was an elder and could be considered a knowledge keeper or tribal historian of the Wahpaton Dakota Indian Reserve near Prince Albert (now called the Wahpeton Dakota Nation). I have selected certain of his narratives, particularly those that relate to the Wakáŋ Waćípi society as well as the journey of the Dakota people to the Prince Albert area from Minnesota and the 1862 Dakota War.

PHOTO 1. Robert Goodvoice, 1984. Photo courtesy Shirley Goodvoice, Wahpeton Dakota Nation.

PHOTO 2. Jim Sapa (James Black), photograph taken at Prince Albert, Saskatchewan. Glenbow Archives, Calgary, NA-3878-74.

Robert's family background is *Isáŋti*: his father was Mdewakanton and his paternal grandfather was John Sioux. His mother was Wahpeton.

Jim Sapa/James Black

The fourth strand is somewhat different from the others. It comes from an artist of the early twentieth century who provided forty-five vivid, colored images drawn in two small notebooks: thirty-three in one and twelve in the other. I viewed them and had them photographed in 1968. I refer to them as the Jim Sapa notebooks because Jim Sapa's name is written on the first page of one of the notebooks and because the notebooks were in Jim Sapa's possession until his death. It is probable that he was the artist of the images in both notebooks. Most of the images include many subjects: persons, mammals, plants, tipis, horned creatures, arrows, guns, wavy lines, and unidentifiable objects. Two other signatures appear later in the same book in which Jim Sapa's name appears: JA McKay (or JS McKay) and Dan Melvin.

Although twelve of the images are accompanied on the same page by statements written in Cree syllabics, we have determined that these sentences have nothing to do with the images and appear to have been written later. That is the conclusion of Arok Wolvengrey (e-mail to DB,

September 14, 2013) after carefully examining the photos and translating all the syllabics. Several of the Cree statements refer to Jesus. They are possibly an attempt to practice or repeat a Christian catechism, using any available paper to write on at a time when paper was not readily available.

Because the cost of printing the forty-five color images would be prohibitive, this book provides a sample set of twelve of the images in black and white.

The purpose of the images and their connection with the *Wakáŋ Waćípi* remain unclear. Although the connection of the two notebooks with this book may not be immediately obvious, we include them because Sam was certain that they were used, and by Jim Sapa, in the *Wakáŋ Waćípi* ceremonies in Saskatchewan. Perhaps further analysis may reveal a connection with the songs.

In this strand we feature the songs we assume Jim Sapa and others sang in the *Wakáŋ Waćípi* ceremonies over the years, as transcribed by Henry Two Bear and translated first by Sam, later by Louie Garcia, and finally by Jurgita Antoine. As part of this strand, Jim Sapa's account of his experience in the last known complete *Wakáŋ Waćípi* ceremony, as reported by Sam, is presented. Also included in this strand, in part 4, is the paper I wrote and published in 1987.

The *Dakóta Oyáte* (Dakota Nation)

In this volume several terms are used to describe the Dakota Sioux. *Wapahaska*, the Whitecap Dakota First Nation, one of the three Dakota First Nations in Saskatchewan, describes the Dakota Nation this way,

> The Dakota Oyate, or Dakota Nation, is a large and diverse nation of Indigenous peoples whose traditional territories spanned modern-day United States and Canada. They occupied a territory extending from modern-day western Wisconsin and Minnesota west to beyond the Missouri River and north-west to Ontario and the prairie provinces. (Danyluk et al. 2016, 2)

The Standing Buffalo Dakota Nation says, "According to oral history of the Dakota people, there was an organizational structure of all the Dakota Oyate. This structure encompassed the Seven Council Fires . . . also known as the Oceti Sakowin" (*The Story of the Dakota Oyate and the People of Standing Buffalo* 2015, 4). As Standing Buffalo oral historian Clifford Tawiyaka further explains, "The original was 12 Council Fires. . . . Then five broke away, then there were Seven Council Fires. The seven who remained a united group were: The Wahpekute, Sisseton, Ihankton, Ihanktonwanna, Teton, Wahpeton and Mdewakanton" (4).

By the time of first European contact in present-day southern Minnesota about 1650 they had already divided into three major groups: the Dakota or Santee or Eastern Sioux, which comprised the Mdewakanton, Wahpekute, Wahpeton and Sisseton councils; the Yankton-Yanktonai or Middle Sioux; and the Lakota or Teton or Western Sioux (see map 2). They all speak the same language and call themselves *Dakóta* or *Lakóta*, depending on their dialect. The Santee speak the Santee-Sisseton dialect and call themselves Dakota; the Yankton and Yanktonai speak the Yankton-Yanktonai dialect and also call themselves Dakota; and the Teton speak the Teton dialect and call themselves Lakota. In this book we sometimes use the term Sioux as Sam does to refer to the larger entity of all three groups (all seven councils) and the terms Dakota (*Dakóta*) and Santee (*Isáŋti*) for the Eastern Sioux. The word *Dakóta* means friend or ally and comes from the word *kodá* in the Dakota dialect.

The term Sioux was not what the people called themselves, nor is it today in Canada, but came into English from the abbreviated French plural form of the Ojibwa (Chippewa) name, *Nadoues-sioux*. This word has been widely assumed to mean a lesser adder, hence an enemy.[2] The people themselves and many writers use the term Dakota (or Lakota) in preference to Sioux because they consider the term Sioux to be derogatory. The term Sioux still is widely used, however, by governments, academics, and others.

The locations of the Dakota or Santee reservations in the United States and the seven (formerly eight) reserves in Canada are shown on map 3. Many Dakota also live off reserves in urban centers. The Dakota have dwelled continuously in Canada since the mid-1860s, but they occupied the region intermittently long before that (Marino 2002, 251).

Despite early and ongoing claims to the contrary, the Yankton-Yanktonai do not call themselves Nakota (Parks and DeMallie 1992, 234). The Assiniboine and Stoney do call themselves Nakota or Nakoda but are not considered Sioux. Although their dialects share a common origin with the three Sioux dialects, several hundred years ago and before European contact they separated and began evolving to be distinctly different, so much so that the Stoney dialect may now be considered a separate language (Parks and DeMallie 1992, 21).

The Sioux form the largest nation of the Siouan language family, which also includes the Assiniboine, Stoney, Crow, Mandan, Hidatsa, and others on the Plains as well as the Winnebago in Wisconsin and, formerly, the Biloxi in Mississippi and the Tutelo and several other small groups in North Carolina and Virginia. The Siouan language family extends from what are now South and North Carolina, Virginia, and the Gulf region to the upper Mississippi and the Plains and into Saskatchewan and northwestern Alberta (see map 1). Dakota stories in this volume suggest that this wide distribution might be the result of westward migration in ancient times, possibly from North or South Carolina, then a dispersal in different directions, including movement by the Dakota to the upper Mississippi River area in Minnesota. This was followed in historic times by a westward movement of the Lakota and Dakota from the edge of the woodlands toward the prairies and the plains.

First contact of the Dakota with Europeans was in the mid-1600s with the French, who claimed possession of all the interior of North America and exercised control from 1534 to 1763. What they called Canada or New France extended up the St. Lawrence River through the Great Lakes and down the Mississippi to Louisiana. Jean Nicollet in 1640 first records the presence of the Sioux when visiting the Winnebago in present-day Wisconsin, calling them the *Nadisieu*. In 1660 the explorer Pierre-Esprit Radisson was the first who actually contacted the Dakota, in present eastern Minnesota, calling them the Nation of the Beefs because they made their livelihood by hunting buffalo (DeMallie 2001, 719). In 1680 a longer contact was with Father Louis Hennepin, who was captured by the Mdewakanton Dakota, the most easterly Dakota group (Elias 1988, 5), He was taken to their village near the mouth of the Rum River on Mille Lacs Lake, in north-central Minnesota east of the Mississippi River (see maps 2 and 4). A map drawn in 1697 by Franquelin based on information provided by Le Sueur shows twenty-two villages and labels "Sioux of the East" and "Sioux of the West" on either side of the Mississippi River. "In the mid-1600s Sioux territory stretched from the coniferous forests around Mille Lacs, through the deciduous forests and open grasslands-forests that followed the Mississippi and Minnesota Rivers, and across the tall-grass prairies of western Minnesota and eastern North and South Dakota to the Missouri River" (DeMallie 2001, 719–20).

The estimated population of the Sioux nation declined from about 38,000 at the time of first contact with Europeans to about 25,000 in 1805; much of this decline was due to epidemics of disease brought by the Europeans, particularly smallpox, to which the Indigenous people had little or no resistance (Anderson 1997, 22).

Through the 1700s there was a general movement westward of all three Sioux groups for several reasons: to follow the buffalo, which had ranged east of the Mississippi but were contracting westward in their range; to move away from the Ojibwa and Cree, who were better armed and were pressing in from the north and east; and to get closer to French and other traders, who were coming up the Missouri and tributaries. By 1736 most of the Sioux lived west of the Mississippi (DeMallie 2001b, 722).

The seven tribes or councils (*Očéti Šakówiŋ*) are listed here, using both the common anglicized names and the names spelled with the Dakota orthography, indicating proper pronunciation, used in this volume.[3] Assuming their main location in the early 1800s, and going roughly from east to west, from the Mississippi River in present-day Minnesota westward to beyond the Missouri River (see maps 2 and 3), they are:

Eastern Sioux, Dakota or Santee (4 councils)

Mdewakanton	*Mdewákaŋtuŋwaŋ*, Spirit Lake dwellers
Wahpekute	*Waȟpékute*, Shooters among the deciduous leaves
Wahpeton	*Waȟpétuŋwaŋ*, Village among the deciduous leaves
Sisseton	*Sisítuŋwaŋ* or Village among the fisheries

Middle Sioux, or *Wičíyena* (2 councils)

Yankton	*Iháŋktuŋwaŋ*, Dwellers at End Village
Yanktonai	*Iháŋktuŋwaŋna*, Dwellers at Little End Village

Western Sioux or Lakota (1 council)

Teton	*Títuŋwaŋ*, Dwellers on the prairies

The general name for the Dakota people (*Isáŋti*, *Isáŋati* or Santee, meaning dwellers at the knife), was derived from a lake they called *Isáŋtamde* (Knife Lake), southeast of Mille Lacs Lake in Minnesota (Pond 1986, 175). The term *Isáŋti* applied first to the particular Mdewakanton band located at Knife Lake, and then to all the Mdewakanton for a time. Then the term Santee came to be used by the Teton and the Europeans ("whites" or *wašíču*) to apply to all four Dakota or Eastern Sioux councils (Oneroad and Skinner 2003, 60–61). The Mdewakantonwan council took its name from the lake called *Mde Wakáŋ* (Spirit Lake), which is now called Mille Lacs Lake in Minnesota (Pond 1986, 175).

Trade and their "middleman" role in trade were very important for the Santee (Dakota). In the 1790s and the early 1800s, and probably earlier, an annual trade fair took place in May, generally on the James River in what is now eastern South Dakota (see maps 2 and 4). All seven councils or tribes came, and they camped at specific positions in one or two large circles, as many as 1,200 or 2,000 lodges and about 3,000 men bearing arms.[4] They referred to themselves then as the Seven Council Fires (Maroukis 2004, 12).

The gathering served as a time of social and spiritual renewal in addition to being a trade fair. The Tetons from the west and the Yanktonais came bringing horses and leather items—buffalo hide tipi coverings, buffalo robes, and antelope skin leggings and shirts—to trade with the "middlemen" Santees for guns, iron kettles, and other European trade goods (Maroukis 2004, 12), which the Santees had obtained from Canadian traders from the Montreal-based North West Company in exchange for furs (McCrady 2006, 2). Although the most westerly tribes depended very much on the buffalo, all four Santee tribes participated in one or more buffalo hunts in the summer.

The creation and maintenance of alliances also were important to the Dakota Nation. As the Whitecap Dakota First Nation states,

> Negotiating space with other Indigenous peoples, and later with European powers and settler populations, was integral to the continued success and prosperity of the Dakota. Intermarriage with other nations enabled the Dakota to strengthen their alliances and make peace with their neighbours. From these personal family bonds came powerful relationships and alliances between nations: these relationships also encouraged trade and collaboration. This practice continued with the arrival of Europeans into Dakota territory. (Danyluk et al. 2016, 5)

The Dakota made a number of treaties of peace, friendship, and trade with the French and later the British rulers of what became Canada, treaties that were sometimes accompanied by military support (see appendix 1 for selected events on a Santee history timeline). It was to protect their economy, territory, and sovereignty that the Santee supported the British militarily against the Americans in both the American War of Independence (1775–83) and the War of 1812, including the seizing and holding of Michilimackinac (McCrady 2006, 9). A number of Dakota chiefs, including *Húpa Iyáȟpeya*'s father Flying Thunder, received King George III medals in recognition of their loyalty and support. *Húpa Iyáȟpeya* was later to lead a group of Santee from the northern Minnesota borderlands to Prince Albert to establish a new home.

The alliance of Dakota Nations with the British Crown in the War of 1812 is a central part of the history of Saskatchewan Dakota Nations. In her discussion of the First Nations alliance with the British Crown in the War of 1812, Danyluk argues that "promises made during the War of 1812 were an extension of a long-standing treaty relationship between the Crown and First Nations, whereby the former recognized the autonomy, sovereignty and territory of Western [First] Nations" (Danyluk 2014, 241). She shows "how the Crown's promises constituted a treaty from a First Nations perspective" (241). In a speech delivered by Robert Dickson at a council at Michilimackinac in January 1813 he declared, "The object of the war is to secure to the Indian Nations the boundaries of their territories" (243). As Danyluk maintains, "In the minds of the First Nations people, these were solemn treaty promises. With the signing of the Treaty of Ghent [in 1814], however, the Crown's promises were left unfulfilled. The territory of the Western nations was handed over to the Americans" (243). British commander Lieutenant-Colonel McDouall called this a breach of faith. As Danyluk says, his words indicate the blatant disregard of promises to protect the sovereignty, territory, rights, and privileges of these allies (246). As discussed later, this betrayal was further magnified when the Dakota came north across the forty-ninth parallel after the Dakota War of 1862.

McCrady (2006, 2) maintains that it is useful to recognize the Sioux not only as American Indians but as people of the Canadian-American "borderlands," both in terms of their political relationships, as already mentioned, and as regards the territory of which they made use.

Regarding the extent of traditional Dakota territory, two perspectives are recognized in this volume. The predominant view in the academic and popular literature locates this territory mainly if not entirely in what is now the United States. According to this view, the Dakota or Santee territory of greatest use in the early 1800s, as shown in map 2, includes the southwestern two-thirds of what is now Minnesota, and the adjoining portion of eastern North Dakota and South Dakota, as well as a portion of western Wisconsin and a part of northern Iowa.

Many Dakota in Canada hold a different perspective. As stated in the recent Wahpeton Dakota Nation Community History,

> The history of the Dakota in Canada as described by non-Dakota scholars differs markedly from the oral history passed down by the Dakota people themselves. A central disagreement has to do with territory. Dakota in Canada maintain their traditional territory has always included part of what is now Canada. . . . In addition to oral history, there are written historical accounts, treaties signed between the Dakota Oyate and the French and British Crowns, Dakota language place names, and archaeological sites that all support the Dakota territorial claim. (Wahpeton Dakota Nation 2012, 14–15)[5]

The Dakota maintain that they had a substantial presence in Canada: that in the mid-1800s, those Dakota who came north into Canada were returning to a territory with which they were familiar and following their former routes used in hunting, trading, and war raids.

Whitecap Dakota First Nation has developed educational lessons and instructional resources for Kindergarten to grade 8: "Exploring Dakota History, Language and Culture." Included in the material on "Historic Dakota Territory and Land Use" are maps that show numerous locations of Dakota presence in what is now Canada from 1750 to 1900. The unit also explains,

> Written sources from European newcomers cannot be relied upon as accurate descriptions of Dakota territory, as areas such as the Great Plains and the Missouri Coteau were unoccupied by settler presence until the 1870's. Since much of the research on the Dakota has relied on written European sources, this has skewed the perception of Dakota patterns of land use. (https://dakotalessons.ca/wp-content/uploads/2018/01/Dakota-Territory-Information.pdf)

Archaeological and archival evidence indicates that in the 1700s, although Minnesota remained the primary land base for the Dakota, their territory of frequent use was considerably larger, particularly before the smallpox epidemic of 1781–82 on the northern plains.

Pond claims that when first discovered by the French, many Dakota were living northwest of Lake Superior (Pond 1986, 174). At various times during the 1600s and 1700s the Dakota occupied and controlled the area from Lake Superior in the northeast to Lake Winnipeg and the Red River in the west.

Excavation of the Rum River site near Mille Lacs Lake revealed pottery, mentioned by Hennepin, made by the *Isáŋti* and named Sandy Lake ware by archaeologists. Sandy Lake ware has been found in thirty-four sites in Wisconsin, Minnesota, western Ontario, and eastern Manitoba, indicating Dakota presence. This is supported by reports by "the earliest [European] travellers in the western regions of the Great Lakes [who] placed the Dakota in the territory that Sandy Lake ware was found" (Elias 1988, 3–5).

The Dakota also had a presence farther west in present western Manitoba and Saskatchewan during buffalo hunts, trading expeditions, and war raids, as indicated by place names, fur trader records, and Cree and Dakota oral tradition. Much of this was related to the trade and diplomatic relations they had with the French until 1763, and then with the British.

In 1670 the British had established the Hudson's Bay Company (HBC), chartered to operate in the Hudson's Bay watershed they called Rupert's Land. In the same period the French traders in the Montreal-Indian-French trading network entered the area as competitors. This rivalry had a significant impact on the Dakota and their relationship with their northern neighbors, the Assiniboine and Cree, who had established a "middleman" role in the HBC fur trade (Ray 1974, 14).

According to Cree oral history, place names, and interviews, the Dakota went on numerous war raids in northern Saskatchewan in the 1700s.[6]

Another consideration regarding the territory of the Dakota in the 1700s was the great smallpox epidemic of 1781–82. It was devastating in its impact on the American and Canadian northern plains and western woodland region. "By 1783 it had reached the Indians of the West, killing much of the population" (Cadotte 1985, 587). This depopulation massively disrupted whatever earlier Dakota occupation might have existed in what is now Saskatchewan. "In 1781, the estimated Dakota population was 25,000. By the end of 1782, approximately 95 percent of the Dakota population was decimated by smallpox, with a remaining Dakota population of 4,200" (Dwayne Stonechild, quoted in Omani 2010, 105). This led to huge population shifts as survivors moved south and other groups moved in, particularly the Cree and Ojibwa, from the east and northeast, in the early 1800s. "By the early nineteenth century, the Dakota had withdrawn from these northern territories" (Elias 1988, 6). Some of the Dakota survivors intermarried with the Cree.

Omani (2010) claims, based on his oral history interviews, that *Húpa Iyáȟpeya's* Wahpeton ancestors in the 1700s occupied territory along the Saskatchewan River and Churchill River in north-central Saskatchewan until they were almost wiped out by the smallpox epidemic in 1781–82 and withdrew to their traditional Lake of the Woods territory. After the 1862 war it was from this region in the deep woods of northeastern Minnesota that *Húpa Iyáȟpeya* had led a group of Wahpetons and Mdewakantons back to the Prince Albert area in 1876 (Elias 1988, 29).

Despite the major population loss from smallpox, written journals of U.S., British, and French Canadian fur traders from the 1790s to 1820 make reference to the presence of the Dakota or Sioux as occupying territory above the 49th parallel along the valleys of the Souris, Red, Assiniboine, and Qu'Appelle Rivers in present-day southern Manitoba and Saskatchewan (Omani 2011, 18), "although whether other aboriginal occupants recognized the territories as theirs cannot now be established" (Marino 2002, 253).

Samuel Pond was a missionary who spent considerable time with the Dakota in Minnesota. He spent time at Lac qui Parle and Lake Traverse in 1834. In his ethnography *The Dakota or Sioux in Minnesota as They Were in 1834*, he describes the five councils with which he was familiar (he does not describe the Ihanktonwanna or the Teton, who lived farther west). He says:

Although the language, manners, and dress of the different divisions were not precisely alike, they were essentially one people. Nor were these people of Minnesota separate from the rest of the Dakota nation, but were closely connected with those living farther west. They considered themselves as forming part of a great people, which owned a vast region of country, extending from the upper Mississippi to the Rocky Mountains.

They thought, and not without reason, that there was no other Indian nation so numerous or so powerful as the Dakota nation. . . .

The reader will bear in mind that the Dakotas or Sioux of Minnesota formed but a small fraction of the nation to which they belonged, and were not distinct from the rest of their people. (Pond 1986, 4)

In the early 1800s the primary ecosystem of the Dakota was the zone of mixed grassland and woodland of the upper Mississippi watershed: the upper Mississippi Valley, the Minnesota River Valley, and several large wooded oases. At that time the four Santee tribes had a highly successful mixed economy based on this ecosystem, depending primarily on hunting, fishing, and the harvesting of wild plants, with a very limited amount of horticulture (Marino 2002, 22). Wild game was still relatively abundant. They were highly mobile, but they returned to specific localities for certain resources at certain times of the year, creating an annual cycle of movement. This included harvesting wild rice in the lakes and wetlands and their planted corn in the fall, hunting deer in the northeast forest in the late fall and winter, procuring fish and returning waterfowl near their semi-permanent villages along rivers and lakes in the spring, and hunting bison on the prairie grasslands in the southwestern part of their territory in the summer (Anderson 1997, 2–7).

This ecoregion, transitional between the boreal forest and the prairie grasslands, extends northwest from Wisconsin through Minnesota to Manitoba and Saskatchewan. When many of the Dakota and Lakota moved north after 1862 and 1876 to what is now Canada, they eventually obtained reserves in similar ecological surroundings to what they were skilled in using: the Mdewakanton at the edge of the boreal forest, the Wahpeton in forest and parkland, the Sisseton in parkland and prairie, and the Teton on open prairie (Elias 1988, 29).

Regarding food, Pond states, "Before the sale of their lands east of the Mississippi in 1837, the Dakotas of Minnesota lived almost exclusively on the products of the chase and fishing, with such vegetable food as grew spontaneously" (Pond 1986, 26). He reports that they did raise corn at Lake Traverse (26–28). They gathered considerable quantities of vegetable food they found growing wild. The most important were *mdo* or *bdo* (wild potato, more like sweet potato); *psincha* (a spherical root) and *psinchincha* (an egg-shaped root), both growing at the bottom of shallow lakes; wild turnip; water-lily; and wild rice (26–28). Ruth Landes, who did field work among the Mdewakantonwan in Minnesota in 1935, refers to the traditional foods Pond mentions as well as "berries, cherries, plums, nuts, and plants neglected by whites." She reports that foods gathered by the Prairie Island women in 1935 included wild potatoes (*bedo*), wild onions, turnips (*tipsina*), and wild beans obtained by raiding the underground storehouses of field mice (Landes 1968a, 202–3). Eastman reports: "When our people lived in Minnesota, a good part of their natural subsistence was furnished by the wild rice, which grew abundantly in all that region. . . . The wild rice harvesters came in groups of fifteen to twenty families to a lake. . . . Some of the Indians hunted buffalo upon the prairie at this season, but there were more who preferred to go to the lakes to gather wild rice, fish, gather berries and hunt the deer. There was an abundance of water-fowls among the grain; and really no season of the year was happier than this" (Eastman 1971, 200).

In terms of culture the Dakota were considered Plains Indians but were influenced by Woodland Indians, for example in their use of floral designs and their practice of the Medicine Lodge (Deloria 1998, 17). By the early 1800s the Dakota villages in Minnesota were relatively settled. Pond estimates the Dakota population in 1834 as about 7,000, living within the area of Minnesota and in the part of South Dakota closely adjoining Big Stone Lake and Lake Traverse: 2,000 "Medawakantonwan" and "Wahpekuta," 4,000 "Wahpetonwan" and "Sissetonwan," and perhaps 1,000 "Ihanktonwan." This figure does not include those tribes living farther west, the "Ihanktonwanna" (Yanktonai) and the "Titonwan" (Teton). The Teton population had grown to make up more than two-thirds of the total Sioux nation by the mid-1800s (Landes 1968a, 13).

In 1834 the Mdewakanton lived the farthest east on the lower Minnesota River and nearby upper Mississippi River (see map 4) in seven distinct bands (Wallis 1947, 9). They hunted deer in the forest areas, used canoes for wild rice harvesting (often traded from the Ojibwa for guns and blankets (Westerman and White 2012, 115), and lived most like woodland people. The homes in their large summer villages were rectangular and made of wood and bark, while their winter homes were tipis of hides, which they moved often.

The Wahpekutes, a smaller group, were in villages southeast on the

Cannon River (near present Faribault) with about 150 warriors. They lived much like the Wahpeton.

The lower Wahpetons were located on the lower Minnesota River. They lived more like the Mdewakanton than like the Sisseton. Although they participated in summer buffalo hunts on the plains to the west, they spent time in the forests to the northeast hunting deer in the winter and used the numerous small lakes for fishing, duck hunting and wild rice harvesting in the spring and fall. The upper Wahpeton villages were on Lac qui Parle on the upper Minnesota River.

The lower Sissetons occupied the region around Traverse des Sioux, Swan Lake, and the Cottonwood River, extending west to the Coteau des Prairies (see map 4). The upper Sissetons lived farthest west on the upper Minnesota River on Big Stone Lake and Lake Traverse (Wallis 1947, 9) and on the prairies and the coteau west of Lac qui Parle, Big Stone Lake and Lake Traverse in present South Dakota. They hunted buffalo, used horses to some extent, associated with the Yankton and Yanktonai farther west, and lived most like plains people and least like woodland people.

There was considerable intermingling and intermarriage among the four Santee tribes, some with the Yankton-Yanktonai (particularly by the Sisseton), and even some annual contact with the Teton who lived farthest west, mostly on the plains west of the Missouri River.

The population soon declined drastically, however. After the smallpox epidemic of 1837 and the disappearance of most game and fur-bearing animals from their lands, the Indian agent Taliaferro reported that the population of Wahpetons was only 750, of Sissetons was 1,500, and of Wahpekutes was 325 (Anderson 1997, 162), for a total of 2,575. This compares with the figures of 7,000 for 1834 and 25,000 for 1805 cited earlier.

In the mid-1800s another drastic change occurred as the pressure from Americans for land increased. "The Santee moved from a state of self-sufficiency and autonomy to one of destitution and dependence" (Albers 2001, 769). Dakota were forced to give up most of their territory in Minnesota through treaties, particularly the Treaty of Traverse des Sioux and the Treaty of Mendota in 1851. Most Dakota then were confined to the Lower Sioux Agency and Upper Sioux Agency, a narrow strip of land along the Upper Minnesota River (Elias 1988, 3–6). By another treaty in 1858 the portion (about half) of that reservation northeast of the river was also ceded and opened for settlement.

In 1862 a small number of Mdewakanton Dakota could no longer endure the ill treatment, food shortages, and treaty violations, and they staged an uprising against the *wašíču* (white men) in an attempt to regain their lands. They killed traders, Indian agency employees, and white settlers, men, women and children. At least four hundred civilians (and possibly six hundred or more) lost their lives, and about one hundred women and children were taken captive during the four days. The Dakota War of 1862 began at Acton, Minnesota, on August 17 and had been crushed in the settled areas by the American troops and militia by September 23. Of the Dakota who surrendered and were tried by a military commission, 303 were condemned to death. The federal government in Washington intervened, Abraham Lincoln selected thirty-nine men for the death sentence, and thirty-eight were hanged at Mankato, Minnesota, in the largest mass execution in American history. The remaining Dakota in captivity then were removed from the state. Some were imprisoned. Many died of starvation or exposure before or after being put on reservations on the prairies along the Missouri River (Anderson 1986, 139, 164–65). The desire for vengeance by the *wašíču* was strong. The Sisseton and Wahpeton who were not involved in the uprising fled Minnesota somewhat later, when it became apparent that Minnesota Governor Ramsey "intended to make real his vow to eliminate every Dakota in the territory" (Elias 1988, 20). The Dakota treaties were revoked unilaterally and the land was confiscated. Anderson in his book *Little Crow* (1986) discusses the causes of this uprising. These include a desperate shortage of food, even verging on starvation, suffered by the thousands of Dakota in the Upper (Yellow Medicine) Agency and the Lower (Redwood) Agency along the Minnesota River in early 1862, exacerbated by the tremendous increase of white population just outside the borders of the reservations, settlers who harvested what little game remained. There was also dissatisfaction among the Dakota that the government annuity cash payment and promised food were overdue, exacerbated by knowing that the traders' stores were full of goods and food while the government warehouse was empty (except for some food kept for the white employees and for farmer Indians). There was anger with the manner in which the government agent handled annuity distributions of money and food; anger at traders for ongoing unjust practices and for denying credit; and a growing perception that the traders were ignoring their kinship responsibilities (all had Dakota wives) and were treating their trade only as a business. Another factor was development of a soldiers' lodge of angry young men who, particularly after the killing of the settlers near Acton, wanted to launch a full-scale war to drive the whites from the Minnesota Valley.[7] They wanted to recapture their hunting ground and destroy the hated farm program that divided the Dakota people into farmer Indians and hunter "blanket" Indians. Pertinent, too, was the willingness of Little Crow, as chief, to join the young men in going to war and to sacrifice his life for his community, even though he believed it was the wrong decision (Anderson 1986, 116–34). The 1862 Dakota War is also known as the Minnesota Uprising, and its causes are discussed also by Elias (1988, 16), Howard (1984, 25), Oneroad and Skinner (2003, 8), and Westerman and White (2012, 193 ff.).

About four thousand Santee, fearing retribution, fled from Minnesota into Dakota Territory. Generals Sibley and Sully led campaigns to pursue and capture them. At the Battle of Whitestone Hill in 1863, for example, Sully defeated one village, killing or wounding hundreds of Dakota, men, women, and children. The Yanktonai Chief Two Bear, who played a role in the battle, was the grandfather of Henry Two Bear, who moved to the Wahpeton reserve in Canada and is featured in this book.

By the 1867 Treaty of Lake Traverse the Lake Traverse Reservation or Sisseton Reservation was established, primarily in northeast South Dakota, mainly for those Dakota considered loyal to the U.S. government in the 1862 war.

Perhaps a thousand Dakota moved north and crossed the "medicine line" that separated the British and the Americans, some in 1862 and some later. The Sissetons and Wahpetons, most of them innocent, had fled before the advance of General Sibley, and led a nomadic life in Dakota Territory and in Canada's Northwest Territory. They sought the protection of the British, initially in the Red River settlement at Fort Garry, and the right to be on British soil. They said King George III had promised the Dakota help because of their support for the British in the War of 1812, and they showed medals given to them to recognize that support.[8] The Dakota were allowed to locate and eventually obtain reserves in what became Manitoba and Saskatchewan (Elias 1988, 3–6).

Of the nine Sioux First Nations (Indian Reserve) communities in Canada, eight were established by the Santee Dakota (with some Yankton-

Yanktonai) who came north after the Minnesota Uprising of 1862: five in present Manitoba and three in Saskatchewan. The remaining one was established by the Teton (Lakota), remnants of those who came north with Chief Sitting Bull, the Hunkpapa Lakota leader, after the Custer Battle of 1876: that community is near Wood Mountain, Saskatchewan.

The government of Canada regarded the Dakota as American Indians, as refugees from the United States, and therefore refused to enter into any treaty with them, but granted them some land for reserves on a humanitarian basis, although less land per family (80 acres) than that granted to treaty Indians (640 acres for Treaty 6); as noted in the recent Whitecap community history, "To the Dakota, there is a bitter irony in this: the Dakota had joined forces with the British to help successfully repel the Americans, only to then have their land abandoned by the British and given to the Americans as part of the peace that followed. The Dakota only became 'American Indians' against their will and as a result of their betrayal by the British Crown."[9] As expressed by one elder from Whitecap in a recent oral history study, "our older Dakota people used to say, . . . we didn't cross any borders, they crossed us!" (Omani 2010, 147). The Canadian government eventually applied similar policies to them as to the treaty Indians, including the Indian Act of 1876, except for the annual treaty payments and the much smaller land base. (see appendix 1) The three Santee reserves in Saskatchewan were Standing Buffalo (Standing Buffalo Dakota Nation), Moose Woods (later called Whitecap Dakota First Nation) and Round Plain (later called Wahpeton Dakota Nation).

As explained by the Provincial Archives of Saskatchewan (PAS) in their Documenting the Dakota exhibit, the Canadian government thus not only denied the Dakota people treaty status but by calling them Indians under the Indian Act denied them the right to obtain land as non-Indigenous settlers did through purchase and the provisions of the Homestead Act (https://www.saskarchives.com/Dakote_Land).

Reserves for treaty Indians were established in Saskatchewan in the 1870s through the "numbered treaties," particularly Treaty 4 in 1874 at Fort Qu'Appelle and Treaty 6 in 1876 at Fort Carlton. Reserves for the (non-treaty) Dakota were established in the 1890s: Standing Buffalo and Whitecap (at Moose Woods) were surveyed in 1880 and 1881, and Wahpeton reserve was established in 1894.

By the mid-1870s the population of the Santee (Dakota) in western Canada was about 1,780 (Elias 1988, 37).

After 1862, for about twelve years, the Dakota (mostly Sisseton) led by *Ṫaṫáŋka Nájiŋ* (Standing Buffalo) the Elder and *Wapáhaska* (Whitecap) had been able to carry on a nomadic, hunting lifestyle on both sides of the international boundary, particularly in present-day southeast Saskatchewan. As McCrady points out, as "borderlands people," not only did they cross back and forth many times in hunting buffalo and trading but they exploited the boundary tactically (2006, 3–4). For example, they could obtain firearms and ammunition, contraband in the United States, from Metis Canadian traders. Knowing the American troops could not follow them across, they could remain close enough to the border to evade the American authorities if they were pursued. By the mid-1870s, however, as the buffalo population dwindled and settlers began to trickle in, and as Treaty 4 was being negotiated by Canada with the Cree and Saulteaux (Plains Ojibwa) in 1874, they realized they needed to obtain their own lands. Chief *Ṫaṫáŋka Nájiŋ* (Standing Buffalo) the Elder had led his Sisseton band from Minnesota after 1862. After his death in 1866 his son, *Ṫaṫáŋka Nájiŋ* (Standing Buffalo) the Younger, led the band and chose the present location of the reserve near present-day Fort Qu'Appelle, Saskatchewan.

In 1878 these two separate bands (about two hundred and one hundred persons respectively) briefly attempted to occupy the land selected by Standing Buffalo where the Jumping Deer Creek joins the Qu'Appelle River, but they did not get along together. So Whitecap and his band, including his son *Bdo* (or *Biddow*), moved north to another location Whitecap was familiar with along the South Saskatchewan River (*Bdo* continued on to Prince Albert). The two reserves were surveyed, and after delays in receiving the farming equipment and other support promised by the Canadian government, they began to be self-supporting (Elias 1988).

As Elias points out, the Wahpeton Dakota Reserve near Prince Albert was formed by three different groups. One group was led by *Bdo* (considered as a headman, not a chief, by the Dakota), was mainly Sisseton, and was the band for whom the Round Plain reserve on the Shell River northwest of Prince Albert was secured. A second band was led by *Ahíyaŋke* and were Wahpeton who had come from Fort Ellice. These two groups lived together much of the time, although they saw themselves as separate entities, and moved into the present reserve initially about 1894 to 1898. A third group, led by Chief *Húpa Iyáȟpeya*, were Wahpeton and Mdewakanton. They had arrived in the Prince Albert area first, in 1877, but were moved later, after 1917, from the Little Red River 94B site to the Round Plain 94A site (Elias 1988, 204–210). Elias says the documentary record for the *Ahíyaŋke* band disappears in 1894; Leo Omani claims that when the children went to an Indian residential school in Regina, many got scurvy and died, and the few remaining were absorbed into the other two groups (Omani, interview with DB, September 13, 2007; the school was probably Regina Indian Industrial School, 1891–1910).

To conclude this discussion of the history of the Dakota Nations in Canada, the question of sovereignty and treaty status still has not been resolved, at least not yet. "Canadian Dakota claims to aboriginal occupation north of the 49th parallel have been central in their relations with both the Canadian and the US governments" (Marino 2002, 253).

The Dakota communities have long sought to negotiate improvement in their situation, to obtain recognition, land, and other resources. "It is important to note that because they have not signed a treaty, Whitecap Dakota First Nation has not ceded any of their Aboriginal rights and title" (WDFN Whitecap Dakota lessons 2019). A framework agreement for a Whitecap Dakota treaty to advance Dakota reconciliation was signed on January 22, 2018, between Whitecap Dakota First Nation chief and councilors and Canada's minister of Indian Affairs and Northern Development (see 2018 item in appendix 1). According to Chief Darcy Bear, "The main objectives for the First Nation in treaty negotiations are to acquire a larger land base for sustainable growth, money for economic development, capital projects and protecting language and culture and to be recognized as a Treaty First Nation" (Whitecap Dakota First Nation signs framework agreement for treaty with Canada, January 22, 2018).

Early Migration Theories

In this book Sam and Robert take us back many generations, to the distant past, to the very early times of the Dakota people on the eastern coastline, their migration from the ocean westward, their dividing and dispersal in four directions, and the settling of the Wahpeton in present-day Minnesota. There are several other accounts, some also suggesting an eastern origin of the Dakota. There has been considerable debate and speculation about a Sioux homeland and evidence from oral tradition for an eastern origin of the Sioux, but the question is still unsettled.

Oneroad (Jingling Cloud), a Sisseton-Wahpeton man from a Dakota community in South Dakota, related the following "Migration Tale" in 1914: "The Eastern Dakota claim that the Sioux originated in the north, and came south, until, somewhere to the southeast of their starting point, they were stopped by the ocean, where they scattered and went in different directions. They fought many tribes, and finally grew stronger, and then travelled northwestward toward the prairie. When they reached Minnesota and eastern South Dakota, they came upon the Cheyenne, whom they drove out upon the prairies" (Oneroad and Skinner 2003, 191).

Among the Yanktons there are widespread oral traditions concerning an eastern origin of the Dakota people. In a 1912 speech a Yankton elder related knowledge "as is handed down by our tribal historians from generation to generation from time immemorial up to the present. They had migrated from afar. Centuries before the time of Columbus they lived near, or upon the Atlantic seaboard in what is now North Carolina." He went on to describe the migration through the Ohio Valley and westward. Another Yankton highly respected for his knowledge of the Yankton traditions, at eighty-nine years old, told an interviewer that "our Dakota Indians came from the eastern seaboard and finally they got to the Mississippi River" (Maroukis 2004, 6).

McGee in 1897 reported on several writers (Hale, Dorsey, and Gatschet) who noticed a resemblance between the Dakota language of the Plains and the tongues of the Tutelo and Catawba peoples near the Atlantic coast and showed the languages to be of common descent. Although it first was supposed that the eastern tribes "were merely offshoots of the Dakota," Hale claimed evidence that their language was older in form, "and consequently that the Siouan tribes of the interior seem to have migrated westward from a common fatherland with their eastern brethren bordering the Atlantic." Subsequently Gatschet and Dorsey also studied the language of the Biloxi of the Gulf coast of Mississippi and established its Siouan affinity (Dorsey 1897, 158–59).

More recent linguistic research confirms the Tutelo (first reported in the area near the present Virginia-North Carolina border) and the Biloxi (first reported on the Gulf coast of Mississippi) as part of the Siouan language family. There is also a tribe called Santee who were located near the Santee River in South Carolina, but their language was Catawba, "a group of languages distantly related to the Siouan languages" (Rudes, Blumer, and May 2004, 301).

Regarding the migration, McGee claims the movement was westward and northward: "Some five hundred or possibly one thousand years ago the tribesmen pushed over the Appalachians to the Ohio and followed that stream and its tributaries to the Mississippi . . . ; and that the human flood gained volume as it advanced and expanded to cover the entire region of the plains. . . . The reason was the food quest . . . with the buffalo at its head" (McGee 1897, 199).

The *Wakáŋ Waćípi* (Holy Dance) and *Ćaŋkú Dúta* (Red Road) in Comparative Perspective

The *Wakáŋ Waćípi* (Holy Dance)

The *Wakáŋ Waćípi* was derived from the Ojibwa or Sauk or other nearby woodland peoples like the Menominee, who practiced varying forms of the Medicine Lodge. Central to the initiation, songs, dances, and other practices of this ceremonial society was the reenactment of a myth of the origin of the Dakota people. As Samuel Mniyo describes in this book, the *Wakáŋ Waćípi* society sought to foster, maintain, and perpetuate the values, beliefs, and practices of the *Ćaŋkú Dúta* (Red Road) way of life in Santee (*Isáŋti*) Dakota society. This close connection between the *Ćaŋkú Dúta* and the *Wakáŋ Waćípi* is emphasized by both Robert Goodvoice and Samuel Mniyo, but is not mentioned by others who describe the *Wakáŋ Waćípi* or Medicine Dance. Also as Sam describes, the Red Road Journey or Red Road Pilgrimage and Lifestyle is not only a way of life but a physical movement, a migration westward.

Although the *Wakáŋ Waćípi* seems to have disappeared by the 1860s among the *Isáŋti* in the United States (Skinner 1920, 262), remarkably, it persisted until the 1930s among the *Isáŋti* Dakota in Canada, as Samuel Mniyo describes here. The present volume seeks to tell the story of the Red Road and the *Wakáŋ Waćípi* particularly from the point of view of *Isáŋti* who came to Canada after the Minnesota Uprising of 1862 and their descendants. It is about both the time the *Isáŋti* Dakota lived mostly in what is now the United States and the time after they settled in what is now Canada.

The Ċaŋkú Dúta (Red Road)

For many Indigenous people to follow the Good Red Road simply means to live in a good way. Blair Stonechild, of the First Nations University of Canada, in his discussion of Indigenous spirituality, refers to the importance of living the "good life" or "following the Red Road." (Stonechild 2016, 5)

For the Dakota, as Robert Goodvoice said, "This is the good path of life. . . . The red path leads to life everlasting" (Howard 1984, 130). For Samuel Mniyo, the Red Road, running from east to west, was a central belief of the *Isáŋti* Dakota.

With the Dakota the "good red road" also was an important symbolic concept and was related to the concept of the sacred hoop or medicine wheel. In his discussion of the Red Road (*Ċaŋkú Dúta*), Howard (1984) says the equal-armed cross symbolizes the four directions or four winds, the corners of the universe:

> Each of the two arms of the cross is also symbolic. The arm extending from east to west is called *the canku duta*, the "red road," the path of good. The arm extending from south to north is the *canku sapa*, the "black road," the path of war and calamity. . . . Both roads are travelled during life, and although the red road is the better and the preferred path, the warrior must travel the black road to protect his family and tribe.
>
> The cross may be superimposed upon the circle to produce a characteristic Sioux design called the cankdeska wakan "sacred hoop," called the "medicine wheel" in English. (Howard 1984, 103)

As Howard points out, the sacred hoop is the result of combining two important religious symbols of the Sioux: the cross and the circle. The hoop or circle, he says, illustrates the completeness and interrelatedness of all things in nature. As Sam Buffalo commented: "The circle is the most *wakáŋ* design of my people. It reflects the way we do things. My people dance in a circle. They used to camp in a circle with the *tiyótipi* ['soldier lodge'—Howard] in the center. Indians always sit in a circle when they are councilling or even just visiting" (Howard 1984, 103).

According to Sam and Robert, the *Wakáŋ Waċípi* and *Ċaŋkú Dúta* were closely related: for Sam, the *Ċaŋkú Dúta* or good red road was the way of living in a good way, the way of peace and harmony and right relationships, while the *Wakáŋ Waċípi* was the ceremonial vehicle or means to perpetuate and maintain the *Ċaŋkú Dúta*. Robert appears to regard them as one and the same thing. Although there are numerous descriptions of the *Wakáŋ Waċípi* by other observers, I am not aware that any of these connect the *Wakáŋ Waċípi* to the *Ċaŋkú Dúta* (Red Road) or to any migration westward by the Dakota. In 1972 Sam Buffalo and Robert Goodvoice described the origin of the medicine dance of the Dakota to Howard. We begin with that account, as reported by Howard (1984; Howard's 1972 field work was not published until 1984). Robert's account tells of the *Uŋktéḣi* or Water Spirits whose role in the origin story is explained later. This is followed by a general description of the *Wakáŋ Waċípi* and its significance and several accounts of the origin story of the *Wakáŋ Waċípi*, then a detailed description of its performance and physical layout, and finally reference to the song board used in the ceremony.

The Origin of the Medicine Dance (Holy Dance) and the Red Path (1972)

"Robert Good Voice (Round Plain) stated that the 'red road' was an important symbolic concept in both rites [the Medicine Feast and the Medicine Dance]. He commented, 'This is the good path of life. One hundred and fifty different roots are used in the various medicines found in the medicine bags. The red path leads to life everlasting'" (Howard 1984, 130).

"According to Robert Goodvoice (Round Plain) the *Uŋktéḣi* are everlasting. They live in the sea, toward the rising sun. One is an old man and one is an old woman. In appearance they are giant panthers with horns. Mr. Goodvoice stated that it was the *Uŋktéḣi* who gave the Medicine Dance to the Sioux and showed them the good red road" (106).

Howard says:

The following is a composite of Mr. Goodvoice's and Mr. Buffalo's separate accounts, which complemented one another.

"Many years ago the Dakota people landed on a peninsula on the east coast of North America. They were surrounded by waters and could go no further, so they prayed. Finally, in response to their prayers, they heard a great voice, and above the surface of the ocean, in the direction of the sunrise, they saw the heads of two spirits. These were the *Uŋktéḣi* [Underwater Panthers]. One was male and *sota* ['grayish-white'] colored. The other, a female, was the color of a buffalo calf [reddish-brown]. They were like giant panthers in shape, but had horns like a buffalo.

"These spirits told the people to travel west, following the *c'aŋku duta*, the 'red road'. [In other words, to perform the Medicine Dance and to follow the teachings of the organization.] This road, they said, has four divisions [the four groups making up the society?]. The promise of the red road, the *Uŋktéȟi* said, is as true as what you can see. The people looked toward the west and saw that their path seemed to lead into the sea. They feared that they would be drowned, but they had faith and followed the red road.

"When they came to the water, one man stepped on it, and it parted, revealing a dry path. The rest followed. The red road led the Dakota west to the Minnesota country and they kept up their *Wakáŋ Waćípi* from that time onward. Some men here still know the songs and we still believe in its teachings." (137–38; brackets are Howard's)

Although "Mr. Robert Good Voice stated that it was the *Uŋktéȟi* who gave the Medicine Dance to the Sioux and showed them the good red road" (Howard 1984, 106), Sam makes no reference to the *Uŋktéȟi* in the three versions he gave to me (in 1977, 1985, and 1997) and which I present here in part 2. Although Sam did mention the *Uŋktéȟi* briefly to me once (August 1996) as an underwater god, he did not relate it to the *Wakáŋ Waćípi* and claimed it was more a Yankton and Teton idea (Mniyo, June 13, 1988).

As is shown in parts 2 and 3, Mniyo and Goodvoice see that one purpose of the *Wakáŋ Waćípi* is to promote long life and to recognize the gift of plants and herbs. Mniyo emphasizes the notion of long life, or the completion of the promised human life span, as a reward for following the way of the Red Road, and claims the proper human life span was longer in the early times. He sees the performance of the *Wakáŋ Waćípi* as playing a key role in demonstrating and maintaining that good Red Road way of life.

In one of his narratives, Eli Taylor, a Wahpeton elder of Sioux Valley Dakota Nation in Manitoba, recounts an ancient story. Although it makes no direct reference to the *Wakáŋ Waćípi* or the Red Road, it bears some similarities to the narratives of Sam and Robert. He tells about a group of Dakota men who were on a long journey to find the end of the land, in the direction where the sun sets. They encountered a different kind of man, a human but perhaps a spiritual being, who explained to them how they were to live on the earth, saying, "Have compassion for one another, know your relatives, honor your relatives, respect them, and treat each other as relatives." He then showed them grass and grass roots and how to use them for medicine for various illnesses. He showed them the woods and how to depend on them. He gave them the gift of horses. He told them to remember these things he was telling them, and continue telling them to every generation, to walk in that path of what they remember (Wilson 2005, 74–84).

Although other accounts of the practice of the *Wakáŋ Waćípi* among the Dakota do not associate it with the *Ćaŋkú Dúta* or any westward migration, one report of the *Midewiwin* of the Ojibwa does include clear reference to a westward migration. This is shown in the narrative that follows, collected by historian William Warren in the early nineteenth century: it starts with the suffering forefathers (of the *Anishinaabeg* or Ojibwa in this case) located on the shore of the ocean to the east when they received the gift from the Great Spirit and began their trek westward:

> "My grandson," said he, "the megis I spoke of, means the Me-da-we [*Midewiwin*] religion. Our forefathers, many string of lives ago, lived on the shores of the Great Salt Water in the east. . . . [W]hile they were suffering the ravages of sickness and death, the Great Spirit, at the intercession of Man-ab-o-sho, the great common uncle of the An-ishin-aub-ag, granted them this rite wherewith life is restored and prolonged. . . . Our forefathers moved from the shores of the great water and proceeded westward.
>
> "This, my grandson, is the meaning of the words you did not understand; they have been repeated to us by our fathers for many generations."
>
> . . . These . . . "sacred narratives" were passed on orally from generation to generation precisely in order that the Ojibwa would always know who they were, where they had come from, how they fitted into the world around them, and how they needed to behave in order to ensure a long life. (Angel 2002, 3)

The *Wakáŋ Waćípi* in Dakota Society

The *Wakáŋ Waćípi* was called the Holy Dance, not only by Samuel Mniyo but by Howard (1952; 1953) and Wallis (1947, 69). It also was called Medicine Society (Gillette 1906, 459; Anderson 1986, 20), Medicine Dance or Medicine Lodge (Howard 1984, 131; Pond 1986, 93), Medicine Dance Society (Landes 1968a, 57), and Medicine Ceremony (Skinner 1920; Westerman and White 2012, 75). *Wakáŋ* can mean sacred or holy; it also can mean mysterious or incomprehensible; traditionally it also meant powerful, with power for good or evil.

The *Wakáŋ Waćípi* was performed by the Dakota in former times and "was pre-eminent among the woodland-derived ceremonial organizations of the Santees" (Howard 1984, 131). It was one of the most common forms of public worship, yet a sacred society, the "free masonry of the Indians" (Pond 1986, 93). It was one of the most honorable societies (Wallis 1947, 69).

It was not a post-contact nativistic resistance movement but already existed at the time of contact. "Wallis in 1914 was told by a seventy-year-old man that his grandfather's great-grandfather was a child when the Wahpeton first saw white men and then they possessed only one dance, the *wakan wacipi*, and other dances were introduced subsequently" (Oneroad and Skinner 2003, 83). One of the first to report it was the explorer Jonathan Carver in his journals of 1766–70 (Westerman and White 2012, 75).

The *Wakáŋ Waćípi* was widely practiced among eastern Siouan and Algonquian groups. It was similar to the *Mide* lodge or *Midewiwin* of the Ojibwa (Landes 1968a), Sauk, and other Algonquian-speaking tribes and similar to ceremonies among the southern Siouan groups. This is because the *Wakáŋ Waćípi* came to the eastern Dakota from the Ojibwa Medicine Ceremony or *Midewiwin* (Gillette 1906; Skinner 1920; Wallis 1947; Howard 1985), either by way of the Sauk, Winnebago, or Fox or directly from the Ojibwa (Skinner 1920, 12–13; Pond 1986, 93).[10]

Leo Omani, of the Wahpeton Dakota First Nation, provides a contrasting picture of how and where the *Wakáŋ Waćípi* (sacred dance) was given to the Dakota by the Ojibwa:

Our older Dakota people also talked about *Wakpa-Sa*, which means the "Red River," that's the one at the bottom [south end] of Lake Winnipeg. It was named after a big battle between our *Dakota Oyate* and the Ojibwa a long time ago before the *Wa'si'cu* (Whiteman) arrived. Our older Dakota people said that there was so many killed on both sides, the *Dakota Oyate* and the Ojibwa, that the river turned red from the blood spilled, that's why they called it *Wakpa-Sa* (Red River). They later made peace with each other and the Red River became kind of like a boundary line where we traded with each other. Our *Dakota Oyate* and the Ojibwa also shared certain sacred ceremonies with each other. We gave them permission to use our big round drum in their ceremonies. They allowed us to use what they called the medicine dance, we called it *wakan-wicipi* which means "sacred dance." The Ojibwa also gave us the moccasin game as part of our traditional treaty of peace, friendship and trade. That's before the *Wa'si'cu* (Whiteman) arrived with his fur trade." (Omani 2010, 188)

Sam and Robert never refer to any Ojibwa origin for the *Wakáŋ Wacípi*. "At least three types of the Medicine Ceremony once existed: (1) the Dakotan type, once practiced by the Wahpeton Dakota, Iowa, Winnebago, and Oto; (2) The Omaha type, as practiced by the Omaha and Ponca; and (3) The Algonkian type, as practiced by the Menomini, Ojibwa, Potawatomi, and perhaps by the Cree and Sauk" (Skinner 1920, 11).

The *Wakáŋ Wacípi* (Holy Dance or Sacred Dance) ceremony for the initiation of new members or the funeral of a member often was accompanied by the *Wakáŋ Wóhaŋpi* (Medicine Feast or Holy Feast; DeMallie 2001c, 790), but the feast was observed more frequently than the *Wakáŋ Wacípi* itself. The *Wakáŋ Wacípi Okódakičiye* or the *Wakáŋ Okódakičiye* was the Holy Dance Society, Holy Society, or Medicine Society.

Those who were received into the *Wakáŋ Wacípi* society paid liberal fees for admission. Much food also had to be collected in advance, both by the one who gave notice that he intended to hold a dance and by others. The dance was not held very often, but generally as often as two or three times a year at each village of the Santee or Eastern Dakota (Pond 1986, 83).

Some observers say the dance was highly regarded. Not all Dakota were participants. "Frequently, the old men compare these meetings to church services: as many whites do not join the church, so many Dakota, lest they deceive *Wakantanka*, to whom they pray, do not join the *wakan a tci'pi*. If they join and fail in their higher duties, they thereby make fools of themselves and will soon die" (Wallis 1947, 69). Its members were "high class," religious people, circumspect in their behavior and generous to their fellow tribesmen. Many possessed great power (Howard 1984, 132).

The *Wakáŋ Waćípi* was one of the most honorable societies, comparable in our times to a church, secret society, or fraternal lodge. Both men and women were members. One intent was to make members virtuous. Members were exhorted not to drink whiskey, not to fight or abuse anyone in any way, and not to slam the door of any house; they were told that if they did not follow the injunctions they would become ill and die, but if they obeyed the injunctions, they would have a long life, be strong always. and live to an old age (Wallis 1947, 69).

Some observers are less positive in their reports. Most shamans belonged to the Medicine Dance Ceremony (Landes 1968a, 57). The membership was composed of all sorts of persons, some of the worst and some of the best (Pond 1986, 93). In spite of the ethical teachings that forbade members to slander, steal, commit adultery, etc., the behavior of members did not appear different from that of non-members (Landes 1968a, 59).

Within each village a medicine society existed. The society was composed of four separate groups, or "bands," and there were at least two of these present in each village where the ceremony was practiced. "At a meeting there are four groups which sing in rotation. The average number of songs which belong to each group is stated to be about 12. This is certainly an underestimate" (Wallis 1947, 69).

Among the Wahpeton Dakota, one of the four bands of which the medicine lodge was composed was led by Chief *Mazómani* (Walking Iron), probably at Little Rapids (on the lower Minnesota River about forty-five miles southwest of present-day Minneapolis), a Wahpeton semi-permanent or "planting village"; an archaeologist identified what she believed was the probable site of a medicine dance enclosure there (Spector 1993, 117). Chief *Mazómani's* son *Mazámani II* signed the 1851 Treaty of Traverse de Sioux with the U.S. government, after which the people were moved to the Upper Sioux Council near Granite Falls on the upper Minnesota River.

In the early 1800s the society possessed extreme power in Mdewakanton villages, in what is now eastern Minnesota, where perhaps half the adult population was admitted and virtually every member of the society was recognized as a *wićáśta wakáŋ* or shaman (Anderson 1986, 20).

The fundamental purpose of the *Wakáŋ Waćípi* of the Dakota is suggested by several writers. One claims it was to exhibit the power and virtue of the medicine (Gillette 1906, 472). Landes (1968a) claims the public ceremonies were "for the purpose of magical display and intimidation"

(57). Landes studied the Medicine Dance Society among both the Mdewakantonwan in 1935 and the Ojibwa in 1932–35 (1968b).

The *Wakáŋ Waćípi* ritual was viewed by the Dakota as a way of purifying or cleansing the body of evils coming from outside. The "shooting" of the small missile from the medicine bag served to shoot the good into the body to expel the bad. Further, this individual event was viewed as expiation or exorcizing for the whole group, done on behalf of the group, and essential to keep the world going (David Miller, personal conversation, 2008).

Sam claims that the *Wakáŋ Waćípi* was not practiced by the Teton, Yankton, nor even by the Sisseton, but only by the Wahpeton and other *Isáŋti* Dakota considered as woodland peoples (i.e., the Mdewakanton). At least some Sisseton did participate, however, and some from the other three tribes or councils did as well. Martha Tawiyaka, a Sisseton of Standing Buffalo, who was eighty-eight in 1972, says "I used to see the *Wakan Wacipi* 'Medicine Dance.' I saw it four different times. One time the [Catholic] priest saw some of us girls there and scolded us. My mother belonged to the *Wakan Wacipi*" (Howard 1984,.46–47).

The Yanktonai and probably the Yankton practiced it traditionally (DeMallie 2001c, 789), and some of them, like Jim Sapa, did practice it in more recent times. "The Medicine lodge ceremony (*Wakan wacipi*) of the Yanktonai, though highly regarded, was rarely performed, and disappeared early in the reservation era" (Howard 1966, 16).

The Teton also practiced the Holy Dance, referred to as the *Waćípi Wakáŋ* or Holy Dance by the shamans, who also stated, "*Uŋktéȟi* gave the *Wacipi Wakan*" (Walker 1980, 118). He quotes a head chief of the Oglalas in 1896, "The sacred dances are the Dance for the Dead, the Scalp Dance, the Holy Dance and the Sun Dance" (Walker 1980, 67).

Origin Stories

Skinner (1920) gives a detailed description of the Medicine Ceremony of the Wahpeton Dakota and others (Menominee and Iowa), including the origin myth, initiation ceremonies, and funeral ceremonies, and gives briefer notes on the ceremony as practiced by the Bungi Ojibwa. He notes the importance of the *Uŋktéȟi* (Water Spirits) in bringing knowledge of medicinal plants and herbs to humans in the *Wakáŋ Waćípi*. Here is my paraphrase (with quotations) of Skinner's account of the "Origin Myth" of the Wahpeton rite:

> *Wakáŋ Táŋka*, the Great Spirit, before there was any earth, only water, came down and stood upon the water. He tore out a rib from his right side, threw it into the sea, and it became a male *Uŋktéȟi*. Likewise, from his left side his rib became a female *Uŋktéȟi* monster. (273–74)
>
> The *Uŋktéȟi* cause muskrat to dive under the waters and bring them mud, of which they create the earth. They then originate the medicine-lodge with the assistance of the animals, who form bands of their own species. The birds and beasts later appear to the Indians in dreams and instruct them in the rites of the lodge. (302)
>
> In that first medicine lodge, it was the *Uŋktéȟi* who sang the medicine songs, and the animals of all kinds, which had taken on the nature of human beings, came in groups of their own kind and sang. They shot each other with birds and eagle-claws, but they could not bring their victims to life, so the *Uŋktéȟi* taught them to substitute shells (the Ojibwa *migis*) as their missiles. (276–77)
>
> The two *Uŋktéȟi* then went down under the earth and lay with ears open to hear the Indians' prayers. "From the hairs of these monsters come the grass and herbs and shrubs that are used to compound the medicines utilized by the Indians to cure sickness and heal wounds. . . . When you go to dig these plants, first bury red and white down to clothe them, and sing the song that belongs to the medicine before you dig them up." (277–78)

For a more detailed summary of the Wahpeton rite as described by Oneroad and Skinner (2003) see the endnotes.[11]

There are two references to "rib" and the "mystery of the rib" in the songs in the Henry Two Bear notebook that was used in the *Wakáŋ Waćípi* ceremony in Canada until the 1920s and first translated by Sam: see Jurgita Antoine's translation in part 4.

Pond claims that the chief object of worship of the Dakota in the mid-1800s was *Unkteri*, the mammoth, a species they described as resembling the buffalo or ox but of enormous size. "They supposed that the race was still in existence, and, as they were not seen on land and their bones were found in low and wet places, they concluded that their dwelling was in the water" (Pond 1986, 87). I assume he is talking about *Uŋktéȟi*. Mammoths were a large ice age mammal: most died off at the time of the last glacial retreat about 10,000 years ago.

The area at the confluence of the Minnesota and Mississippi Rivers, called *Bdóte*, was considered a sacred place. "Missionary Samuel Pond learned from Dakota elders that this was the dwelling place of *Unktehi*, a powerful underwater spirit" (Westerman and White 2012, 92). The hill overlooking this location, known as Pilot Knob or *Ohéyawahi*, also was considered sacred, mainly because of its association with the *Uŋktéhi*. "The health-giving Wakan Wacipi, or medicine ceremony, was sometimes performed on this hill.... The ritual teachings of the Wakan Wacipi were said to have come from Unktehi" (186; this location is near Fort Snelling, Minnesota).

The Dakota soldier and artist Seth Eastman painted an image of a medicine ceremony that may have taken place on that hill in 1847 (see cover of this book). The hill is located near the historic Fort Snelling, half-way between the modern cities of Minneapolis and St. Paul.

Performance

The *Wakáŋ Waćípi* ceremony, initiation ceremony, feast, physical layout and other details are described by Gillette (1906), Skinner (1920), Wallis (1947), and Howard (2014, 120–26).

In Skinner's account, the night before the initiation ceremony the four leaders give the candidate instructions. The first tells him the myth of the origin of the society; the next, the ritual; and the third, the Ten Rules of Life. The latter rules include: You must not quarrel; respect your lodge and respect and welcome visitors who come to your lodge; love your neighbors; respect the fellow members of the *Wakáŋ Waćípi*; the members of the *Wakáŋ Waćípi* are as one and should regard each other as equal (Skinner 1920, 280–83).

Each member had an animal skin medicine bag, used in the ceremony, and a yarn medicine bag, in which his or her medicines were kept, which was not usually brought to the ceremony. The medicine bag (*wakáŋ* sack) contains four kinds of *wakáŋ* medicine and represents fowls, herbs, trees, and quadrupeds (Oneroad and Skinner 2003, 83), represented respectively by female swan down, grass roots, bark from tree roots, and hair from the back or head of the buffalo (Gillette 1906, 464).

The paraphernalia used in the Wahpeton rite also included the deep water-drum, gourd rattles and feather plumes. The medicine bags were furnished with double-pointed oblong objects cut from white or yellow shell, used as medicine arrows during the "shooting" part of the ceremony. Carved wooden bowls and spoons were used for feasting. Quantities of red and white swan- or eagle-down were strewn on the floor of the lodge. (Skinner 1920, 26–66, my paraphrase)

The ceremony and the contents of the medicine bag demonstrate a central theme in the *Wakáŋ Waćípi* origin myth, namely the key role of animals, first the *Uŋktéhi* and then the other animals, to pass knowledge about plants to humans. "It is believed that animal nature helped to create humans and that animals have always served as humanity's mentors in coming to know the nature of the world" (Cajete 2000, 151).

The *Wakáŋ Waćípi* ceremony of the Dakota was performed by an organized ceremonial group. A main feature was the magical "shooting" of a small object into the body of the initiate and its subsequent removal by "magic" means (Howard 1984, 131). The object shot in Ojibwa ceremonies was a *megise*, a cowrie shell or a small seed, whereas Wahpeton ceremonies used "curious double-pointed oblong objects which seem to be cut from yellow or white shell, and these are used instead of the small shells which are the medicine-arrows of other tribes" (Skinner 1920, 265). "*Migiis* shells are small white cowries that grow only on reefs in the South Pacific ocean. . . . In Ojibwe religious and cultural thought, *Migiis* [*miigis*: Angel 2002, 69] is a great white shining cowrie shell in the sky, which led the *Anishinaabeg* [Ojibwa] on their long migration from the shores of the Atlantic to the west, around the Great Lakes. *Migiis* represents the sun" (Giese 1997).

The following is a summary of the initiation ceremony as practiced in Canada, based closely on the description by Howard.

The candidate applied to the leader of one of the groups making up the organization at a feast that the applicant had prepared. If accepted, he was given instruction and the origin legend was recounted. The applicant was lectured further at a sweat lodge ceremony and would give valuable presents of blankets to the leaders: all information had to be paid for.

On the first day of the ceremony the main lodge was constructed and the tipis were erected, the one for the leaders at the west end and the one for the *akíćitas* at the east end. That evening was a practice singing session.

On the second day the leaders took their places at the west end of the lodge, and the groups making up the organization entered at the east end, one at a time, facing west, sang one of their sacred songs, marched west in a clockwise direction and took their seats on one side or the other of the lodge. The ceremony began with a pipe ceremony, offering the pipe to the four directions, zenith and nadir, and then passing it to those present. The drum and gourd rattle were given to the first group, four members of which sang while the remainder danced, simply bobbing up and down in place. When they finished there was a feast. This was repeated for each of the four groups with a feast after each dance.

On the final day of the initiation the famous shooting occurred. The candidate was seated in the center and the membership, one person at a time, charged down on him, holding his medicine bag extended head first toward the candidate. The shooter stopped a short distance away, shook the animal skin in the candidate's direction and uttered the sacred cry. This was supposed to propel the "medicine arrow" (a small shell) from the bag into the candidate's body. The candidate would retch violently and bring up the shell. Then it would be repeated, with each group shooting in turn, followed by a general shooting (1984, 132–35).

Howard describes the physical layout of the Medicine Dance (*Wakáŋ Waćípi*) ceremony of the Dakota in Canada:

> The ceremony was held in a brush arbor about forty feet long and ten feet wide, rounded at the ends. This arbor was open at the top but covered on the sides to a height of about five feet. It was oriented east and west, with openings at either end. At the west end, blocking the west door, a tipi was pitched opening into the main lodge. Here the leaders of the ceremony were seated when not otherwise engaged. A short distance from the eastern doorway, another tipi (in later times a wall tent) was pitched. This was the headquarters of the *akíćita*, a group of warriors selected to keep order in the vicinity of the lodge while the dance was in progress. . . . A stone, shaped like an artillery shell set on end, was placed in the center of the ceremonial lodge. This was the symbol of eternal life. (Howard 1984, 132)

The physical layout is shown in two pictures. The photo on the cover of this book presents an 1847 painting of a Medicine Dance of the "Sioux or Dakotah" near Fort Snelling (in present-day Minneapolis), by Seth

PHOTO 3. "Great Medicine Dance (*Wan-ni-waci-pu*) of the Sioux in North Dakota about 1879." View of a dance ceremony in progress, with the dancers in the center of the enclosure. The enclosure is formed by blankets hung from ropes on the two sides of the space, with the tipi for the *akíčitas*—police or guards—guarding the entrance at one end (near left) and the tipi for ceremony leaders closing off the far end, assumed to be the west end, of the enclosure (center right). Photo CL 275, George W. Ingalls Photograph Collection, Huntington Library, San Marino, California.

Eastman. Photo 3 shows a Great Medicine Dance (*Wanniwacipu*) of the Sioux in North Dakota about 1879. This may be one of the only two photos in existence of this important Dakota rite.[12]

Songs, Song Boards, and Song Sticks

The songs are a central part of the *Wakáŋ Wačípi* ceremony. Singers, seated near the west end of the lodge, sang a planned sequence of songs, accompanied by drumming, during much of the ceremony. This guided the dancers who moved around the oblong area. "The drum used in the ceremony was a Woodland style water drum, which was beaten with an 'L' shaped stick. A large gourd rattle (*wakmuha*) was shaken in time with the drum" (Howard 1984, 133). One would expect this singing and drumming to have a powerful effect on the overall atmosphere. To identify the precise songs of a Medicine Dance and sing them in the proper sequence, the singers would use a wooden song stick (*dowáŋpi*), also called a song board (or with the Ojibwas, a scroll of birch bark) on which they had inscribed pictographic records. These were memory aids, not words but symbols or mnemonic representations of animals, people, arrows, etc. referring to the various songs, "which assisted the singer to remember the correct sequence of songs in the medicine dance. The picture merely suggested

FIGURE 1. Wahpeton Dakota song record (obverse and reverse) used in the Medicine Dance. Among the songs identified and numbered on this song stick are: 1. Buffalo song and 2. Sun song (on obverse side); and 4. Fish song and 5. Spider song (on reverse side). From Skinner 1920, 270. The song stick is located in the American Museum of Natural History, Anthropological catalog #50.1/79840.

the subject matter of the song to those particular singers" (Howard, letter to DB, April 19, 1967). The singers would sing the songs on one side of the board, then the songs on the other side (Skinner 1920, 267–68).

For a diagram of one of several Wahpeton and other song boards shown by Skinner (1920) see figure 1. For a description, photo and tracing of the song stick belonging to Henry Two Bear of the Wahpeton Dakota Reserve, see figure 9. Hoffman (2005) provides a detailed description of the songs used in the *Midewiwin* of the Ojibway before 1891, with music ledger notes and the pictographic symbols that serve as mnemonic aids to the singers.[13]

Organization of the Book

Using the notion of four strands, this book is organized in four parts. Part 1 is my editor's introduction. It introduces the four authors or voices, the Dakota nation and its history, and the two central themes—the Red Road and the Holy Dance. It also includes discussion of the orthography used for the Dakota words in this book.

Part 2 presents the oral history narratives by Samuel Mniyo/Sam Buffalo. It begins with an introduction in which Sam talks about why and how this story was written, outlines the four eras in Dakota history, and identifies those who taught him the stories he is passing on to younger generations. The chapters in part 2 follow a chronological order, starting with the distant past and moving toward the present. The main focus is the evolution of the Holy Dance and the Red Road, a story that ends in part 4.

What Sam calls "The Era of the Red Road Journey or the *Tiwópida Oíhduhe* era" is about, first, the origin of the Red Road (*Ċaŋkú Dúta*) and Holy Dance (*Wakáŋ Waċípi*), and second, the story of the Dakota people as they begin to follow the Red Road Journey westward from somewhere on the Atlantic coastline. This chapter attempts to reach away back into the mists of time to talk about events that some might consider supernatural or mythical.

What Sam calls "The Dakota Turning Point: The Dakota Divided (Three Versions)" is about when the Dakota people divided into sub-tribes and moved apart in different directions. This may not only explain the location of the Dakota at the time of contact but may help explain the wide distribution of the Siouan languages, from the Biloxi in the south through the plains to the Stoney in the northwest.

What Sam calls "The Circle Power Era (*Tiyóti Oíhduhe*)" is a period of several hundred years that extends until somewhat after the time of contact with Europeans. In "*Tiyóti Oíhduhe*: The *Tiyóti* System (The Circle System) in Dakota Society," Sam examines the complex ways in which the circle was a central feature of life and social organization. In "The Sacred Hoop: Learning and Teaching over the Life Span," Sam examines learning and teaching through the human life span and relates several stories that illustrate principles of the *Tiyóti Oíhduhe* system.

What Sam calls "The Trading and Reserve Era" could also be called "The Christian Era and Adjusting to Life on Reserves." Sam here discusses beginning life on the Upper Sioux reservation in Minnesota and the end of the *Tiyóti* system. After referring to the Dakota War or Minnesota Uprising of 1862 he describes his family history, how the *Isáŋti* people came to Canada, and how the Wahpeton Dakota reserve was established. The narratives in this chapter, and in other chapters, are based mainly on what was told to Sam and Robert by their grandparents (and other elders) based either on their own direct experience as eye-witnesses or on what their grandparents and great-grandparents passed on to them.

"The Present Challenge" focuses on life on the reserves and the breakdown of traditional practices.

"Samuel Mniyo's Own Story" includes accounts of various life experiences, including his account of four meetings with his spiritual guide; a discussion of his collaboration with me ("Sam and Dan"), and a timeline of his life.

The last days or final stage of the *Wakáŋ Waćípi* with the Dakota people are discussed in part 4.

Part 3 presents the oral history narratives of Robert Goodvoice, which complement Samuel Mniyo's material. "Traditional History" includes stories of the origin of the Red Path, of living under the circle system, the division and dispersal of the Dakota tribes, and becoming a member of what he calls the Red Path Society (referring to the *Wakáŋ Waćípi* society).

"Relations with the White Men" begins with the period before and including 1862.

"The Move to Prince Albert" deals with the aftermath of the 1862 Dakota War and describes how the *Isáŋti* people came to Canada, including his own family history.

Part 4, the fourth strand of this book, is about the *Wakáŋ Waćípi* in Canada in the twentieth century and features materials in which Jim Sapa figures prominently. It begins with my 1987 essay "A Prairie Puzzle: The Wakan-Wacipi Dakota Song Stick." This shows a scale tracing of the song stick that belonged to Henry Two Bear and may once have belonged to *Mazámani*. Transcriptions by Henry Two Bear of *Wakáŋ Waćípi* songs follow, together with their translation initially by Samuel Mniyo and later by Jurgita Antoine. Next, Mniyo presents the description by Jim Sapa of the last performances of the *Wakáŋ Waćípi* in Canada.

The next portion of part 4 reproduces some of the images from the two notebooks of pictographs that belonged to Sapa. Their purpose remains unknown. These pictograph records are unique, the only examples known from any of the Dakota or Lakota groups. A sample of twelve images in black and white images is presented, representing the forty-five color images from the two notebooks.

The appendices provide a variety of supporting materials, including a Santee history timeline; Sam Buffalo's family tree; a summary description of the Wahpaton [*sic*] Dakota Oral History tapes; biographical sketches of persons most involved in this book; and an example of how Sam's oral history was used in a Regina high school lesson as a case study.

Maps show the locations of most of the places referred to in this book. The bibliography includes both published and unpublished sources, and the glossary explains Dakota words used.

Note on Editing and Orthography

For the names of the tribal divisions and dialects of the Sioux Nation, I use the common anglicized terms—for example, Wahpeton, Sisseton, Dakota, Lakota, Santee and Sioux—and the English plural forms for Dakota words. For the greater Sioux Nation itself, I use the terms Sioux, *Dakóta Oyáte* (Dakota Nation), or *Oćéti Śakowiŋ* (Seven Council Fires). The term Siouan refers only to the Siouan language family.

Words in Dakota are transcribed phonemically and printed in italics: for example, Isanti or Santee (with some exceptions) is rendered as *Isáŋti*, tiyoti as *tiyóti* and Wakan Wacipi as *Wakáŋ Waćípi*, unless quoted from a published source. Dakota personal names (except Mniyo and Sapa) and Dakota renderings of place names are also italicized (except in the figures, where no italics are used). In the figures, pronunciation marks are used in most but not all cases.

The Dakota tradition of writing Dakota personal names that consist of a noun and adjective as one word is followed: White Cap or Whitecap becomes *Wapáhaska*, and Red Arrow becomes *Waŋdúta*. In other situations the two words are separated: Red Road becomes *Ćaŋkú Dúta*.

In most cases I have capitalized the first letters of *Wakáŋ Waćípi, Midewiwin*, Medicine Dance and similar terms as proper nouns or names.

The Ojibwa, a neighboring tribe, is referred to also with several terms: Ojibway, Chippewa, Saulteaux, Bungi and Anishinaabe.

Captions for photos, figures, and maps are mine, but photo captions in quotes indicate the official title provided by the source museum or organization. All headings are mine, as are all endnotes, and I have also added comments in bracketed asides in the text, identified by my initials, DB. When some Dakota words were first introduced in the story, we also provided the translation in square brackets to help readers follow the story.

The sources of material from Sam Buffalo and Robert Goodvoice are broadly identified in square brackets at the opening of each quotation

[SB 1977], [RG 1977], with more detailed citations in parentheses concluding the text segments, so (Samuel Buffalo 2, 1977, 5) means Samuel Buffalo oral history audiotape number 2, 1977, transcript page 5; (Robert Goodvoice 2, 1977, 2–7) means Robert Goodvoice oral history audiotape number 2, 1977, transcript pages 2–7). Quotes from my own interviews with Samuel Mniyo are identified in opening with the [SM 1987] format and in closing with his name and the interview date, for example (Mniyo, May 31, 1997).

Sam used many Dakota words and terms in this narrative: there may be over 230 if we count those used by Robert. Sam gave his English translation, and readers should bear in mind that the meanings he gave to some words may be particular to a place, time, and group of people. Some of his words, perhaps two dozen or more, are not in common use or are not listed in Dakota dictionaries.

As earlier noted, Sam spelled out Dakota words to me using the Roman alphabet letters commonly used in English, with no accents or diacritics (pronunciation marks). In part 4 Henry Two Bear, in transcribing the Dakota songs used in the Holy Dance, used the Riggs spelling system familiar to most older speakers and readers of Dakota (Riggs 1890).

In this volume an attempt is made to present the sound of the Dakota words more accurately. The Dakota orthography here is based on the system developed by Lakota educators in 1982 (White Hat 1999, 4). We marked stressed syllables of Dakota words with acute accents throughout the book, hoping to help Dakota learners and readers who are not familiar with the language. This spelling system or orthography and a Guide to Pronunciation are in the appendices. With the risk of over-simplifying, in this system *Wakáŋ Waćípi* is pronounced wah-KAHN wah-CHEE-pee, where the *áŋ* has an acute accent indicating an accented syllable, ending in a nasal sound, and the *ć* with a dot over the c indicates a "ch" sound as in chin. Similarly, *Ćaŋkú Dúta* is pronounced chahn-KOO DOO-ta. The Dakota words that appeared only in the written form and are not commonly used in contemporary Dakota (e.g., some personal names) are left unstressed, since we did not hear storytellers pronounce them.[14]

Although every effort has been made to achieve consistency in editing and orthography, some inconsistencies may be expected.

Part 2

The Narratives of Samuel Mniyo (Sam Buffalo)

Introduction

[SM 1997] I will introduce myself to you. My name is Samuel Mniyo. But my full Dakota name is *Mniyódowaŋ*, which means, as I translate it, rhythm in motion. [*Mní odówaŋ* literally means "water song." DB] Ten years ago my name was Samuel Buffalo, the name I went by before. I am a member of the Wahpeton Dakota Reserve 94A located ten miles northwest of Prince Albert. My birth date is October 29, 1929. I lived most of the first fifty years of my life at the Wahpeton.

Since February 26, 1979, I have been living here at the Sherbrooke Community Centre in Saskatoon. Due to my condition, I need special care on a daily basis. Since 1990 I have lost quite a bit of my physical ability, mainly with my hands and arms. I use the wheelchair. In June 1993 I got on a machine called MRI. My illness was diagnosed as syringomyelia, and it is progressing. [Samuel Mniyo died on November 28, 1999, at seventy years of age, at his home in the Sherbrooke Community Centre in Saskatoon, after a lengthy illness. His funeral and burial were on December 2 at Wahpeton. DB]

Why and How This Story Was Written

I will introduce this book to you and why and how it was written. I want to tell you the story of the Dakota people as my elders and sponsors gave it to me. This book will be for the younger generation of Dakota to look at, to learn about who they are and where they came from, and for other people who are interested. Only back in May 1993 my nieces visited me here one day. We were talking about this, and they were questioning me about the Dakota history and how the Dakota religion ended, and who their god was. So I was telling them these stories. And they suggested to me that I should record these holy stories now because those people who asked me not to record them have all died, and whenever my time comes, all these stories would come to an end too. They said I should write them in the form of a book, that it can be used in the schools, maybe not only

Dakota reserves but other reserves. So I was thinking about that. Then last year Dr. Dan Beveridge brought the subject up again about writing this book. Then last December we talked about this again. Then I got very interested to resume my recording about the Dakota history. And now that's what I intend to do. What I know is that there are three parts of the Dakota history: the Red Road era, the Dakota turning point, and the *Tiyóti Oíhduhe* (sacred hoop) era. And I can also come into the reserve era. [So that makes four eras. DB] So this is what I'll [have in] this introduction.

This book includes stories that I recorded at three different times: oral history interviews in 1977, and interviews with Dan Beveridge in 1985 and 1997 [also four with notes but not taped, 1986, 1987, 1988, and 1996. DB]. Before that in 1971 [1972] I recorded stories with Dr. James Howard. He was an American anthropologist who wrote a book on the Canadian Sioux [*The Canadian Sioux* (1984; 2014)]. (Mniyo May 10, 1997).

[SM 1985] In 1974 [1972] I took Dr. James Howard up there [to Round Plain], and he came two summers. Once he spent three weeks with me, going to pow-wows on the weekends, where he danced and sang. He was at the Oklahoma State University at Stillwater, Oklahoma. . . . He speaks Wahpeton. (Mniyo May 1, 1985)

[In September 1977 at the Wahpaton Dakota Reserve Sam recorded four oral history interviews which were transcribed into typed form (Wahpaton is the former spelling, later changed to Wahpeton). He introduces the third one. DB] [SB 1977] Since last June, I have wanted to record several topics of Dakota history for Robert Goodvoice, a councilor at Wahpaton Band now doing research work for the Saskatchewan Archives. . . . I have been compiling materials for textbooks and Dakota language courses because there is a prospect that Dakota language courses will be held on every Dakota reserve. I am very interested to do this type of work; besides I am a physically handicapped person and I have the time to study and train in the field I have mentioned. So writing Dakota stories is my choice (Samuel Buffalo 3, 1977, 1). [That is, Samuel Buffalo, tape 3, 1977 oral history, transcript p. 1; see bibliography and appendix 3 for additional detail. Robert Goodvoice, now deceased, is referred to by Douglas Elias (1988) as the tribal historian for the Wahpeton Dakota First Nation. DB]

[SM 1997] I met Dan Beveridge in 1962 when he was visiting the four Dakota reserves in Saskatchewan as part of the research for his master's degree. In April and May 1985 in Saskatoon I tape-recorded interviews with him some time after he went to work at the University of Regina. After he typed and edited these, I added more material during several unrecorded interviews up to September 1987, and he produced a manuscript in August 1988. After a long pause we started talking about it again in 1996 and I got very interested to resume my recording about Dakota history. Dan combined material from the 1977 oral history interviews and came up with a second manuscript in March 1997. Then in May 1997 in Saskatoon I recorded more new material with him.

At least one of the stories from my earlier 1977 oral history interviews was picked up and translated into French, to appear in a Saskatchewan grade 8 French Immersion school text book, and brought home from school by Dan Beveridge's son Danny about 1990. [See "Etude de cas," appendix 5. It was in a textbook or resource book used in Grade 8 French Immersion in Saskatchewan, probably in *Sciences humaines*, in 1990. These 1977 recorded and transcribed interviews make up part of the series collected by Robert Goodvoice, summarized in appendix 4 and cited in the bibliography. DB] (Mniyo late 1997, edited by DB)

Four Eras in *Isáŋti* Dakota History

[SM 1985, and SM 1997] In this book I talk about the Dakota history. What I know is that there are four parts of the Dakota history:

• Red Road Journey and Lifestyle [*Tiwópida* era]
• Dakota Turning Point
• *Tiyóti* Journey and Lifestyle or *Tiyóti Oíhduhe* (Sacred Hoop) era
• Trading and Reserve Era.

The **Red Road** (*Ċaŋkú Dúta*) **era** is the period of the westward Red Road Journey or the Red Road pilgrimage and lifestyle, searching for the Hill of Truth and following the promise of the mystery voice (or *Wakáŋ Waċípi*, which meant mystery motion, or later, holy dance). It also could be called the *tiwópida* era, when people lived in rectangular shaped dwellings arranged in a line but not in a circle. [*Wópida* means "thankfulness, gladness, joy"; *tiwópida*, "place of thanksgiving, gladness," refers to the tent of the elders or leaders of the *Wakáŋ Waċípi*, at the west end of the oblong arbor where the *Wakáŋ Waċípi* took place. DB]

The Dakota **turning point era** is when most of the people turned away from monotheism to worship many gods, divided up into different groups, and went away in different directions.

The *Tiyóti Oíhduhe* **era** or *tiyóti* journey and lifestyle era is the **era of the circle power**. [Mniyo uses the term *tiyóti oíhduhe* to refer to the lifestyle or type of social and cultural organization of that era. Mniyo also calls the *tiyóti* a cult movement (Mniyo May 1, 1985). Literally, *tiyóti* or *tiyóti típi* or *tiyótípi* refers to the soldiers' lodge. "This is established for the purpose of making laws and providing for their execution. The object is generally to regulate the buffalo chase" (Riggs 1890/1992, 471). *Oíhduhe* means "to have one's self, or citizenship." The expressions seem to imply organizing social life by creating a soldiers' lodge to maintain order. Normally the *tiyóti típi* would be set up in the center of the encampment. DB]

Tiyóti Oíhduhe was the name given to the sacred hoop that symbolized the mystery voice, the Dakota principles and rules, and the Dakota life span, which I will explain. [See The Circle Power Era (*Tiyóti Oíhduhe*), later in part 2. DB] The *Tiyóti Oíhduhe* also meant the "home within home, life within life" system. "Home-within-home" refers to the community aspect of the circle power, with a mutual relationship between the people around the camp circle and the men at the center of the circle. "Life-within-life" refers to the personal aspect, meaning the real "you" inside your body. It was a long period of several hundred years, when encampments were circular in formation and other things in their society were based on the circle. Most of the plains Indians accepted living in a circle during that time.

The **trading and reserve era** is the era after contact with the non-Indian society, up to the present time.

So this is the story of how the Red Road [or *tiwópida*] era began, how it developed, how it ended in the Dakota turning point; and also how the *Tiyóti Oíhduhe* or era of the circle power started, carried through a long period, and ended in the reserve era.

When I talk about the Dakota people I really mean the *Isáŋti* people, those who speak the Dakota language. The *Isáŋti* had eight clans originally, including the *Waȟpétuŋwaŋ* (Wahpeton), the *Mdewákaŋtuŋwaŋ* (Mdewakanton), the *Sisítuŋwaŋ* (Sisseton) and others I will mention later on. Some call them the Eastern Sioux. The Western Sioux or *Títuŋwaŋ* (Teton) speak Lakota. In between were the *Iháŋktuŋwaŋ* (Yankton) and the *Iháŋktuŋwaŋna* (Yanktonai), who also speak Dakota but were not

Isáŋti. (Samuel Mniyo narrations, May 1, 1985, and May 10, 1997, tape-recorded, transcribed, and edited by DB; these accounts are cited here-after as Mniyo with date.)

Who Taught Me These Stories

[SB 1977] And to finish this introduction I will tell you about my sponsor. An old man named *Ité Wapíkida* was my sponsor who taught me about the Dakota development in the old traditional *Tiyóti Oíhduhe* meaning home-within-home, life-within-life system. The Dakota child discipline commenced when a child reached the age of two years old. The parents will select an elderly man and invite him to their home. After serving him food, gift, and a filled pipe to smoke, the mother of the child will ask him to *waékiya,* meaning sponsor her child. The sponsorship will continue until one party dies. They will associate together as often as possible and the boy must visit his sponsor even just to have a conversation. Whenever they are well acquainted, then the teaching starts.

[*Ité Wapíkida* was very real to Samuel Mniyo but may not have been a human being in the normal physical sense. As discussed later, his four appearances to Mniyo could perhaps be described as visions, but this is not at all certain. See Visions and Dreams, later in part 2, where Sam describes visions, a spiritual guide, and spiritual teacher. DB]

In my case, I saw my sponsor four times in my life. The first time I was very young. As I remember what happened, I saw a blue sky, birds, heard a man harmonizing over the hill. I stood there and saw an old man, tall and slim, sitting there cross-legged on a little hill. He played a flute, then he started to hum. I looked at his face. He looked very old, yet beautiful, face copper, not creased, with white hair, thin short braids, leather laces across his forehead. His hair was parted right in the middle. He had put a red ochre paint line down the middle where he parted his hair. He talked to me and said, I am *Ité Wapíkida* (*ité* means face, *wapíkida* means appreciation). In each hand, he held several objects I cannot identify. In front of his folded knees he placed a hoop with markings on it. This hoop was the *tiyóti owíhduhe.*

He told me the hoop was the symbol of the mystery voice that prom-ised our ancestors a new generation in the land where the sun descends. This hoop was the *tiyóti owíhduhe.* That our grandfathers lived by its prin-ciples and rules. This hoop was the Dakota life span that provided them with good health, good home and hunting and pleasure. This hoop was the sacred hoop that developed the Dakota [principles of] belief, identity, skills, and appreciation [thanksgiving or *wapíkidapi*].

Another man who taught me was James Black, better known as Sapa [*sápa* means black], now deceased, on our reserve. He was a *Ċaŋdójuha Yuhá* meaning principal member of the *Wakáŋ Waċípi* meaning Holy Dance society. In the fall of 1951, I used to visit him every evening and do his chores for him. He would tell story after story until late at night. He told me a number of stories concerning the Holy Dance Society. He taught me about Dakota religion and some accounts of Dakota history. I also heard stories from others relating to the Holy Dance Society. [*Ċaŋdójuha Yuhá* literally means "tobacco bag owner," apparently referring to the medicine bags carried by members of the society.] (Samuel Buffalo 3, 1977, 2)

[SM 1997] My first interview with him was in the later part of October and [then] all November and early December in 1951. He was teaching me with the *Isáŋti* traditional teaching, based on repetition. He was asking, "What is it I told you?" So I have to answer him and tell him word for word what he said to me. Then he'd say, "No, I didn't say that, I said so and so," and he keeps correcting, that was the way they learned about the Holy Dance Fellowship (*okóta* = fellowship).[1] But in his time it was called a Holy Dance Society (*okódakiċiye* = society), and later on, in the Reserve Era, it was changed to Holy Dance Religion (*wóċekiye* = religion).[2] (Mniyo May 31, 1997)

[SB 1977] The Dakota bands resid[ing] on seven small reserves in the provinces of Saskatchewan and Manitoba . . . did not rebuild the *tiyóti* formation, but . . . employed many ideas from the *Tiyóti Oíhduhe*. But the Santee, commonly called the Sioux camp, located two miles north of Little Red River park at Prince Albert, were known to be the last with *Tiyóti Oíhduhe*. . . . The flu epidemic in 1919 corrupted the last working *tiyóti*. About a dozen families survived and were moved to the Wahpaton Reserve 94A about 1921. (Samuel Buffalo 2, 1977, 8)

[SM 1985] Dr. James Howard told me, "Your sponsors gave you these stories to write them." (Mniyo May 1, 1985)

[SM 1997] And so I am passing on these stories to the Dakota people, to learn about who they are. (Mniyo May 10, 1997)

The Era of the Red Road Journey (*Tiwópida Oíhduhe*)

The Red Road Journey of the Dakota People, 1977

[SB 1977] It began in far eastern lands. From there our ancestors came in search for the new generation. The journey extended to many, many Dakota generations. The journey had trained Dakota people to share knowledge and support one another. The promise of a new generation had trained the Dakota people to centralize their confidence and hope in one sacred circle. The sacred circle was in harmony with the circle powers of nature. Our Dakota elders interpreted their history as: "We are the survivors of the *Tiyóti Oíhduhe*. We are the descendants of the eastern generation. We will be the ancestors of the new generation. We will find mutual relationship and kinship in Dakota history. When we look around, we will find friendship. When we look ahead, we will find sponsorship of Dakota elders for Dakota children." This was the way of the Red Road leading to the promised new generation. (Samuel Buffalo 3, 1977, 2–3)

The *Wakáŋ Waćípi Oḱodakíćiye* (Holy Dance Society) and
Ċaŋkú Dúta Owíćimani (Red Path Journey), 1965

[SB 1965. Sam Buffalo delivered this speech on Flower Day, Sunday, May 30, 1965, at the Wahpaton Reserve cemetery. Henry Two Bear also spoke (in Dakota), and singers sang songs on this occasion. Sam recorded the event on a tape recorder. Dan transcribed Sam's speech many years later. In this speech, at age thirty-five, Sam expresses his deep desire to preserve the untold history of the Red Path Journey. He also declares his belief that the Red Path Journey was intimately interwoven with the Holy Dance Society. He advocates doing a study to gather more information. Perhaps this book is the result of that conviction and that hope. DB]

That day has arrived when a dominant culture has gradually vanished and will return no more. I am here to witness this sad event. Yes, I possess the knowledge to speak the language, the skill to interpret the signs and colors, and the memory of many good interesting stories that I heard in my childhood days. Therefore the least I can do is to preserve what little can be told about the vanished society that once made the Dakota nation strong and courageous. The composition I intend to prepare is to review the untold history of the *Ċaŋkú Dúta Owíćimani* meaning the

Red Path Journey. . . . However, this . . . depends mainly on two factors, first, how much information can be collected about the pre-European organization known as the *Wakáŋ Waćípi Okodakíćiye* (Holy Dance Society); secondly, to find a person who will interpret the signs, colors and arts expertly into a formal language. . . .

A strong interest motivates me to make a study of the [Dakota] nation's path from an unknown point in the east leading westward.[3] The study will be performed by interpreting the principles and the songs of the Holy Dance Society. The group in Holy Dance Society had all spoken of the Red Path Journey. According to the *Ćaŋdójuha Yuhá* (special member) of the Holy Dance Society . . . , at the extreme point in the east where the land meets the ocean, it was at this place where the *Ćaŋkú Dúta* was introduced. The people stood [by a deep water] and it spoke with the voice of a higher power. The voice assigned them to a westward journey to seek for a good reward. The reward of this journey is the promised land which lies far beneath the western horizon.

The [journey] consists of four eras, as: early day, mid-day, late day and dusk.[4] The people accepted the message to explore the vast unknown land. They [acted on] the promise by organizing the *Wakáŋ Waćípi Okodakíćiye* [Holy Dance Society, and commenced the journey] to search for the promised land. Unfortunately this . . . dominant society with the *tiyóti* administration, referring to the circle system, does not exist with us anymore. The last known *Ćaŋdójuha Yuhá* (special member) died only a short time ago at Oak Lake Reservation in Manitoba.

Still though, much information can be found in several ways. There are several books written about the *Wakáŋ Waćípi Okodakíćiye*. A number of antiques belonging to the *Wakáŋ Waćípi* society can be found at a museum of a university. Other informants available are as follows:

(a) Contact the other people whose father or mother was a *Ćaŋdójuha Yuhá* (special member) of the *Wakáŋ Waćípi* Society. These are the people who are familiar with the *Wakáŋ Waćípi* principles and songs; [they] are very few residing throughout the North American continent.

(b) Only one song stick and a few copies of song sticks and scrolls are found in Saskatchewan. There are many more to be found. The importance of these songs is depicted on these sticks or scrolls. Recently some of these songs were translated into words of the Sioux language.[5] The interesting part of these songs describes conquering animals, location of residences, and the acts of people.

(c) The study can be focused on the designs of art: arrows, spears, and cooking methods, the pattern of homes and transportation, new communications they acquired as they advanced on their journey. Perhaps . . . the songs or arts may describe one of the heroes and their drastic changes.

The *Ċaŋdójuha Yuhá* (special members) declared that it was on this continent when the third era had occurred, that their people had gradually moved along the Atlantic coastline to the location of *Mniháħa* [*mni* water, *haħá* falls. DB] which we know today as Niagara Falls. That movement [then] directed westward to the region of the *Tiatowana* [Teton], meaning plains dwelling [and] in a large circle pattern they were moving westward to the area of *Wazí Pahá*, meaning Cypress Hills, Saskatchewan. [Sam originally used the word *rijutoha* for Cypress Hills. We were not able to decipher this word in this form, and since it was used in a letter, there was no way to hear it spoken. Therefore we chose *Wazí Pahá*, which is a place name commonly used by the Dakota for Cypress Hills. DB] [They came together in] Minnesota. Western settlement broke up the cycle movement; people dispersed in Canada and the United States and the *Wakáŋ Waċípi Okodakíċiye* slowly vanished to near extinction at our present time.

One of the principles we share, to live in harmony, is considered to be the most important. Others are skills, philosophies, *tiyótis*, circle administration. Now if these formations of the *Wakáŋ Waċípi Okodakíċiye* are [gathered], organized and written into books, [they] will not only preserve the native culture but also provide a role in social education and provide very interesting reading. (Buffalo May 30, 1965)

The Song Stick (*Wakáŋ Dowáŋpi*), 1966 and 1967

[SB 1966. Sam Buffalo wrote a letter to me on December 27, 1966, about the "song stick" (*dowáŋpi*) and its relationship to the *Wakáŋ Waċípi*. We approached faculty members at the University of Saskatchewan with a written proposal for doing research on the *Wakáŋ Waċípi*, but nothing came of it and I forgot the matter for many years, until about 1985. The letter follows. DB]

The proper name in the Dakota dialect is *Wakáŋ Dowáŋpi* [song stick for *Wakáŋ Waćípi*].... This stick is a specially treated piece of wood usually about 15 inches long, 2½ inches wide, and ½ inch thick. There are numerous small arts [pictograms] on each side, single thin line carvings of man, animals, fish, lodges, the world, bow and arrow. These inscriptions represent the meaning.... The combination of these meanings describes the insight relationship between higher power, spiritual, mental, physical, and action of man....

The song sticks are very rare among the Dakotas in Canada....

The owner of a song stick is a member of the *Wakáŋ Waćípi* (holy dance organization). The member of this organization usually dedicates his own life as a partaker in an essential body of the Dakota nation. In fact, there are four inner groups in this organization. The names as follows: *Ṭaodé, Ćaské Pos'íŋ, Wahpé Atúŋwaŋna,* and *Apéhota.* The four groups practiced the same doctrine of the *Wakáŋ Waćípi.* [Sam later also gives these same names to the four groups into which the Dakota people divided in the Turning Point era. DB]

According to the tradition of the *Wakáŋ Waćípi* there are several items passed on from one generation to another generation. The items are: *ćaŋkójuha, ćaŋksá, waksíća, waćíŋhe,* and *wakáŋ dowáŋpi* (song stick). Basically, this is done to avoid any change in the fellowship of the organization....

The secret code among the arts [characters, symbols, pictograms] is important. Members are warned to take all precautions to keep it from the public and other Indian tribes. The only time when some codes are simplified and announced to the public is at the annual meeting in the midsummer. This event is known as *Oyáte Ókiju* (public unity)....

We know there are several methods used for communication.... On the song stick of *Wakáŋ Waćípi* are some arts [pictograms] explaining how to commune from the image of man to a higher power. These two arts give the best illustration. The art of a man erected upon a circle or globe and the art of a circle or globe upon a man, this is how the communication is modified.

Nature's pattern of movement is in a circle and everything [is] performing in harmony with one another. Likewise, the Dakotans have adapted such a system into their livelihood and developed a strong faith, confidence, and wisdom in the path of unity with nature and with higher power.

The general principle of the song stick is to preserve the Dakota culture. In the arts, codes, message, and communication, we find the science of living in harmony. . . . There is just one constructive pattern of motivation as: surrender, survive and conquer. This is the common practical cycle in every span of life in the individual, friend, family, clan, society, inner tribe, organization, and nation. The prayers, arts, crafts, and homes all centralize around the circle, for it is the circle that is fundamental to the Dakota culture. (Buffalo December 27, 1966, edited by DB)

[SB 1967, telephone conversation]

Q. You mentioned that there are several articles passed on from one generation to the next, other than the song stick, according to the tradition of the *Wakáŋ Waćípi*. What are they and what do they look like?

A. There is the *Ćaŋkójuha*. It is a sort of leather pouch, with arts [pictograms] and codes on the outside. Then there is the *Ćaŋská*. It is a wooden stick about 2 feet long with a few arts on it. Also there is the *Wakśíća*, which is the bowl. Most of them are wood, with some arts on them. There are some made of stone or sea shell, but very few made of clay. Then of course we have the *Wakáŋ Dowáŋpi*, the song stick, which has the most arts so you can tell the most from it. (Buffalo January 1, 1967, edited by DB)

The *Wakáŋ Waćípi Okodakíćiye* (Holy Dance Society) and *Ćaŋkú Dúta Owíćimani* (Red Road Journey), 1977

[SB 1977] Originally, a disaster had dispersed people into strange lands. A small group fled to save their lives. They encountered the ocean. So they travelled along the coast for a suitable hiding place. One was found and temporary homes were built. But happiness did not dwell with the people. Many were frightened and [too] insecure to look ahead. Unfriendly activities prevented them from associating together. This condition made them long for a better life.

Four eldest men were chosen to find a new life for the people. A narrow peninsula wedged far into the sea. At the very tip, the four elders made an altar. They prayed and fasted days and nights. Then one day at dawn, they saw the strangest event in their lives. Near them on the sea, the water sank down forming huge foot shapes. Above was like a massive bright star's falling. The elders' eyes were closed by the glow of the light.

Then a voice spoke to the elders that echoed throughout the sky. The voice described 150 herbs to refresh their health. The plants were shown to the elders. The voice explained four principles to organize their people. The voice gave them new survival methods to be carried out in many ways. The voice promised a new generation in the land where the sun descends. The voice commanded the elders and their people to journey to that *Ċaŋkú Dúta* meaning Red Road. A very heavy fog fell upon the elders for a short time. The scene concluded with a reddish circle that disappeared westward.

The Red Road Journey Westward. The elders were happy and quickly returned home. They delivered the good news to their people. Many . . . details were kept secret by the elders. On the coastline in the unknown eastern land, people rejoiced. They were blessed with new tidings on a most beautiful day. Four crowds seated in circles. At the center stood an elder teaching to people. These elders were busy in preparation activities.

The fourth day after hearing the holy voice, at dawn the first *omníċiye*, meaning circle ceremony, was conducted. In each direction, an elder sat facing one another [meaning four elders sitting in a circle]. At the center, a folded material was placed. When it was unfolded, a red circle [was] at the center of the material. The elder seated in the east commenced to talk about one of the four gifts. Then the elder representing south spoke of the second gift. It continued with the elder in the west followed by the elder in the north. The procedure closes with meditation and singing. A large crowd formed a large circle. . . . Dancing, yelling, and using musical sounds were performed. It was their way of expressing appreciation in refreshed life. The word *ḳodá* meaning friend was adopted. The four elders addressed one another with *ḳodá*. The title means the elders were dedicated members of the circle ceremony. Thereafter, every *omníċiye* (circle ceremony) closed with these words: "*Ḳodá úŋṡimada pó,*" meaning, "Friends have mercy on me." It was strongly believed that exchange of mercy promoted friendship. In *omníċiye* the friendship was an essential need. More and more people were accepting the big challenge. They were working hard in final preparations.

Another day full of excitement had arrived for the people. After a long time of preparing and waiting for this very special day, the journey commenced on the Red Road. The four elders led the file of people called *oúŋhdake*, meaning movement—the westward movement in search for the new generation—the new generation with good health, adorable homes, many arts to be learned, and pleasure for everyone to enjoy. This was the heart of the movement as the Red Road progressed step by step.

The Red Road was not followed every day of the year. It was [guided and] measured by the seasons. Each season of the four in the year had different assignments. Still the journey kept advancing westward. One important season was *wétu*, meaning spring, a period of refreshing body and mind to strengthen health. New growth of plants provided fresh herbs for them to use. Every seasonal circle ceremony, the diet changed too. There were four types of diet available to avoid famine. Flesh-eating animals and fowls were forbidden to be eaten by people. According to the *wakáŋ dowáŋ*, meaning holy songs, the Dakota ancestors were vegetarians. One other notable season was *bdokétu čokáŋyaŋ*, meaning midsummer. The elders selected a suitable campsite for one purpose, a pleasure for young and old, in terms of laughter, singing, dancing and games. This annual event was understood as rehearsal for the new generation. Most men's games were based on accuracy in spear and in shooting arrows. . . .

The recording of the journey distance by *očéti*, meaning campsite [camp fireplace representing a campsite], and *ómaka*, meaning season, was [ended] because the Red Road [Journey] had lengthened into generations. So, *čaŋyáwa*, meaning generation counter, was introduced. A piece of wood was measured longer than the length of a hand and an arrow; one side was flattened and smoothed. Two pictorial writings representing season and moon were sketched into the flat surface. Each *čaŋyáwa* equals one generation.

The Wakáŋ Wačípi Practice: Ceremony and Physical Layout. The traditional [system of] four members in the circle ceremony of friendship [became] outdated. The elders' duties accumulated beyond what four men could manage. Expanding [the] membership to share knowledge and support one another was favored. Any gray-haired men and women qualified to join the circle ceremony. So the membership increased creating [the need for] a structure change. A waist-high oblong wall of posts staked closely side by side was made. The size depends on the number of members participating within the structure. On each end a tipi was placed about twenty steps away from the main lodge. The [siting was that] the three lodges were erected in line from east to west. The tipi at the east represented the first altar. The *akíčita*, meaning guardian members, dwell in these [east] tipis during the ceremony. The main lodge represented *okó-dakiċiye*, meaning society. The tipi at the west represented the promised new generation; the *Ċaŋdójuha Yuhá*, meaning principal members, were in the oblong lodge [west].

The duties of the four gifts were distributed among the principal members. Every member was thoroughly taught about the Dakota movement.

The four principles given to the Holy Dance Society were arranged for organizational development. These were: belief, identity, skills, and attitude. The first known belief was their encircled encampment in harmony with *Wakáŋ Ťáŋka*, meaning most holy circle in the universe. Then the circle power of earth, meaning nature. They constructed their homes as circled tipis according to their *wówiċada* meaning belief. Near the center of each tipi was the sacred circle *oċéti*, the fireplace. (Samuel Buffalo 4, 1977, 2–5)

The *Wakáŋ Waċípi Oḱodakiċiye* (Holy Dance Society) and *Ċaŋkú Dúta Owíċimani* (Red Road Journey), 1985

[SM 1985] The words *wakáŋ waċípi*, or "holy dance" originally meant "mystery motion" (*wakáŋ* = mystery, and *waċípi* = motion). So *Wakáŋ Waċípi Oḱóta* really means "mystery motion fellowship."[6]

Long ago, when our ancestors were far on the eastern coastline, on a peninsula wedged far into the ocean, the man *Iyá Owáśte* (Speaks Well) was praying there to God. The name for God was *Ajúhowa* or *Júhowa*: creative-voice-being (*jú* = to decorate or beautify, *hó* = voice, and *wa* = being).[7] *Iyá Owáśte* was a spiritual seeker, searching for the Hill or Knoll of Truth (*pajódaŋ iyéċetu*), going from hill to hill. The others were afraid to pray to God since they thought God had afflicted them: they had lost the main body of their people due to some disaster.

This group had escaped the disaster, and had wandered like gypsies from one group of people to another, since no group wanted to take them in. They had become good traders, excellent bowmen, fearless fighters, and skillful in making things with their hands. Moving eastward searching for a country with fewer people, they had come to the ocean. Some were dying from strange diseases. They were divided: some wanted to return to their country, and some did not. These small groups were enemies to each other. Each small group had an idol and prayed to different gods.

Four men still believed in one god: among them were *Iyá Owáśte* and

Izó Ċaské [*izó* = peninsula, *ċaské* = name of firstborn child, if a son]. *Izó Ċaské* also was one who always prayed to God, who believed all the praying to idols by the others was not doing any good, and whose own group living on that peninsula was healthy. *Iyá Owáśte* believed that if they did renew their relationship to God their prosperity would be restored. *Iyá Owáśte* went to *Izó Ċaské*, who suggested he fast four days and four nights, praying only to God, so they did, the four of them.

They made an altar at the very point of that peninsula and fasted there four days and nights. Finally, at the end of the fourth night, at dawn, a light came to them, in a circle, like a halo, a light which was in motion, going small and big, small and big. A voice spoke to them from there, telling them to journey westward, to the land where the sun descends, saying "There you will find *oúŋ*," a place or condition where people will live together, share equally in good health, work and prosperity, and become a nation. *Oúŋ* means homeland, not land itself but home (community, people) also expressed by *ókiju*, where people come/stay/keep together.

The Red Road Journey Westward. After discussion, preparation, and fighting among the people, *Iyá Owáśte* took the lead and managed to lead some of the people westward on the Red Road Journey [Red Road Pilgrimage and Lifestyle]: *ċaŋkú dúta oúŋ hdámni k'a oíhduhe* (*ċaŋkú* = road; *dúta* = red; *oúŋ hdámni* = pilgrimage; *k'a* = and; *oíhduhe* = lifestyle). The four men, including *Iyá Owáśte* and *Izó Ċaské*, remained together. Not all people moved with them, only those who believed in *Iyá Owáśte* when he visited them in their camps: the others stayed behind.

Iyá Owáśte and the three others became elders of the Red Road Journey, the journey to that *oúŋ* which God had promised them in the direction the sun descends. These four leaders camped west of the main body of the people (this was before the Sioux split up into different groups). They pitched a shelter tent, and before sunrise all home-owner-men (household heads) would go there and pray together. The elders would give the message of the day and tell what the routine of the day should be (they were not travelling every day). They would return to their huts (oblong buildings with the roof going down to the ground) and tell their families the routine and work. As they carried on this way, constant, they began to have better health, community consciousness, and fellowship. They lived as allies, not enemies, and began communication and trade with others. The word *kodá*, which now means ally or friend, really means co-believer in the *Wakáŋ Waćípi* and its promise, not doubter. In those early days they believed and trusted in finding *oúŋ*.

Iyá Owášte was the last of the four elders to die. To succeed him as leader he appointed *Hokśíŋ Wamná* (the Orphan Boy). [*Hokśíŋ Wamnáda*, "Respected Boy"; the word for orphan is *wamdéniĉa*.]

This boy had been there with the four elders and his grandmother, and had volunteered help. His name was *Waŋdúta* (Red Arrow) [*waŋ* = arrow, *dúta* = red], a name that reappears throughout history as a hero. He developed the *Wakáŋ Waćípi* as a religion; that is, he gave people the freedom to join the *Wakáŋ Waćípi* society or not. They could still remain in the Sioux group, but were no longer forced to be a member of the *Wakáŋ Waćípi* society. Since then not all have become members. After that time whenever they appoint a baby boy as leader, they give him that name, *Waŋdúta*.

Not all the Dakota followed the Red Road Journey. They split up into smaller groups or clans, each with its own medicine, altar, icons, etc., competing with each other, saying "our clan has better medicine than your clan."

The Wakáŋ Waćípi Practice: Ceremony and Physical Layout. [In later years] the people came together each year for two to four days for a commemoration of the *Wakáŋ Waćípi* or mystery motion of the light and voice. They demonstrated their thanks-living by giving their testimony that throughout the past year they have gained so and so or have lived this way. There would be singing, praying, giving of testimonies, and demonstrating gifts such as medicines, all for the purpose of giving thanks or thanks-living (*wópida-ikíni uŋ*).

The tent of the elders was called *wópida* (wo = seventh sense, source or part of the divine power, referring to divine, not earthly mystery; *pi* = channel; *da* = to ask for something more in life; *wa* = sixth sense, in between wo and the person, ordering the mysterious things on earth).[8] In this tent lived those who had reached their life span. At the time of the *Wakáŋ Waćípi* gathering, there would be constant praying, day and night, in thanksgiving. They saw the *Wakáŋ Waćípi* as mediator between man and God.

East of the *wópida* was the main structure called *oyáte anóka* ["people on both sides"] where the other believers gathered for the *Wakáŋ Waćípi*.

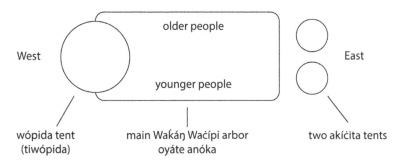

West   older people   East

younger people

wópida tent   main Wakáŋ Waćípi arbor   two akíćita tents
(tiwópida)   oyáte anóka

FIGURE 2. Layout of lodge for *Wakáŋ Waćípi* during Red Road era. This drawing, made on Sam's instructions, shows several main features: an east-west orientation (possibly symbolizing the east to west Red Road pilgrimage); an oblong or oval ceremonial dance enclosure, called the *oyáte anóka*, with walls chest high and no roof, with the older people seated on the north side and the younger people on the south side, and the drummers, singers and flutists in the two corners at the west end; the *Wópida* tent, closing the west end of the dance enclosure, half-open on the east side, housing the leaders of the ceremony; and the two *akíćita* (guard or police) tents guarding the open (entrance) east end of the enclosure. I believe that dancers moved around the enclosure in a clockwise direction, symbolizing the circle of the life cycle, from birth and young age to old age and death, and birth again. Drawn by Daniel M. Beveridge, Danny Beveridge, and Molly Seaton-Fast.

They stood still in an oblong shape inside this oblong structure (running east-west) which had walls chest high and no roof. [See figure 2.] The door was in the east end. People were situated according to their age: the younger people were along the south side, to the left of the entrance, and the older people were along the north side: this was according to the *nióbe* of their life span, and the *tiyóti oíhduhe*. . . . The drummers, singers, and flutists were in the two corners at the west end. The leader or host was called the *ćaŋdójuha yuhá*. The area inside the door [east end] was where the faith-walk or *owítaŋ ećáŋ* took place.

East of this [long main arbor structure] were the tents [two tipis pitched together] for the *akíćita*: the police and servants who would cook, supply food, keep the fire going and the water. Others would bring food too.

Non-believers would be outside the camp, having a sports meet and practicing their skills. (Mniyo April 30, 1985)

[Sam's description of the physical layout of the *Wakáŋ Waćípi* is consistent with the descriptions and photos provided by Howard (1984) and others in part 1. DB]

PHOTO 4. Chief *Tama*, a chief at Wahpeton Dakota Nation. He was a Mdewakanton, the youngest brother of John Sioux (*Aŋpétu Waśíċuŋ*), who came with his six brothers and with Chief *Húpa Iyáhpeya* to the Prince Albert area in 1877. Courtesy Leona Anderson, Wahpeton Dakota Nation.

The *Wakáŋ Waćípi Ok'odakíćiye* (Holy Dance Society) and *Ċaŋkú Dúta Owíċimani* (Red Road Journey), 1997

[SM 1997] Among my Dakota informants, three were members of the *Wakáŋ Waćípi Okóta* (Holy Dance fellowship) or sometimes they call it the Holy Dance religion. Well, when they're talking about it, these three men, that was Chief *Tama*, John Campbell, and James Black [Jim Sapa], they all start at the same point by talking about the search for the Hill of Truth, that's where they always start with the Dakota history.

In those days a destruction or disaster occurred in that region where our *Isáŋti* ancestors lived. At that time they were living in the far eastern lands, in the ancient time of Dakota history. After the destruction occurred, there was a man known as a *waáyate* (which I translate as a seer or prophet of God). His name was *Wahóbe Adéde*. This old man was telling the people the destruction came upon them to punish them because of their cruel practices and their belief in polytheism, or worship of many gods. Many were fasting and calling themselves holy men. This old man went on to tell them that he had some good news, and this good news was about the search for the Hill of Truth. Whenever they find this [Hill of Truth] they will find four things: *wówičada* (belief), *wósu* [faith], *wótawa* (personal spiritual belongings, what you can claim from God, live as follower), and *wówiyekiya* or *wičóiyekiyapi* (identity). These four things make up *wópiye* (new medicine bag), and with these four things they will find what the word *odákota* means. He said they will make a lifestyle called *odákota* which means the people who have these four things can say, "I am a Dakota, you are a Dakota, we are Dakota." He said, not until then can we call ourselves *dakóta*: we have to find this Hill of Truth.

This *odákota*, when we find it, we'll find a new way of living or lifestyle. So he and the believers, and remember that they were the people who were trained to worship one god, were the ones to live through this destruction, they went around looking for the Hill of Truth in all directions in that area. But they couldn't find it. This man died. Then they appointed another man who took over.

No one really knows how many generations they were searching for the Hill of Truth. But many generations thereafter they came to an eastern ocean, with a peninsula wedging far into the ocean. It's a narrow piece of land. And that's where they dwell first. And they call this place *Izó* or *Isáŋ Izó* (sharp-edge peninsula). [*Isáŋ* = sharp, *izó* = peninsula.] That's where the name *Isáŋati* or *Isáŋti* came from.[9] And while they were living on this piece of land there was a child born there and they gave him the name *Isáŋ Izó Časké*. *Časké* is the name for the oldest boy in each family [if a firstborn] and *Winóna* is the name for the oldest girl [if a firstborn].[10] As he grew up his grandfather was the one who taught him about the heavenly god and the belief that goes with it.

So as he was growing up, they always have this *iŋhdépi*, an altar made of stone, a pile of stones. [*Íŋyaŋ hdépi*, "rocks piled up."] On top of that they put some sweetgrass, they burned that. That old man will be praying to God and asking to direct him to where the Hill of Truth is. Because by that time the people were now again going back to where they were. Each person was starting to fast and all that. All the people were starting to have their own gods, and even some human beings, children, were worshipped. I don't know exactly the ways they're doing it, but they usually worshipped some man, some beautiful girl, or a child. So when they were starting to do this, *Izó Ćaské* started to pray about it and [was] always asking.

And there was a man named *Iyá Owáśte*, and he was also looking for the Hill of Truth. He was going to pray to wherever he sees a hill, he goes up there, on top of that hill he'll see another hill someplace, and he's looking for it, believing he'll find it. Then in his vision he was told to go down to *Izó Ćaské* and make one of these *íŋhdépi* (altars). So he went there and told *Izó Ćaské* about his vision. And they elect two other old men who also had the same belief as *Izó Ćaské*. So these four men went to the very point of the *Isáŋ Izó* and they made an *íŋhdépi* (altar) and there they fasted. They fasted two days or four days.

It was the last morning when a voice came from a ray of light, as the voice told them to go westward, that's where the sun descends. Below that there is a new land, no one lives there. Now this new land has a river. On the north side of the river he told them to dwell, until they find that Hill of Truth. So that's what they did.[11]

Before coming to the river they came upon a land where it has many lakes, or it has many islands, they didn't know which is which. [This could refer to the area northwest of Mille Lacs Lake in Minnesota, which has hundreds of small lakes, on both sides of the upper Mississippi River. DB] So they stopped, and the scouts went ahead. And some time later on they returned back to the people and they told them, it's quite a ways from here, we found the river, so we're going to go up there, I believe that's the river. So the journey continued on. Again I don't know how many days it took them to go down to that river. But finally they arrived there. And that river has a lot of fish. And in that area it has a lot of *psíŋ* (wild rice) so the leader said we should stop here. So we'll rest for a while, then continue our journey. So they stopped there. Then a few years thereafter they continued to look for the Hill of Truth for a while.

Along the river [they were] going up and down. This man was telling them that they are forgetting about the purpose of this journey, that is, to search for the Hill of Truth. But then, he says, if we don't move on and look for this particular place, then we're going to be punished. But the people didn't listen to him. So one day he told them, I am moving westward to search for the Hill of Truth. I'm going along this river.

He says, up to this point the heavenly god called this as *čaŋkú dúta oúŋ hdámni oíhduhe* (the Red Road Pilgrimage and Lifestyle). So he said, I will resume this pilgrimage. So anybody who believes me can follow me. Then he went westward along that river. Now this river they call it *Miníhaha Wakpá* (river with many falls) known today as the Mississippi River, that is supposed to be the blood line of this continent. So they turned westward. (Mniyo May 31, 1997)

[SM 1997] While they were beside the Mississippi River they forgot the Red Road. Only a few were dedicated to it. When a prophet/seer called a *wičášta wakáŋ* (messenger to people from God) told them if you don't move westward searching for the Knoll of Truth, you'll be punished and the Red Road will be disappeared. There was a four-day storm. On the fifth day all the land east of them became ocean. All those living out on islands died. (Mniyo May 10, 1997)

[SM 1997] Several days after they left, a severe thunderstorm came to them, and so they had to stop. This severe thunderstorm was east of them. After that storm was over, this old man told the younger boys, go back to where we started off, he says, see what happened. So they went back to where they were. And they found out that where they were, from there eastward, the Red Road was sunk far deep into what is known today as the ocean. Well, so all these people where they once dwelled were gone under the ocean. Nearly every little island there was people living on there. They didn't know whether it was a big lake with many islands or a land with many lakes, at this particular point where the Mississippi River drains into the ocean. All eastward, all the people who lived there were all gone. No one was left. That's the way they reported back to the people who were coming westward. (Mniyo May 31, 1997)

The Legend of Corn, 1997 and 1999

[SM 1997] Soon after they came to the Mississippi River and were living there, one particular group of people had an orphan boy named *Wamnámna*. He had no parents or grandparents. So he lived here and there, sometimes he lived in a dog house, he lived among the dogs, lived in the bush, and so on. And then there was an old man there who took him, washed him, clothed him and said, "You may stay with us and I will adopt you as my grandson." He was an elder of the *Isáŋti tiwópida*.

So after that he advised *Wamnámna* to meditate on the hill, to meditate concerning the Hill of Truth. "You may fast in the name of *Ajúhowa*," he said. By this time, they named the heavenly god as *Ajúhowa*. So while the boy was fasting and praying to *Ajúhowa* the heavenly god, then one early dawn of the third morning a large bird came to *Wamnámna*. He identified himself as a *hezá*.[12] This bird will be coming to an end. There's something about that bird that people use it for the feathers, although this bird was only a vulture. So due to the people, *hezá's* flock was getting smaller and smaller. And the *hezá* said to the boy *Wamnámna*, "One day you are going to die, like me, soon I will die and the *hezá* flock will be no more. And perhaps you someday are a descendant of the *Isáŋti*, and your *Isáŋti* may come to an end too. Therefore I have an idea I want you to consider. I want you to go and get two plants, then bring them to me, pound them together, and then I'll give you something that you've got to mix with it."

So after his fast was over, the boy went to look for these two particular plants and brought them to him, together, and he went away. Next morning *Wamnámna* went back to get the pounded up mixture, there on top of what he had left there was a big pile of the manure of the vulture. So he mixed them together and sowed them into the ground. From there grew a strange plant. It had a large stalk. He was expecting fruit, but there was something else that grew on there. Eight ears grew on that plant.

Then again he met in his sleep this *hezá*. The *hezá* said, "Now is the time. Those ears, fruit of that stalk, are ripe to be picked and eaten. Now," he said, "if you take those eight ears, you eventually will learn to cook them in different ways. Put them into water and boil them and then eat them, with honey. But before you cook them, take eight kernels from each ear, then next spring in the spring moon, put them in the ground, plant them, and you will get more."

The *hezá* said, "We'll combine our names together, that will be the name of this new plant. And you should use that corn to develop *odákota* in the name of your heavenly god with other people. There are many other people that you have not met, southward and northward. So take this corn to other people and tell them about this heavenly god, and tell them about the pilgrimage the heavenly god has guided you on. Tell them about the voice that came from the circle of light, which told your people to go westward to find a new land where the sun descends, to follow the Red Road pilgrimage and lifestyle, to search until they find the Hill of Truth." (*Odákota* means fellowship through one belief. Its purpose was to find the Hill of Truth.) "If those other people accept that, they'll also search for the Hill of Truth and pray to the god *Ajúhowa*."

So that is why the boy was taught how to grow the corn, he's supposed to make *odákota*, to bring peace to other people who were there. There was deep underlying tribal prejudice, different tribes praying to different gods, saying, "Our god is better than your god." *Odákota* is to stamp that out, to lead the people to have one god and one belief, to share a common spiritual belief quest, identity and fellowship.

So *Wamnámna* cut the ears off and when he cooked them, put honey on them, took this corn and gave it to the *tiyóti* old people and told them about this. So *Wamnámna* told the elders that the *wópida* (the place of meeting to give thanks to God) should continue on, that as long as they use this corn they should also leave the *tiwópida* in their *wićóti* (community). No one ever ate this [corn] before. Up to then there was no name for that plant. So the elders accepted corn as a food given from God. So that's why the elders called that corn *wamnáheza*, the boy and the bird, in the *Isáŋti* language, and so today.

After that, when they have this *wamnáheza*, they started to plant, every household cultivated its own small plot of land for corn, and they find ways of cooking it. Always the *Isáŋti* people have corn as their staple food. The next one is that wild rice, *psíŋ* they call it.

Those days, when the *Isáŋti* had a stomach ache, they often died, because I suppose corn and rice give lots of stomach ulcers. Some *Isáŋti* avoided corn.

And with the corn, the way they use it is they take it and introduce it to other natives, northward and southward. That's the way they made their friendship between different tribes, using the corn. They're evangelizing their god *Ajúhowa* along with this corn. So people accept this corn. If they accept this corn they should also accept *Ajúhowa* as their God.[13]

After that, they kept this up until the *tiyóti* era, then they started using tobacco and pipe.

As they went around, later on [in the *tiyóti* era] still with the *tiyóti* circle and lifestyle *ohóċokaŋyaŋ*, then they make these landmarks of a circle—they put stones in a circle and then that was a landmark to show how far they have evangelized their god and their corn. They were introducing the corn and trading things with corn on the Mississippi. (When the *tiyóti* big tent is in the middle and the camp is in a circle around it, the space in between is called *ohóċokaŋyaŋ*). And that is the legend of the corn.[14] (Mniyo May 31, 1997, and July 1999)

The Dakota Turning Point: The Dakota Divided (Three Versions)

The Red Road Journey Continues, 1997

[SM 1997] And then they keep coming westward again. Some of them again felt reluctant to go any farther westward. They didn't like to leave that country because it has a lot of game, a lot of plants, fruit. So some of them will remain [and] there's an antagonism between [them]. So at one particular point along the Mississippi River they decide to break up into four parts: one is to go westward, one is to go southward, one to go northward. . . .

So the ones who went westward kept coming west, always, came to a point where two or three rivers were draining into the Mississippi River. So they took the one that kind of went northward. And after journeying so far they came to a lake, and their leader said that we're going to dwell at this lake. From this point we'll look for the Hill of Truth. Then we're also going to go westward along that river. Maybe this is not the river that we came on. So the people who dwell at this particular lake, they call it *Isáŋ ta Mdé* [*isaŋ* sharp, *ta* at, *mde* lake]. *Isáŋ* is a sharp-edged lake because their ancestors came from the ocean, a peninsula, a very narrow peninsula, where it's into the ocean, call it *isáŋ izó*. So that's why they call this place [that].

My maternal great-grandmother [who became the wife of *Waŋdúta* (Red Arrow)] was a descendant of the *Isáŋati*, and she grew up at this lake [Knife Lake].[15]

I started off with the search for the Hill of Truth. Now this Hill of Truth really ended when they came to dwell at that peninsula in the ocean. From there on, thereafter the activities on the journey they always call it the pilgrimage. That's where the westward Red Road pilgrimage and lifestyle started. And that account come[s] to the Mississippi where the people divided in four ways. And that particular place, or after that era, they call it the turning point in life for the Dakota people. Because we did not take the name Dakota: you cannot take that name until you find the Hill of Truth. But . . . they're still searching, their pilgrimage is still searching for that Hill of Truth.

And then, after dwelling at this particular lake, the ones who went westward kept going westward until they came upon a mountain range lying north and south. And from there they sent their scouts ahead again. And when they returned sometime thereafter [the scouts] told them beyond this mountain range there's the ocean. So we made one big circle back to the ocean. So I don't think we can ever find this Hill of Truth. So that particular group broke up, some of them said they were going to remain at that west coastline. Some of them went toward the ocean, others remained at the foot of that mountain range, some of them went southward, some went north, some returned, backtracked themselves back again. And in later years they found these people living at the *Isáŋ ta Mdé* [Knife Lake]. And then these people remained there, these three men that I mentioned, they think that those people who returned and remained where the three rivers meet, they became the fishermen, they live on fish diet, and they were the *Sisítuŋwaŋ*, who today are known as the Sisseton. . . .

This turning point originally was where people were starting to disagree with each other, and there again, the *Isáŋti* nation was getting to be too big for one leadership [and for one region]. And they were getting into . . . polytheism. So what they did is that by a river they made a big landmark in a circle, a big landmark of bones, turtle backs, turtle shells, stone, wood and earth. This is where each went in different directions.

They divided into four groups, *Ṫaodé, Ċaské Poś'íŋ, Ẇahpé Atúŋwaŋna* (*Wahpeton*), and *Apéhota*. After this turning point took place, the *Isáŋti* [lost] their belief, the Red Road . . . pilgrimage. They still had their religion called the *Wakáŋ Waćípi Wikótin* [*okóta*], meaning Holy Dance fellowship. Later on they were known as the Holy Dance religion [*wóćekiye*].

Another reason why the *Isáŋti* tribe broke up into four groups, including the Wahpetons. The Wahpetons will [get] credit whenever they find the Hill of Truth. So if we make a *wićóbe* (encampment) and our *wićóbe* finds the Hill of Truth, we'll be the ancestors of their new way of life called *Odákota*. And also our descendants will be adopting the name *Dakóta*.

The ancient god named *Ajúhowa* ordered them to do that. But while they were living, during the Red Road Era, they're not supposed to have any other gods. But they do have their gods themselves. If this happened then their plans will fall apart and the descendants of the Red Road *Isáŋti* will be abolished from this Earth. So that was the big fear that they had, they didn't want to be abolished. So again, jealousy came among them as to which one, which *wićóbe* will find the Hill of Truth?

So the ones who went northeastward were the *Waȟpé Atúŋwaŋna* [Wahpeton]; the ones who went northward were the *Ćaské Poś'íŋ*; *Ṫaodé* went southward; and this other group, *Apéȟota*, went westward. So the *Waȟpé Atúŋwaŋna* continued with their Holy Dance fellowship, still looking for that Hill of Truth. But up to the *Tiyóti Oíȟduhe* era, which means *Tiyóti* Circle and Lifestyle era, and up to the Trading and Reserve Era, that Hill of Truth was never found (Mniyo May 31, 1997).

[SM 1985 and 1987] As they journeyed westward they came to find a mountain range lying north and south. They sent the scouts ahead to find a mountain pass to go through. Several years later the scouts returned and said, "Beyond this mountain lies the ocean. So all these generations we have journeyed we have made a big circle and have come back to the ocean. So after all, that voice lied to us." They still had not found *oúŋ* [home place, see glossary].

The people were divided there once again. Some said, "Why don't we look for that Hill of Truth?" So they started fasting in caves, mountains, hills, islands, and some dug into the ground and fasted in the ground. The number of temporal gods they used in their religious ceremonies multiplied. They prayed no longer to God, but to the four directions, to grandmother Moon, grandfather Sun, and grandmother Earth. They became polytheists, or worshippers of many gods.

They divided up into four main groups and went different ways. Some went south or north along the mountains. The group that went north was called *Ćaské Poś'íŋ*. They searched for the Hill of Truth, and sometimes made markings, possibly at the "growing hill" (*Ićáǧa*) between Fort Qu'Appelle and Griswold, the east end of Turtle Mountain (Canadian side), the east end of the Cypress Hills (*Wazí Paȟá*), and perhaps even the medicine wheel at Saskatoon.[16] Maybe the Assiniboines descended from this group. Some stayed there at Morley, Alberta, the Stoneys. I have heard that the Okanagan Indians at Vernon, B.C. have a center which they have named the Red Road Centre. The Stoney Indians at Morley, Alberta also talk about the Red Road and use Dakota words like *wašté* (good), *wakáŋ* (holy), and *nína* (very or most). (Mniyo May 1, 1985, revised August 3, 1987)

[SM 1987] The legend is that one group (named *Ćaské Poš'íŋ*) went north along the mountain range and across the ocean, searching for *oúŋ*, but we don't know if they returned.

The group of *Wakáŋ Waćípi* religion members turned back east, thinking they must have missed *oúŋ* somehow. They remained true to God and looked for the four spiritual treasures (beliefs, identity, quest, fellowship) as well as for health, home, career, and community. They went down the Mississippi River all the way to the ocean, and then back up the river. Now a large number of people, they were on the edge of starvation. They decided to divide into four groups, and whichever group finds *oúŋ* first will tell the others and they'll all come together there.

Two groups went south and west onto the plains. Another group, led by *Ṫaodé*, went east, came to a great waterfall, came back to the Mississippi River again (around Iowa), and went west up another river coming from the north. Another group went northeast into what is now Minnesota. One of these was the *Waȟpétuŋwaŋ*. (Mniyo September 30, 1987)

[SB 1977] During the *Akípa ikpákpi* era, meaning when the Dakota nation was reduced to people at the *wićóbe* or small encampment level, they had many gods. The problems they experienced were relating to their motto, "we share and we live in harmony."

The largest [or outermost] circle of homes and the circle next to it were made up of the strong men and women, capable in providing for survival needs. The third inner circle, they were employed in preparing material needs, storing and preserving food. The fourth or smallest circle were the homes of the *Wizí* (old folks and orphans living with their grandparents) and the *Ṫiókiti* (physically handicapped persons, mostly blind). This formation, which identified the Dakota nation, came to an end. [For Robert Goodvoice's similar description see figure 8 in "Living in the Four Circles" in part 3. DB]

It was separated in four equal parts according to four holy dance religion practices. They were *Ćaské Poš'íŋ*, the second one, *Waȟpé Atúŋwaŋna*, the third band was *Ṫaodé*, and the fourth group were known as *Apéȟota*. These were the four bands separated after the Dakota nation reached its height.

Since then, when an encampment grows too large, they will separate in equal parts. It was the way to avoid problems among themselves and externally. To share everything was hard to do, as a nation living all together [in one region] struggling with famine. The problem extended to their religion group practices. Each group was competing in making miracles, which led to threatening with *kičíčuŋza*, meaning cursing one another, and finally *kičíhmuŋǧa*, meaning killing in a secret way. The external problem can be described as the nation was too big to remain in one region for a full season. To maintain [a large group] in harmony with nature was hard to do. But *Wičóti*, meaning a community approach, was easier to do, without much hardship. So the process of dividing continued on.

However, the subdividing process among the Dakota did not make extinct the annual gathering called *Oyáte Ókíju*. Each summer season, the *Ókíju* were held at many locations by the *Dakóta Ošpáye* [band]. The annual Under the Big Top Celebration held on many Dakota reserves today is an old Dakota idea. It will trace back to the *Oyáte Ókíju* based on the activity known as *Itúh'aŋ* or donating. Still today, *Itúh'aŋ* is active as ever in the sense of pride but the original meaning is lost.

The sub-names of Dakota were developed according to a region or their costumes. One Dakota encampment received its name when a traveller came upon a *wičóti*, an encampment, which was erected on flat land without a pond or lake or river in sight. The visitor, curious, searched for their water source, and asked the crowd, "Where is your water hole, or do you people lick the morning dew?" Since then the people of the encampment were known as *Ćusdípa Oyáte*, meaning people of dew lickers. Cook Ironside [of our Wahpaton reserve] is a *Ćusdípa*.

The Dakota also had a second name, *Isáŋ Atúŋwaŋna*, meaning knife dwellers, to date abbreviated as *Isáŋti*. Some say the name "knife dwellers" [was taken] by Dakota people finding the material suitable for a cutting tool. Others say the eastern Dakota contacted the white traders at the Gulf of the Mississippi and obtained knives from them. The term Sioux was recently developed.

[As Sam has stated in this section, the initial close connection between the Red Road and the Holy Dance was almost lost in this era. In the next section, the influence of the Red Road is greatly diminished but the practice of the *Wakáŋ Waćípi* (Holy Dance) ceremony continues in the era of the circle power. DB]

The Circle Power Era (*Tiyóti Oíhduhe*)

[For Sam, *tiyóti* refers both to the large tipi at the center of the encampment and to the sociocultural system based on that *tiyóti* as its sacred center. DB]

Changing from the *Tiwópida Oíhduhe* to the *Tiyóti Oíhduhe* (part 1)

[SB 1977] In far off eastern lands, our ancestors journeyed westward. The Dakota people possessed a small [article], folded and preserved. At certain times it was unwrapped for their circle ceremony, placed open at the center of four elders. It contained only a thin line, depicting a circle. That was the sacred object called *iwósu*, meaning the seed or their purpose of life. The encircled elders spoke, prayed, meditated, and refreshed how to live. Then the circle ceremony closed with much excitement and joy. The Dakota informants claimed it was the symbol of a promise by a mystery voice, a promise of a life beneath where the sun descends. The life awaits with adorable homes, many arts to learn and pleasure for all. The Dakota people moved and [sought for] the new generation.

A new formation was made a long time after the start of the journey. The homes were placed side by side, forming a large circle. At the center was erected a big tipi called *tiyóti* [council tipi, soldiers' lodge]. It had two literal translations, which were "home and home" or "life and life," usually described as "home within home" or "life within life." The people protected the *tiyóti* to exist. In turn, [the] *tiyóti* protected the people to live. This was the beginning of their mutual relationship. The selected men conducting *tiyóti* duties were called *Tiyóti Yaŋká* meaning *Tiyóti* residers. They made decisions for the people. Every day men of the Dakota movement visited the *Tiyóti* to hear the latest decisions and plans to be carried out. This was their way of life for many, many years.

Again, many, many generations passed before another change was known. The *Eyáŋ*, meaning the herald man, went around the encampment informing the people, "We are the survivors of the Dakota minority movement. We are the descendants of the eastern generation and we will be the ancestors of the new generation. People be stern and be observant. You will live for the reward of the circle of life with fourteen *nióbe*," meaning phases. [Phases of life: 14 x 7 years = 98 years life span. DB].

The newly developed life span was measured by: one day and one night, one winter and one summer, four seasons, 12 moons, 24 times,

40 times minimum and 48 times maximum, meaning complete. (Samuel Buffalo 2, 1977, 2–3)

[SM 1990] Our early Dakota ancestors were pilgrims. Their westward Red Road Journey to *oúŋ* could be called *wiyóȟpeyatàkiya ćaŋkú dúta oúŋ hdamni k'a oíhduhe wihduhe* (Westward Red Road Pilgrimage and Lifestyle).

Legends played a part in the Red Road Journey. During the *Tiwópida Oíhduhe* era people believed then that [the] monotheistic god *Ajúhowa* spoke to them through the legends, geese [or other animals], etc. Spiritual well-being was [their] pursuit of life they learned at the Red Road Journey era time. But in the *Tiyóti* era, they started to worship the animals, the god of spring, the god of lakes, the god of hills—polytheism. They prayed to the White Buffalo, coyote, owl, bull elk, snakes, eagles, meadowlarks, geese, nighthawks, pelicans, the God of Two Maidens, clowns (*heyóka*), horses, dogs (some tribes). My mother worshipped horses. This was not the case before. But they also learned the spirit of Satan, [which] comes to them at the time of fast, [if] they do something bad, [like] worship their oldest or youngest son or daughter. (Mniyo March 20, 1990)

Changing from the *Tiwópida Oíhduhe* to the *Tiyóti Oíhduhe* (part 2)

[SM 1997] When they broke away from the Red Road, the *tiwópida* [tent] was outside the circle. But later on they quit that and brought that *tiwópida* into the circle and called it *tiyóti oíhduhe* (*tiyóti* lifestyle). It was in that pattern until they came to the reserve era or in 1862 when the uprise took place. The *tiyóti oíhduhe* was starting to break up after that.

Before the *tiyóti* era, this oblong formation [of the encampment], the main thing is they were praying to one god and all the people had the same beliefs. But suddenly they find out that each person can have his own beliefs, such as fasting. And then it happened, then each person start[ed] to have his own beliefs. This developed into several generations before this *Tiyóti* Fellowship [formed]. The *Tiyóti* Fellowship is a religious group. Before the members said OK we have to change because we're not praying to one god any more, we're having our own, we're inventing our own god. So therefore we have to change it, and someone came with the idea of a circle, *tiwópida* would be on the west side, outside the circle. Then that's the way they had the formation, a new formation. Those eight men who were operating the *tiwópida* [were] supposed to be the leaders of this Dakota movement, this *tiwópida* movement. But later on again, they said that wasn't good, you left the Red Road, the Red Road era was many years ago, so let's abolish the *tiwópida* and use a big round tent [*tiyóti*]. That's where the eight men, they cut it down to four men, four leaders.

Then the people's attitude changed. They had a mutual relationship with the *tiyóti* and the *tiwópida* people. And *tiyóti* [was] supposed to have a new relationship with God and God with the *tiyóti*. They put that *tiyóti* in the middle. *Tiyóti*: a large tipi in the middle with the four leaders in it. That was the last change they made.

But this *tiyóti* movement lasted more than two hundred years. My grandfather *Biddow* said they were living with that, with that *tiyóti* lifestyle.[17] My dad [Herbert Flying Buffalo], my grandfather *Biddow*, my great-grandfather Whitecap used to talk about this. Great-grandfather and his grandfather, they were all *tiyóti yaŋká* [*tiyóti* leaders]. . . .

My grandfather, *Biddow* Buffalo, said they were living like that just before the reserve era, said there's about 400 to 600 tipis in one encampment. And then Chief *Tama* [said when they had the] fiftieth year anniversary of Treaty No. 6, at Carlton, the old Carlton Agency, back then there was over 5,000 people there and the camp was quite big. [Treaty 6 was in 1876; its fiftieth year was 1926. DB]. And Chief *Tama* said, "It's just like when I was young. I used to come out of our tipi and this is just the way I see it." There are that many. They're not small camps. . . .

[But] the *Wakáŋ Waćípi* [ceremonial enclosure] retained its oblong shape during the *tiyóti* era, the last two hundred years of Dakota history. That remained the same. But that only lasted four days. Most of these *Wakáŋ Waćípi* ceremonies lasted for two days or four days, in the middle of the summer. It's always been that, two or four days. But there's one man who will make a *Wakáŋ Waćípi* ceremony. When it stops, another one will make theirs; and another. This is why they call it *Oyáte Ókíju*, meaning people coming together at one particular place in summer time, July or August. (Mniyo May 31, 1997)

[I show some of the differences between the two eras in the following table; Sam shows key differences in figures 4 and 5. DB]

Characteristic	*Tiwópida Oíhduhe* era	*Tiyóti Oíhduhe* era
Belief	belief in one god	belief in various personal gods
Layout of camp	linear or circular	circular
Layout of *Wakáŋ Waćípi* lodge	oblong or circular	circular
Leaders	*tiwópida* (four elders initially)	*tiyóti* (one group, cult movement leaders)
Location of leaders	*tiwópida* (tent on west side of camp)	*tiyóti* (tent at center of camp)
Number of niobes in life span	16 (16 x 7 = 112 years)	14 (14 x 7 = 98 years)
Faith walk	ends in *tiwópida* tent	ends in *tiyóti* tent

[SB 1977] In the *Tiyóti* system, the time called *Tu* was measured by twelve moons, especially by four seasons. Every season the Dakota moved to a certain region for a different purpose. For example, during the summer season the Dakota people had their *Oyáte Ókíju*, meaning people gathered together, in a sense of annual celebration to perform different dances and games for young and old folks. The main event was the holy dance [*Wakáŋ Waćípi*] religion ceremony. Within the body of the holy dance were four circles. It began with one circle of encampment and one *Tiyóti*. Later one circle had doubled and then tripled and a fourth one was constructed. So the Dakota encampment had reached the stage of four *Tiyóti*, one representing each direction, [in] a circle and facing each other. Each had a circle encampment. (Samuel Buffalo 2, 1977, 4–5)

[SM 1987] The *tiyóti* tried this and laid out their encampment in that same way, but it became a cult movement, praying in the four directions, earth, moon, morning star, not really praying to God. The elders of the *tiyóti* spend most of the day there [in the big tipi at the center of the *tiyóti* circle, the center of the encampment].

There was always an opening on the east side and on the west side of the encampment circle, three feet wide. (Mniyo September 30, 1987)

[SM 1985] Under the *tiyóti* cult movement, one group took control, claiming to have more power and to be braver. Now all people lived not around the sides of an oblong [as in the previous era] but in a circle. The *Isáŋti* Sioux had one large *tiyóti* tent (40 buffalo hide size) there in the center of a large circle of tents (20 to 25 buffalo hide size). But they saw the *tiyóti* as something like one big [invisible] tent covering the whole camp [wičóti] and protecting all, and also as a mutual relationship protecting one another.

The men of prayer in the center did the discussing of what to do, the thinking for the betterment of all, and most essential, the praying: they prayed expectantly, believing that what they prayed actually would happen. They were all old men, white-haired. They were twelve to fourteen in number, one for each nióbe of the human life span. If one of those in the tiyóti tent died, the others inside would elect another person from the camp to replace him. This would be not just anyone, but someone who had experienced an answer to prayer. It was the eldest daughter (winóna) and the eldest son (časké) of each family [if firstborn] who would take food to them and help old people particularly.

Under this tiyóti cult, the Dakota people didn't pray to God any more, and lost two nióbe from their life span, bringing it down to 98 years [14 nióbe]. Under the tiyóti they commemorated the Wakáŋ Wačípi annually, and called it Oyáte Ókíju (when all the people come together, for four days). The people had other ceremonies also, like the Sun Dance and the Buffalo Dance, since not all were Wakáŋ Wačípi members. (Mniyo May 1, 1985)

Tiyóti Oíhduhe: The *Tiyóti* System (The Circle System) in Dakota Society

[When Sam uses the term "sacred hoop" or *tiyóti oíhduhe* he makes no reference to the popular modern concept of "medicine wheel" used as an instructional tool for personal development, aimed at the physical, mental, emotional, and spiritual development of the individual, using four colors and referring to the four directions. DB]

[SB 1977] *Tiyóti Oíhduhe* was the name given to the sacred hoop that symbolized the mystery voice, the Dakota principles and rules, and the Dakota life span. It also meant the "home within home, life within life" system. "Home within home" refers to the community aspect, with a mutual relationship between the people in the circle and the men at the center. "Life within life" refers to the personal aspect, meaning the real "you" that is inside your body. (Samuel Buffalo 3, 1977, 2, edited by DB)

[SB 1977] The four principles given to the Holy Dance society were arranged for organizational development. These were: belief, identity, skills, and attitude. The first known belief was their circular encampment in harmony with Wakáŋ Taŋká, meaning most holy circle in the universe. Then the circle power of earth meaning nature. They constructed their homes as circular *típis* according to their *wówiċada*, meaning belief. Near the center of each *típi* was the sacred circle *oċéti*, the fireplace. . . .

An important identity in a *típi* was the invisible partitions. When entering a *típi* one should turn to his left. One should never turn to his right, in respect of the lady who lives there. (Samuel Buffalo 4, 1977, 5)

The Seven Circles

[SB 1977] The smallest circle in a home was *oċéti*: the fireplace was constructed of stones placed in a circle at the center of the tipi. Next, was the *típi* in round form. Then the *wiċóti*, a large circle visualized as one huge tipi protecting people and their sacred center, *tiyóti*. The Dakota *wiċóti*, meaning encampment, now in modern terms means community. Following this was *siŋtómni*, meaning the area as far as you can see around you. The final biggest circle was upward as far as you can see, was *Wakáŋ Ṫaŋká*, meaning moves mystery, commonly translated as most holy. There was one other circle of knowledge called *Wa* available for any purpose. So there were seven circles in harmony one with another. [See figure 3.] This was the power of the Dakota minority movement. And this was believed to be the central formation on the road to a new generation. (Samuel Buffalo 2, 1977, 3)[18]

The Sacred Hoop: Learning and Teaching over the Life Span

[SB1977] The Dakota life span was designed like a hoop [this hoop was the *Tiyóti Oíhduhe*]. The first half was for learning, and the second half was for teaching. On this sacred hoop there are fourteen markings called *nióbe*, meaning phases. Each *nióbe* consists of seven *ċaoéhde*, meaning steps, translated as seven years. The thirteenth and fourteenth *nióbes* are called *sagyé oéhde* meaning cane markings. (Samuel Buffalo 3, 1977, 3)

[SM 1987] The Circle of the Sacred Hoop is divided in half with a horizontal line from east to west, the Red Road or "path of goodness," with seven *nióbes* in the bottom half (age 0–49 years) and seven *nióbes* in the top half (age 50–98 years). The vertical line from south to north, which is the Black Road or "path of evil" is Teton only, not *Isáŋti*. (Mniyo September 30, 1987)

[SM 1985] The circle of man's life span may be divided up into *nióbes* or seven-year periods to a life span of 16 *nióbes* or 112 years in the Red Road Journey era (which was reduced to 14 *nióbes* or 98 years in the *Tiyóti Oíh-*

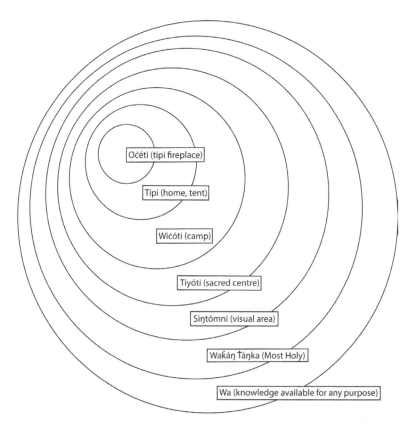

FIGURE 3. The seven circles of the *Tiyóti* system. Drawn by Daniel M. Beveridge, Danny Beveridge, and Molly Seaton-Fast.

duhe era). The first half, or up to age 49, was for learning, and the second half was for teaching. (Mniyo May 1, 1985)

[SB 1977] Every Dakota child from birth to seven years old, will learn about belief (*wówiċada*). Age seven to 14 will learn about identity (*wiċoiyékiyapi*). Then 14 to 21 years old will learn about skills (*wiċíoni*). And 21 to 28 years old will learn about attitudes (appreciation or *wapítkidapi*). The learning process concluded at the end of the seventh *nióbe*, or 49 years old. The eighth *nióbe* [49 to 56] was for analyzing and organizing all the things being learned. Then one began with the ninth *nióbe*, or age 56 to 63, teaching his selected subject relating to Dakota human development. The teaching process concluded at the end of the 14th *nióbe* or 98 years old. Thereafter the time is for preparing and meditating on the Red Road to a new generation. (Samuel Buffalo 3, 1977, 3–4)

[SB 1977] The spiritual aspect of the life span was measured by seven *ċaoéhde*, meaning stamps, translated as seven years or one *nióbe*. After 13 *nióbe*, or 91 years, it was measured by *sagyé oéhde*, meaning cane mark. The total years was 98, or 14 *nióbe*, which was the life span of the circle of life. The meaning of the circle of life was translated as birth child returns to old age child. . . .

An individual Dakota had one *nióbe* or seven years to search for his identity. His services were in this order: *Oċéti*, *Tiyóti*, *Wiċóti*, and *Siŋtómni* (visual area).[19] His work experiences in those four areas will provide one personal interest, will develop a personality and a name. In supporting his identity was *Dakóta* and the knowledge called *Wa*. The term *Wa* was only utilized in meditation and a four-day fast. A man must follow the procedure as discussed. For a girl the choice was to follow or restrict herself to home and community, because the identity difference between a boy and a girl is as follows: the male intelligence was evaluated on how strong and steady the feet demonstrated themselves; a female intelligence was evaluated on how active and attractive the hands demonstrated themselves. Only a foolish person will be concerned about facial appearances or posture. (Samuel Buffalo 2, 1977, 2–4)[20]

[SM 1987] Chief *Tama* did teach and made a feast in our reserve. Rose [my elder sister] said when she was a little girl the school kids were asked to go there. He took out a piece of cardboard with drawings on it.

The hoop can be made of flat wood, in 14 pieces, like a jig-saw puzzle. The 14 pieces are v-shaped, one for each *nióbe* [seven-year segment of the 98-year life span]. Each one has two parts, the physical aspect and the spiritual aspect. They can be one half inch wide, blue.

I only saw one in a vision with "this man" [*Ité Wapíkida*, my spiritual teacher]. It was red, flat, two and a half inches wide.

It could be a hoop with a round mirror hanging in the middle on a string from the top curve or north. (Mniyo September 30, 1987)

Teaching and Learning Skills under the Tiyóti Oíhduhe System [SB 1977] Now, what skills did a *tiyóti* produce? It commenced with the oldest child of the family. [If the firstborn], every oldest son was named *Ċaské* and usually was trained to help old-age people and handicapped, and every oldest daughter was named *Winúna* and they had the same training. The *tiyóti oíhduhe* had two types of poor people: called *wizís*, meaning the old folks, or orphans living with grandparents; the next one is *tiókiti*, meaning the physically handicapped persons, mostly blind. The *Ćaské* and *Winúna* duties were gathering fuel, hauling water, packing their belongings when moving the camp. *Ćaské* will hunt for *wizí* and *tiókiti* dwellers. *Winúna* gathers vegetables and does the sewing and things like this for them. In earlier times Dakota people were vegetarians—some say 148, others say 150 plants for vegetables. Many stories mention *wahúwapa* or *wamnáheza*, both terms meaning corn. It seems corn was a staple food for the Dakota people.

The *tiyóti* system developed a good understanding of mutual relationship. Kinship became so important that people found a method of keeping a record of family trees and that was a skill of everyone's concern. Another skill that every young man was encouraged to learn about was *siŋtómni*. They study [the] land formation, seasonal changes, and all its inhabitants. It was believed that the knowledge of *siŋtómni* will maintain, in harmony with *tiyóti*, a recording method known as *ćaŋyá*, meaning wood counting. One of the *Tiyóti Yaŋká* kept a record of *wićóićaġe*, meaning generations. Each *Tiyóti Yaŋká* recorded once in his life. Pictorial writing of songs and messages were preserved. This was the reason why the Dakota language has the words *toktópawinġe*, meaning one thousand. The next word is *wóyawa táŋka*, meaning one million. The Dakota people extend their counting method to a million.

The *tiyóti* system educated its people in skills in the following order: *wićóuŋ*, meaning the work and the relationship between the home encampment and *tiyóti*, including homecare practices. The next one was *wićózani*, meaning health preserving methods. This was the most important science in the *tiyóti* system. And *wićóḣtani* applied to everyday living and food gathering and performing work that was part of maintaining life in harmony. *Wićóimaġaġa*, meaning the social activities. Dancing was considered to be important. Next to it was the games and the social meetings and visits and so on. I should also mention the term *itúya oḣ'áŋ*, meaning voluntary actions, abbreviated to *itúḣ'aŋ*, translated as donate. The donating practice was developed in *tiyóti* for the sake of the *wizí* and *tiókiti* dwellers. (Samuel Buffalo 2, 1977, 4–5)

[Sam sets forth eight essential learnings or key aspects of life that the Dakota needed to learn in the first four *nióbe* of their life cycle, if the Dakota people were to follow the Red Road Journey and Lifestyle or the Red Road Pilgrimage toward the "promised land" called *oúŋ* (during the *Tiwópida Owíhduhe* era) and *odákota* (during the *Tiyóti Oíhduhe* era). In explaining these to me and also to Louis Garcia (personal correspondence, July 19, 1987), he distinguishes between the tangible and intangible aspects of life as follows:

Tangible aspects of life (*Ṫaŋíŋ*):
Health = *wózani*
Home/dwelling = *tiúŋ/tihdé*
Career/skills = *wičíoni*
Community/encampment = *wičóti*

Intangible aspects of life (*Ṫaíŋšni*):
Belief = *wówičada*
Identity = *woiyékiye*
Quest = *waóbe*
Fellowship = *oyáte ókiju, okóta*

Mniyo emphasizes the notion of long life, or the completion of the promised human life span, as a reward for following the way of the Red Road, and claims the proper human life span was longer in the early times. As proclaimed by the *éyaŋpaha* (herald man) around the encampment in those early times, "We are the survivors of the Dakota minority movement. We are the descendants of the eastern generation and we will be the ancestors of the new generation. People be stern and be observant. You will live for the reward of the circle life with 14 *nióbe*" (Samuel Buffalo 2, 1977, 3). One *nióbe* was seven years, so the proper life span was 14 *nióbe* or 98 years whereas in the earlier times it was 16 *nióbe*. DB]

The Red Road and the Faith Walk. [SM 1997] During the *Tiwópida* era, that path that goes right to the *Tiwópida* was called *Ċaŋkú Dúta Oúŋ Hdamnípi* (Red Road Pilgrimage Path). The Red Hoop Path (*Ċaŋhdéška Dúta Oómani*) was the first translation of that. It ran from the opening at the east side of the encampment west to the *tiwópida* (meeting and prayer refuge) on the west side of the encampment. The tipis are in a circle, but they always leave an open area at the east side. During the *Tiwópida* era they always leave the west side of the encampment open. They always visualize the *Ċaŋkú Dúta* [running through the encampment].

But then after that, when they abolished that *tiwópida* and changed it into that big tent (*tiyóti*) in the center of their camp, that's when they called it Ċaŋkú Dúta Wówaċiŋye Amánipidi (Red Road Faith Walk).

When someone dies, they believe they take the short walk to the *tiyóti*, in spirit, and from the *tiyóti* they go to heaven. They think there is a Red Road Nation (Ċaŋkú Dúta Towiyhe), a nation of the Red Road. Other natives call it the happy hunting ground! There are people [who think those who die] go to the *tiyóti*, since the *tiyóti* has a mutual relationship with God, from there they go on the journey to the Red Road Nation. These beliefs were in both eras, when one died, they would go on a spiritual walk, on the Red Road Path to the *tiwópida* or to the *tiyóti*, [then] to the Red Road Nation. [When] anybody dies—a lot of people do not meet the 14th niobe—but when every one of them dies, they die with the belief that they're going to come to this *ċaŋhdéśka* (hoop) they go around, come to this Ċaŋkú Dúta, then they walk to [the] *tiyóti*, when they go into [the] *tiyóti*, then their god will receive them and take them to the Red Road Nation. That's what they believe. [In 1985 Sam states, "The area inside the door [east end of the *Wakáŋ Waċípi* enclosure] was where the faith-walk or *owítaŋ eċaŋ* took place" (see figure 2).]

[That is] something I always believed in all my interviews, because I was told not to record these things, but in recent times I came to realize that these stories are of some value to the Dakota children to know where they come from and who they are. And that is why I want to include this part. (Mniyo May 31, 1997)

[SM 1987] At the age of 84 (12 *nióbe*) the old people were called *bahá* (curved over). When you reach the age of 98 (14 *nióbe* or full life span), you were called *wiċáȟċa* (true mature, bloom) and you would take the Red Road faith walk. (Mniyo September 30, 1987)

The Sacred Hoop: Comparing the *Tiwópida Oíhduhe* and the *Tiyóti Oíhduhe*

[Toward the end, Sam wanted very much to show in visual form simultaneously how the different features of the Sacred Hoop were integrally related. Let us repeat one of Sam's key earlier statements. DB]

[SB 1977] *Tiyóti Oíhduhe* was the name given to the sacred hoop, which symbolized the mystery voice, the Dakota principles and rules, and the Dakota life span. It also meant the "home within home, life within life" system. . . . The first known belief was their circular encampment in harmony with *Wakáŋ Taŋká*, meaning most holy circle in the universe (Samuel Buffalo 3, 1977, 2, edited by DB).

[Sam also wanted to show how the *Tiyóti Oíhduhe* era differed from the *Tiwópida Oíhduhe* era from which it grew, particularly:

- the physical or spatial layout of the *Wakáŋ Waćípi* ceremony;
- the physical or spatial layout of the Dakota encampment;
- the ideal life cycle of the individual Dakota person, with the essential learning tasks for different ages;
- the "Faith Walk" when a person dies; that is, the spiritual walk to the spirit world, the Red Road Nation.

Figures 4 and 5 are very similar in showing the central importance of the Sacred Hoop, but they show two important differences between the two eras, namely (1) the removal of the *Tiwópida* lodge shown outside the circle in the *Tiwópida* era in figure 4 and its replacement with the *Tiyóti* (*típi*) at the center of the circle in the *Tiyóti* era in figure 5; and (2) the removal of the Red Road Pilgrimage Path shown in figure 4 and its replacement with the Red Road Faith Walk in figure 5. Figures 6 and 7 are my own attempts to show only the spatial layout of the encampments during the two different eras. They may or may not match Sam's idea. DB]

Learning and Teaching over the Life Span: Belief, Identity, Skills, Attitudes

[SB 1977] A Dakota child who followed this life process would have exciting adventures throughout his life. A child must learn to listen with an open mind. A child must learn to observe everything. A child must learn to respect the elders and his sponsor. A child must understand the power of sacred objects, places, and names. The sponsorship was the basic training for *kićí*, companionship. It was an important practice in *Tiyóti Oíhduhe*. Learning to be a good companion will lead to having many friends. Later a man will be a member of an organization so the understanding of companionship and friendship will teach a man about membership.

Discipline commenced soon after birth; the child will have parental training. This early training was to prepare the child for his sponsor. The sponsor will teach generally about the *Tiyóti* system but his main concern will be the Dakota belief. By the end of the first *nióbe* at seven years old, the child will acquire a fair knowledge of the spiritual aspect of Dakota

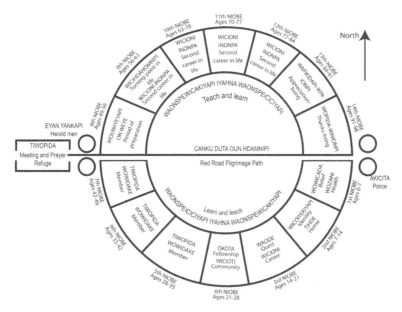

FIGURE 4. The Sacred Hoop during the Red Road or *Tiwópida Oíhduhe* era. Drawn by Daniel M. Beveridge, Danny Beveridge, and Molly Seaton-Fast..

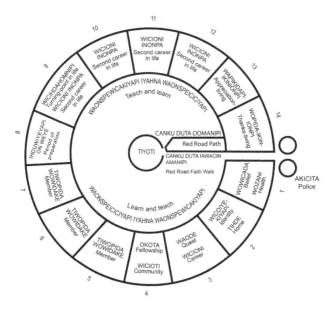

FIGURE 5. The Sacred Hoop during the *Tiyóti Oíhduhe* era. Drawn by Daniel M. Beveridge, Danny Beveridge, and Molly Seaton-Fast.

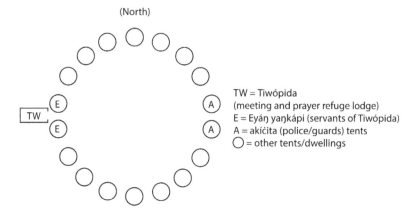

(North)

TW = Tiwópida
(meeting and prayer refuge lodge)
E = Eyáŋ yaŋkápi (servants of Tiwópida)
A = akíčita (police/guards) tents
◯ = other tents/dwellings

FIGURE 6. Encampment layout during the Red Road or *Tiwópida Oíhduhe* era: 10 to 100 tipis (tents) or dwellings in oblong-shaped or circle-shaped layout; *Wópida* (meeting and prayer refuge lodge) just outside and at west side of encampment; tipis of the *Eyáŋ yaŋkápi* (heralds or criers, servants to the *Wópida*) between the *Wópida* lodge and the main encampment; one or two tents of the *akíčitas* at the east end of the camp. (The layout of lodge for celebration of *Wakáŋ Wačípi*, a temporary structure erected at least once a year in summer, was similar: oblong, east-west orientation, *Wópida* tent at west end, *akíčita* tents at entrance at east end.) Drawn by Daniel M. Beveridge, Danny Beveridge, and Molly Seaton-Fast.

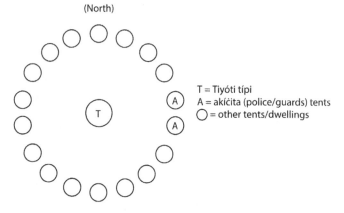

(North)

T = Tiyóti típi
A = akíčita (police/guards) tents
◯ = other tents/dwellings

FIGURE 7. Encampment layout during the *Tiyóti Oíhduhe* era: A circular layout, with 10 to several hundred dwellings in a circle; *Tiyóti*, a large, round tipi for leaders in center of camp; two *akíčita* tents at east side of camp. (The layout of the lodge for celebration of the *Wakáŋ Wačípi*, a temporary structure erected at least once a year in summer, however, was similar: oblong, east-west orientation, leaders' tent at west end, *akíčita* tents at entrance at east end, same as in *Tiwópida Oíhduhe* era.) Drawn by Daniel M. Beveridge, Danny Beveridge, and Molly Seaton-Fast.

development. The following story illustrates about belief or *wówićada*, to be developed during the first seven-year *nióbe* [age 0–7].

Belief: The Story of *Kas'ákuwiŋ*

An old lady was sponsoring a seven-year-old girl named *Kas'ákuwiŋ*. She and her parents left Long Plain, Manitoba. Several other families joined them to journey to *Wazí Pahá*, now known as Cypress Hills, Saskatchewan. When they reached *Maka Owíću*, now known as Gravelbourg, Saskatchewan, they visited some of their relatives who lived there. This was early in the spring to do *maśtíŋpazí* [this may refer to a special method of rabbit hunting — Sam did not translate; DB] and trapping fur-bearing animals at *Wazí Pahá*. So one early morning they left *Maká Owíću* for their destination.

When they arrived at their selected place, the following morning three cousins of *Kas'ákuwiŋ* — the men were in their twenties — suggested going *maśtíŋpazí*. *Kas'ákuwiŋ* saw one of her cousins walking out of their tent with her father's double-barreled gun. The three men went a short way from the lodges and loaded their guns. Then they sang *wakté*, meaning victory song. After that, one spoke loudly, addressing her father, "You are one of the few who started a fight at Minnesota called *Wóśiće*. Your foolishness scattered Dakota people in strange regions. You made many of us orphans and many families broken never to be together again. But today, you and your family will pay for it." They came forward toward the lodge and started shooting. *Kas'ákuwiŋ* held onto her baby brother. Her parents and brothers were shot. The three men quickly disappeared soon after the murdering action. Meanwhile, the old man [her father] called *Kas'ákuwiŋ* to bring her brother. When she knelt down with her brother seated on her knees, they were close by their father and suddenly he drew his knife but she pulled away quickly. With her brother, she managed to dodge the swinging knife.

Kas'ákuwiŋ took a small pail, a bundle of pemmican, her mother's sewing bag, a hatchet and a knife. She put her brother in a blanket and pulled him over her back carrying the other bundle. Both were crying as they left the scene. She followed back along the country that she barely remembered. The first nightfall, she selected a clump of bush. She prepared her bedding with old stumps. She stamped on them until the stumps were in small pieces and spread them out. There she placed herself on it very carefully with her baby brother, covering with one blanket but her feet were wet and cold. She started to cry as the memories of the fatal incident were coming back to her. But again she started praying and directing her mind to the spiritual aspect of life. *Kas'ákuwiŋ* lay there with little warmth.

Then she heard a man walking up to them. His clothing was decorated with small jingle bells. He stopped a short way from the children and said, "Your grandfather heard you and knows what happened to you. He appointed me to guide you children back to your people so fear me not. I am here to keep you children warm and throughout the day, follow my footsteps for strength and speed. Tomorrow, a little way from here, a fat duck will be given to you. You cook the duck so both of you may avoid hunger." The stranger came and lay down at the children's feet. Soon afterward, the warmth reached the children and they slept very heavily.

Kas'ákuwiŋ woke up by the sound of movements nearby. She quickly changed her brother's diapers, once again placed him in a blanket and on her back. She pulled the blanket ends tightly around her and tied them together. Then the other bundles and a pail she carried in each hand. When she came out of the bush, she saw a coyote trotting away, so she followed the coyote half running. After travelling far from where she started out, they came up to a pond. She found a large fat mallard tangled in the tall dry grasses along the pond. She killed it and prepared it and cooked the duck. She fed her brother and drank the broth. From there *Kas'ákuwiŋ* felt strong and eager to get back to the camp at *Maká Owíċu*. The following day, she did—went back late in the evening. The strange experience in reply to her prayer, it strengthened her Dakota belief.

Later, some families escorted *Kas'ákuwiŋ* and her baby brother back to Long Plain, Manitoba. They lived in that region with their uncle. She became a reliable helper to many families.

Her brother grew up to be a fine, intelligent boy but he was always in search for his family's murderers. One day, he found two men sleeping in the hills. He snuck up to them and took a double-barreled gun from them. He examined the gun and found the markings on it. He knew it was his father's gun so he shot one in his sleep and shot the other one while running down the hill. Soon after that incident, he found the third person. He walked up to him and gunned him down. Thereafter *Kas'ákuwiŋ*, her brother, and the whole family of her uncle moved away to another band. Then her brother joined another band and she never saw him again. *Kas'ákuwiŋ* married Ozepshunkov and moved to Prince Albert, Saskatchewan. She lived to a very old age at Wahpaton Reserve. While visiting her son Alex Swifthawk at Pelican Lake, Saskatchewan, she took ill and died at Pelican Lake Reserve. Most of her teaching to children was based on Dakota belief. She lived a healthy and a long life. And this is the end of the story of *Kas'ákuwiŋ*.

Identity

The next aspect of Dakota life was identity or *wičóiyekiyapi*, to develop during the second *nióbe* (age seven to fourteeen). A person doing a deed for a Dakota band was highly valued in those days. The people of that band were praised for it. Even if one person made a new discovery that the Dakota people would benefit from it, the Dakota band would be credited instead of the individual. The eastern Dakota or *Isáŋti* had learned to make baskets out of young willows and birch bark. The plains Dakota had horses before the eastern or the northern Dakota people. But through the annual *Oyáte Ókiju* meaning people gatherings, this is the place where they would share knowledge and help one another.

Now, the Dakota skills [called *wičóni*] were developed for the boys during the third *nióbe*, commencing at the age of 14 [age 14–21]. The boy would leave his home for good for long periods of time. He associated with other boys of his age. He continued to visit his sponsor for advice. Soon, he will join with other bands and travel with them. He knows that the seven years of skill searching and practicing adventures must be done. He was learning to survive in every circumstance of the *tiyóti* system. If he failed to do this, then people will identify him as one of the poor. They were known as *wizí*, meaning round-tipi dweller, or *tiókiti*, meaning living-within-his-own-tipi dweller. This was considered an embarrassing way to live. But some Dakota people had no choice but to live as *tiókiti*. (Samuel Buffalo 3, 1977, 3–6)

[SM 1985] I have tried to follow this teaching. I was supposed to go on a pilgrimage of seven years between the ages of 14 and 21. But when I left, my parents put the Mounties [Royal Canadian Mounted Police or RCMP] after me, caught me up, and sent me back home, and again a second time. I didn't bother after that. (Samuel Mniyo May 1, 1985) [This did bother

Sam considerably throughout his life. He often told me he regretted not being able to carry out this pilgrimage that he was supposed to do. DB]

Skills: The Story of *Tióde*

[SB 1977] Now this is the story of a fourteen-year-old boy named *Tióde*. His sponsor visited him often and encouraged him much with many exciting stories. But he knew he matured by adventures away from home or his encampment. The other boys of his age did not associate with him because he was blind and a *tiókiti* (physically handicapped person). But an idea came to him that prompted him to action. When his sponsor came and *Tióde* told him about his secret ideas, his sponsor was very glad and helped *Tióde* to make a plan. The following day the sponsor led *Tióde* to the hills. Later in the day, he would bring *Tióde* back home. This continued throughout the whole summer. Whenever the encampment moved to a new area, they would quickly find a suitable place for his skill development. During the winter months *Tióde* stayed indoors and practiced his skill secretly. He was very eager for the spring season. *Tióde* and his sponsor made more plans for the following summer months. As soon as the spring season arrived, he commenced his skill training. His practices were long and nearly every day. The sponsor wanted two full summers of training before introducing *Tióde* to the people.

In the third summer his practice extended only to the *Oyáte Ókiju*. At that time, the Dakota were engaged in three new activities: peace-making missions, trading adventures, and territorial fights. So, at the *Oyáte Ókíju*, the sponsor introduced *Tióde* as a singer and song-maker for the Dakota *Ohítikapi*, meaning Dakota heroes. Our *Ohítika* (hero) will approach *Tióde*, telling him about his daring action. *Tióde* will summarize the story to a song of twelve to sixteen words, including the *Ohítika's* name. This new style of promoting the men, created by *Tióde*, was well accepted. His skill was introduced at the proper time. He made his name *Tióde* well known in a short period. He received many gifts and payments for it, [and] that satisfied him. The following years were prosperous, having his own large tipi and married to a kind and a helpful girl.

His singing and his song-making skill led him to another skill. *Tióde* was paid for a song with a young colt. It later became a fast running stallion named *Pikána*. *Pikána* won many races. *Tióde*, the blind man, became a horse raiser, selling and exchanging horses with the pioneers coming westward.

Tióde, supported by his sponsor, freed himself from being *tiókiti* to become a respectable man of success. He died of old age. He sponsored many young boys into their manhood with good reputations. His teaching led to skill development. *Tióde* showed skill as presenting a new arrangement of old Dakota ideas. (Samuel Buffalo 3, 1977, 6–7)

[Later, in a letter to me in 1986, Sam used the story of *Tióde* to explain the two concepts of outcast and skill. *Tióde* was the father of *Wapáhaska* (Chief Whitecap) and a great-great-grandfather of Sam. DB]:

[SM 1986] The skill or career of selling or trading was so important to our forefathers. . . . The Holy Dance religion encouraged its members to develop this skill. After all the Red Road journey and lifestyle progressed by the skill to trade. By their hands they became artisans and produced something to trade with other people. In this manner they found favor and friendship with other people as they made their journey westward. This is the reason the term *Odákota* originated and became popular among the Dakota people.

According to the *tiyóti* rules, if any person young or old is considered unreliable to the encampment, he is an outcast. The *tiyóti* officials will tell that person's family to prepare him for passive euthanasia. Such experience happened to my great, great grandfather when he became blind before he was fourteen years old. He knew in a few years his family would prepare him to die. One morning he woke up with an idea—how to survive. He asked his brother to lead him into the hills. When he was alone he started to train himself to be a singer and a drummer. In three years, from spring to fall he practiced every day.

In the fourth year during the spring celebration, he introduced himself as a singer, and his new songs. Thereafter he became a paid singer. Someone offered him a mare and its colt for his singing payment. So he accepted the offer and later on that colt became the fastest running horse and a beautiful stallion. The owner was blind, yet he raised and trained his horses to be fast runners. Also he survived to a very old age. [He was] the first blind person to do that among the Dakota people. By one skill, they trade or sell to make one's own career and be a part of *Odákota*. (Mniyo, letter to DB, January 26, 1986)

Attitude

[SB 1977] *Opíič'iyapi*, meaning attitude, was the last of the seven-year training phases, the fourth *nióbe*, from age twenty-one to twenty-eight years old. *Dakóta opíič'iyapi* was the combination of skills to be practiced throughout one's life. In the case of the blind man, *Tióde*, his attitude extended into horse trading, peace-making missions, and giving fine race horses as gifts, fast running horses used in territorial defenses and successful *wanása*, meaning the buffalo hunts. In the case of *Kas'ákuwiŋ*, her attitude extended to the art of meditation and *haŋbdé*, meaning four-day fasting. She gave much advice in these areas. *Kas'ákuwiŋ* developed a special touch in caring for sick children. Both had attitudes relating to the art of appreciation in life. And in Dakota you call that *opíič'iyapi*.

Friendship: The Story of *Siŋkpé*

The next story was a common children's story about friendship. It was a slim-bodied little animal with a large flat tail named *Siŋkpé*, meaning muskrat. He was preparing to leave his river home to a lake. Just then a strange animal swimming down the river was approaching *Siŋkpé*. He stopped close to *Siŋkpé* and said, "I am *Čápa*," meaning beaver. "Why do you look so sad?" *Čápa* asked. "My name is *Siŋkpé*. I am sad because I am forced to leave my river home. The river is drying up and leaving my feeding places without green grass." *Čápa* stretched his large muscular body and swung his long narrow tail a few times and said, "*Siŋkpé*, do not worry or move away to the lake. I will dam the river to deepen the river." *Čápa* assured, "You will have many feeding places with new growth of green grass." *Siŋkpé* was glad and he stayed at his favorite river home. He was amazed at the hard work of *Čápa*. The dam was finished and water was slowly rising. *Čápa* suggested, "I will build my home close to yours. We will visit one another and we will live as good friends." So they did for a long time after that.

But the third party arrived and made his home near to them. He introduced himself as *Ptaŋ* meaning otter. He roamed around and enjoyed sliding into the river. He was a fisherman. He laughed a lot and visited *Siŋkpé* and *Čápa* too often. He visited *Čápa*, the beaver, and said, "You are strong and a hard worker. Your body pulls you as a proud *Čápa* but your long and narrow tail degrades you. If only *Siŋkpé* would lend you his big flat tail, you would do more work and faster too. You will be able to dam the biggest and the strongest river in this land with a flat tail."

Ćápa thought for a moment and refused. So the otter left and visited Siŋkpé. The otter suggested, "You should lend your tail to Ćápa. He will improve this place for you to enjoy. That big tail spoils your appearance. But you will look better with a long, narrow tail." But Siŋkpé got angry and said, "Go home, Otter, and visit me no more. You are trying to break my friendship with Ćápa." So Otter left quickly from Siŋkpé's home. But Otter continued his steady visit to Ćápa. He kept repeating his suggestion with the same words. At last Ćápa had a strong desire to trade tails with Siŋkpé. So one evening Ćápa interrupted Siŋkpé and said, "I want to extend our friendship as long as I can. I will make a better place for you to enjoy." He paused and continued, "I want to dam the biggest and the strongest river in this land with your flat tail. When I complete the dam, I will return to give your tail back to you." Siŋkpé remained silent with his head down. But Ćápa continued to beg with the same words. At last Siŋkpé gave in and traded tails with Ćápa. Siŋkpé said to Ćápa, "We visited each other, we talked freely to one another, we journeyed together. These are the reasons why I value our friendship so much and that is why I don't want to lend my tail to you." Ćápa said, "I felt the same way as you do but you will be proud of your new home."

At dawn, Ćápa left for his new assignment. Siŋkpé noticed the otter deserted his home too. Siŋkpé waited and waited for Ćápa to return home. The dam got so old and broken down, drifting with the river. At last the river went dry again and then Siŋkpé, the muskrat, left to search for Ćápa. He journeyed down the river singing these words, "Ćápa, give back my tail. I will give back yours." To this day, Siŋkpé waits on the dam for Ćápa. They still live near to each other but without friendship. The otter goes on living his own unfriendly life.

The Dakota elders reminded the children about the message of the story. Just as you are—[is your] only chance to have true friendship. Never allow a third party to interfere with your friends because the third one is always tempted to break up a friendship. Or avoid being the third person to other friendship. Do not lend anything away to your friend because you may find yourself waiting and you will lose important time. Perhaps lose friendship too. The friendship plays a large role in developing the art of appreciation and life. The Dakota people taught their children the important parts of development of people. This is the end of the story about trading and losing a good friendship. (Samuel Buffalo 3, 1977, 7–9)

[SB 1977] The Dakota child discipline has been discussed and the basic information about child training in the *tiyóti* system has been mentioned. We should reveal one other main point before concluding. The circle that had been used throughout the Dakota history ceased in the reserve era, but not completely. In the first place, the circle was used as a symbol of the mystery voice that promised the Dakota people a new generation in some unknown western land. Have the Dakota people reached that land now? According to *Ité Wapíkida*'s teaching, a woman moaned and prayed to the most holy circle, "Have mercy on my grandchildren. Protect them well. I arrange myself in a new position. Our grandmother the earth will move any time now."

Arranging ideas and presenting them in a new way was the *tiyóti oíhduhe*. It was an illustration of principles and rules working together. These were applied in a mutual relationship between the circular homes and the *tiyóti*. The elders rearranged these ideas showing a clear way as a life span. The fourteen markings on the circle were the rules. Any Dakota respecting these rules will [find this revealed] in good health, home, hunting, and pleasure. The word hunting can be changed to job or occupation or career in our time. The life span of ninety-eight years had three major stages—learning, refreshing period, and teaching. This way, the whole lifetime of a Dakota will practice the art of appreciation in life.

Another arrangement was the sacred circle interpreted as *Wakáŋ Waćípi*, meaning holy dance, and *okódakićiye*, meaning society. This *okódakićiye* provided four principles—belief, identity, skills and attitude. A person must be older than twenty-one years old to join the society. Then he becomes a *Ćaŋdójuha Yuhá*, meaning principal member, or an *Akíćita*, meaning guardian member. *Kićí* literally means with other, but refers to companion. The word *kićíwa* was understood as co-worker in the old *Isáŋti* language. Man and wife addressed one another with the word *kićíwa*. So, it interpreted the marriage as man and woman working together to keep their home existent.

Dakota progress was measured by these numbers: 2, 4, 8, 12, 16, 24, 40, and 48. Only a Dakota life span was measured by the number 7. Dakota language is one of the few native languages that has the word *wóyawa táŋka*, meaning million. It would be interesting to know what it was in Dakota history that extended their counting into millions. *Ćaŋyáwa* was the method of counting generations of Dakota. But Dakota elders quit the *ċaŋyáwa* early in the reserve era.

One other subject that should be included in this discussion is students' "dropout." In grades three and five [they] show the first sign of dropout. A chart may indicate the highest rate will be at grades eight and nine. There are many suggestions for solving the problem. These are good and have helped many students. According to *Ité Wapíkida*, he spoke about the young Dakota training process. The training period was divided in four equal parts. It can be measured by day, moon, season, or year. In our modern time, we can include hour and week. If we consider school is training a student measured by year, the training will be complete at the end of the sixteenth year. A two-year-old child possesses a mind with the desire to explore. This was the proper time to have a sponsor or instructor other than parents. Exploring a subject, let's say carving, the training would be in four parts, and exploring is the first part with four meetings. The second part is to recognize carvings in four meetings. This is done by identifying carving pieces and knowing his own carving ability. The third part is application. A child must apply carvings in everyday life, such as repairing his toys or decorating his room or making bird houses, etc. The fourth part is observing the mind about carvings. This will be done by discussing, review, practices, and teaching. A child must know carving is the purpose for convenient time structuring in life.

I was two years old when *Ité Wapíkida* taught me in the following procedure. Subject, the sacred circle, two meetings, eight sessions and sixteen hours. Bear in mind an old Dakota saying, numbers three, five and nine—will not do any good for you. (Samuel Buffalo 3, 1977, 9–11)

The Trading and Reserve Era or the Christian Era and Adjusting to Life on Reserves

[The traditional territory of the four Dakota groups in the U.S.A. was ceded or sold to the U.S. government for settlement through several treaties, including the following:

- By the 1837 Treaty the Mdewakanton lost all their territory east of the Mississippi River; the other three Dakota (*Isáŋti*) groups were all living west of the Mississippi by that time.

- By the 1851 Treaty of Mendota the Mdewakanton and the Wahpekute lost their territory in eastern Minnesota and were moved to the Lower Sioux Agency along the Minnesota River (near Redwood Falls).

- By the 1851 Treaty of Traverse des Sioux the Wahpeton and Sisseton lost their territory in southern and eastern Minnesota and were moved to the Upper Sioux Agency along the Minnesota River (near Granite Falls).

- By another treaty in 1858 the portion (about half) of the 1851 reservations, the whole strip northeast of the river, also was ceded and opened for settlement.

- By the 1867 Treaty of Lake Traverse, Sisseton and Wahpeton bands that remained loyal to the U.S. during the 1862 war received the Sisseton Indian Reservation in northeast South Dakota. DB]

Beginning Life on Reserves: Upper Sioux

[SM 1997] The Wahpetons broke away from the others. These people went eastward and dwelled maybe somewhere around Indiana. And they also went to *Wíta Wakáŋ* which is Manhattan Island today. So in that area that is where the territory of the Wahpetons [extended]. But the immigration came along and kept pushing them westward to Minnesota. Because as I said before, in northern Minnesota there is a lake, *Isáŋ ta Mde*, meaning sharp-edged lake, that is where the *Isáŋti* dwelled. [There is a Knife Lake not far from Mille Lacs Lake, which is shown in map 4; *mde* means lake. See also note 16 to part 2. DB] My grandmother's mother lived there. They had a lot of timber for lumber and good soil for farming. They moved them westward to a big reserve. . . .

My maternal great-grandmother was a descendant of the *Isáŋatis*, and she grew up at this lake. [She became the wife of *Waŋ Dúta*, Red Arrow; the lake was called *Isáŋ ta Mde*. DB] And when she was fourteen years old she remembered taking a pilgrimage from that lake back to the Mississippi River and they go down to the ocean. She always tells there are two delicacies of the *Isáŋati* people: that is the last, the second last egg of the alligator and then the meat in between the back of the ocean turtle. These were the two delicacies the *Isáŋati* people had.

Why they go back to the ocean, they take all their fourteen-year-old boys and girls, they go back to that ocean. She was telling them about it, it takes them over 30 days to get to the ocean by their canoes, then it takes them over 40 days, something like 50 days, in her case it took them 53 days to came back from the ocean to *Isáŋ ta Mde*. Grandma's mother lived there. Grandma lived in Upper Reserve as a child. [Sam's grandmother was Mary Duta of the Upper Sioux Reserve in Minnesota. DB]

They moved them westward to a big reserve. I don't know the name of that big reserve in Minnesota but they call it Upper Sioux and Lower Sioux. My grandmother and her group lived there at the Upper Sioux. The lake there has a French name, maybe Lake Traverse. I think it is mentioned in the 1864 treaty, revised in 1905 or 1910. [Sam may mean Lac qui Parle, also on the Minnesota River, about seventy miles southeast of Lake Traverse. He may mean the 1867 treaty, which created the Sisseton Reservation nearby in South Dakota (Oneroad and Skinner 2003, 9), but more probably he means the 1851 treaties at Traverse des Sioux and Mendota, which created the Lower Sioux and Upper Sioux Reservations and were revised in 1858. See maps 3 and 4. DB]

The Dakota people were starting to divide, even among the *Waḣpé Atúŋwaŋ* (Wahpeton), who divided into four groups: the *Aŋbdó Wapúskiye* (people who carried drying clothes or drying meat on their backs when travelling); the *Psiŋ Hu Atúŋwaŋna* (or *Psiŋ Hu Wakpá Atúŋwaŋna*, who used wild rice stems woven into mats); the *Mdewákaŋtuŋwaŋ* (Spirit Lake dwellers); and [unclear word]. In some books they say that *Waḣpé Atúŋwaŋ* and the *Waḣpekute* are two different tribes but it's not [so]. They are both the same tribe. *Ċaŋkúte*, that's a different one. So the Lower Sioux consisted of four *Isáŋati* tribes: the *Mdewákaŋtuŋwaŋ*, the *Aŋbdó Wapúskiye*, the *Waḣpé Atúŋwaŋ* and the *Ċaŋkúte*. And the Upper Sioux was all *Waḣpé Atúŋwaŋ*.

At that time the missionaries arrived. I believe the Presbyterian Home Mission was built in Upper Sioux. Most of them were Wahpetons at the Upper Sioux. My [maternal] grandmother's mother, she was among them, working at that mission. [Missionary Thomas S. Williamson established a mission at Lac qui Parle on the Minnesota River in 1834 or 1835.[21] DB]

The Wahpetons were always planting potatoes, *píksina* (turnip), *paŋǵí* (carrot), *waḣpé*, *wamná-heza* (corn), *psiŋ* (onion), in their gardens at that home mission. Where they got the onion I don't know, or the carrot or turnip. They say there are wild turnips in those areas or even here in Saskatchewan, and *paŋǧí* (carrots).

The End of the *Tiyóti* System: The Christian Church as *Wópida*

They were not living any more in the *tiyóti* circle [perhaps *hoćoeya tiyóti?* DB]. They were starting to get away from that, going back to the original way of life in the Red Road Era. My grandmother used to say that while they were living in Minnesota, they were living in two rows facing each other, running east and west, just like the way they used to do in the Red Road Era. Facing each other, they had to make a mutual relationship. Another reason was *anúka anapikíćipi*, which means sort of guarding each other. She said that at the east end of the village (outside it) were the *akíćitas* (meaning police) in two tents, one on each side of that main east-west path. And outside the village at the west end of the village was the Presbyterian Church.

By then they were using the Presbyterian Church. The church replaced the *wópida* because they knew that they cannot live the way their ancestors of the Red Road lived, they're going to have to change to that small piece of land called Indian Reservation. So there's one thing they did do—they adopt the Presbyterian Church as *tiwópida*. They go there and they pray together and they can give thanks to God. And there were no servants in tents on each side of the path between the church and the camp [like before]. They didn't do that anymore—the servants were from each home [instead]. And [a separate place for] the old people, the poor, the sick people, some people who got into accidents, or blind, that was abolished too. At one time they used to live outside of that row of tents [*wizíoti* for the old and *tiyótiki* for the sick and crippled] but that fashion ended. No special place for them anymore. Back to the main society, the main camp. Because they were starting to live with that goal. So it was Wahpetons who were the first ones who broke away from the *Tiyóti* circle.

And soon after was the 1862 uprising caused by the Lower Sioux. And they were also in the Reserve Era.

So originally the people, the believers or followers of that old man *Wahube Adede* set out to look for the Hill of Truth. They are our *Isáŋti* ancestors. The *Isáŋti* people are the Red Road [people], they are our ancestors. Now originally that man had a message of good news, whenever they find the Hill of Truth they will find four things: *wówićada* (belief), *wósu* (faith), *wótawa* (personal spiritual belongings), together making up *wópiye* (medicine bag).

John Campbell would say that in place of *wótawa* he would use *wičoiyé-kiyapi* (meaning personal identity). But James Black argued that *wówičada* (belief) was the first thing or main thing, that every person should have, the same *wówičada*, to have mutual relationship in community.

All these phases, milestones of the Dakota history, always have the search for the Hill of Truth in their minds.

James Black thought that since they didn't find the Hill of Truth, he was beginning to agree with what Chief *Tama* and John Campbell said. He said, I think the reason why they changed that *Tiwópida* and adopted the Presbyterian Church is for the people to go to pray and to praise God.

They adopted the Church because it's in the Bible where the Hill of Truth can be found. Now after I became a Christian on February 18, 1981, then I'll always remember that and come to agree with them, that we the *Isáŋti* can say we have found the Hill of Truth, because what they call the Hill of Calvary or Hill of God, it's in the Bible, in the New Testament where Jesus went. What does Jesus say? I am the Way, the Truth and the Life. So from there the New Testament Bible came. Prior to that, Christians were unknown and so was the New Testament. But the first Christians were the twelve apostles and also the apostle Paul. They were the first ones to call themselves Christians. Now I'm [content], this whole history of the Hill of Truth. Put these together and you'll find the new *Odákota*. It'll be a mystery until you find the Hill of Truth. Now the Bible will become real to you, I am the Way, the Truth and the Life. I am that *Dakótide*. We can use that as the foundation of our faith, our Christian faith. And the *Oíhduhe*, or the Mystery, they didn't know what *Odákota* means, and today we can say we have found the Hill of Truth in the Bible, and our new *Odákota* is the way of Christianity or Christian living. That is the Good News of that destruction that [took] place many generations ago. (Mniyo May 31, 1997)[22]

The Minnesota Massacre

[SB 1977] The conclusion of [the *Tiyóti* era began]. It began with territorial clashes among the Indians. The eastern and the southeastern country were inhabited by settlers. Different tribes started moving closely together as the U.S. developed westward. The natives fighting each other can be observed as clashes, not wars. The Dakota term *ozúye* [means] an attack process to strike the target and return without a stop. The *ozúye* tactics were carried out. The next was the territorial losses. The settlers, army posts, missionaries, traders, and gold diggers were claiming lands. The treaties were violated by illegal traders. Soon Dakota people were forced to take a stand for their limited land called reservations.

It only happened once to the Dakota people in Minnesota when a small party of Dakotas were involved. They fought with white settlers in what is now known as the Minnesota Massacre. [For more on this see part 3. DB]. Soon after, the U.S. Army retaliated against the whole Dakota nation. Many sub-bands had no knowledge of the fight that took place in Minnesota but the U.S. Army attacked any native encampment as long as they were Dakota. By that time many Dakota bands were settled on reservations in Minnesota and North Dakota.

They dwell in log and brick houses pursuing farm and stock raising occupations. Even they were included in some of the raids by the United States Army.

What was left of the *Tiyóti Oíhduhe?* The Dakota people were disorganized and language was silenced in confusion. [Silenced were] the proud words that used to be, "We are the survivors of the Dakota minority movement. We are the descendants of the eastern generation. We will be the ancestors of the new generation." But now, the Dakota people were scattered and fled, fleeing to survive. The Dakota who are now residing in Canada won this right in the Seven Fire (*Oċéti Šakówiŋ*) treaty with the British government in 1812. And this is why there was no hesitation for some of the Dakota people to enter into Canada. (Samuel Buffalo 2, 1977, 6–7)

My Family History: How the *Isáŋti* People Came to Canada

[SM 1986] When the Sioux Indians moving westward on their Red Road journey hit the mountain range, the *Wakáŋ Waċípi* members turned around and went east, hoping to get where they started from. They came to a river and followed it to a fork of three rivers. They followed the Mississippi River to the ocean, and back up to the Green River. A Kentucky knoll or hill was a landmark going both down and back up the Mississippi River.

My mother and her side were Wahpeton. Her father was a Goodvoice.

My maternal grandparents ate turtles and fish for meat. They hardly used red meat, they were more vegetarian . . . their staple foods were wild rice and corn. My maternal grandmother [Mary Duta] had a women's hand game, with eight pieces carved from cherry stones and a flat wooden bowl. It is like a dice game, the oldest form of gambling among the Sioux. It was made for her grandmother by that grandmother's uncle." (Mniyo April 28, 1986)

[SM 1985 and 1986] In their travels, some of the Sioux had come upon a French colony along or at the mouth of the Mississippi River, made peace and stayed a while to work there, picking up agriculture. These Wahpeton Sioux started gardens and grew corn, potatoes and turnips. The French colony gave fifty French girls to the Sioux boys to marry, and the Sioux in turn gave fifty Sioux girls to the French to marry. That's how my maternal grandmother's grandmother or great-grandmother was a French girl from France.[23]

My maternal grandmother's father was French, and her mother was Sioux. [But Sam said his maternal grandmother's father was *Waŋdúta*, so Sam may mean one or two generations earlier. DB] She and her brothers and sisters grew up among the Sioux in Louisiana near the Mississippi River. There was a treaty between the French colony and the Sioux, where French girls married Dakota boys and [one hundred?] Dakota girls married into the French colony.

I heard recently that the French government found documents showing the French made treaties with the Sioux Indians in many places, including Canada, and including the area between the river running north and south and *Wazí Pahá* (the Cypress Hills), away back in the 1700s! After the French and British fought in Quebec, the treaty said the British will have to honor all treaties made by the French with the Indians. [Probably the Treaty of Paris, 1763. DB] That will upset all those Crees!

The Wahpetons started using quite a lot of chickens, eggs and potatoes, which came in with the French. Shortly after 1808, their first treaty with the U.S. government, the Wahpetons became Christians and started going to school, so by 1862 they were already quite civilized. [Sam may mean the Treaty of 1837, since there appears to be no 1808 treaty. DB] My maternal grandmother's parents had a log house, chickens, and their nomadic life was over.

My dad's side was half Sisseton and half Wahpeton. My great-grandfather (my paternal grandfather's father) was a Sisseton named *Wapáhaska* (White Warbonnet) who became Chief Whitecap. He came from the Sisseton Indian Reservation in South Dakota, where agriculture was being taken up. [Also referred to as Lake Traverse Reservation, see map 3. DB] Some families were living in brick houses, and had chickens and all, until militia riders came shooting, and they left.

He was already living in a brick house on the Sisseton Indian Reservation in South Dakota. His father, *Tióde*, was a blind man who became a horse raiser, selling and exchanging horses with the pioneers coming westward. "Give us four horses, then go down there, we'll order you bricks," some said. At that place where three rivers came together there were lots of houses, it was already a city. He came to the dock, he paid so many cents a brick, and bought lumber, there was a big lumber mill there, sawing logs from Minnesota. Two white guys in exchange for four horses built him a large brick house.

Whitecap became chief there on that reserve, and there was a treaty. Then he went into farming, with corn and potatoes, oats, and several hundred horses. He left everything when the American militia came and started shooting and they left. The Sissetons were still nomadic [or nomadic again? DB] at that time, going with the buffalo herds. He went to the Missouri River, up to a place between Culbertson and Poplar, Montana. (Mniyo April 30, 1985, and April 28, 1986)

[SB 1977] Now, about the major challenges of the coming of the *wašíču* [white man]. . . . Tangible aspects were the United States Army, famine, and diseases. The three created only a shadow of death on the Dakota people. My great-grandfather [was] *Wapáhaska*, known as Chief Whitecap, and his band story is as follows. The region they occupied was the western part of the Dakota plains along the Missouri River and northeastern Montana. The messages that were brought to his *wičóti* (encampment) were hard to believe. But he continued roaming his territory, grazing his herds of horses. At that time they were engaged in horse trading with other tribes. Their Dakota *woókiya*, meaning peace-making, extended to other tribes. In the meantime, a message reached them that drew their attention. A short distance away, the *Isáŋ Táŋka*, meaning Big Knife, referring to the U.S. army, approached and destroyed a Dakota encampment. The

PHOTO 5. Chief *Wapáhaska* (Whitecap) in 1885. After 1862 he led his band from the United States. He secured and settled a reserve at Moose Woods in 1879 (surveyed in 1881), close to the South Saskatchewan River, now the Whitecap Dakota First Nation. He was a Sisseton, born about 1840, one of Sam Buffalo's paternal great-grandfathers. Glenbow Archives, Calgary, NA-1940–3.

army was known as *Pehíŋ Háŋska*, meaning long haired, referring to General Custer. So Chief Whitecap sent his scout out to investigate but was turned back by the army. So without delay, the encampment dispersed in different directions. That was the final end of the Whitecap *wičóti* in the sense of the *tiyóti* system. They left behind their property including the herd of horses. They came straight and fast to Canada. They roamed around in the area of Cypress Hills, Saskatchewan, to Fort Garry, Manitoba. Finally the Canadian Government granted him a reserve near Saskatoon, Saskatchewan.[24]

The hardships of diseases, famine, and the United States Army were experienced by Chief Whitecap without doing anything wrong to the United States government. The Dakota people in Canada made themselves a good reputation of being willing to work and learn. For this reason they had no problem with the Canadian government to settle on the reserves. (Samuel Buffalo 2, 1977, 7–8)

[SM 1985 and 1986] They came north to the border and met a big caravan coming down, building the international border.[25] There were some Sioux interpreters there, who said, "There's a large number of Sioux refugees in Fort Garry, they're living well there under the French governor" [*sagada* means French, *sagadashe* means English].[26] So they said, "'Let's go there," and passed Turtle Mountain.

So Whitecap, with his son *Biddow* Buffalo, who was my paternal grandfather, went [east] to Fort Garry. My grandfather went to school there four or five years in a French school taking agriculture.

They were accepted by the French governor at Fort Garry who opened an agricultural school for the Sioux Indians in exchange for breaking land for the French. They were taught to make cheese, butter, bread.

Then he [*Biddow*] came together with Whitecap to Sintaluta and then to Fort Qu'Appelle. Whitecap and Standing Buffalo did not get along together, they started to break up, so my grandfather *Biddow* came to Prince Albert.

The Wahpetons were already there. They had left Fort Garry for Prince Albert with [James] McKay as early as the 1870s before there were any Indian Reserves. His sons were James and William McKay.[27] William's grandson is still living. My grandfather *Biddow* Buffalo married a Wahpeton. My grandmother's name was *Tiwákawiŋ*. Then he married her sister *Ṫaṫé Waṡṫé* (Good Wind); it was common to have two or three wives at the same time who were sisters. My father Herbert Buffalo was their son. He married *Ho Wašté* (Pansy Good Voice). (Mniyo April 30, 1985, April 12, 1986, and April 28, 1986, edited by DB)

[SM 1997] Then the people were scattered all over toward Canada. Most of them landed at the Long Plain Dakota reserve near Portage la Prairie in Manitoba. About 4,000 or 5,000 of them landed at Fort Garry. My grandfather [*Biddow*] and his brothers, Thomas *Tama* and his brothers, many of them spoke French and wrote French and got agricultural courses there. The Dakota men broke up a big piece of land in that Fort Garry area. [The Fort Garry area is now the city of Winnipeg; note that *Biddow* and *Tama* were not brothers. DB] (Mniyo May 31, 1997)

The Dakota Bands in Canada; the Little Red River
Sioux Camp and the Last *Tiyóti Oíhduhe*

[SB 1977] The Dakota bands reside on seven small reserves in the provinces of Saskatchewan and Manitoba. In Saskatchewan they are Wahpeton located ten miles northwest of Prince Albert, White Cap near Saskatoon, and Standing Buffalo near Fort Qu'Appelle. In Manitoba they are Bird Tail Reserve near Birtle, Sioux Valley near Griswold, Pipestone Reserve near Pipestone, and Long Plain Dakota Reserve near Portage la Prairie. [Initially there was also a small reserve called Dakota Tipi I.R. 1, close to Portage la Prairie (Elias 1988, 188). DB]

The seven reserves did not rebuild the *Tiyóti* formation but employed many ideas from the *Tiyóti Oíhduhe*. But the *Isáŋti*, commonly called the Sioux camp, located two miles north of Little Red River Park at Prince Albert, were known to be last with *Tiyóti Oíhduhe*. At this location, one section of land was given to them for a reserve. But later, one section was reduced to one quarter for some unknown reason. The Dakota people numbered about one hundred. The elders appointed Mr. Willie Gun, better known as *Húpehaŋ*, to be a *Tiyóti Yaŋká*. His leadership ended about 1920.

They selected a small suitable area for residence along the Little Red River. Their little log cabins were built closely together forming an oblong circle. Near the north end, a hollow was erected for social events. [Sam showed me this hollow in the mid-1960s. DB]

They resided there only in the winter season. In the spring season, about the end of March, they move to south of Prince Albert. In the spring, trapping muskrats, being farm hands, planting gardens and odd jobs in Prince Albert were done by the Dakotas. In the summer season they continue with casual labor and picking berries for income. One or two days of dance will bring them together at the little opening area called *Tiṇtáṇ* near their reserve. Then one day of the Prince Albert fair in July welcomed the Dakota people living nearby to provide one of the main attractions of dancing performance. In August, the ones who owned horses will go to their hay meadows for winter feed. Work was performed in group. After completing their hay-making they will return to work as farm hands and harvesting work in the autumn season. The *Tiyóti Yaṇká* Mr. Gun called a meeting for all able men. They will discuss the home preparation for the oncoming winter. Usually before the first snow storm all homes were prepared for the winter. The wood fuel was gathered and distributed to the homes. Their old folks and widows with children were given extra care. Meanwhile, several boys will go hunting big game. On their return, they will distribute the meat to every home. All the activities [followed] the seasons. This new adjustment with *tiyóti* principles was good while it existed.

The flu epidemic in 1919 corrupted the last working *tiyóti*. About a dozen families survived and were moved to the Wahpaton Reserve 94A about 1921. Their reserve consisting of one quarter of land at Little Red River was referred to as Wahpaton 94B. [The spelling Wahpaton was used until the 1960s and later. DB]

Let's review now. The *Tiyóti Oíhduhe* progressed from a small circle sketched on a material as a symbol. Then developed a *wićóti* (encampment) formation with a mutual relationship. The Dakota belief was that the *tiyóti* was inspired by circle powers in harmony. An individual Dakota felt secure to understand the circle powers. His knowledge acquired at different stages is identified in the *Tiyóti Oíhduhe*. Whatever skill a Dakota chose to do, it will be based on the "we-share" idea.

All accomplishments were evaluated on the *tiyóti*'s approval because the *tiyóti* had a custom of praising a person, known as *iwákći*. All the daily work was reported to *tiyóti*. For the ones approved by *Tiyóti* members, an elderly man will sing, including the doer's name with the wording of the song. Then he will announce what that person had done. This was the way an individual developed pride in developing a skill. Without *iwákći*, there was no pride. Every person was educated to be *wićóti akíkta* meaning encampment wise because the *wičóti* [encampment] functioned based on four things: health, home, hunting, and pleasure. These areas need an exchange of constant attention and advice. If neglected the *wičóti* problems will prevent appreciation of living.

The last surviving *Tiyóti Yaŋká*, Mr. Willie Gun, better known as *Húpe-haŋ*, he purchased five acres of land to make his permanent home at Cloverdale District. He became a faithful taxpayer for over twenty years. In October 1944 he died at the Wahpaton Reserve 94A. (Samuel Buffalo 2, 1977, 8–9)

The Little Red River Sioux Camp I.R. 94B, the Establishment of Wahpeton Dakota Reserve 94A

[SB 1977] Chief *Ahíyaŋke* had about ten families. And he was requesting, to the federal government, a reserve where he and his band can reside. And in 1894 the reserve was granted. And August 1894, the reserve [had] been completed as far as the surveying. [Elias (1988, 208–10) explains that three different bands came together to live at the Wahpeton Dakota reserve 94A: the Sissetons under *Biddow*, the Mdewakantons and Wahpetons under Chief *Húpa Iyáhpeya* who lived at 94B until 1921, and the Wahpetons under Chief *Ahíyaŋke*. DB]

Now, the people here dwell on this reserve and spend most of their time away from the reserve. There was no reserve farm development until four years after the completion of the surveying. My grandfather *Budown Ṫatáŋka Kiŋyéyapi* [*Bido, Biddow, Bdo*][28] moved in the spring of 1898 on the reserve to farm [see photo 6]. He was with his son, eight years old, Herbert Buffalo [see photo 7]. And after that, they were engaged in farming. And at that same time the home mission and the school was built on the reserve. The home mission was operated by Miss Lucy Baker, better known by her Dakota name, Missy Baka. (Samuel Buffalo 1, 1977, 8)

[In 1967 or thereabouts, Sam described to me how the two different groups settled on the Round Plain reserve. DB]

[SB 1967] In 1898 many families, all Wahpetons, moved to the present site of the Round Plain Indian Reserve No. 94A and began farming. They included Chief *Tama*, Ironside, *Biddow*, Iron Buffalo, Good Shield, Sioux, Spoonmaker, and *Skúye*. Some had had previous farming experience, gained at Fort Garry or Portage la Prairie. They co-operated together,

PHOTO 6. *Bdo* or *Biddow* (Flying Buffalo). Sam's older sister Rose is the child in front; the woman at left is Miss Mink, the teacher. One of Chief *Wapáhaska*'s sons, he was a Sisseton headman who led a group of Sisseton to Prince Albert. With others, they obtained a reserve, the Round Plain–Wahpeton Dakota Reserve, in 1894 and settled. He married a Wahpeton woman and was Sam Buffalo's paternal grandfather. Courtesy Leona Anderson, Wahpeton Dakota Nation.

PHOTO 7. Herbert Buffalo, son of *Bdo* and father of Sam Buffalo. Courtesy Leona Anderson, Wahpeton Dakota Nation.

raised crops and livestock, and also hunted, for [making] pemmican and dried meat.

In 1921 the RCMP made the Sioux living at the "Sioux Camp" near Prince Albert move out to Round Plain. They were related but were *Isáŋti, Ċaŋkútes* [Mdewakanton and Wahpekute]. They had been living on the 160-acre Indian Reserve No. 94B just northeast of Prince Albert. They included (Robert) Good Voice, Four Star, *Wadítaka*, Henry Crowe, *Ománi*, White Cloud, Good Wind, James Black [Sapa], Henry Two Bear, *Tupete*, Swift Hawk, George Norman. The 1919 flu epidemic had already killed way over half of them: there had been sixty-eight houses, but only twelve houses were left to move to Round Plain 94A.[29] Then the trouble [between the two groups] started: they had different customs, they were not farmers but hunters, the men hunted spring and fall, and the women worked in Prince Albert housecleaning." (Buffalo, 1967)

The Present Challenge

Dakota Elders' Predictions about Reserve Life; Living Well and Living Disorderly; the Early Promise of Reserve Life

[SB 1977] The Dakota elders predicted, "In the future, the Dakota people will live insecurely." These elders lived far apart in different regions. Perhaps some of them had never met each other. Yet their forecasts consist of the same words. It indicates that their seventy years of reserve living are alike. . . .

The elders spoke of the reserve era in two stages. I quote, "In the past the Dakota people lived well. Today we live disorderly."

They give numerous stories as references. . . . [For example] the Dakota language not developing with the people on the reserve. Yet, our ancestors advanced and developed pictorial writing. They preserved their language, songs and messages, depicted on wood and hide. Today, many Dakota cannot speak their native tongue.

The growth of the Dakota minority movement expressed [the motto], "We are the descendants of the eastern generation and we will be the ancestors of the new generation."[30] The Dakota were organized by the *tiyóti* system and we shared the motto and we lived in harmony. But this prosperous lifestyle has been confronted and rejected by the reserve era.

The original Dakotas' reasons for residing on the reserve were:

1. To live a healthy life.
2. Construct permanent homes.
3. Learn farm development.
4. A school for the children.
5. To work together.
6. Red Coats to protect them and their property.

These reasons can be [summarized as]: Their basic purpose for a Dakota Reserve was security. [They had] a special need for the freedom to develop a new way of life with old Dakota ideas. The government granted them a reserve and promised to assist in their new adventure. The reserve era commenced with men building log cabins and stables for each family. They extended their work in preparing garden plots and crop fields. In May times, the ladies were marketing willow baskets, rugs, quilts, and wild berries. Some worked as housekeepers at the nearby village or town. These activities demonstrate [how they could] fulfill their reasons for reserve life. Most men had seasonal job experience as farm hands, supply freighter, river boat, stock yards, and warehouses. A few advanced in carpentry and as brick layers. The archive documents provide evidence that the Dakota people were willing to work and to learn.

Social activities were a weekly dance, chat meeting, religious feast, and hand games. The ladies' game, *kaŋsúkute*, meaning shooting dice, provided evening entertainment for the lady folks. At this early stage, several elderly folks equipped themselves with drums, rattles, bells, and sometimes a flute. So often they make their rounds house to house and this is called *tiódowaŋ*, meaning home singing. They sang and danced, encouraging each family with a new motto: "We live and we work together." (Samuel Buffalo 1, 1977, 2–3)

Rule by Indian Agents, Breakdown of Traditional Practices, *Kahómni* Dance, Disorganization and Organization, We Live Disorderly, *Odákota* Is Confused

[SB 1977] But this fresh and active start was short-lived, because two major interruptions occurred within a decade of reserve life. The Indian Agent rules and the home mission teachings were introduced.

The [Indian Agent] rules interfered with the Dakota group management. The Agent used threatening tactics to prevent men from working together. A Dakota must learn to manage and control his own farm without [his] neighbor's help. The sales permits control the grain and hay and product of a Dakota farm. The iron brand with I.D. initials, meaning Indian Department, registers the Dakota reserve stock as crown property. When a Dakota wanted to market or butcher a steer, he must have permission. Quite often the Agent refused to issue the permit. The vegetables, poultry, and hogs are recorded. The Indian Agent's rules decreased the interest in developing farming.

The home mission and school prohibited Dakota language on their premises. A student was punished for speaking their Dakota language. The children were told to avoid certain persons or families because they engage in Dakota traditional activities. These doings were called "evil doers practice." Food rations were issued to the old-age folks but if one was dedicated to the Dakota ceremonies, his needed rations will be reduced for punishment. This type of treatment, by favoring one group and neglecting the other one, divided the people.[31]

Soon thereafter, an internal problem among the people was noticed. It was called *okičiyúȟpapi*, meaning "pull one another down." The term and activities still are well remembered by the older members of these reserves. A person showing business competence higher than the rest, he became a target to be discouraged, to give up his occupation, and this usually happened. [Sam often remarked on the difference he noticed between Indians and non-Indians in the way they tried to level the differences in wealth. Non-Indians tried to "keep *up* with the Joneses," so if someone in the neighborhood bought a certain type of appliance, his Saskatoon landlady wanted to have one too. But Sam claimed that on the reserve, if someone started to get ahead farming, neighbors would try to knock him back *down* to their level, by putting sugar in his tractor gas tank or causing other damage. Or an Indian who got a job in the city received visitors from the reserve who stayed until the food was all gone. DB]

Then in the 1930s the Depression decreased the reserve's living standard to a very low point. By this time, from *Ċakúsa* [probably a location in North or South Dakota or Montana: see Howard 1984, 98. DB] beyond boundary came a slow beat dance called *Kahómni* meaning "rotate swing," a very suitable dance for the younger generation who are idle and restless. The *Kahómni* dance usually reached its peak during winter months. Sometimes the dance will continue every night for weeks.

An old man started to criticize *Kahómni*. He informed the people that *Kahómni* cannot be considered as an entertainment, but a way of inviting troubles and unhappy experiences because every song wording consisted of one of these—a sad heart, I am crying, you left me, I am in jail, we are drinking, and so on. "If you hear these words too often, eventually it will condition your mind to do these activities," he warned. But very few pay any attention to his warnings. As the years went by, the *Kahómni* gradually changed to violence. There were more and more drunk brawls at the dance. Broken homes, family negligence were increasing. Young people were directed toward jail. The death rate among children was upward. The people were unhappy and socially disorganized. Some families confined themselves in far corners of the reserves. Others moved away from the reserve. The interest in community activities was next to none. Likewise the *Kahómni* dance ceased. But it was too late. The period that the Dakota lived well had been swung away with the *Kahómni*. The aforementioned description of Dakota reserve life was experienced by each reserve at different times. The elders observed that the *Kahómni* started early in the twenties [1920s]. It reached a high performance throughout the thirties and declined to an end in the late forties.

The old age pension, family allowance, social welfare allowance and land lease payment were extended into the reserves for the first time. This financial support augments the reserve's standard of living. It provides some means to advance in managing and controlling business in private, co-op and band operation. These enterprises had shown new potential income for the people. But the access to social and welfare allowances was too easy. More and more people were becoming social and welfare recipients.

This was the beginning of what our elders called "today we lived disorderly." The elders agreed that the welfare has a meaningful purpose. It assists unemployed men with families, sick persons, and especially neglected children for immediate care. But the reserve's unemployment problem created a misunderstanding about income. Since no temporary job programs were available to the young people, the social and welfare assistance became the only steady income for them. The job-hunting and job-holding ambitions were lessening. But monthly assistance increasingly progressed through the years of the fifties and the sixties; this problem being supported by the liquor outlet for Indians in 1957. The long desired privilege advanced in support of disorderly behavior. The rock bottom life depressed many into themselves. Suicide among teenagers climbed and the rate is high at the time of recording this tape. The Dakota people are in a bad situation whether they are living on or off the reserve. The earlier motto, "we live and we work together," is now in question.

The sixties commenced with the faint sound of the beating drum. The beats became louder and louder, attracting the Dakota people to a new entertainment. This is called "Under the Big Top Celebration." Each summer the Big Top extends to a different reserve. It provides an opportunity for people to meet each other several times every summer, visiting one another abroad, constructing a better understanding of reserve life. The Big Top motivated competitive activities between reserves and among the attendants. The Dakota community interest expanded with group singers, group dancers, fund-raising projects.

There is a method called *tidówaŋ*, meaning home singing, commonly used for every family canvas. . . . *tidówaŋ* is conducted by a group of singers and dancers, including other means of musical sound-making. They visit each home to provide a short entertainment of singing and dancing, usually performed outside and near the door, unless the homeowner invites them indoors. The M.C. makes his announcements in the first moment of silence. He will tell the family of the next Big Top Celebration's date and month. He will continue, to say it was their reserve's project to broaden friendship and develop talents. But Big Top can only accomplish this by every family's support. So naturally, a family will donate money or something that can be auctioned. *Tidówaŋ* is repeated several times in a year. One other progress is the revival of *Dakóta Péjí*, meaning grass songs and dancing costumes. Many fine arts of designs, beading, and other needlecraft were displayed by younger people.

Others found new opportunities in the research work of the Dakota identity development. The Dakota people are preparing to have Dakota language classes in their schools on the reserves. There is much language developing to be done for the literature of the reserves. The Dakota language is an impressive dialect because of its many verbs. Nouns will be the main concern in updating the Dakota language. Another area is producing text books. There are sufficient interesting Dakota stories suitable for reading. The aforementioned activities were advanced by the "Under the Big Top Celebration." It provided a chance to exchange ideas and information for the Dakota people. Often one will see men seated in small circles. They are discussing many reserve problems; and how to solve them is usually suggested. This can be observed during the Big Top days.

One important change has developed. This is the Canadian Dakota reserves organized themselves. Here again "Under the Big Top Celebration" should be credited for it. Exchanging visits brought the seven Dakota reserves to one body. It is used for organizational approaches in claims and research. It is called the Dakota Association of Canada. This association was established in November 1969. So far, the association progressed in two fields of work: the Mississippi Santee claims, and Dakota history. There are other interesting areas proposed to investigate. The Dakota people have advantages through their own association. Their full support can empower new organizational privileges. Also, it can be adopted as *tiyóti* to provide external services. So the seven Dakota reserves will be organizationally wise with a desirable future prospect.

But sad to say that the promoter [of] Under the Big Top Celebration is struggling to exist. Our Dakota elders forecasted this would happen because Dakota reserves are in the stage "we live disorderly." Sooner or later, the disorder activities will extend to the Big Top attraction. This was seen as Big Top dueling with alcoholism, since it is truly a conflict of interest that gradually separates people within each reserve. "Don't come to the Big Top drunk." In reply is, "Don't come to my home for Big Top support." This internal disorder produces a trend in Big Top Celebrations. One by one, the reserves will pass the summer without Big Top attraction. However, by this time, the Dakota cultural recovery will be so great that experience will perpetuate in other new adventures. Whatever happens, the basic need should be challenged. That is security. If Dakota reserves are structuring time for security, we may avoid our Dakota elders' predictions.

Now this is a summary of what has been discussed:

The Dakota reserve is used to test the Dakota elders' predictions. It consists of two stages. The first one was referred to as, "In the past, the Dakota people lived well." Why do these elders say they lived well in the past when we observed them with many hardships? That is true, but internal corruption did not dwell with them. The Dakota movement into the reserve was in one united body of families. The first motto, "We live and we work together," was clearly [shown]. We live, meaning the reserve is used for a survival purpose. How they are going to use it is shown by "we work together." One other point that can be made is the reserve visualized as a *tiyóti* as far as they are concerned, because their spoken words, *tiyóti uŋyáŋpi*, illustrate that. So the first settlers of the Dakota reserve knew who they were and what they were going to do, and how they were going to do it.

The second stage has been noted as, "Today we live disorderly." Originally this had been started by interferences. Official permits must accompany their work. This limits and controls their action and accomplishment. Freedom to work in *Odákota*, meaning Dakota belief, identity, skill, and attitude, was incomplete because of confusion. The constant dual issue of money and alcoholism maintained the Dakota people on the road of confusion aiming for the elders' predicted future of living "disorderly." Meanwhile, Under the Big Top attraction existed as a puzzle picture of *Odákota*, which drew some attention with the desire to put the picture together. While others go on as, "we dance and we will compete with one another," these last two interests barely promote the Big Top for [securing] popularity. But the strengthening of *owíyahaŋtùkeśni*, meaning unpopularity, will build the freeway to our Dakota elders' prediction: "In the future the Dakota people will live insecurely." (Samuel Buffalo 1, 1977, 3–8).

The Present Challenge

[SM 1985] Once again we, the Dakota, are divided and fighting among ourselves. We are like our people when they were living at the eastern coastline, not praying to one God but worshipping all sorts of idols. We too are making ourselves extinct, at least in our language and culture; the road to our extinction is straight and downhill now: that's the way I see the Dakota reserves. My aim is to show the Sioux people what they're doing, that they're not getting anything out of it this way: that now there is no respect for one another or the law, the homes are all broken.

What we need now is another Turning Point, back to worship God. What I say here is based on the New Testament (Acts 17: 26–27).[32] The promise of *oúŋ* wasn't really a lie, it was really the voice of God that spoke to our ancestors, but it was misunderstood. *Oúŋ* was not land but salvation in Jesus Christ, who went to Calvary Hill and paid for our sins. The Hill of Truth means that we have the chance to turn to God once again, to repent from our sins, and to ask for forgiveness; we have the chance to put our hope, our salvation, and our future in Christ which I will name as *oúŋ*, that which *Iyá Owáśte* and our ancestors were looking for. (Mniyo May 1, 1985)

Samuel Mniyo's Own Story

Three Events in My Early Life Experience

[SM 1985] One day in August when I was about ten months old I was sleeping. My mother said I woke up, jumped up called out and came running across to her. As I remember what happened, I felt I woke up, heard voices, saw a blue sky, birds, heard a man harmonizing over the hill (where Danny . . . later had his house). I stood there and saw an old man sitting there cross-legged, face copper, not creased, short braids, leather laces across his forehead. He talked to me and said I am *Ité Wapíkida*. . . . He said when I wake up I'll feel I was floating in the air, I'll see a woman, he said to call her Mother (*Mihúŋ*). Then I woke up. I was already able to walk by holding the bench, but this time I walked and ran as if an older child! The old man had said, "Be skillful, do not sidestep. Do you know your master (lord) has planned a wonderful life for you?" I said no. Then the old man told me stories. Seven-year pilgrimage . . . (Mniyo April 30, 1985)

[This part was preceded by the following. DB]

I've mistepped. At age fourteen, I was supposed to go on a seven-year pilgrimage, but didn't. When I left my parents put the Mounties after me, sent me back, I left again. My parents didn't have confidence in me that I could survive. But I had a good friend Ole Carlson, down in California, I wanted to see him and explore and see the world, but that never happened.

At age sixteen, I was returning from feeding horses. A little light whirlwind passed on my left side in the moonlight, and my watchdog took off. My mother said my skin was paler on the left side. Once playing soccer suddenly my left leg failed and I fell. That was temporary, but by age 28 or 30 I had no control of my left leg or left arm. (Mniyo April 30, 1985)

[In 1997, Sam describes these three events again this way. DB]

[SM 1997] On June 30 we were ready to move up that night to [Prince Albert] to set up the Indian Dakota camp at the agricultural exhibition (Dad was responsible for the Indian pony racing, etc.). Mother had a headache, was asleep, moved me on top of a trunk below the window.

Then [it happened, I was spoken to:] "Boy, listen to me, hear me well. My name is *Ité Wapíkida*. I have a message for you from your heavenly grandfather. God has a wonderful plan for your life." He repeated the message to me when I was a boy of eight years old on that hill.

When I reached the age of fourteen to twenty-one, I must leave my parents' home and start travelling around to meet and associate with different people in different church [denominations?], not to return home until I'm twenty-one. I missed that spiritual quest. I became idle like other boys, started the wild side of life, drinking.

When I was fifteen years old I saw this strange thing, late at night, on the path between our house and barn. Dad said, light a lamp and go check on the horses. I went. On my way back I saw this strange thing. A little whirlwind about four feet high, looks like an ice cream cone, spinning and making a noise, coming on the path I'm on, came close. I made one step, I froze. It passed me on my left side. At that moment, one thought came to my mind, I'm off my track, I'm not doing what *Ité Wapíkida* asked me to do.

After I got inside the house, I woke up my mother, I told her, "I want to talk with you." I described to her what I saw. I don't feel right since then.

I remember *Ité Wapíkida* said, this is what will happen if I don't follow the instruction and go on the pilgrimage. During my pilgrimage some spirit will be with me and guide me. I was upset with my mother at that moment because she never said a word. But in thought I knew I'm off my track.

But the following night my mother asked Alex Swifthawk who was a shaman in those days, invited him to come and find out what that wind was. So Alex Swifthawk came and gave his ceremony which takes about one hour. After he sat down he said you saw a whirlwind but that was a person, warning you that you are not doing your assigned mission (to go on my pilgrimage away from my home seven years). (Mniyo May 10, 1997)

Visions and Dreams: Four Meetings with My Spiritual Guide

[Some parts of this section may seem to lack coherence; as Sam recalls his experiences, visions and/or dreams and puts them into words, the memories do not always come forth as complete grammatical sentences, and some spoken words I was unable to understand and write. DB]

[SM 1987] In my life I saw *Ité Wapíkida* four times [the name *Ité* means face, *Wapíkida* means appreciation].

The first time was when I was only eight months old, when I saw him and I walked! My mother was getting ready for the Prince Albert Exhibition, to put up the tent the next day which would have been August 29, 1930. I saw him sitting on a little hill. In front of him was this big hoop. He played a flute, then he started to hum. I looked at his face. He looked very old, yet beautiful, with white hair, short braids, braided leather tied around his forehead. His hair was parted right in the middle. He put a red ochre paint line down the middle where he parted his hair. He was sitting on [skins?] I remember! He started talking about "Wake up and share in the joy of creation. Get up, stand up, stand firm. Enjoy this very day." I looked around, I heard all kinds of birds in the sky, I heard one talking in the [bush?] language . . . meadowlark. . . . He told me to take care of my foot. He rubbed my foot. His hand was so warm. I felt strong. He said "Go here. When you see a woman she's your mother. Run to her, say 'Mother, Mother,' put your arms around her." I woke up, I had to, mother said I was sleeping on a trunk. I was at the stage of not quite walking. She said, "You woke up, sat up, you said clearly 'Mihúŋ, mihúŋ'" (Mother, mother). I jumped off the trunk and ran to her, placed my hands on her knees, jumped right up on her lap and embraced her. She said, "You jumped off and ran toward the door, I followed you. You looked up in the sky, ran toward the hill" (the one south of our place, where Chief *Tama* used to live). But in my dream I didn't see the houses. "Then you started to cry," she said, "I lifted you up and carried you back."

The second time I saw him he took one of the objects, the pipe, lit it, and he prayed. I didn't hear him but saw his lips moving. He turned to me and said to take two draws on it. I did it. He said blow, smoke it, I did. This was also in a vision, before age two. I woke up then, my mother said, and started to cry. "Čaŋdí, čaŋdí" (tobacco, tobacco), I said. "You want to smoke?" she said. I nodded. She filled her pipe and gave it to me. I drew on it twice, two long draws, blew it out. "You didn't cough," she said, "You lay down and went to sleep." "Next day you woke up and spoke fluently and started questioning old people."

The third time I met him I was four years old. This was before I was named *Mniyódowaŋ* (rhythm in motion, or motion like whirlpool ripple within singing or rhythm). He was telling me about life and how to live my life, to prepare myself for the age of seven. (Last October [30?] I was 57. I started my 58th year, so this October 29th I'll be 58 years old.) When

I'm seven years old, my birthday complete, next day I'm in development of my eighth year. Entering that period he told me to be on the watch for survival in community, my role in home, community and survival.

The fourth time I saw him I was in my seventh year. I don't know the exact date, it must be my birthday, when I was seven years old. "Tomorrow you'll have turned, reached a stage, first step toward the 14th age." Before my 14th age I'll have contact with the opposite sex, my mind and body is going to change. "Look," a young lady is coming toward me, a screen, like a shadow, watch her so you'll recognize her in the future. I did, how she moved her body, her head. Later in your life you'll see her, meet her, she'll be your *kičíwa* (wife). (*Kičíwa* = co-worker, the old term for wife in the old *Isáŋati* language; now we say *tawíču* = this is my take). She disappeared. The man talking never looked at me, only facing straight ahead with eyes closed, looking east. I never saw his [eyes?]. I'm always attracted by his face, no wrinkles, but looks so old. He said, "Look." I looked and saw three little girls, two the same height, one shorter, . . . more stern look. Later in your life these will become your daughters if you follow my instructions. He emphasized for me to take the pilgrimage when I reached age fourteen to twenty-one. But I made two attempts, but my parents, especially my mother, got me back, I gave up.

Two years after that, I saw this strange thing, this whirlwind, came [and it came] to my mind, "I'm off my track." I woke my mother up, "I want to talk. I saw a very strange thing outside." I don't feel right since then, this is what will happen if I don't follow the instructions and go on pilgrimage. Sure spirit will be with me and guard me. She never said a word, just sat smoking a cigarette. I knew I'm off my track. Alex Swifthawk was a kind of medicine man, did ceremony an hour or so. He said I saw a [person?].

From then my whole life was changed! I don't feel the pep, seems I had a great loss somehow; prior to that the future was so important to me, follow-up after I'm twenty-eight.

(The fourth time he [*Ité Wapíkida*] gave me a little cup, my whole body changed, I feel I can jump up and down. Later in life I drink. Beer didn't attract me; wine, I took as a soft drink, not care whether I drink or not. I drank Bristol Cream, sherry wine, gave me the same lift. Then a few years later I drank Lemon Hart rum, gave me the same feeling as I had before. He tells me through your whole life you'll live with these. Smoking, since my dad died I haven't smoked. I quit snuff until I got crippled. Now and then I have a real desire to have a smoke, and to drink wine or rum. But my experience . . . sometimes I get so . . . I have no ambition, sinks down to nothing. Soreness, sore eye, ankle, more frequent. Eye last week, more frequent physical problem now.

During my fourth time (still age seven) I was watching a very old man, staggering, drunk, fall by two big spruce trees. So beautiful the ground there, [and] horses, trucks, airplanes, cattle, horses, sheep, dogs, chickens, machinery. He fell, got up. I saw that was him, but in flick of an eye that was me. A girl came along but in fiftieth white hair left beautiful small short lady. I remembered that smallest of three girls. She pulled me into her arms, I lay against her bosom. She put her arms around me, she started to hum at the same tone *Ité* had when I was eight months. She reached, pulled out a flat bottle from my suit jacket, red mark and label. I said I want to take a drink. I took a big swig of drink. She put it back. I felt so relaxed, same as the fourth time, when he gave me that drink. I saw a bull whip on this (right) side, and on the left side a Luger gun. I felt so good, I dropped against her left chest, jumped up on my feet, jumped up and down, like when I was eight months old. I saw strange country, same as the first time I saw Ité sitting. I looked back, saw her still holding me in her arms. Like the end of my life.

I told all to my dad. I did want to hear more. He grabbed me across cement bridge over Lacroix Creek, swampy country, swung me around, slid me onto tall weeds and grass. I was by there and saw frogs and garter snakes, going out to see muskrat traps. In 1978 I was turning forty-nine, nice fall day October 29, I asked Peter Bushroad [who used] wheel chair skis, found place by river, I stayed all afternoon by a narrow creek. Rock still there in 1978. That was my dream vision of life.

I saw Pete LaSuisse, a medicine man. He took a paper, here's your house, here is where you met this strange object, person. Could I at age thirty-one go back to my original path? On Thanksgiving, Saturday, I'll be back: Fort Qu'Appelle. Come on Tuesday, for four nights. But he got killed in car accident. (Mniyo September 30, 1987)

Sam's Birth

[SM 1997] The doctor had said, "Your son will never walk."

When my mother was pregnant with me seven or eight months, women usually used to ask Mrs. Campbell, a shaman woman, to do a half-hour ceremony, give a prediction boy or girl and other prediction, what to do with the new child, what to name the new child. My mother did. She came. She told Mother I'm going to be a boy, but something strange about him . . . problem. He's not going to be normal, not going to lead a normal life. He has a mission, he was called to do a mission to do with the Dakota people. So my mother was worried about this. All day and night, ladies helping to deliver her, couldn't do anything with her. So Dad went to the schoolteacher, woke her up, wife, nurse, came and examined Mother, admit to hospital even. "She'll bleed. She's quite weak right now." The ambulance came and took her right to Holy Family Hospital under Dr. Cheesman. He tried that day. Early afternoon he came to be, "We must try to save you or you'll bleed to death. See his head. But not mov[ing]. So forceps to deliver. Skull three places, spinal cord, neck bone. Deliver. You had a boy, but he's gone." Basket. He left.

Change shift, different doctor, examined me, turned to Sister. "This boy is alive." He shook me . . . mouth, then I started to bawl. My head was shaped like an egg from the jaw up. He pushed my head, reshaped, repositioned it, put a tight cap on my head. [So I had an] Injury at birth. Had to have a neckpiece. Couldn't hold my head up. Took me to hospital once a week for 15 weeks, then once a month for 15 months for examination and support. But after June 30 no more. (Mniyo May 10, 1997)

Sam and Dan

BY DANIEL M. BEVERIDGE

Adapted from a story written for and presented to a University of Regina Seniors Education Centre class, April 25, 2007

It was May 1, 1962, in the early evening when I first met Sam. He and his father, Herbert Buffalo, came out and were standing in front of their house, a one and a half story log house with square dove-tailed corners and a steep shingled roof. This was my first visit to the Round Plain Reserve, about ten miles northwest of Prince Albert. I was visiting the four Dakota Sioux Indian Reserves in Saskatchewan as part of the research for my master's degree in sociology. I was twenty-four years old, a bit nervous, awkward and silent at first as Will Littlecrow introduced me, trying to explain who I was, here to see Round Plain. Herbert said, "Yes, here is

Round Plain, there, there and there," as he made wide gestures in three directions toward other homes located around the edge of a large clearing surrounded with bush and forest. I also shook hands with Sam, who limped and moved awkwardly, the result of some crippling disease like polio some years ago. We went inside to talk, as Herbert was almost deaf and had to put on his hearing aid. He was solid and stocky. Sam was heavy-set, thirty-two years old. I talked mostly with Herbert first, about the reserve and the different families. He was pleased that I already knew his sister Eva (wife of Charlie Hawk) at the Moose Woods Reserve near Saskatoon. I began to talk more directly with Sam. He soon surprised and impressed me with his speech, coming out with statements like, "That family no longer resides on the reserve." Before we left he told me that he wanted to write a book, a book with stories about the history of the Dakota people.

I made many visits to Round Plain (now called Wahpeton Dakota First Nation). Sam Buffalo helped me a great deal in making contact with people, attending community events and getting information. After my master's research was finished two years later in 1964 and I joined the work force I still kept in touch and visited once in a while for several years. Sam told me about the Dakota custom of the vision quest, where the young man fasts for four days and four nights. I figured I'd like to try it myself, a shortened version I could squeeze into a weekend, preferably in a location where I might see some of the little people, the elves Sam had told me about, so I drove up to see him. When Sam saw I had a few prunes and crackers in my pocket he decided I wasn't really ready for a vision quest! He did take me to the nearby Sturgeon Lake Reserve, but we didn't see any elves nor talk to anyone Sam said had seen them.

I was impressed with Sam's desire to improve himself and his community. He had notions of community and economic development. I attended a meeting in his house of a youth group he tried to start on the reserve. Sam also got me to drive over to an Alcoholics Anonymous Roundup at Crutwell, a nearby Metis village. I took my old vw van with a bunch of young guys from the reserve in the back loudly beating their drum as we drove through the forest reserve. The aa Roundup was a rousing event with fiddle music and old-time jigs. Alcohol was a serious problem in the area. Quite a few aa groups were starting up in Prince Albert and the area and lots of folks were joining.

I tried to help Sam start a forest products business. Sam and his dad spent quite a bit of their time, both summer and winter, living in the bush several miles from their house on the reserve. They lived in a tent in the forest reserve adjacent to the Indian reserve. I often remember Sam saying his favorite month was the month of May, when the weather is good, the ground and forest is green, you hear the raindrops falling on the canvas tent roof, and the mosquitoes aren't bad yet. Herbert had a team of horses, a wagon and sleigh. Often with the help of a young man from the reserve, he cut jack pine poles, sixteen-foot corral rails, which he sold to truckers who sold them down south. I remember one night I spent with them in the winter in their tent. It was very cold, even with the little stove going. Sam told me a few weeks later it got so cold their cat froze to death inside their tent. That's when they quit cutting, took the team and moved back to their house in the reserve. I lent Herbert money once to help buy a horse.

Sam thought cutting rails could benefit the community more than it did, if they owned the business themselves. I knew absolutely nothing about business or managing a business, so I asked a friend of mine in Saskatoon, where I was living, for advice. He said, "How much money are you willing to lose?" I didn't know but I figured it was worth it to try something anyway. I got another acquaintance interested. This was Mervin Milne, the inventor of the pyramid bale stacker, and the owner of a business. He had a truck, I found a buyer, so we drove up, loaded up a truckload of rails and sold them to a lumberyard in Poplar, Montana. Merv or his hired man picked up a few more loads that winter and we were able to get quite a bit more money into the pockets of those who cut the poles. The main costs, aside from the cutting, were the stumpage fees paid to the government and the transport.

Sam and I then got more ambitious. Sam looked around and chose another site, west of the Shell River and west of the reserve, where there was more jack pine for poles. We decided to cut and sell 10,000 rails. I arranged the selling and transport, getting a semi-trailer outfit this time. I also provided the finance. Sam was the manager of the cutting at the forest end. He hired young fellows from Round Plain and nearby reserves. Our rail project should have made a surplus but it didn't. We lost money, or more precisely I lost several thousand dollars, because of poor management at Sam's end of the project.

I didn't realize at the start, but soon found out, that Sam had a bad drinking problem. When I heard that while he was drunk out at the bush camp he shot a rifle bullet not far over somebody's head, I drove up from Saskatoon and helped him get enrolled in a three-week residential course in Regina run by Dr. Saul Cohen at the Saskatchewan Alcoholism Commission. This helped Sam a lot. Then he was able to get help from the federal Indian Affairs Branch to further his education. He took several classes at the Western Co-operative College in Saskatoon where I was an instructor, and upgrading classes and other classes as well.

Sam and I probably made a strange pair. Although I never drank alcohol, and had a very different background from Sam, we were friends and our relationship did last a lifetime.

At that time Sam was able to walk. Because of the paralysis in his left side, he had limited use of his left arm and left leg. He used no crutches or cane, but swung his left foot in an arc.

Once, in 1966, Sam told me he heard that Henry Two Bear had died on the reserve and we should go up there right away in case his family was going to throw out some valuable items. Henry was an elder who had been a participant in a religious society called the *Wakáŋ Waćípi*, or holy dance. We arrived just in time to rescue books, diaries, two medicine bags and a song stick. Of special interest was a book with songs used in the holy dance ceremony and a song stick which served a similar purpose. A wooden board about a foot long, with human figures and other figures inscribed around the edge on both sides, it reminds the singers of the songs.

In 1969 I got married and my wife Angelina and I left to work in Africa for several years. I was an extension specialist at a church-sponsored community development training center in Congo-Kinshasa, later called Zaire. When we returned to Canada we lived in Regina where I obtained work in University Extension at the University of Regina. I deposited most of the Two Bear materials in the Saskatchewan Archives, where they were organized by Louis Garcia, a Dakota-speaking tribal historian from North Dakota, and made available to the public. A number of Dakota people have gone to see the items.

Sam returned to live at the reserve and to work on various projects. In 1971 or 1972 Dr. James Howard, an American anthropologist, visited Sam and recorded stories and information. After visiting the nine Sioux reserves in Canada (four in Saskatchewan and five in Manitoba), he wrote a book, *The Canadian Sioux*.

In 1977, as part of an oral history project at the Wahpaton Dakota Reserve coordinated by Robert Goodvoice, one of Sam's uncles, Sam recorded four oral history interviews. One thing Robert Goodvoice said in his tapes is that Sam would have been chief of the reserve if the hereditary system had not been abolished by the government.

Sam's great-grandfather (his father's father's father) was the Sisseton *Wapáhaska* or Chief Whitecap, who obtained the reserve at Moose Woods now called Whitecap Dakota.

Sam's father's father, *Bdo*, was the leader of one of those groups who formed the reserve at Round Plain. Sam's father, Herbert, was a shaman and also an elder in the Presbyterian Church. Sam's mother was a Wahpeton.

In 1979, at about age fifty, Sam lost consciousness for a while, collapsed in front of his house on the reserve, and lost much of his mobility. He went to live in the Sherbrooke Community Centre in Saskatoon where he could receive the extra care he needed. He wasn't happy with his father's name, Buffalo, and took a Dakota name, *Mniyódowaŋ*, which he translates as rhythm in motion. He went by the name Samuel Mniyo. Sam told me that he became a Christian in 1981, although he had been a nominal Presbyterian since childhood.

In 1985, after quite a long period without contact, I went to see Sam. He used a wheelchair and had lost quite a bit of physical ability with his hands and arms. He had not made much progress in writing the book he had hoped to, but he still wanted to tell the story of the Dakota people and pass it on to the younger generation. He started to tell me these stories, and I tape-recorded them on two occasions. After I typed and edited these, I added more material during several unrecorded interviews up to 1987 and produced a manuscript in 1988. We then had a long pause in the writing.

In 1993 two of his nieces came to visit him one day. They asked him about the history of the Dakota people and how the Dakota religion ended, and who their god was. So Sam began telling them these stories. They suggested to him to record these holy stories now because those people who asked Sam not to record them have all died, and whenever Sam's time comes, all these stories would come to an end too. They said he should write them in the form of a book, that it could be used in the schools, in Dakota reserves and maybe other reserves. As Sam said, "I want to tell you the story of the Dakota people as my elders and sponsors gave it to me. This book will be for the younger generation of Dakota to look at, to learn about who they are and where they came from, and for other people who are interested."

So about 1996 Sam got very interested again and we resumed working on it. He obtained and began using a computer. I combined material from the 1977 oral history interviews, recorded more new material from Sam, and came up with another manuscript in 1997.

As Sam's pain increased and his ability to proofread the manuscript declined, Sam agreed that his niece Alvina should take responsibility to work with me to read, revise, and complete the book. She had library experience, computer skills and keen interest. I was so pleased to meet Alvina and discuss this with her how to do this. We wanted Sam to feel comfortable with the text, satisfied that it was saying what he intended. We planned to put some of it in a larger font size on the computer to make it easier for him to read.

Less than two weeks later Alvina died tragically in a car accident. We were devastated. Sam got pneumonia, weakened, and died on November 28, 1999. He was seventy and I was sixty-one. I was an honorary pallbearer at his funeral, where I pledged to complete the book we had worked on together for so long. It is still, as they say, in progress, but inching closer to completion . . . I would like to give you just a glimpse of the kind of story or stories that Sam learned from his elders and how he learned them. These are Sam's words.

[Here I included a section from Sam's introduction to this book, telling about his sponsor *Ité Wapíkida*, Jim Sapa, and Dr. James Howard.]

Samuel Mniyo's Time Line

BY DANIEL M. BEVERIDGE

1929	Sam Buffalo was born at Wahpeton
1930s	probably went to day school on the reserve, up to grade 2
1945	whirlwind incident and beginning of paralysis (age fifteen)
1951	visited and learned from James Sapa (Jim Black)
1961	became physically handicapped

1962	met graduate student Dan Beveridge
1963–64	took eleven-month work-training at orthopedic shoe shop, Handicapped Training Centre of Saskatchewan Council for Crippled Children and Adults, Saskatoon
1964	began study of grade 4 textbooks, studied grade 5 and 6 by correspondence school
1965	gave speech at Wahpeton cemetery proposing study of Red Road and *Wakáŋ Wačípi*
1965–66	shared management of Round Plain Rail Project (to cut and sell corral poles) with Dan Beveridge; his alcohol problem became more serious
1966	with Dan, obtained song stick, song notebook, and other items after Henry Two Bear died
1966	took three-week course at Saskatchewan Bureau on Alcoholism, Regina, with Dr. Saul Cohen
1966	wrote letter to Dan about song stick and proposing study of Red Road and *Wakáŋ Wačípi*
1966–67	started Adult Upgrading School at grade 7 and completed grade 10 Vocational Certificate
1967	took nine-week Handicraft Employee Course at Western Co-operative College, Saskatoon (with employees of Inuit and First Nations handicraft co-operatives)
1967–68	took grade 11 classes
1969–72	did research work with Dakota Association of Canada
1972	met anthropologist James Howard
1974–76	hospitalized twenty-one months in Victoria Union Hospital, Prince Albert
1977	had oral history interview with Robert Goodvoice
1979	moved to nursing care home in Saskatoon at age fifty
1981	became a Christian
1981	changed name to Samuel Mniyo
1985	had taped session with Dan
1997	had taped session with Dan
1999	died at age seventy; at the funeral, Dan promised to complete the book we had begun

Part 3

The Narratives of Robert Goodvoice

Traditional History

Introduction: Learning Traditional Knowledge and
Skills from the Older Generations, and the Loss of Culture (part 1)

[RG 1977] Now these are the kinds of stories that my grandparents tell to other people and other people tell different stories to them. I used to sit there and listen. That's how I can tell lots of these stories. There are men of my age, the same age as me, that can't do these things because they lived with their parents who were young and they don't seem to care for what the old people say or what the old people know. This is where I kind of (I wouldn't say I am ahead of them), but this is where I know what they don't know because I lived with the people who know these things and saw these things. How they cure meat and how they cure food for the winter, I have heard all this and I have ate a lot of it. My grandmother used to cure meat and wild fruit and how they tan hides. They used to live without going to school or learning anything from a teacher. They learned these things from their own parents. This trade (or whatever you might call it) has been handed down from one generation to the other and they don't change it. Whichever way they have done a certain piece of work, and if it is good, well that's the way it is done all the time. They don't change it at all. (Robert Goodvoice 2, 1977, 10) [That is, Robert Goodvoice oral history tape 2, 1977, transcript p. 10; see bibliography and appendix 3 for additional detail. DB]

[RG 1977] A fellow asked me the other day (he said he was going up north) and he asked me if I could go along and dry meat for him. Well I guess I could try, but I don't know whether I could make the dry meat as my grandfather and grandmother used to make it. I don't know how to do it.

Animal meat, like the buffalo, they dried the meat. They get the meat and then they treated it in some way that it tastes different. They dry it all right enough but then some of it they dried over a fire. Some of it they dried maybe ten feet up and let the air dry it, the heat from the sun and the air. That tastes different. Things like that, you know it is very interesting. We don't know anything about it at this time. That's lost.

So it's lost, those things are lost and we will never find what we don't know now. We will never find out. There aren't very many Indians living today who know these things and if you ask them — "Oh yes, I heard my grandfather say something about it." "Oh, yes, I heard my grandmother say something about it, but I don't know." That's the answer you get. At least that's the answer I get. I have been getting that for the last two months now and it is very hard for me to tell stories and put it on tape.

What I am saying is what I heard from my grandfather and grandmother, but there is nobody to testify of what I am saying and I would like to get somebody who would elaborate on what I am saying, if possible. But there is nobody here. I have one man here who is older than me, but he is not interested in a thing like that and I am. I asked him a couple of times and he said, "I don't know. I'm doing all right," he said. This is what he said. He has a pension and when he wants medicine he goes to the drugstore and goes to the doctor and that's it. He doesn't have to worry about what is gone and what has gone out of sight. And he doesn't have to bring in his presence his grandmother or grandfather and he is not criticizing himself for not knowing this or he didn't ask his grandmother, grandparents about these things, which was good to them. It was their livelihood in those days. But now he doesn't know and he still enjoys life, as he says.

Really, I would like to know and remember everything that my grandparents used to tell me and used to say. They never depended on anybody but themselves. They knew what to do and if they had a sore foot or a headache, they knew what to do to cure themselves. I am having a hard time to find out things. (Robert Goodvoice 2, 1977, 10–14)

The Origin of the Ćaŋkú Dúta (Red Road or Red Path) and
Wakáŋ Waćípi (Holy Dance or Medicine Dance), 1972 version

[As James Howard notes of the Medicine Feast and the Medicine Dance, "Robert Good Voice (Round Plain) stated that the 'red road' was an important symbolic concept in both rites. He commented, 'This is the good path of life. One hundred and fifty different roots are used in the various medicines found in the medicine bags. The red path leads to life everlasting'" (Howard 1984, 130). Howard notes of the water spirits: "According to Robert Goodvoice (Round Plain) the *Uŋktéȟi* are everlasting. They live in the sea, toward the rising sun. One is an old man and one is an old woman. In appearance they are giant panthers with horns. Mr. Goodvoice stated that it was the *Uŋktéȟi* who gave the Medicine Dance to the Sioux and showed them the good red road" (106). Howard says:

> The following is a composite of Mr. Goodvoice's and Mr. Buffalo's separate accounts, which complemented one another.
>
> "Many years ago the Dakota people landed on a peninsula on the east coast of North America. They were surrounded by waters and could go no further, so they prayed. Finally, in response to their prayers, they heard a great voice, and above the surface of the ocean, in the direction of the sunrise, they saw the heads of two spirits. These were the *Uŋktéȟi* [Underwater Panthers]. One was male and *sota* [grayish-white] colored. The other, a female, was the color of a buffalo calf [reddish-brown]. They were like giant panthers in shape, but had horns like a buffalo.
>
> "These spirits told the people to travel west, following the *ċaŋkú dúta*, the 'red road.' [In other words, to perform the Medicine Dance and to follow the teachings of the organization.] This road, they said, has four divisions. The promise of the red road, the *Uŋktéȟi* said, is as true as what you can see. The people looked toward the west and saw that their path seemed to lead into the sea. They feared that they would be drowned, but they had faith and followed the red road.
>
> "When they came to the water, one man stepped on it, and it parted, revealing a dry path. The rest followed. The red road led the Dakota west to the Minnesota country and they kept up their *Wakáŋ Waċípi* from that time onward. Some men here still know the songs and we still believe in its teachings." (137–88; bracketed asides are Howard's). DB]

The Origin of the *Ċaŋkú Dúta* (Red Path) and
the Gift of Medicinal Plants, 1977 version

[This story is most remarkable: it takes us back in time seven generations, to the time of the great-grandfather of Robert's grandfather. It portrays a slightly different version of the story already told in part 2 by Sam of the origin of the *Ċaŋkú Dúta* and *Wakáŋ Waċípi*. DB]

[RG 1977] This has something to do with a person who stood on the water and told them about this Red Path. The Dakotas don't know why they did this. One time all the Dakotas out of Dakota, they gathered by the seashore. There was nothing there for them, nobody asked them to gather there but they all gathered there on their own will and they camped there and there was a bunch of them. Lots of them.

And one morning it was—they say it was a nice bright morning. There was no wind on the sea. And somebody happened to look toward the sea and they saw a person. They saw a person standing on the water. And this story was told to my grandfather by his great-grandfather, not his grandfather but his grandfather's father. My grandfather's great-grandfather's grandfather told this story. He said that is a long ways, way back. He said the beginning of time, *toká wičóičaǧe*, the beginning of the human race. When they first come into existence. That is the time he said that this happened. This man stood on the water and told them that there is a path from where he is standing on the water, that is the beginning of the path. And this person called it the Red Path, *Čaŋkú Dúta*, that means the Red Path. And it is toward the west. And at the end of this Red Path, there is a crown of white—*watéśdake ska*, that means a headgear of white— over there for you. Work for that. And if you get to that crown at the end of the Red Path, you would receive this crown of white, the headgear of white. And from there farther west, there is a land there above this land. And that on that land, there is no end. Life—there is no end to life there. There is no end to happiness.

Now, later on there is a man translated what this man said who stood on the water. And he said that is a spirit world. The crown of white, the headgear of white, is a man's hair. His hair will turn white. And if you are good, you are kind and honest, you will live to a happy old age. Your hair is not going to be black, it will be white. And the clothing has no seams and it will never wear out. They say that is an old man's skin. It is kind of loose but then it will never wear out there. And the world above this one is the spirit world. This is the way that was translated by a man. He heard this and saw this in his dream.

And this man who stood on the waters and told them about the Red Path also showed them 150 different kinds of roots. Roots, leaves, flowers, and the stalk plant that is good for every part of the body. Now take it and use it. While you are taking it, while you are digging it up, remember the most holy, the *Wakáŋ Táŋka*. There is life in that plant. And that is what you are taking and that is what you are going to administer to other people.

A life that the most holy provides and placed it on this earth. That was once. And then each year, these plants, they come. When it is time for them to grow, they grow. And that is the life you take, you consume that and you use that for your health and you have health by using these plants. Roots, herbs, leaves, and the flower and the tender part of the stalk. Now this is the instructions that the Dakotas got about four or five generations before my grandfather. My grandfather's great-grandfather, they tell this story to each other, from one generation to the other.

And of course, as my grandfather said, it is no use him telling me this because I wouldn't pay any attention to it. He said, "You boy, you people today, you are among the whites, the white people, and they are going to take control of you and you will fall for them and you will believe them and you are going to use their medicines, whatever it may be. But you are not going to use these roots, herbs of all kinds. You will never use them, my grandchild." He told me this himself, which is right. We have no— what the white men call our people—the medicine man. We have none of them but we have some men that still know a few roots and they practice using them and they get good results from these roots that this man show[ed] the Indians, showed the Dakotas standing on the water. And they saw him standing on the water and he disappeared. They didn't say, they don't know whether he went in the water or in the air or where he went. (Robert Goodvoice 6, 1977, 11–12)

[Robert Goodvoice's paternal grandfather was John Sioux (*Aŋpétu Wašíćuŋ*). A Mdewakanton, probably aged seventy-one in 1912, he came to the Prince Albert area with his six brothers and Chief *Húpa Iyaȟpeya* in 1877. They lived at the Little Red River Sioux Camp. DB]

Becoming a Member of the *Ćaŋkú Dúta* (Red Path) Society

[In speaking here about the *Ćaŋkú Dúta* or Red Path (Red Road) and the Red Path Society, Robert certainly is describing what Sam calls the *Wakáŋ Waćípi* or Holy Dance Society. DB]

[RG 1977] I am going to speak on the *Ćaŋkú Dúta*, the Red Path a little bit yet as my grandfather told me. My grandmother also repeated the story many times. *Ćaŋkú Dúta* is a word used, a livelihood to the— let's say to the high points of civilization and to Christianity. Not as the

Bible recorded or the Bible states but in their way, in their own way, as my grandfather said, everything that is good in their minds and in the human minds relates to the top of this *Ċaŋkú Dúta*, the Red Path, the end of the Red Path.

To be a member of this society, you have got to be good. You have got to be honest. You have got to help others at all times. And you have got to be faithful to your partners, chiefly your wife or your husband. And first, you have got to think of your family, your children, and then the others who need help, you have got to be there to help them. Once you drop off—once you do wrong or say wrong, as he tells me, you drop off—then you still belong to the *Ċaŋkú Dúta* society but then you are not going to travel on the *Ċaŋkú Dúta* as fast and get to the top as quick as the honest and faithful members. If you are not a faithful member, you would struggle. Your soul would struggle here and there on the way to the top of this *Ċaŋkú Dúta*. Therefore, you have to be good.

To start with, to become a member of this society, you have got to ask the principal members of this society to become a member of this society. They won't say yes or they wouldn't say no but they would say they are going to watch you for four moons or four seasons. Four moons means four months. Four seasons means a whole year, they will watch you. There might be fifteen or twenty members of this society in the camp in which you live. There will be twenty watching you. No matter where you go, no matter what you do, there is somebody looking at you. They know how many good deeds you have committed and how many bad ones you have committed. They know how many times you have failed to help your companions and how many times you have helped them. And when you finish, they will tell you. "We'll watch you for four moons or four seasons," and at the end of that appointed time, when you finish your time, then you go before them. And you tell them the truth that you have lived a clean, honest, reliable life for that period of time and you intend to carry on that life from that time to the end of your days. Then they will bless you and pray for you to the *Wakáŋ Ťáŋka* [Great Spirit], asking him to help you to be good. And if you fail, if you get angry and you fail to live up to what you promised—that is, to be good, honest, and reliable—if you fail that, if you fail, then you are not a true member. But then you still could join them in some of their feasts and some of their gatherings like the real *Ċaŋkú Dúta* members' meetings and dances.

They dance to the—they have a dance. It is not a dance where—like the dances that you see today. It is a kind of a ceremonial dance. And it is sacred. All the food that is going to be consumed within that lodge, each piece, like a pail of meat or soup or whatever it is, each one, an individual would pray with that and they would put it over there. And then another one would pray for another dish or whatever it may be and they would put it over there. Everything that is in there is blessed and the people prayed with it, asked the good Lord to bless it and that when they consumed that they would they take it as consuming medicine and good for the body. And beyond that, [it would] give them strength to follow this *Ċaŋkú Dúta*, the Red Path faithfully, willingly, honestly. And then they would pronounce you, they pronounce one a member of the society but he is not in the front. He is at the back seat. He has got to work by his good deeds to get in front.

And when they get in front, my grandfather said that two or three men, mostly two men, would take this new member into the forest or on a hill someplace and they will fast there with him and ask him, the *Wakáŋ Táŋka*, to give the new member extra power to heal sick and to make the sorrowful happy. They stand there, that's wherever it is, on a hill or along the river bank or in the forest. It doesn't matter where but they have got to be alone with him. They will pray for him and he will pray for himself to obtain some gift of some kind to—or else, [as] I said, extra power to heal [the] sick and cure people from their sicknesses and diseases and this and that.

Some people they feel—they feel their body change. They say they feel their body, starting from the feet up till they get to the top of their head, they said they feel warm. Just warm. They change. The heat comes from the earth and it penetrates through their body right to the top of their head and to the tip of his fingers. When that happens, he is supposed to tell these two men that are there with him and pray for him and ask the *Wakáŋ Táŋka* to give him a gift, the ability to heal sickness and anything that a man is suffering. When that feeling is over, this man, they say he is happy. He has changed. His body has changed and he is very, very happy. While they are there for a day or two days or two nights they don't drink, they don't eat, they don't sleep but they stand there and they pray. Their mind is wherever the *Wakáŋ Táŋka*, the God is, that is where their mind is most of the time. They have got to do this in order to receive some help or some power.

Some stand there and carry on for three or four days and their body never changed. They never have no feeling, no different feeling in their body. Or they don't see anything or they just want to go to sleep and they are getting hungry and they can't forget that, they can't forget their hunger. All they think of is food. All they think of is a place to lie down and sleep. Well, this kind of people, their mind is just, is not where *Wakáŋ Táŋka* is. His mind is not in harmony with the power above. But he is just wanting to go to sleep and eat. But this man here could stand there for twenty days and never get no blessing or no gift of any kind at no time. Because his mind is, just a minute now, what do they call that now? His mind is on the earth. But not upwards. This is the way they call that. And once they do that, when they find that out, that his mind is not toward the power above, they just take him home. And yet he is still a member.

Next year, this man here that fasted for three days or two days and see or hear nothing, next year, about the same time, they will just go there and tell him, "Here, you come. You have to go through that procedure that you went through last summer. Maybe your mind has changed this time. Maybe you changed your mind. Maybe you have changed into another feeling or you would get some help so you got to come." Some refuse. "I was there once and I never got nothing, I am not going." Well then, they condemn him. They condemn this man here that refused to give a second try, they condemn him to the earth. They condemn him to the earth. And you should struggle day in and day out, all the days of your life on this earth. This is the way they cancel a man out of the Red Path Society.

But if he goes the second time, if he goes the second time and they perform with him upon the top of a hill or in the forest or along the river or someplace away from the camp, this time he will be there two days. Maybe he will hear a voice, a voice way far away. Somebody yelled at him or something. He will hear a voice. Chiefly it is about . . . and most of them they say they get scared when they hear that. There is nobody in sight, there is nobody about there and yet a voice come to him telling him to brace up and receive, prepare to receive what is coming. But then this person who is trying to obtain extra powers by fasting, they get scared. Prepare to receive. What is it? It is a voice that they hear. How is he going to prepare? These things come in their mind and lots of them . . . just then they will hear the voice again closer, more loud, louder than the first time. Some of them, they tell these two men that are there with them, "Well,

I can't stand it. I can't receive that voice, I can't." And they just pick up whatever they have and then go home. Well, he heard a voice. That means that something had paid attention to him. Some power had paid attention to him and this power let him know by hearing. By making this noise, saying a few words, they warned him. That is a kind of a warning that they.... He is approached by some extra power, a power from above. This is what grandfather said. They called that a power from above. And then, well, he ran away. Of course they let him go. That goes on till next year.

The same time next year they take him back to the same place and they try him and this time if he failed the second time, third time, well they took him three times but the third time if he fails well, next year they will take him and put him through the same procedure. That is to try and get some extra power from the Almighty, the *Wakáŋ Ťáŋka*. And the fourth time, the fourth time, if he can carry out the orders that he is just about to receive from above or from the power of the air or the spirit of the air or at night, the spirit of the night or the day, then he would know at the fourth try.

And each time, if he hears something strange, at the fourth try he would stand it and he would accept it. Then of course he would go on out, he would drop to the ground. But they won't touch him. He would lie there and then in that trance, he is in a trance, and then while he is in that trance, then he receives the instructions and what to do, how to do it, and all that. Then when he comes to it, when he comes to, rather, and wakes up, he has got everything. He remembers everything: the words that he is supposed to say when he is praying and the direction that he is supposed to face when he is looking over a sick body, maybe his head to the south or his head to the west or his head to the north. Whichever direction that body, he saw in his trance, that is the way the body has got to be if he is trying to doctor it through this power given to him, through this invisible instructor, I would say. And then when he sobers up and comes to, his mind is clear. He understands these things clear. He might hear four sacred songs, he would remember them. And the prayer that he is supposed to say, he would remember it.

And this man would come to the camp and then he is among his people. Four tries, that means four years, and then they would accept him back into the Red Path with that extra power and then everybody depends on him. And the more sick people that he cured, the healthier he is and the healthier his family, his grandchildren will be. This is the reward he gets. But when a sick person goes to him and if he cured him, well that sick person, when he is better, he might give him a gun or a Hudson Bay blanket or a tent or whatever he has that is worth having. They would take that and give this to the medicine man. Naturally he would accept it. Then he is paid for what he did. A gun, traps or one thing or another, blankets, tanned hide, he is paid for, so he is not gaining anything for his grandchildren or himself or his sons and daughters. He received the payment in materials, not in good health. And there is lots of these men, they wouldn't accept anything like any manufactured materials as a payment. They would heal this person and then he don't take no pay for his work. But then his children and himself and his grandchildren, he gains health for them. This is the understanding, way in the beginning of these here people receiving extra power, gaining extra power by suffering for three, four days asking for this power.

And when they get the power, then they start receiving payments, taking the blankets from the poor, sick person. Or take his tent or his gun but a person like that, he is—they don't consider him as a man with extra power to help people but he does—he gained that for his own personal gain. And when they find out a person is like that, well, nobody goes to him. And when people don't go to him, but he has got that extra power for the people but nobody wants it, so he has got that in him and it is no good for him. He is always suffering in some way.

But if he helped the people . . . as my grandfather said, there is a man. He had extra power like that. It took him four days and four nights out in the wilderness to gain that. All this time he prayed and he cried and he prayed and prayed to the *Wakáŋ Táŋka*. When his prayer was answered, he got an extra power. He come back to the camp. If he hear anybody's sick, you don't have to call him, he will get up and he will walk over there and perform over this man, touch him, lay his hands on him and pray for him, lay his hands on him. Wherever the pain is, he will lay his hands on that pain, sore spot or . . . and then he cures them. He never, never take nothing for his work from a human hand to his hand. But then this man here, he was a good trapper you see. He was always trapping and hunting. When he goes out into the bush, just a little ways from home, he will go hunting. He don't go very far. There is an animal standing there watching him, looking at him. Shoot him and that is his. He has got his:

his hunting is over for that day. And when he sets traps for fur-bearing animals, he gets them by the dozens where other people don't get nothing. And they figure he cured people, helped them, but never take payments, never received payments from his family or from his sick person's relatives. But he gets it back in some other way.

Now this is the duty of a man that is a member of this here Red Path Society. It is hard, it is very, very hard. You have got to be good and you have got to have patience and anybody make you mad, you are supposed to leave him and you are not supposed to get mad or fight. You have got to be good, that is all there is to it. Then you gain this and then you will reach the end of the Red Path and from there, life everlasting. This is what the Red Path leads to and the teaching of the Red Path, if you follow it, it will take you there. You will reach the high points of civilization and Christianity. (Robert Goodvoice 6, 1977, 13–18)

Learning Traditional Knowledge, Skills and Medicine
from the Older Generations (part 2)

[RG 1977] Another thing, it seems to me that my grandparents, my grandmother said that she was a good swimmer. So they must have lived in a place where there is lots of water. [Probably Lac qui Parle. DB] She said when she was a little girl she used to dive and swim. They mastered the water pretty well. She doesn't remember hearing of anybody telling about anybody getting drowned. They go to the lake and swim and play in the water and this and that but they seem to get into the lake or river but they would all come out. So that's something. I look at my grandmother and the way she looks at age of around ninety, she doesn't look as if she can swim at all. But I guess she could. My grandfather said water doesn't mean anything to him. He said he can swim against the waves. He said he likes water, he likes swimming and he likes hunting. He showed me how and he told me how to hunt and how to trap and how to snare this way and why he set his trap this way and all that. He said the animals are going to come there and you've got to understand this thing, you've got to understand what move the animal is going to make after he steps over this log, or to go around this clump of willows. What is he thinking when he is going around? Is he going to look right down or is he going to take a far away look? My grandfather used to tell me all these things, which is very good.

There is one good thing that I know, by him telling me, "There is a certain time of the day when all the animals, like the jumpers and the deer and elk, there is a certain time of day when they are sound asleep. You could walk right up to them," he said. "They are just sound asleep." There is a certain time of the day, and that's when he said he gets his animals, is when you catch them right in their beds sleeping. They didn't have horses or anything to haul their meat home so they packed everything. They are good packers. They could pack quite a few pounds.

They seemed to have a feeling of tomorrow, what sort of a day it is going to be tomorrow. They seemed to feel it today. They watched the stars and they watched the sunset and they watched the weather and they seemed to guess. But most of the time they seemed to know what they are saying when they speak of weather. Today, nobody knows anything about the weather, only what we get over the radio.

Another thing, a person getting sick, they don't go to a doctor and they don't go to a nurse because there was no doctor or no nurses in the camps. But then they would dry roots, herbs and leaves and this and that. Not any kind, just a certain kind of plant that is a medicine. It is good for the wind and it is good for the muscles and so on. There is something for every part of the human body, as they always say. If we have a headache today, what do we do? We take an aspirin. If they had a headache in those days they would take a piece of root, a dry root and they will get a piece of charcoal and they will put this dry root on that red hot charcoal and it would smoke up and they will inhale that smoke through their nostrils and then they would cover their head and lie down and their headache is gone. It never came back to them again. Now things like this, if I tell them to my grandchildren, they won't believe it. They won't believe it. If that root, the smoke of that root could kill headache, why couldn't a cigarette? This is the answer they will give me. I know they would.

To hear them talk and when they show you what they did to live and how they lived and what makes them do these things to live, it is wonderful. They have a reason. It is pretty hard for me to explain. They have a reason. They never go to a doctor, they never go to a nurse as I said before. There are no hospitals. They catch cold, sure they catch cold and they break a bone once in a while. They cured themselves and nothing else sets in. Today, if a person breaks a bone, there is some other thing which sets in before the bone heals. But in those days they put some kind of root, leaves and this and that and they make poultices of it and they wrap it around it and they put bits of clay of some kind. They put that all around it. Today, it always comes to my mind when I see a man with a cast on his arm or his finger, or his leg, I often remember what my grandmother and grandfather used to say about this clay that they put on their arm or leg to keep it in shape. It doesn't go out of shape, it keeps it there and in so many days they cut it, they chip it some way and they take it off and the bone is healed and it is healed the way it should be. All these things, they would talk about it and they believe in it.

Another thing that I find very good is, my grandmother and grandfather, both old, if they have toothache well they take a root. They soak a root in warm water until that root is soft and then they put that in their mouth wherever the tooth is aching they put it there and then they will bite it and then they will cover their face and lay down and tomorrow, no more toothache.

The same thing—they've got an eyewash. My grandmother, she is ninety-three and she can thread a needle just as good as anybody else. So does my grandfather. Some old people, once their eyes give they just give, give, give and they go blind. But most of them seem to have good eyes right up to old age.

As far as living and medicine and looking after the body is concerned, this is the way they talk and there is a lot of medicine they get from the ground and from the trees, from the flowers, the bark and the leaves and the flower and the root. But us Indians today, we don't know nothing about those things that my grandfather and grandmother used to live by using these things. Now we don't, we don't know what these roots are. Where can we go to get them? What are they, how do they look? (Robert Goodvoice 2, 1977, 10–14)

How the Dakota People Began the Sundance

[RG 1977] Now, I am going to tell a story that my grandfather told many times. And he heard this story when he was a little boy. But he said he remembered the story as his grandfather told it to him.

Once upon a time, many years back, the Indians, the Dakota, camped at a certain place and there was a slough there and they used that slough for drinking water. And one day it commenced to go down and finally it dried up. And then they started searching for water, here and there.

They come to a slough, camped there and it would dry up. Another place, dry up. Come to a creek, it has dried up and there is little water left. At the deep places where the water can't get out . . . they camped there and used that water until that dried. It was getting serious. After all, they can't find any water. The land was dry. And they sent boys, strong boys, strong healthy men in every direction seeking for water. The boys come back in the evening without finding any water. And they moved about, the whole camp, quite a few families, they moved about and sometimes the older people, the old people, they commenced to play out and they can't move anymore. So they put them in one place and from there, the boys, the young strong men, they are still searching for water. Animals were running back and forth searching for water. They come to a river but that river was dry. Only the curves where it is deep, there is a little bit of water there. But anything that lived in the water are all gathered there, snakes and lizards and frogs and fish and whatever lived in the water, they are all gathered there. That water is not fit for a human to drink but they drank it anyway. That dried up. And at the curve of the rivers where the water was and then it dried out. So you would see that there, that place there, full of dead fish and other animals. Other creatures like frogs and lizards and snakes and things like that. This went on for a few days. He didn't say how many days. Pretty soon there is no water at all. They followed the riverbed but they can't find any water. By this time, most of the old people played out and they just kept them in one piece. And one fellow, one old one of the leaders, he picked little pebbles, it is a kind of a blue sort of little stone. About the size of a large marble and it is round. He picked a lot of them. And he put one of these pebbles in the mouth of the old people. And they say that keeps the mouth from drying up. And they moved about. They went in every direction looking for water. And pretty soon these strong boys that they chose to go and seek for water, they will go but they will return in a short time. They can't find any and they are getting weak. So they can't stand the travelling no more. Their mouth is dry and they are just dying for a drink of water.

So they, the chiefs and the leaders, the old men, they all got together. And they got together and they say there is something wrong someplace, that they are punished, that the world is going dry. They are punished, for something that they did or something that happened; that the creator of heaven and earth didn't approve of their transactions so he is punishing them by cutting them off water. So these Indians, the Dakotas, they say they are going to stay there and they will die there. They can't move on any more. So they went and brought the old people that played out and that are too weak to move, they brought them to this same place. They were all there.

And these old people, the old men, they choose four of them and they ask them to pray for water; ask the Creator to lead them to water or cause it to rain so that they would have water. My grandfather said his grandfather who told him this story was just a small boy. He didn't say how old he was but he was small. And he remembered very well these four men stood side by side facing the south and another four men stood side by side facing west. Another four men facing north and four more facing east. There is four men, each group of four facing in four directions of the wind, east, west, north, and south. The people that are facing the south, they are the number one. They prayed. They prayed; and the west, the north, and then the east. They all prayed and they—when they finished praying in groups then they all prayed while the others of the tribe, they were sitting on the ground. And they made a space in the middle where these men stood. And they prayed and cried and prayed and cried.

Pretty soon a cloud appeared in the west, a long ways, appeared and then it was coming toward the east. As it approached them, the cloud seemed to spread across, wider and wider and then they saw lightning, here and there but not a big clash of lightning, just a little bit. You can see it is lightning and that is all. And then when they saw that, they know it is going to rain. They know they are going to receive water from above. So they prayed some more and then they asked everybody to stand up and put their hands up toward this black cloud, which they all did. Sure enough you can see the sign of rain. In no time, it rained upon them and then whatever they have, birch bark cups and dishes, whatever they could catch water in, they would spread it out. And even the rawhides, they make it in a way that it will hold water. And they dug holes in the ground where the water would run in. And this happened when they started praying and when they started to gather together in one place. And when they started praying, they say it was just before midday. And then when it happened, it is halfway between midday and sunset. And that is when it rained, the same day. And then it rained until evening, until the sun went down. And then the rain stopped.

By that time, all the sloughs and all the hollows in the area were full of water, the way it had been before. And when they saw this, they were pleased and they thanked the Lord, the Creator. And they faced the south, they stood in a circle and they sang a song of thanksgiving and they prayed and they stood, everybody stood facing the south. And they started clapping their hands and when they sang this song of thanksgiving and clapped their hands, everybody did that, and they started dancing facing the sun. And they were happy and then some cried and some sang with the elders and some just stood there praying. And they are still dancing. They stood in the same place and danced. Kept time with the clap of their hands (claps his hands). Like that, they kept time. And some of them started whistling. They whistled, and some of them, they had whistles. What made them, how they come to have those whistles they don't know but anyway, they had whistles made out of bone and made out of wood. So they put these whistles in their mouth and blow it and keep time with the clap of the hands and the singing. And they danced until dark.

They had all the water they want to drink. And they had food. They carried their food and they ate and drank and danced. And the next day, they still stayed at the same place. They stayed there four days. And then they went to move on to some hunting grounds for they were getting short of food. But they sent four boys, strong men, to see how much water there is in the country. They told them to go this way, to keep going, until such time and then they could return. "And you go this way and you go this way." So these boys did and as far as they know, every hollow and every slough refilled. There was water for them no matter where they go, water for the animals. And all this time, while they were on dry land, there was no water. For a few days, they didn't see a bird. Not a fowl, not one. The animals, they saw them running this way and this way searching for water. And they saw them dead too. So they didn't say how long that happened but that happened. And just before they scattered to different — back to their hunting grounds — the elders got together and they say, they said the way they danced and the way they returned the good Lord thanks for the water that they received, and they stand in a circle. All those that could take part, they stand in a circle, facing south. And they made up some songs. They worded their songs as thanksgiving, thanks to the Creator for the water that they received from above. They thanked him for saving their lives. They thanked him for saving the lives of animals that were their food and causing the plants to grow that were their food. And the fruit, the wild fruit on the trees, they thanked him for that. And then they stood in a circle in a horseshoe shape facing the south and they danced . . . half a day, they danced half a day and they were going to break up in the evening and then they were going to move on. But the elders, they say, "We thank our Creator during the day. We must thank him during the night, under the moonlight, under the starlight and in the dark," and this is what they did. They danced that night until sunrise and they all faced the sun as it came up and it slowly turned to south. When it was midday, that is when the dance broke up.

And my grandfather says from that time, this dance is called the Sun Dance. They don't call it the Rain Dance but they call it the Sun Dance. And by performing this kind of a dance in that fashion, they received blessing by obtaining water from above. So they figure that their prayer was answered by performing this kind of a dance and the songs that they sang and the songs of thanksgiving. The way they worded their songs, they figure that the Creator heard them and saw them and granted them what they prayed for. And this is what my grandfather said that is what he was told, and he saw his grandfather perform a Sun Dance once.

There are others performed. When a child is sick or a man is sick or anybody is sick, they offer a prayer. And they say, "If I reach that season," but it's always when the poplar trees—when the leaves on the poplar trees are the size of a quarter, that is a twenty-five-cent piece, it would be about an inch in diameter, when that season comes, that is the Sundance season, that is when the Dakota perform Sundance if they are going to perform one. So if anybody is sick, they go outside with the sick person facing the rising sun just as the sun rises. They stand out there facing the rising sun and pray to the Almighty God, the Wakáŋ Táŋka, the most holy. That is what that means, Wakáŋ Táŋka means the most holy. They prayed to him and they looked at the sun and they prayed to him again and again until midday. Then they make a promise and say if they reach that season when the leaves on the poplar tree are about the size of a quarter, they would perform. And they would leave all their earthly habits like eating, drinking, sleeping, whatever habit they have, they would leave that for a day and one night. They make that promise. Sure enough the sick person recovers to good health and they live on until they come to that season.

And this person who was sick and the person who made the promise to perform the Sundance, them two enter the Sundance lodge first and then the rest of the people. They take their position on the north, inside the lodge on the north side facing south. On our part, on our Dakota way, the singers, the music makers, they sit on the west side of the lodge, inside the lodge only on the west side. And to begin, they always remember and they always mention the day when the Indians, when the Dakotas were dying of thirst and they asked the *Wakáŋ Ṫáŋka* to shower some blessings and water upon them that they would live and it happened. They always mention that first. And then whatever is to follow, it follows. With pipes and other ceremonial articles, rattles, and drums, and drum sticks, and all these kinds of things that they have as sacred things, then they bring these into this here Sundance lodge and this is where they open them up and — they are always kept wrapped — and then they bless them with a smoking of this here sweet grass. When they do that, they burn this sweet grass and when the smoke rises, they put these things over it and they smoke it. And then they say that is purifying it. And then the spirit of the air, the spirit of the day, the spirit of the night, they respect that very transaction. This is known, a person was sitting in the lodge after sundown and it was dark and the others retired. They move outside of the Sundance lodge and they are still sitting there but this one Indian, Dakota, he sat inside the lodge with all these sacred articles. And this is what he found out and this is what he saw done with a pair of hands taking these things and smoking them and they are purified. That is why they do that, my Dakota people. They do that right up until today. And this is the way the Dakota people begin the Sundance.

And at times there are men, women, they go out, away from the camp onto a hill with their sick person, sick baby or sick brother or sister or sick relative, they go away from the camp with their sick person and they fast overnight one day or maybe one day and night. And a voice, a voice would — they would hear a voice telling them that they cried and their prayers were heard. And they made a promise that if this child or person is better, they would make a Sundance — as they say it, make a Sundance — and they would leave their earthly habits for a length of time. And then they understood that that would be accepted. And the sick person becomes healthy and gains his health and is just as strong as the rest of them when that, the appointed time rolls around. So this Sundance, as my Dakota people call it, it is a very, very, very—they respect that highly. They figure and they say it is a fact, when the Sundance lodge is made and things that are used in there are in there and the people are in there, the Gods would be there with sincere, high minds, with all their power. Toward *Wakáŋ Táŋka* , toward God. And they prayed. And then their prayers are answered. This is the belief they have. It never failed, you see.

At one time, at the beginning, it never failed. Women, men, children, of all ages, they are cured from their health. Some of them, something happened to their leg that they can't hardly walk, they stay in that Sundance lodge for two days. And then they come out of there walking just as perfect as they were one time before they got hurt. People lose their sight. Some accident or something that they lost their sight. They are in there and they gain their sight and come back. They see everything the same as the other people with their eyes perfect. Of course, anything that is broken—like if a finger is cut off, that is gone—but if the bone is broken, it could be together. They pray and if they say they would perform a Sundance, if that arm or leg is back to perfect, back to its perfection.

They don't ask nobody to go there. They don't invite nobody but they know they find the people and if they want any blessings or any help to gain good health, they go there on their own. They go there with a sincere heart that they would come out, come out of that Sundance lodge with a perfect body. This is the idea and it happens as they say. They depend on that greatly. (Robert Goodvoice 6, 1977, 2–7)

Uŋktómi, Dakota Spirit Helper

[RG 1977] And this is something my grandfather didn't—he said this. Lots of people, lots of elders didn't agree with this. He said nobody asked this, this what we call *Uŋktómi,* and the Crees, they call this being, *Wičáȟke-čaȟ.* But this *Uŋktómi* is a human, looks like a person but nobody touched him. Nobody ever get close to him and touch him but he speaks. They speak to him where he lives and where he come from, nobody knows. All at once he appeared to them in the camp amongst them. Now this is where in this Sundance Lodge, this *Uŋktómi,* I don't know what you would call him in English, but he appeared to them and he showed them and he guides them. He tells them there will be an epidemic that is going to raid the camp this winter. He tells them to prepare by digging up this root and that root and this and that and keep it and do this and do that.

And pray in this fashion. Use these words. And this is the way *Uŋktómi* guides the Dakota people. And they do as he gives orders or commands them to do. And the epidemic did raid the camp but they never lose anybody. They all lived through it.

Now, as my grandfather says, he said, he never saw this *Uŋktómi*. Or in the Cree way they call him *Wićáḣkećaḣ*. Maybe that is the same. I wouldn't say *Uŋktómi* and *Wićáḣkećaḣ* are both the same because the way *Wićáḣkećaḣ* acts with the Crees, it is different from what *Uŋktómi* acts with my Dakota people. He is a guardian and he is an advisor. And he never, he never hurt nobody. And when he leaves the camp, they don't know where he is. Nobody ever met him out on the hunting grounds or in the forest or along the lakes and sloughs or anyplace, nobody ever met him. But all of a sudden, there he is again. He dressed the same as they dress, talked the same language, built the same. Talks and laughs, he eats with them but nobody knows what kind of a home he has if he has any. It is a mystery to the Dakota people, this *Uŋktómi*.

Nowadays, today's generation, we don't, we never see him or we never see it. But what is it? We don't know. That is a lost thing for us. It is a mystery to our people. Today it really [has] disappeared from our sight. We don't understand him but they did. They obeyed him and they trusted him and he never misled them. This *Uŋktómi* is a dependable person. And he will tell them to camp at this certain place during the winter. And if they did, there was no enemy would raid them. And *Uŋktómi* never joined a warpath with the Dakotas when they were on the warpath. And he never told them to go on the warpath. He never mentioned that part of their life is to go on the warpath against another human.

These things my grandfather said, they sit in this, it is a lodge in the middle of the camp. They generally have four of them, four tipis pitched up in the middle and that is where they make decisions and anything happened, anything that is a problem, they take it there and the men in there, they kind of solved the problem the best they could. And they call this place *tiyóti*. That is one, but to refer to the four of them, they say *tiyótipi*, that means more than one. Now, they take their problems to this *tiyótipi* and the people in the *tiyóti*, many times they talk about this here *Uŋktómi*. Why is it that he talk their language? And eat with them? Talk with them? Laugh when he is among them? But he will not allow nobody to touch him. Why is that? What if they do touch him? All these questions, they ask each other these questions, and they are left unsolved until *Uŋktómi* disappeared.

Maybe he is still in existence in some way among the Dakotas. And I believe, and as my grandfather said, these are the words he used, "I believe he is yet because there are times a Dakota would be downhearted, his heart is broke by losing his knife or his gun or part of his gun or something or traps or something like that. He lost them. And which are very valuable to him but he lost them, well, his heart is broken. He lay down to sleep and thinking of his lost article. A man would appear to him in the night and show him where that lost article is, the ground, the sign, there would be a big tree or whatever it may be, it is close there. This broken-hearted Dakota would wake up in the morning and he would keep seeing the place. So he will go there and sure enough, whatever he lost, he found it there." Now, my grandfather says that *Uŋktómi* is still among the people only is invisible. He is still an invisible ruler or a helper or a guardian among us, he says. That we don't know.

Now I heard grandfather tell of these things and the hard times. There are times where my grandfather, he addressed him as "partner," *kodá*. That means a partner or a chum, a friend, a helper. That is what that word means, *kodá*. Some evenings my grandfather used to recite a prayer and ask the Creator to send this *kodá* to him to show him this and to help him to get rid of a severe cold that he has got or there is something that is bothering him. He asks for help to the Creator, asks him to send this *kodá*, the *Uŋktómi* to help him to solve this problem. And I often hear my grandfather say, "*Wakáŋ Táŋka*, send *kodá* to me. Ask him to help me to find out this and to do this," and so on. Now I often wonder, who is this *kodá*? Now in the olden days, as he said, that is the way the people used to address him, as *kodá*, their friend, their helper, their partner, their chum. And I think, as he says, it is no use calling him brother or uncle or father or cousin but *kodá* is the right word. He is a helper, not only to one person, not only to a certain class, but everybody—women, children, men, of all ages. This *Uŋktómi* is a helper. So this *Uŋktómi* is on our side of the—of his life, he is a good man.

But other people, other people, other tribes they call him—I wouldn't say he is the same person because he don't act the same—he acts different with them as he acts different with us. He acts with the Dakota people in kindness with mercy and with knowledge. But with the Crees, he seemed to act as a clown. He even, I understand that he [would] even take away—take a pretty lady away from the camp and go and live with a pretty lady. But on our side with the situation as far as *Uŋktómi* is concerned, those things are not known to him and he don't show these things to anybody.

Where [does] he come from? Where is his home? This is the thing that is left unsolved. And my grandfather of course, my grandfather was a kind of a—he was man who liked to see everything where it came from and what were the results of it. If he acts this way or if he did this thing this way, what is the result? And he was kind of an inquisitive sort of a person. Now, I come to *Uŋktómi*—my grandfather, he believe in him, real, real. He really believed in him and he said he is still among us, among the Dakota people, only we don't see him. He might be still the same age, the same looks, the same, but we don't see him no more. He don't appear to us. We don't see him no more. And in them days, in them days, a blind man might lead, might go away from the camp, away from his home and then he couldn't get back to his home. He is lost. Maybe he is only a few yards from home but he can't get to his home. And then he will hear this voice, "Come this way. Come this way." And when they hear that voice—this blind man never saw *Uŋktómi*—but when they hear that voice they know it is *Uŋktómi* who is talking to him. So whichever direction the sound come from, the blind man would go that way, make his way that way, that way, pretty soon he will come to his tent. Now this happened many, many times as they say.

So these are the kind of things that my grandfather tells in the evenings. I might be there with two or three boys or there might be full-grown people there and he will tell these stories to them. Of course, my grandfather's home was my home, so I'm there in the evenings and I hear a lot of these stories. And I am repeating it as I remember it. I know there is some parts that I forgot but the idea, I haven't forgot the main ideas of the story. I heard it more than two or three times. But then I, I got it pretty well, I remembered pretty well. But when I am making these records, sometimes I am all alone speaking into the recording machine but my mind is not—I don't seem to concentrate too well. But if there is a man looking at me, somebody looking at me and if I am telling the story to him, that is when I remember things and it seems to come as it was told to me by my grandfather. It seems it comes in place, just like reading a book. You read a book and you put it away and five years after you take it, it is still there, you read it, it is still the same. But when I am all alone, there is nobody around and yet I am talking. This is what I—it keeps me thinking to try and concentrate on what I am doing. I never have nobody with me when I am recording these stories because they are all busy and they are all away and I am all alone. But anyway, this is what—this is the stories that my grandfather told me. (Robert Goodvoice 6, 1977, 7–11)

Living in the Four Circles, the *Tiyótipi*, Dividing into Sub-tribes, Moving Northeast

[RG 1977] My grandparents used to talk about their childhood days. . . . I find this very interesting and when they speak of this or tell this story, they tell the story over and over and this is the one that I like to hear. They say they used to live in circles. There is a big circle and there is another one within that big circle and then another. That's three. The fourth one, it is a small circle and in this small circle there are four lodges there. That's where all the decisions are made.

In the big circle, they say if you stand at one side of the circle and look straight across, the tent at the other side looks just about the size of a thimble, so that must be at least or almost a mile across. There is another circle in that and another one. So there are quite a few [concentric] circles. There are quite a few families living in these four circles. [See figure 8.]

In the first circle, the big circle, there are all the young men and strong men and good hunters. So is the second one. They are all able-bodied people.

The third one, they are still strong people but then they are men around fifty or sixty years of age. Now the first circle and the second biggest, whatever they get in the line of food they feed the people that are living in the small [third] circle because they are the old people and the people who are crippled, blind or children, orphans, women with children, widows.

The people in the first two circles, whatever they get as food they feed the rest. That's the way they help each other. Whatever clothing or hides (they used to have hides, deer hides and coyote hides and all that kind of hides), they used to tan them and that's their clothing. The stronger people used to do that and help the old people, the weak people, in the line of food like berries, wild berries and wild turnips and wild carrots (there are a lot of wild things, vegetables that grow wild) and wild rice

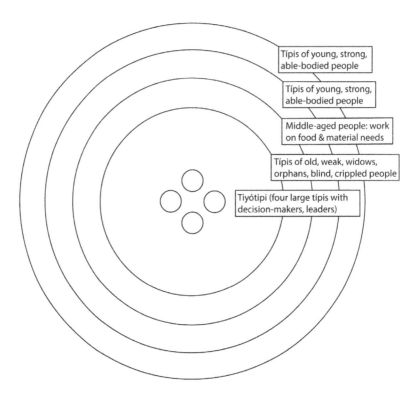

Típis of young, strong, able-bodied people

Típis of young, strong, able-bodied people

Middle-aged people: work on food & material needs

Típis of old, weak, widows, orphans, blind, crippled people

Tiyótipi (four large típis with decision-makers, leaders)

FIGURE 8. Circular layout of Dakota encampment: Four circles and four *Tiyóti*.
Drawn by Daniel M. Beveridge, Danny Beveridge, and Molly Seaton-Fast.

(that's a very good food, they say). They lived together, but there were so many of them so whatever is edible in that territory in two or three days it is all gone. So they are always under the shadow of starvation. (Robert Goodvoice 2, 1977, 8–9)

[RG 1977] These things my grandfather said, they sit in this, it is a lodge in the middle of the camp. They generally have four of them, four tipis pitched up in the middle and that is where they make decisions and anything happened, anything that is a problem, they take it there and the men in there, they kind of solved the problem the best they could. And they call this place *tiyóti*. That is one, but to refer to the four of them, they say *tiyótipi*, that means more than one. Now, they take their problems to this *tiyótipi* and the people in the *tiyóti*. (Robert Goodvoice 6, 1977, 8)

[RG 1977] One time the chief, all the chiefs and the councilors, the head men of each circle, they gathered in these four lodges. As I said, they gathered there and they came to a decision that they should divide — so many people as a group to move one direction and so many others, just spread out so that the food could be more plentiful. In this way they wouldn't be moving camp every other day. So this was agreed by all people and that's where lots of these groups got their name.

We will say there is a group that went a certain direction and they came to a lake where there are ducks and fish and wild rice and other things that was food to them was theirs. So they camped near that lake and after dark they say they used to see sparks and lights and things like that passing over the water. They called it a sacred lake — *Mde Wakáŋ* they called that lake. [*Mde* = lake, *wakáŋ* = sacred, holy.] But the people lived there. They would stick around that sacred lake. So they called them *Mde Wakáŋ Atúŋwaŋ*. Today we still call them the *Mde Wakáŋ Atúŋwaŋ* [Mde-wakanton]. There is another group who went a different direction and they came to a creek, a creek where there is lots of wild rice and there are some beavers and other things and food to eat. So they stick around there. Now that creek, we call it *Wakpá* [*wakpá* = river, stream] and the people living there are *Atúŋwaŋ* [*atúŋwaŋ* = living, staying.] so the people were called *Wakpá Atúŋwaŋ*. That's how lots of them got their names, by moving, when they spread out, by the divisions of the tribe.

I asked this question of one man in Manitoba, who is my uncle. He is about a year older than me. I asked him if he heard of that and he said he thought he heard some old person mention that and I told him to tell me as he heard it. He said he can't, he said he just heard it and that's all.

There is another people. They went to the prairies. They live right in the prairie. Well the prairie, we call it *tiŋtáŋ*, but the people live there so we call them the prairie dwellers *Tiŋtáŋ Atúŋwaŋ* [Teton]. This is where a lot of these people, most of these people, got their names.

There was a group who went northeast and they landed in a place where there are big hills and lots of timber and lots of lakes. So they were called *Ḣe Mni Ċaŋ*. "*Ḣe*" means hills, "*mni*" means lakes and water, "*ċaŋ*" means timber. So they put those three words together, *Ḣe Mni Ċaŋ Atúŋwaŋ*, dwellers. There are lots. I can go on and say lots of how they got their names, but it is pretty hard to translate those things word for word. I would like to do that all right enough and I am doing my best to translate the easiest ones. (Robert Goodvoice 2, 1977, 9–10)

The Names of the Twelve Months

[RG 1977] Every season they go by, summer, autumn and winter, just the same as they do today. But there are no calendars. They named the months. Like January, they name that the Hard Month; February, they say, it's *Wičáta Wi*, that means the Moon of the Raccoon. The raccoon, in the month of February, they commence to travel from one nest to the other where the females are and that's February; March, they call it *Ištá Wičáyezaŋ Wi*. That means there is something in the air in that month that gives the people sore eyes, so they call it *Ištá Wičáyezaŋ Wi*; April, that's when the geese come from the south and they commence to build a nest and lay eggs, so they named April, the moon of April, the Goose Moon or something like that; May, they named it, that's when the grass grows, so they named it the Moon of the Time the Grass Grows; June, at the end of June the strawberries are ripe, so they named that June moon, Moon of the Strawberries; July, Midsummer Moon; August, everything is ripe. July, they call it *Bdokétu Čokáŋyaŋ Wi*, and August, everything is ripening and fully matured so they call it *Wasútuŋ Wi*; September, the leaves commence to change color. They commence to dry out, so they call it *Čaŋwápa Ġi Wi*, where the leaves are brown; October, they call that *Ptaŋyétu Wi*, that's beginning of the Autumn. They call it the Moon of Autumn; November, that's when the deer mate, breeding season for them so they call that *Takíyuha Wi*, which means breeding season for the jumpers, for that special deer. Not all animals, but the deer, that's the mating season for them in November; December, they call it *Tahéčapšuŋ Wi*, which means all the animals lose their horns, or they knock them off. Anyway, the elk and the jumpers, they lose their horns, they drop off so they call it *Tahéčapšuŋ Wi*. That means the moon where the animals lose their horns. Back to January, *Witéhi Wi*, the hard moon. That way they keep track of the days. (Robert Goodvoice 1, 1977, 12–13)

Relations with the White Men

First Contact with Europeans

[RG 1977] This story that I am telling is told to me and a few other boys by my grandfather. My grandfather said that this story was told to him by his grandfather.

As I have said before and I am going to say again, that is a division of the Dakota Tribes that live in a big circle and another one in the big circle. There are three circles. The time came when they divided into groups and they scattered here and there. Shortly after the division was made, the people, some moved eastward and they saw the white man.

There was, one day, a man walking along the seashore and he saw something strange in the water. He took a good look at it, but it was something strange. He had never seen that in his life and he sneaked up to it, to make sure that it was not a living thing. He wasn't going to investigate, but it don't look like a living thing. But anyway he sneaked up to it and got close enough and on the land close to this thing in the water, he saw some people. They looked strange. They walked upright on two legs all right enough and their arms, their head, everything and all the motion of the bodies was the same as anybody else. He figured they are people, but at the same time their body was covered with something that he never saw.

On their head was a funny looking thing, on their head. So anyway he got closer and closer and finally he got close enough that he could hear their voice and he listened and it was a human voice. But then the words that they spoke [he could not] understand what they are saying. But then he kept getting closer and getting closer toward them until he got close enough and he saw their faces. They were human, they were human, that is for sure. He stayed there quite a while watching them. They had a fire going. The smoke was going up and they fed the fire. There was one thing that he found very strange, these people walked on water. From the dry land they just walked right into the water. They go in it and out and walk on the water onto the dry land. They don't sink in the water. So this was very, very strange to him.

Anyway he came back to the camp and he went right straight to the middle of the camp where there were a couple of tents set up for the head men to take these kind of things into consideration and they make decisions there. This is called *tiyótipi*. So he told them about it and they didn't believe him. The next day this thing was the main topic for the rest of the night and the biggest part of the day. They decided that they were going to see and find out. So about thirty of the Indians got ready and the man who was acting as the leader, and he took them to where these people were.

Sure enough that strange thing in the water was still there. On the shore, on the land, the people were there. They would walk back and forth into the thing in the water and, of course, that was a boat but they didn't give a name to it and they just called it the thing, something in the water. They went to it and inside and out and onto the dry land. They never took their clothes off to do that because they had some kind of a bridge or a ramp or whatever made to do that.

They took about thirty of them to see and find out for sure what this was that was in the water and if they were real people. They got ready and went to the seashore. The leader then, of these thirty men, he was quite old. They say he was an old fellow and he told the young boys, "When we get to this place I want you fellows to stop far enough away and leave your clubs, your spears, your arrows and whatever you have, and your blankets, and dress light so that you can run if they come after you. Come to where I will be sitting with what you leave with me to look after for you until you return. Then we will try to stop them or hold them. We will not take them to the camp or we wouldn't show them where the camp is," he told us. Then he said, "I am going to repeat something to you people, which my great grandfathers have told us. This is a prophet. He is a man who tells things that is going to happen in the future. So far, things that he forecast, or prophesied, it all happened."

"Now," he said, "this prophet said there is a group of people coming to this land, coming to this world in which we are living. These people are going to come here with power in speech and in every way. In every walk of life they are going to come with power and under their feet we are going to be slaves for a length of time until another group—it will be the same kind of people as the first group—they will come and they will take us out from underneath this first group's feet. They will put us free from slavery. The second group would be a group with mercy and peace-loving people, and peace-making people.

"These people, the second group, would make us even with the first group and everybody else. This might be the first group so don't let them touch you. If you see them, if there is anything that you can see about them that is not human, don't bother them. But if they are human, the way they walk and the way they bend down, the way they talk and the way they act, if they are human go to them, but don't let them touch you. Don't go within the reach of their breath to you, because they will reach you with their breath. They are liable to draw you and they are liable to hypnotize you and you might stay there."

"These people they have power so don't let them touch you or don't go within the reach of their breath. As I have said, they might hypnotize you and if they do you will stay there." But anyway before they got to them, these thirty men divided into three groups. The middle group are the ones that were supposed to go to these people, approach these people first, which they did. They stood close to each other. They tried to talk to each other, but they didn't understand each other. They smile, they laugh and they have a happy look in their faces. These Indians could see that. They are not afraid of them. They had no feeling of fear, but they liked to see them and they liked the way that they were dressed and all that. They were happy that they got into close contact with each other.

Then, these Indians tried to make them understand by using their hands and speaking at the same time and making motions. There was another bunch over here and this Indian called the group that was on his left side and they came up and they showed up and so did the others. They were all happy and they gave them something to drink, but they didn't accept anything from them. They gave them something to eat that looked strange, but they didn't touch anything that they touched. They didn't shake hands or anything, nothing of that kind. They stood far enough away from each other.

After this, they stayed there quite a while and then they came back to the camp. They told the people in the *tiyótípi* what they saw and they told them they were human, only they can't talk to each other due to the fact that their language was different. Anyway, they were told not to go back there anymore until such time. The days went on and for quite a while they didn't go back to the seashore.

One day they were told to go and see if they were there yet or not. So a few men went to the place and that strange thing in the water was not there anymore, or the humans that were on the dry land, they were not there no more. Where they went, they did not know. So they came back to the camp and they told the people there that there was nobody there.

Anyway this went on and the people lived on, the same as usual, until quite a while after they heard of white men, *wašíču*. This is how they called the white men. There was *wašíču* here and *wašíču* there, there are lots of *wašíču* landed on this world, as they called it—this continent, they called it the world. They came to occupy the dry land and live on it. They made their living the same as anybody else by whatever they got out of the land. They made homes for themselves. They lived in groups the same as the Indians. They stayed together closely.

This went on for many years and the *waśíću*, the white man and the Indians are mixed. They are pretty well together now and they trade back and forth whatever they have to sell or trade. They made deals with each other and they got along good. (Robert Goodvoice 1, 1977, 1–5)

[RG 1977] All this time my grandparents used to talk about their childhood days. My grandfather and my grandmother talk about Niagara Falls and they talk about the territory where the city of New York is situated today. They didn't call it New York at that time but they called it *Wíto Wakáŋ*. Now I didn't know where that was until this summer. I met some people from the southern part of the United States and I mentioned this to them. They said that the Indians used to own that. *Wíto Wakáŋ* means "holy island." The Indians used to own this holy island but the white man took it and I don't know who owns it now, but they told me that it is called Manhattan, something like that. I just can't pronounce that word right, but anyway that's just the way they told. So my grandparents in their childhood days, they came from way south. (Robert Goodvoice 2, 1977, 8)

The War of 1812: Alliance with the British; Promises and Rewards; Seven Boatloads (*Oćéti Śakówiŋ*); The Medals; Boundary Cairns

[RG 1977] I am Robert Goodvoice. My age is seventy-six. I am living on Round Plain Reserve. It is also known as Wahpeton Reserve which is situated about nine miles northwest of the city of Prince Albert. Today is January 6, 1978. I am going to tell a story which was told to me and others many times by a man named Henry Two Bear, his Indian name *Maṫó Núŋpa*. When you translate the word *Maṫó Núŋpa*, that means Two Bear.

Once upon a time as he says, there was a huge Dakota camp. And they heard that the white men were fighting. As his grandfather told him this story and as I am going to repeat it as he told me. He didn't mention any month or date or day or year. He just told the story as he heard it from his grandfather on his mother's side.

Now, as I said there was a huge Dakota camp. And they heard the white men were fighting. The white men from the south and from the north, they were fighting. But the Dakotas had no intentions of joining them. They stayed away. They stayed out of trouble. Until one morning, five men, they were *wašíčus*, white men, came to the camp. They were dressed different from other people. They had different uniforms. And they come there and ask the people that they would like to talk to the leaders of the Dakota camp. They say there was many, many families. So the head men and the older people, they all gathered together with the white men who visit the camp and they had a talk.

And this white man, the spokesman, said to them that they would like the Dakotas to help him fight against the oncoming enemy. He told him that when the war stopped, from that time on, they would be friends, they would look after the Dakotas and they would be friends. So the Dakotas, they agreed to that.

And then they started. They don't fight during the day but during the night. And very few used to go and cut off the supply line of the enemy. And then at night the most of them would go and raise Cain with the enemies. They didn't say—as he said, his grandfather didn't tell him— how long they fought, how many days, but there were two groups. One worked at night and the other during the day. They keep the supply line cut off. Finally the soldiers commenced to move back toward the south so they let them move and they just followed them. And they didn't say how far they followed them but they followed them quite a ways. They were following there for a few days. And these white men who asked for the Dakotas' help come to them and he told them, "As long as they are moving away," he said, "don't fight them. Let them move back and don't disturb them. Let them move back." But these groups that are—their work is to cut off the supply line, food and ammunition and other supplies that the army needs in the front line, but they kept that blocked so they had to move back.

Now they kept working that same style, in that style, until one day, this white man who asked for the Dakotas' help came to them again and told them to stop. Don't bother them at all. The war is over. They made arrangements that they are not going to fight no more. So the Dakotas, they obeyed this white man and they didn't fight no more, they stopped. And they stuck around there, wherever the war ended, they stayed there and moved about you know, the same as they did in the other place. They made camp here and there and hunt and make their living here and there. And they stayed there.

[*Promises and rewards.*] And then the Dakotas were promised, they were promised that there was a reward that they would receive in the near future. And when everything is settled, then they will tell them what their reward is and what it is. But anyway, they are going to tell them what reward they are going to offer them. They are going to tell them in the future. So they waited, they waited, and they told them to stay on that side of the line and if they wanted they could come across, come back on the north side of this here boundary. Go back and forth, back and forth as they like. There is no restrictions. So the Dakotas stayed on the south side there. They were making a good living there. There was lots of game and fish and other things. Their food was plenty there so they stayed there.

And then one day, a messenger come to the camp and told them that all the old, older people and the leaders of the Dakota camp, they were invited to go across the boundary into a certain town. "The white men on that side, the head men, they want to talk to your leaders." So, there was a bunch of them. They say there was over one hundred of them. They got ready and then they came across into this town and they had a talk. And they told them, this man here who asked the Dakotas to help fight, well he did have red hair. So they called him *Pahíŋ Šašá*, the Indians called him that, and his English name was Robert Dickson.[1] He was the commander of the British army but they didn't know this at the time but they know that man's English name quite a few years after. So they give them, each chief got a medal. And his councilors got some kind of a badge. It was made out of some kind of a material. It looks like copper or brass. But anyway, all the councilors got that. And the chiefs, they got a silver medal which is about four inches in diameter. And there is a picture carved on there and they say that was King George III, I think. This was what the chiefs got. There were seven medals that were given to the Dakotas at that time.[2] And this man here, Henry Two Bear as I said, his grandfather, [said that] *Waánataŋ*, he was the youngest chief there and he got one.[3]

And the promises that they got was they were supposed to get seven boatloads of cargo, everything that you can think of, pails and axes and everything. Food, dried goods, seven boatloads. We don't know what size boats they were at that time but then they were seven boatloads anyway. They were promised that and when they used that up, they would get some more and some more. And they give them what they call that now, they call that a pledge on platter. This is whatever the promises were printed on, it's a piece of hide, it is not paper, it is a hide but you can see the writing very plainly. And a medal and this here, the councilors' badges, and flags to the chiefs. And promised seven boatloads of food and clothing and whatever they need. So this is the promise they made.

And then Robert Dickson, Ṗahíŋ Śaśá, told them that they would remember as long as they lived. And they are going to give them a souvenir but then the Dakotas are not going to take that away from the town. They are going to keep it there and they are going to put it someplace and the white men would preserve this. It is a cannon that they are giving to the Dakotas as a souvenir.[4] This was marked that at one time the Dakotas fought side by side with the British army against the enemy. And they paint[ed] this, that is the smallest cannon that they had. It is a small cannon. They painted it yellow and they named that Dakota Čístina. That means Small Dakota or Little Dakota. And it is supposed to be in that town of those days. And Waánataŋ and the rest of the chiefs, I think their name was, they wrote their names some way and it's there, it is not printed on the cannon but it is printed on a piece of metal of some kind and it is there with it.

This is what they call the 1812 battle. Of course, the Dakotas don't know the year and the month and the date and all this and that. At that time, but later on, the history, this is where they get these names and the date and the year. It was in 1812. And then so they left the . . . Dakota Čístina stood there solid and they know they have got a souvenir someplace over there. For many, many years after, they mentioned that. They mentioned the Dakota chief's names. It is over there yet, someplace.

[Seven boatloads: Očéti Śakówiŋ] And this seven boatloads, this is where the [phrase] Očéti Śakówiŋ started. That means seven smoke stacks. They didn't say seven boats because there is one smoke stack on each ship and there were seven of them, so they called it the promise of Očéti Śakówiŋ — the days of Očéti Śakówiŋ — the year of Očéti Śakówiŋ. This is the way they described that. And sure enough, they used to get an annual distribution of food and materials. Powder and guns, very, very few guns. They would give the chiefs a gun each but not everybody. And powder and shot and what they call a cap. These guns were muzzle loaders. And in that town—then they choose a town someplace. They don't know the name of the town but they know where the town is and there is the big, big warehouse. They didn't say warehouse but they said there is a big house and that is full of Dakota property, they owned that. And they used to gather there once a year and get clothing, blankets, and whatever there is there and they would move away. The next year at the same time, the same moon, the same wherever, whatever, the first quarter, full moon, they watched that. They all watched that and they knew. So, when the moon is full, we'll say, they are all there at the same time. And they have done this for many, many years: And then, but then, they never go east to see *Dakota Ćístina* to see if it is there or not. But they know they left it behind. They left it there.

Now this *Oćéti Śakówiŋ*, the word has spread westward right up to the Rocky Mountains and the western part of the United States and those people over there, the Tetons, Oglalas, they use the word *Oćéti Śakówiŋ*, but they translate that in English they say it Seven Council Fires but that don't mean our *Oćéti Śakówiŋ*. We Dakotas meant different. It is a reward, it is the seven boatloads, and that is why they call it *Oćéti Śakówiŋ*.[5] And this Robert Dickson was right there and he was the one who told them, he is the one who asked them to help them to fight and he is the one who asked them to quit fighting and he is the one who told them to stay over there and he is the one who told them any time they want to cross the border back to the north, back into Canada.

They didn't know this country was called Canada then. They used to call it *Ikćé Wićáśa Tamakóće*, the Indian's land, is what they called it, the States and Canada was just one world as they figured. But they think, they think this is of the whole world.

And *Waánataŋ*, the youngest chief there, he remained in the United States, but some of them moved into Canada shortly after that and they moved back and forth, back and forth, they scattered from east right up to, close to Moose Jaw. And they are east and south of Brandon and Winnipeg, around Winnipeg and that is the territory that the Dakotas occupied. But *Waánataŋ*, he stayed in the United States, with that medal, with the Canadian medal, he stayed in the United States and finally, the United States government made treaty with them. And *Waánataŋ* stepped out a chunk of land which I believe is called the Fort Carlton Agency. That is just south of Brandon, not too far into the United States. Close to the border. I think the north boundary joins the international border. *Waá-natąŋ* stepped out a big chunk of land and he was still the chief with that Canadian medal. Of course, the United States government didn't honor that Canadian medal of *Waánatąŋ's* but he kept it.

The medals. And then when *Waánatąŋ* died, I think it is his daughter, the oldest daughter, anyway it is Henry Two Bear's mother had that medal. Until 1925, she was dying and then Henry Two Bear was in Canada then. He got a notice that his mother was very low, so he went back to the United States and saw his mother and she died a couple, three days after he landed there. So she gave this medal to him in 1912. It was either in June or July. And then when his mother was dead and buried after the funeral, then he stuck around there for awhile, a few days, a week or so. And then he came back to Canada with that medal. And he brought that medal to Round Plain and when our chief, *Ahíyaŋke II* [*Ahíyaŋke* the second], also known as *Íto Imáza*, when he heard of this medal, the chief's medal, he wanted it. So he gave a three-year-old pony, it was a nice looking horse, to Henry Two Bear and he gave him the medal. And Chief *Ahíyaŋke II* used to wear that medal to exhibitions and any other gatherings, he used to wear that. And the people used to look at it and sometimes they want to buy it off him but he never sold it. The deal was this, he would wear that and keep that medal as long as he lived. And after, if he happened to pass away that the true owner, who was Henry Two Bear, it will go back to him. Now, this is the deal they made.

But when that time come, *Ahíyaŋke II*, also known as *Íto Imáza*, he didn't want to give it up. He was going sick and he was going down very fast. And he didn't want to give this medal back so what he did is he give the medal to our Indian Agent, John Weir. So John Weir took that medal back to the Agency. And then Henry Two Bear, he knew that John Weir took that medal so he went to town and saw a lawyer, Collin Baker, he was the city solicitor. He told him about it and he wanted that medal. So he wrote to John Weir, and then John Weir when the lawyer was after him, he sent that medal back to Round Plains to our missionary, Reverend J. G. Meek. So he had it. We lost track of the medal for a few months. Somehow, it blew up that Reverend J. G. Meek had that medal. So Henry Two Bear asked Mr. Meek for the medal. He got a lawyer to write a letter to him and Mr. Meek, he sent it back to John Weir and then we lost track of the medal again. And then somehow, the people in Mistawasis [a First Nation west of Prince Albert], they saw that medal in John Weir's office. So Collin Baker, the lawyer, he wrote to him again. And this time he kind of wrote a kind of stiff letter to him. And then Mr. Weir, he retired from the agency and he sent the medal back to Reverend J. G. Meek from the Round Plain Reserve and the Wahpeton. The tribe was Wahpeton that was living on the Round Plain Reserve. *Ahíyaŋke* was the chief. He got it. That is the fellow who gave the medal to the *wašíću*, the white man. And then Reverend J. G. Meek, he was our preacher and . . . . that medal is in that museum in P.A. [Prince Albert]. One of the members of this reserve, his name is Archie Waditaka, was in that museum looking around and he saw this medal and looked it and it says, "presented by Rev. J. J. Meek." So that medal was given to *Waánataŋ* in 1812 and that same medal is in P.A. right today . . . and I just traced that medal and there is lots of them like that [see photos 8 and 9].

So now this *Očéti Šakówiŋ*, let's go back to that. One day, the people were there again to get their food and other things and while they were gathered in front of the warehouse, there was a man. His name was *Wambdína Hótuŋ Máni*, I can't very well translate that but anyway, that is his name. He walked up to this man here who was going to give out the food, make the distribution, he was there. He had the warehouse door open and he was on the platform so *Wambdína Hótuŋ Máni* presented him a letter. So he took the letter and opened it and read it. Read it and then he shut the doors, he shut the warehouse doors and he waved the Indians away. "No more," he said, "no more." He made them understand that he is not going to give them no more. And then the Indians were, they were puzzled—why?

Then later on, there was a man in the United States who had a store for many years and he used to come into Canada with everything that can haul on a boat. Carts, wagons, travois, and he used to take lots of food and property back to the United States to his store. Now I don't know what is the name of this store-keeper in the United States but the Dakotas, they called him *Psiŋčíŋča*. *Psiŋčíŋča*, now that is something, but anyway, that is the way they called him, this store-keeper. And the place where he established this store, the Dakotas called it *Bde Íyedaŋ* [Lac qui Parle in Minnesota]. Now that's—where is that today? What is the English name of that place, that territory today? We don't know. But anyway, that is the

PHOTOS 8 AND 9. King George III medal (obverse and reverse). This medal was one of those awarded by the British Crown to Dakota chiefs for assisting the British against the Americans in the American Revolutionary War or the War of 1812. It is kept in the Prince Albert Historical Museum. Photos by Daniel M. Beveridge.

way the story was told and that is the way I heard it and that is just the way I am telling it as I heard it.

And then, what was said in this letter he said, "The Indians, the Dakotas, are not going to bother about the property that you have in the warehouse that you have for them in Canada. They are going to, they are not going to take anymore. But they are going to haul everything." He told them that he was going to haul everything to his store and all the Dakotas in Canada and in the United States, they are going to live close around there so that they can get their rations, well, that is the way they called it. They can make a distribution every thirty days or every sixty days, not once a year. So he, the letter stated that the food and whatever was in the warehouse is supposed to be kept and they are not supposed to get it no more. So he is going to haul it to the United States and then the Dakotas could go and get it from him over there. The majority of them were in the United States, let's say just about, maybe they figure there is about nine or eight, eight or nine hundred families in Canada at that time. But the rest were in the United States and there was quite a number of them. So this is what the letter said and he said that in the letter it was, he said that was arranged by the majority of the people who are living in the United States and this is what they want. So that is how the Dakotas in Canada lose their *Očéti Šakówiŋ* and property. They never got it after that. And when they see that they are to get it but they are not going to go back to the United States to get it so they didn't pay any attention to it. And it is understood that this *Psiŋčíŋča*, he was making a trip every month during the summer. And then finally he got enough goods over there to keep him going three or four years so he didn't bother with it. He didn't come for no more goods from Canada to run the store in the United States. And as I said, that is how our people lose their *Očéti Šakówiŋ* rights that Robert Dickson had promised them.

The Medals ctd. Now this is a story that was told to Henry Two Bear, and Henry Two Bear died the first week in March, 1966. Either on the fifth or on the sixth of March. He died right on the Round Plain Reserve at the age of eighty-six. And the medal that he got from his mother, she was very, very old. And about this *Dakota Čístina*, they, that little gun, cannon. Around 1908 or 1910, the people in Sioux Valley received a message from some government official in Winnipeg asking them if they want to sell that Little Dakota, the *Dakota Čístina*. If they want to sell it, he would like to have the medals that was given to the Dakotas at the same time as that cannon and this here, what they call Pledge on Platter, gather them and bring them to him. And he was going to give them quite a bit of money. So somebody said, "Let's not do it. Our parents, our grandfathers, they won that by helping the British to fight so let's keep it that way. They made friends and let's keep it that way so let's not sell this *Dakota Čístina* back to the white man, back to the *wašíču*. But then some of them, the younger people at that time, were willing to sell it back to him.

And now, not too long ago, maybe six, seven years ago, there is a man who tried to find that but he can't find no trace of that *Dakota Čístina* or he can't find no record of where the Dakotas received these medals with King George's picture carved on it. There is no record of it no place. But the Dakotas, they have these medals. And these medals were made in England. And a man came from England, across the sea they said, across the big waters and brought them, brought the medals and the councilors' badges and these pledges and give it to the Dakotas. They were not made in Canada, the medal was made in England. So this is the only proof that they have that they are the people who fought side by side with Robert Dickson and his army, but there is no record of it.

And these stories used to be something, you know, people used to tell these stories as I am telling it now. I have heard it many times, different, by different people. And I saw the medals and I am not sure but I think there is one in this here big museum in Calgary.[6] I was there not too long ago, last spring I think, a year ago last spring I was there and I saw one of them medals. But there is no history to it, there is nothing to it and it is in the glass and it was about four feet away from me but it looked like one of them. And so there is one medal in Calgary Museum and the Historical Society of Prince Albert, they have got another one. The one that is in Prince Albert belongs to *Waánataŋ*. *Waánataŋ* was just a young man. They say he was around eighteen or nineteen when he got that. He was the youngest chief. And there were seven of them.

There are two, two I think were held by people in Sioux Valley, one of them, the old man, his name was *Kiŋyéwakaŋ* [Jim *Kiŋyéwakaŋ*] and the other one, I forgot what his name was. And there was one that was held by a man in Pipestone. That's *Ahive* they call him. I think his real name was *Wambdí Iyótake*, Sitting Eagle. And then that is three, and this one in

Prince Albert, that is four, and one in Calgary, that is five. And there are two in Standing Buffalo Reserve. One was held by a fellow by the name of Good Pipe, *Ċaŋnúŋpa Waśté*, and the other one was held by *Iyóȟpaye*. His English name was La Suisse. I just forgot his first name but anyway, his last name was La Suisse [?]. Well, that is the seventh. My grandfather had one of them but he was—it wasn't given to him. He wasn't entitled to it but he was keeping it for this certain fellow. He held it for many years and then he give it back to him.

So that is how, and, the last of these medals was sold about, I'll say about six years ago. That is *Kiŋyéwakaŋ*'s medal. A man came to give *Kiŋyéwakaŋ*, that is the son of George *Kiŋyéwakaŋ*, and he asked him if he still got that medal. And Jim *Kiŋyéwakaŋ* said he has. And he wants to see it so he showed it to him. And this man, he said, "How much you want for it?" And Jim said, "Three hundred dollars." The man, without saying a word, he pulled out three hundred dollars and gave it to Jim and took the medal. So Jim *Kiŋyéwakaŋ* then said, "Now, where you come from? What is your name? Give me your address. I want to know where this medal goes. You got it and I want to know you and I want to know where you come from and your address and all this and that." And the white man says, "No, you got three hundred dollars, you asked for three hundred dollars and you got it and I got my medal and that is it." Then he went away so he didn't know who he sell it to. Now all these medals were bought like that. In the neighborhood of $250, $300, $350. I heard there was one there that sold for $500. So, the proof, our proof that we made treaty with the British way back in 1812, well, we have no proof to show that we did. When all these things that I am saying is not in the history. It is not written no place, but this is what my grandfathers and the old people tell and I believe that they are telling the truth.

It is, at one time, around 1910, 1912, I heard that the Indians used to talk about that and they would go to Ottawa but if they leave the reserve without a permission, at that time they were in reserves already, if they leave the reserves without permission, they will send them back. They won't allow them to go to Ottawa to see the *Dakota Ċístina*, that little cannon called the *Dakota Ċístina*, they wanted to see that. But they couldn't get there because they would leave the reserve without the written permission of the Indian Agent then they couldn't make no headway. They got to, the police would ask them, "Have you got a permission to leave your reserve?" And if they say said no, it don't matter what the circumstances are, if they haven't got the written permission, well, they send them back to their reserve.

So it seems that *Oćéti Śakówiŋ* is a thing that we should know and we should trace, that we might be entitled to something yet. We might get some kind of reward but anyway, even if we don't get anything it should go down in history as it was. But now, our part in that battle, side by side with the British, we lost that. That is not in the history, in the *waśíću* history. It is only in the Dakotas' minds as they said, as the old people said. We remember and we know all these things but we can't write, we don't know how to write so we haven't got [it] written no place. But it is in our minds. We remember these things. This is what they say.

And this here *Psiŋćíŋća*, the fellow who hauled the goods into the United States and established himself there as an agent and built himself a store. The store was still running. The store was still—because it was—it was still as a store selling this and that to the Indians but the man, *Psiŋćíŋća*, he disappeared. He didn't stay there. So this is what we heard. After that, when we didn't go, the people didn't go back there to see the store or anything, but sometimes there is people who come from there, come from *Bde Íyedaŋ* to Prince Albert and they tell the story. They tell the story of *Oćéti Śakówiŋ* and how it ended and how it started we know. We know how it started, that is for sure, but then my people don't know how it ended and how long did that man run that store with the Sioux profit. It is their profit. He hauled it over there and sold it back to them. This is the story my people received. But they didn't want to go back to the United States. They remained in Canada and let the people in the United States [get] the benefit of that. So some of these people in the United States, they have got brothers, uncles, and sisters over this. As long as their relations were getting something out of it, well, they were satisfied. In Canada, they were not getting a thing. But as long as their relations in the United States were getting it, that was fine and dandy.

Now, after, there is a kind of mix-up in that deal on the Canadian side but it didn't last too long. The people we called McKays in Canada here, they all live in the Prince Albert district. They want to get ahold of this *Oćéti Śakówiŋ* in part and they say they will haul it over here, put it in a house here and the Dakotas that are living in the Prince Albert district can go there every now and then and get their clothing and one thing and another. These McKays, they were going strong, they were going to do this. But the Dakotas here, they told them to leave it alone. "It is gone. We can't get it back. It don't matter how hard you try," they told these McKays here, "You'll never get it. It is gone. It is all gone to the United States." And now they said, the McKays said, "There is some there yet for you people. We know it, it is there, we will go and get it and bring it here and you people will have it." But the Dakotas refused for some reason. They didn't want it.

Now that is the kind of deals that my grandparents tell as stories. It is not written in histories or books no place. And as I got the privilege to tell these stories and to put them on record, I am doing it the best I could as I remember it. And as I heard it. (Robert Goodvoice 3, 1977, 1–12)

[*Boundary cairns, placed along 49th parallel in 1873*: RG 1977] They didn't say it was the same year or the next year but anyway, one time there was four boys, four or five boys, young fellows. They come north, these are Dakotas. They come north and they saw a pile of stones, the height of a man's height. That would be about five or six feet. And they are all painted red. And they saw this and they looked toward the west and they saw another one over there and the east they saw another one. So they went up to the one in the east, they saw another one. They followed it and there was no end to it. So they come back and follow it westward, there is no end to it. So they were wondering why those stones were piled up like that, it give them a kind of a suspicious sort of an idea that they are in the enemy territory. So, they went back and told he elders, the leaders of the camp and then they come north across the line into a town. They didn't say what town. They come to a big town. It must be a capital now because they said there is lots of white people living in that town. And that is where these leaders, this man that asked them to help him to fight. He was there. And many others. They had a talk with them. And the white men made them understand that that is a division. The south, that is the people of their own, they have nothing to do with the people on the north side of this here landmark, these red stones. That is the landmark which is known as the boundary between the States and Canada today. That is the way it was first started. Pile those stones and paint them red. The Dakotas call it *Íŋyaŋ Šašá Pasdátapi*. That means a pile of red stones. But many of them. (Robert Goodvoice 3, 1977, 1–12)[7]

The Treaty of 1851

[By the 1851 Treaty of Mendota the Mdewakanton and the Wahpekute lost their territory in eastern Minnesota and were moved to the Lower Sioux Agency along the Minnesota River in western Minnesota (near Redwood Falls). By the 1851 Treaty of Traverse des Sioux the Wahpeton and Sisseton lost their territory in southern Minnesota and were promised land, the Upper Sioux Agency, along the upper reaches of the Minnesota River (near Granite Falls and Lac qui Parle and up to Lake Traverse), where many of them already were living. By another treaty in 1858 the portion (about half) of the 1851 reservations northeast of the river was also ceded and opened for settlement. The Treaty of 1867 created the Sisseton Reservation, of triangular shape on the Coteau in present South Dakota. See maps 3 and 4. DB]

[RG 1977] I don't know how many years from the time they saw the first white man until my grandmother's time — now I am switching over to what my grandmother told me. She said she was a little girl with her playmates playing outside in the circle of the camp and that a few white men came to the people and stayed around there and they talked to a few people here and there and they left. The next day they came back. Each time they came back there are more people came with them until there are about ten of them who came back to the camp. They had an all-day meeting. They met with the older people, the head men of the Indian tribe and later on my grandmother said, "What the white men came here for is to buy the land from the Indians. They say they are going to make a deal, they are going to sell the land to the white men. "Now, my grandmother and her playmates (a girl of maybe eight, ten, twelve years of age, something like that) they are very young ladies. The white man is going to come back and he is going to make a deal. They are going to buy the land. Now these girls they were anxious to see the white man come and buy the land.

When the Indians go to the store to buy whatever they want to buy, the white man takes it and puts it on some kind of a thing and it balances, it's a scale. Then when that thing balances at a certain number or a mark then he takes it off and that's so much. And then another thing, again on the scale. So they wanted to know, for the white man to buy the land, they wanted to know what kind of a scale he was going to bring. What are they going to bring? Sacks, boxes or what to weigh the land as they bought it. This is what they are anxious to see. At that time acres and sections and that was never known among the Indians. Anyway, the deal was made in 1851. They made a deal that they would pay them annually for fifty years, everything, food, clothing, blankets, canvas for tents, thread, needles, everything you could think of, so the deal was made. My grandmother said they got eight and one-half payments and they all say, the older people—the same age as my grandmother, or a little younger or older—they all know it, and they always say that the big knife, the *Isáŋ Ťáŋka*, that means the Americans, owe us for forty-one and one-half payments for our land. Now where this half payment comes in is this. They make a payment of dry goods, food. They make a payment in material. Then ten or twelve days after, then the cash payment comes. Before the cash payment arrived, they received the goods and before the cash payment arrived this here, what they called 1862 Minnesota Massacre, occurred, and that's when that treaty payment was stopped. This is why they say they received eight and one-half payments and the rest they didn't receive. (Robert Goodvoice 1, 1977, 5–6)

The 1862 Dakota War

[RG 1977] Now I am going to tell you, as I heard it from the old people, chiefly my grandparents, that there was one time four guys, very young men—not young boys but young men—went out deer hunting, and they stayed out there three days and three nights and on the fourth day they were coming home. On that day these four boys they were joking and laughing and daring one another and this and that and they took a short cut through the farmer's yard who was living by the road. That's the road that leads to the camp. One farmer's place, they are joking and daring one another and as they passed by this farmer's yard a little black hen was laying on a nest with six eggs under it. She got up and she made all the noise she could possibly make and ran toward the barn. Now the young fellow picked up these six eggs and pitched these eggs at the black hen.[8]

The farmer saw that and he grabbed a broom and came at these Indians, and the one who tossed these eggs at the black hen, he got it. The farmer was hitting him with the broom and he backed up, shielding his face with his elbows. When the farmer stopped hitting the Indian said, "I have a good notion to shoot him down." His brother-in-law said, "Yes, if you have the heart of a man you would, but he pounded you and you backed up and you couldn't defend yourself, so you are a woman. You have no heart to defend yourself. So you are just a lady. A man pounded you and you took it." This man here took his gun and shot the farmer and then they went to the house and they killed all the children, the woman who was in that house, all but a girl. They say she was about eight or nine years of age. She jumped out of the window and ran toward the bush for help. One young fellow took after her but he couldn't catch her. She went into the bush and that's the girl who went to the neighbors and told them what had happened. The neighbors came over. Sure enough, nobody in the house was alive. They were all lying there dead. The four Indians were not there, they were gone.

Now the boy, the man who shot this farmer down, his name is Šuŋkíǧina. That's his name. They went home to the camp and the next day the American police (four of them) went there and they asked the chief and the head man, "Who are the boys? Where are they?" They said, "Such actions are no more to be committed. The police are there to look after people. For anybody to do anything such as this, murder people, kill people, we have to take them and they have to go to jail and we want these four boys. So, where are they? Tell us and we will take them and we will see why they do that. We will see the reason why."

The boys, when they came and saw the police there, they headed for the bush and stayed in the bush. Of course, they were fed and given blankets and one thing and the other were given to them so they stayed out of sight. The police came again and again, and again, for a few days. By that time the story of what happened (settlers being murdered by four Indians—four Dakota people), then the neighboring tribe—they were not Dakotas, they were called Ho Táŋke [Winnebagos. DB] —came to the Dakota camp and they told them, "Don't give up these four boys, four men. If you give these four men to the white men, to the police, they are going to suffer them, they are going to jail them. They will have their legs tied to a rock or something, with a chain. They won't get away from them. And it is not going to be a short time, they are going to be there for a long time. Maybe they will hang them. So don't give them up. You people fight the white people, wipe them out of this country, this world. If you do that, we will help you. We, the Ho Táŋkes, will start over there and you fellows start here. We will wipe them off. We will live in this world all by ourselves. It is an Indian country and we Indians will be here alone once more." This is what the *Ho Táŋkes* said. The people said, "Yes, we will do that." Other people said, "No, they shouldn't fight. Give up these four boys as they shouldn't do that, they did wrong."

The camp was dividing into two, one wanted to fight and the other wanted to give up the four boys, four men. The leader of the party that didn't want to fight, his name is *Ṫawásu Óta*. The other person who wanted to fight, I have forgotten his name. I have heard it but I have forgotten it.

At these meetings, *Ṫawásu Óta* would tell them, "It's very foolish to start war because the *wašíću*, the white man, they've got guns, they've got bullets, they've got gunpowder and shots and the caps and they have food and they have the means of transportation. We Indians," as he said to them, "we haven't got anything. We have to get all these things from the white man and they wouldn't give it to us if we start a war. If we start a war, they will close everything. We wouldn't be able to get anything from them. In two months' time from now it will be winter and if we start fighting, we've got lots of crippled children, crippled people, old people, young children who can't walk, disabled people and we can't take enough grub with us."

The night of the full moon was the last night they had the meeting. That night they decided they would fight.

The next morning was set to start this year 1862 Minnesota Massacre. The meeting lasted until daylight. Daylight came, the meeting broke up, *Ṫawásu Óta* went home but didn't go to sleep or go into his tent, but he sat outside of his tent. Pretty soon he could see a few men going toward the village and some more women, ladies, half of the camp was on the move toward the village. He sat there listening for any reports of guns or some noise of some sort. None. The sun was away up, so he said to his companions, he said he was going there to see what is the holdup. He said, "It is a very, very good thing if they would change their minds. After, if they got there and saw the people and they changed their minds, it would be a very good thing. But I am going to go there and see what they are doing," he said to his companions.

He walked to the village and there were Indians no matter where you looked, with guns and clubs or whatever weapons they could get a hold of. He walked right to the store. In the main part of the town there was a big store there. The man who owned that store there, the Indians called him *Wóṗeṫuŋ Háŋska*, that means the Tall Merchant. He was ready for the day's business. He had his door open and he was standing outside, and the people were here, no matter where you looked, there were Dakotas.

My grandfather, he said he followed him but he didn't follow him right into the store. He got in sight of the village and there he stood. Tawásu Óta walked up to the store. He looked at one man and he was talking to one man and all of a sudden, he pulled out a gun. Those men sitting in front of the store they had their guns covered with their blankets. (Robert Goodvoice 1, 1977, 5–9)

[RG 1977] And there was a man sitting close to the store, the entrance to the store. He looked at him and by gosh, that was the man who wanted to fight. He was sitting there just looking at Wópetuŋ Háŋska, the Tall Merchant. Tawásu Óta got hold of the man who wanted to fight, and Tawásu Óta said to him, this is what he said, "You wanted to fight and I told you not to fight but you insisted that you were going to fight. You have got all these men behind you. You convert these people to fight with you. Now, what are you doing here? You are just sitting here doing nothing, you are not fighting." And this man here had his gun under his blanket. Tawásu Óta grabbed his gun and pulled it out of his hands. And Wópetuŋ Háŋska stood there watching. And Tawásu Óta shot Wópetuŋ Háŋska down and that is what they call—that is the start of the Minnesota Massacre.[9] (Robert Goodvoice 8, 1977, 3)

[RG 1977] The first shot that was done was done by Tawásu Óta and from there they started. They moved southward and they killed everything that was in their path, chickens, dogs, cats, and horses, women, children, anything that was alive that was in their path, they killed it, up to a river. The Dakotas called that river Wáheju Wakpá. What river is that today? I don't know. I have often asked people what is the English name for that river but nobody knows. But that is the name of the river in Dakota language, Wáheju Wakpá. When they got there the American army met them. But they turned back from there and then everybody scattered this way and that way. Tawásu Óta and his bunch moved northward until they came to a river and they made rafts and they crossed that river. All the men who were able to swim swam across that river pulling this raft loaded with men, women, children, sick people, crippled people. They would unload them and go back. They kept on doing that until everybody was on the north side of the river and from there they moved northward until they came to a place. When they came to that place they felt safe so they stayed there and then a few young fellows went back to see which way the army was moving. They said the army was moving westward along the river, south of the river, toward the west and the Indians ahead of them. They caught up to them and there were dead Indians all the way. *Ṫawásu Óta* and his bunch, they stayed there. They stayed there a few days and then they moved eastward. My grandfather and grandmother were in that group. They moved eastward for a few days and then they swung north. They then figured they were far away from the battle zone so they stopped and stayed there for the summer. That's where they spent a few years in that territory.

From 1862 to 1875 they lived there and moved back and forth. Sometimes there would be a messenger from the south telling them to go back to where they came from. I just can't tell you what is the name of the place where this war started. But anyway they told them to go back up into that part of the country and the government would build them houses and they would give them monthly rations of food, clothing. They would build a school there for the children and they would be allowed to have all of their dances and any entertainment that they enjoy. A few times this message was brought to them [and] *Ṫawásu Óta* said that he would go back but not just then, but sometime in the future. Another messenger came and he told them to go back, that there were some houses built already and they were going to keep on building the houses for the Dakotas until all of the Dakotas were gathered there and there would be only one Dakota community. They would be looked after by the United States government. In the future they would have their own teachers, their own ministers and if they want to farm they would help them to do so. So they were asked to go back. As the messenger said, "Nothing would happen to you people. What you did you will be forgiven." But *Ṫawásu Óta* said, "That's not so. What damage we did is great and *wašíċu*, the white man, is not going to forgive us that. They are going to round us up and they are using this system to do that."

"Anyway, if all the Dakotas go to that place we will come, but not right now." This is the answer he always gave them when they came to invite them to go back to where they started from.

They moved back and forth, eastward and west but not too far west until 1875. Then they moved across the border into a place which is now called Portage la Prairie, Manitoba. (Robert Goodvoice 1, 1977, 9–10)

[RG 1977] Then they move about you know, to here and there. And somebody would come to the camp. And this person, he was all over looking for their dad or looking for their sister or brother or somebody. When the war broke out, they all scattered.

Now there is one person, he died in Prince Albert here. He was very, very old. You know, they were talking about fighting, fighting the United States. They were talking about it but he didn't think they would. But anyway, he got his gun and his blanket and one thing and another and he went out hunting. And he camped over there a couple of days. Sure enough, he got an animal so he took the meat and dried it and threw the bones away and when he carried it back, he was lucky. He was going back toward the camp, his name was Ťačáŋ Išóta. He was going back to the camp and there he saw two women coming with bundles on their back and they were running, half running and walking and running. He come close to them, by gosh, he knew them. One of them was his sister and the other one was his wife. He just got married not too long ago. He had been married about three or four months when the war broke out in 1862. So they told him what happened and they told him that the American army is just killing everything that is in their path so we are trying to get away from there. So from there he turned back and went eastward with them. And his father and mother and brothers, they were gone. And his wife's father and mother and sisters, they were gone someplace. But and his sister, his younger sister, she was about sixteen or seventeen when the war broke out, so they decided to stay out of sight for at least ten days or so and then when things quietened down they were going to look for their parents. So that is what they did.

They stay out of sight for ten days as he said, and then they went back and followed the people whichever way they go. You can tell the way the people moved. You can tell the way, the path and the tracks that they make so they followed them. Sure enough they come to one camp. Maybe five or six families camping in the bush someplace in a place where they can't be seen. They asked them if they see their dads, sisters, brothers. No, they never see them. Then they go on this way and back and forth, back and forth, tracking people. They come to another camp. And he asked them if they saw his father and mother and they said they did. About five or six days ago they told him, they saw them going west along the river. And then she asked them, Ṫaċáŋ Išóta's wife asked them if they saw her parents. And they say they did and they went south. They went south with the kids and with the rest of the family. The family stayed together. Her parents went south and his parents went west along the river. Now, she said that she would rather find his parents first and then they can look for her parents. So they went west along the river.

He had his gun and this and that but he don't like to fire a gun. People hear it and the soldiers were still here and there. They see the soldiers. And so they were scared. They never make fire and they never have a hot meal. They just drink cold water and whatever they have to eat, some powdered corn and wild berries and some dried meat. They never made a fire. They were on the move all the time. They kept going. They kept going until they were going for a long time. And then finally things seemed to quieten out, very, very few tracks. All tracks were leading toward the west. Some horse tracks and some people's tracks. You can tell where they camp and this way they figured they would find their parents. And they kept going, they kept going, Ṫaċáŋ Išóta, his sister and his wife, there is only three of them.

One day they come to a valley. There is a little bit of bush in the valley and when they come to that, they can see tracks leading into the valley. So he said to her, "You people stay here, I'll track these through the bush. They might cross over and they might camp here." She said, "We better not separate. We better stay together. Whatever will happen, we will all face that same thing. They might capture you and they might do away with you and then we will be all alone. This is no good. So don't track them, we will stay together." And it could be their parents. Now they are catching up to them. They come to a camp of three or four families. They come to a camp and they asked them if they see their parents and they saw them a couple days ago, going straight. They are still going west. That is Ṫaċáŋ Išóta's father and mother and his brothers and sisters and cousins and uncles and that you know. They were on the go. But anyway, they looked for them. Sometimes they will see a woman and a couple of kids coming, meeting them. They were going east and these other people are going west. They will ask them if they know, if they have seen his parents, "Have you seen my husband, have you seen my brothers," they were all scattered and they were all lost. Some people, they would meet them . . .

One place there, they saw smoke. They saw smoke and they walked there and they come up to him and that is a man and his wife. A man and his wife. And this man here killed two deer, antelope or something, deer. He killed two of them. And he had eight little kids. The youngest one was about seven and the oldest was about twelve, eight of them. These kids were lost. And when they see him, well these kids would run to him. And he would take them and he would tell them not to go away and he kept them and he fed them. And there were, that is the way it was going, people looking for people.

And this Ṫaċáŋ Išóta, his wife and his sister, they were [in the] west. They knew they were in enemy territory so they didn't want to go any further. But again there is some tracks leading west. There is about three groups leading west. So they were going from one path to the other, back again, back again, zigzag. They are quite sure his parents were in that group. So they followed and then finally they lost track of them. Anyway, they kept going and they say they will go till noon. Till midday and then they will swing south and then they are going to zigzag back, toward where they started.

They kept going and they come to a hill, they climbed the hill and just as they got on top of the hill, below there there was oh, Jesus, a big camp, and the Tetons, Oglalas, and Hunkpapas. So they must have [gone] quite a ways west. And when they saw these people on the hill, in no time there were three groups coming at them. They were all on horseback. One group coming right straight at them and another one coming from their left and the other on their right. And they were just, the horses were just running as hard as they could go. In no time they were surrounded. But Ṫaċáŋ Išóta happened to have a little white cloth, he had it and he got ahold of a willow and he tied this white cloth at the end and he had a pipe, what they call a peace pipe. He had one of them so he filled that with tobacco and kinnikinnik mixed and then he had a braid of sweetgrass. So his wife and his sister sat down and he put this white flag up and he stood under it. And these people they come on each side and went right at them. And they stopped, they stopped and one group was talking to the other by yelling at each other. And he understood what they were saying. So he yelled and said, "I am a Dakota. I am a Dakota. I am not an enemy, I am a Dakota, the same as you people."

And then these two fellows got off their horse[s] and they walked toward them. They come right up to them and they said, "Are you Dakotas?" "Yes, we are looking for our dad and our mothers, children, brothers and sisters, and she is looking for her brothers, and sisters, and father and mother and this is my sister, we are looking for them." "Nobody come this far," he said. "We are always on the lookout. When the Indians broke into war with the United States over there, we were always looking, watching out. We have got men over there, we have got men over here, we have got men watching this part. We don't allow nobody to come here. Even the American soldiers, if they come here, we are going to see if we can stop them and if they don't listen to us, well we will make them listen." This is what they told him. But Ṫaćáŋ Iśóta says, "What we are looking for is our parents. We are lost. The whole Dakota people are scattered all over. There is a man over there now, we saw a man there with eight children and none of them were his. They were different. He found them and he called them and he is gathering them and he is feeding them, he is with the kids," he told them.

But anyway, they took them, they took these three to the camp. They give him a tent and they give them dishes and pots and pans and food and they told them to rest, that they would help them to see if they can find their parents. They asked them if they are sure that they come west. And they told them that people told them that their father and mother had gone west, five six days ago, they were gone. That is why they were going west, hoping to find their father and mother. Well, anyway, they kept them there for quite a while and then one fellow, one man, he has a young son and he told him that that is the only child he has got is his son. And he asked Ṫaćáŋ Iśóta [about] his sister, [that] he wants her to marry his son. And he said, "If your sister marries my son, I will give you two horses. One of you can sit on his back and make a travois and you can sit there. You don't have to walk, the horse will take you. And this other horse here, if you see some buffaloes anyplace, you can jump on his back and you can chase them and you'll catch up and you will have all the meat you want in no time." So he didn't know what to say. So he said to this man here, "Well, I'll ask my sister." He said, "I'll ask her and I'll tell her about you giving me two horses. Then I could go further in a day and I might find my father and mother." So he asked her and he told her, "Sister, this is what they want." He says, "If we don't do as they say, they might kill us and they will still take you. They will still take you. So you might as well give in to them and stay with that man. You understand, we understand their language. They are part of us." He said, "Maybe our great-great-grandfathers were once brothers and one family at one time because we understand them today." So she said, "Okay." She said she would stay with them. And she did stay with them and they had a little dog. Just a small little dog.

Well now, they were there and they show him how to put the travois on this horse and what to do to ride the horse. They had never touched a horse in their life. They were scared of them but they were quiet and he handled them and they were all right. He would lead them and he would ride that horse, ride around and he would make him gallop and race him and he don't fall off. He become a good rider in no time. So he said, "All right." So they are going to come back. They are going to come back and go south and back and forth, back and forth until they find some camps and see if their father and mother are there. This is their idea.

Well now, his sister's name is *Kawíŋǧe Wiŋ*. That means turn, turn around, turn back. That is what it means. Turn back, that is what that means, come back. Well, they might as well call her Turner. That is about, there is lots of people called Turner. Well, *Kawíŋǧe Wiŋ*, that is what that means. One, you are going ahead and you turn, *kawíŋǧa*, then you swing back. You turn around and come back, that is what that means. Coming back, turning back that is what that means.

Well, anyway, *Kawíŋǧe Wiŋ* stayed and the day they were leaving, they were going to leave, they packed, they put the pack on the horse and they were leaving and then she said, "Leave me that little dog. I'll stay with the little dog." So they said, "Okay, keep it." She took that little dog and then they [*Ṫaćáŋ Iśóta* and his wife] started off.

Every day the ladies used to—they had some kind of diggers. So they used to go on the hillsides and dig wild carrots and dig some wild—some kind of roots that they had for food. Wild turnip or wild carrots. The ladies dig that and she will go with her sisters-in-law, *Kawíŋǧe Wiŋ*, she used to follow her sisters-in-law and she used to dig that and dry it and boil it and roast it and eat it, the same as what the rest of the people do. And they all, they got lots of buffalo meat. Dried buffalo meat in slabs and they pounded it into powder and they make, what do they call that now, oh, it is a pounded meat [pemmican]. And then they dry fruit, sas-katoons, choke cherries, plums, or whatever there is there, and they mix that. And then they pound this here wild carrot. When you pull the skin off the wild carrot, it is just as white as flour, very, very white. And then they will pound that, pound that, until they pound it into flour. And corn, they pound that into very fine. And then they mix this dried fruit and dried meat and they put this, thicken this pounded root, turnip and corn, they kind of dampen it rather. And then they mix that with the meat and the dried fruit. And then they smash all the bones and they take marrow off that. That oil is different from the fat and then they sprinkle that in it and that is what holds it together and keeps it damp like. So this, she made some of that. She made a nice chunk. She figured she can live on it for three or four days.

Well, whenever they go out on this here root digging, she will take that little dog and she will work her way and she will cross her parents' [brother's] tracks of yesterday, the day before yesterday. And they will come up to there and that little dog will smell their tracks and he wants to follow them and she will call that little dog back. And then the next day, she will do that, she will do that. So, when that little dog gets to their tracks, he wants to follow them although they were gone about three days ago. And on the fourth day, on the fourth day, just as the sun went down, her husband went to a game, some kind of a hand game. He will be there till daylight or the biggest part of the night.

That is when she packed up this here pemmican or whatever they call it and then she—it's a kind of a—some kind of a gut in an animal—they tie the ends together and they fill it with water and it holds water. So she got a couple of them and a little blanket and she wrapped all her food in it and sling it over her back and took this little dog and come to her [family's], her brother and her sister-in-law's tracks and then she asked that little dog, "All right, go."

That little dog followed their tracks and she started. She started running. She run all night until the next day at midday then she stopped and went into a bush and slept, and ate what food she had and fed the little dog and they slept. And then at sundown she started again. That little dog was following these, her brother's and her sister-in-law's tracks. They had four days start on her. She run and run and run. And that little dog was, that little dog stayed right on their tracks. Until, how many days now? I think on the third, fourth day, she caught up to them. She caught up to them and they had the two horses and the travois and that runner, that horse that could catch up to buffalos and they were there, and they were sitting there. She told them that she didn't like to stay there and she told them how she got away and all this and that. "Well, all right, if you don't want to stay there," he said, "We'll have to hit a different direction. They are going to come, they are going to follow our tracks," he said.

So they left the two horses there and the travois and what little bit of harness they had, and they just left everything right there and then they headed for a different direction altogether. *Ťačáŋ Išóta*, his wife and *Kawíŋǧe Wiŋ*, that is his sister. She caught up to them. And they went south. They went south, oh, a long way. And it was getting toward fall and they couldn't find their parents. Some people, they saw them over there but they go to that place and there is nobody there. And somebody would see her parents over there, they go there. They say their feet were sore and they don't—they are always on the go so they walk the full day, they feel weak. So he says, "They might have gone back. They don't know nobody over here, they don't know the land. This kind of land is not the kind of land where we were raised." He said, "Our land is way back there where there are rivers, sloughs, forests, hills. They might turn back and go back so we'll go there. We'll go home. We'll go straight from here."

So they didn't zigzag, they went straight to where they started from and then eastward. They went east and then north and they caught up to the rest of the people like my grandfather, that bunch. They caught up to them. And they say they were gone about, just about, almost three moons. That means three months. They say by the time they caught up to the bunch, it was—the leaves were all dry and it was fall already but no tent, no nothing. So they got to have a tent to live through the winter. They come to a place, the people were not running away no more. They just seemed to settle and the people were hunting and this and that. So he started, he started hunting and his wife and sister, they started tanning these hides. And pretty soon they have a tent, they made a tent. And they had lots of meat. They made it, they made about three or four of these here, what they call pemmican.

And they told, he told the people of his experiences, where he got two horses for his sister and when his sister caught up, well he let the horses go and left the harness and let the horses go. So they must have went a long ways. And all this time, he will shoot a deer and they will take that and that is what they used to have. Sometimes meat three times a day for three or four days. And then they stop and dig some wild carrots and wild turnips and wild potatoes or whatever it is, there is three different kinds of roots that grow in the ground that they dig up. And when they boil some meat they put it in there and they dry it and they pound it into flour and they make some kind of a bannock like. And they picked berries and mix it. When they were on the alert and when they were looking for their parents, they just eat meat three times a day, four times a day. No, well they had a couple of blankets and pillows but no tent, no nothing to cover them when it was raining or anything. In wet weather, they say they suffered.

It is not only him. They met people going this way and going that way and they are looking for their children or their family. Part of their family. But anyway, Taćáŋ Iśóta's parents, he never saw them. That was the last time he saw them. He never saw his other sister and two brothers, he never saw them. Where they went, nobody knows. Maybe they were killed by the American soldiers, nobody knows. But he—that is what they figure, if they were alive, they would find them. They found lots of people. But they were—they see these people, when they mentioned these people they say, "Sure, we saw them over there, over at that place." But they go there, there is nobody there.

At that time, in 1876, they started for Prince Albert. They started for Prince Albert in March and they landed in Prince Albert in August. They walked every step. And Taćáŋ Iśóta and Kawíŋǵe Wiŋ, that is his sister, and his wife, the three landed over there and they stayed together and they all passed away over there at a very, very old age.

And then there is one [they met], he is a Dakota but he is a preacher. His name is Máza Wakíŋyaŋ. Máza Wakíŋyaŋ now, that was his name. He is a Presbyterian minister. He went over there and people asked him, "Have you seen this person, that one and this one? That is my dad, that is my uncle, my brother, we left him behind. If you ever see him . . ." Máza Wakíŋyaŋ, Reverend Máza Wakíŋyaŋ said he saw Taćáŋ Iśóta's parents. He lived close to them for a few years and he said his mother died. "And then about five years after, your father died. And your brothers, I don't know where they are." This is what the preacher told this here Taćáŋ Iśóta. And there is people over there, there is one person, he was in Prince Albert and his sister was in Santee, Nebraska. When the [1862] war broke out, well they ran away, well a few kids they ran, they stayed together and they run this way out of sight and their parents run the other way, that is how they come to miss each other.

One day, Lucy Baker, this was in 1918. [Lucy Baker died in 1909. DB] Lucy Baker was on the reserve, the same one here. She received a letter from the United States asking her if there is a man in the Prince Albert district, a Dakota by the name of *Tuŋkáŋ Apápi*. Well, Lucy Baker saw the name and sure there is a man here. And that was his sister in Santee, Nebraska. That is how far they parted. They parted from, oh, she went south and *Tuŋkáŋ Apápi* went north. Brother and sister, the war had separated them and they never see each other. And they were very young when the war broke out. That was in 1862.

Oh yes, that period of time, there is people, people there—a man would go to my grandfather's camp looking for his wife and children. No, never seen nobody and never seen them. So he would stick around there for maybe a couple of days and then he would leave and go someplace else looking for his family. Sometimes a woman would come along with a bundle on her back, maybe two kids with her, looking for her husband or looking for her father and mother, looking for her brothers and sisters. Some of them were in very, very poor shape. Barefoot, no moccasins, no nothing. Clothes all torn, very, very bad shape. (Robert Goodvoice 3, 1977, 17–25)

The Kidnapping and Pursuit of Dakota Leaders after 1862

[RG 1977] And another thing that was ... [connected to the] ... 1862 battles in what they call the Sioux uprising I think. . . . One day, a Dakota came from the village. This is in Canada, in Manitoba. He came from the village and he went to a man by the name of *Iátokča*. He is not a chief but he is a very, very nice man. He was a very, very popular person in the camp. He is well respected and he is a wise man. So this messenger says to him, "*Iátokča*, there is a white man, there is a *wašíču* wants to speak to you tomorrow in town where the white men are." That means the village. He said he would go. Now, early in the morning, he put on his best. And he walked out in the circle, they lived in a circle. He walked out in the middle of the circle and he stopped. And he said, "I am wise. A white man called me to go and talk with him and I am going. But he is not going to fool me. He is not going to deceive me. I am a wise man." He said that, and he walked on a little ways and stopped and repeated the same thing. And the third time he was just about to the other end of the camp. And from the north, his brother-in-law, *Ṫaté Ićásna Máni*, joined him and volunteered to go with him. And that is the two who went to the—someplace—Winnipeg or someplace. They didn't mention the name of the towns. They don't know the name of the towns. But they always say to refer to a town, they say, "Where the white men are." That is what they always said, *Waśíću tib he*. That is what they said and that means a village where lots of white men are. Or they will say, "Where the stores are." They don't say Winnipeg or Brandon or New York. They don't use them. They don't know how to say them words and they don't know what the towns were called.

But anyway, this *Iátokća* and *Ṫaté Ićásna Máni*, they went to town. And they went to this man's place who invited them. It was, they say it was a kind of a cold morning. So when they went there, when they landed there, the first thing they did was they gave him a drink of whiskey. And then they give him a meal. And then another drink of whiskey and when they finished their meal, they put him in a room and this fellow, this servant says, "The man is going to come, you sit here, you wait here. He is coming." So they sat there and they both fall asleep. And when they fall asleep they wrap them up in warm blankets and this and that and put them in a toboggan, these two men, *Iátokća* and *Ṫaté Ićásna Máni*. They load them in toboggans. This was with two dog teams. And they say they took them to New York. And the white men who shipped them to New York under the influence of liquor and chloroform or whatever you call it—it is something that made them sleep. They were doped so that they fall asleep. He got five hundred dollars for each one of them. Now, how did the Dakotas know that? There was a halfbreed—they call them Metis today but at that time they called them halfbreeds—and this halfbreed worked for this man and he knew the Dakotas and he could speak their language fairly well. And he is the one who give them this whiskey, and he is the one who fed them, and he is one who give them this here dope to make them, to put them to sleep. It is a knock-out drink. He is the one who did that and he is the one who told them to sit in the room and wait for the boss, the man to come and speak to them. . . .

Ṫaté Ićásna Máni's brother and *Ṫaté Ićásna Máni's* wife, they both come to Prince Albert and they stayed in Prince Albert, around Prince Albert rather, and in 1922, *Ťaté Ićásna Máni's* wife, *Ťaté Ťáŋka Wiŋ* — that is her Indian name — she died. I think it was in the month of February. And she often told how her husband was kidnapped with *Iátokēa*. They were taken away by dog teams to New York.[10]

Iŋkpadúta. And *Iŋkpadúta* had four sons.[11] And when he was sick and going down, they were at that time, they were just, they were camping west of Prince Albert at a little town called Macdowell. That is today's name. They call that Macdowell. That is today's name of that town. Well, west of that, toward the Saskatchewan River there was an Indian camp there. There wasn't too many there. About fifteen or twenty families camping there and that is when this here *Iŋkpadúta*, Red Top, he was really low. And he had four sons. And night came and the sun went down into dark. In the morning, when the rest of the camp awoke, Red Top [and] his sons, they were all gone. They moved away from there during the night. And they never showed up, they never come back to the camp for at least ten days. Now this is the story my grandfather had told me. He was in that camp. Red Top and his sons disappeared. They never showed up for ten days, about ten days. And when they did show up, their dad, the father, wasn't with them. He died and they buried him.

And when these boys came back — they were not young men, they were around thirty, thirty-five years of age. They were men already, they were not young, young twenty-year-olds. And they said, my grandfather said when they came back, they didn't camp in the same place as where they did camp. They camped a little ways from there and one of them, I think he said the oldest one, that evening, he made a feast, put up what food he could and gathered the people, the older people of that camp and they all answered his invitation. They all went there and that is when he told them. He told them that their father, their father is wanted by the white man, especially the United States people, the United States government. They wanted Red Top. And they say that is the reason why they are not too closely associated with the rest of the camp most of the time. They can't help but have to live with the rest of the families in winter time but in summer time, they used to go away from the camp and they used to stay away, out of sight. For the people are after their dad. There is a reward for Red Top's head. The reward was to be paid by the United States government. So they didn't want to see their dad's head cut off and taken and somebody get money for it. They didn't want that so they watch him very close. At night, there is somebody, while the old man is asleep there is somebody sitting beside him awake. And they had two vicious dogs. They watch him day and night. And when he was getting low they took him out of sight and when he passed, they buried him someplace and they leveled off the grave and there is no sign of nobody digging him up. Now this is what they told the people. They said that is what they did with their dad's body. That he died a natural death and he is going to lie there as the rest of the people. Nobody bother[s] them once they are buried and he is the same. Once he is buried, nobody is going to find the place and nobody is going to bother him. . . .

There are many people who, as my grandfather says, there are many people who are wanted by the United States government. And he says that everybody was in the wrong at the time of the Sioux uprising in 1862. That is when lots of children are scattered. Families, half of the family is gone this way and the other half this way. Maybe one is left and has gone someplace else. He says that happened. With them, they moved northeast after the war broke out, they moved northeast and they remained close to the border, south of the border but close to it. [Probably in the Red Lakes area in northwest Minnesota, southeast of Pembina. DB] They lived and they hunted and they don't go and work for the white man too much because that white man might be an American and he will report them or he might give them away. This is what they were afraid of so they didn't go out and work for the white man too much. And they said they had a hard time. And all that time, while they were south of the border, short distance, just so they could make it to the border and cross the border over a night's travelling. That is the distance they stayed. That will be about, oh, not much more than ten miles. And he said they watched themselves all, every night there is somebody on the watch. Quite a way from the camp, the road that leads to it, they watched the road and they watched the camp that nobody bothers them.

And he said while they were on the alert like that day and night, somehow the messengers would come from the south and ask them to go back to the United States, that nothing would happen to them, they would be received and they would be back home, they would be back to where they started from. But they would never go back. They never did, they don't believe in that.

And finally, [in] 1876, that's when they left. There is about twelve years there. Well, he didn't say twelve years, he said quite a while they roamed back and forth, close to the border. And all that time, he said they had one dance. Somebody made a dance and they, the people gathered there to dance but he said it wasn't like a dance. They didn't want to take part in it. The music, they would make music by singing and beating the drum but then, no, it wasn't in them at all. They didn't want to. So they had a feast anyway and then they quit. That is the only dance that they had in that length of time.

While they were on the alert, back and forth along the border, there was one death. A man took sick and before morning, he was gone. And that man, that man went to the village, to where the white men are and he worked there. He did some work there, all day. And he slept in the bush and he went back the next day and he did the work and when he finished he came home quite early and toward evening, this man here who worked for the white man, he took sick. Oh, he was sick and he was in pain you know, and he couldn't hardly move and before morning he was gone. Well then they moved away from that territory altogether. And he said they took that corpse and buried it someplace in the bush.

At that time they never used to bury people unless somebody is murdered, they bury him. And if a person murders, they bury him. And any bad actor who dies, they bury them. And the good people, when they die, they put them on a scaffold. He said, "There is five things that make the human body." This is what my grandfather said. He said, "There is the water, heat, earth," and what else now. Water, heat, and earth, there is something else now. And he said, "The main thing is this. The main thing that keeps us Indians alive and moving is something from the sun," he said. And he named it but I forgot the name. "It is something from the sun," he said. "That, as long as you get that into your body and lots of it, you are strong and you can go. Never, never, never weaken. As you grow older, you lose this and you lose that. And then you grow older and then you pass out. You come from the air, water, heat, and earth, and the something from the sun." Any good person who dies, they put him up on the scaffold. You put him up there, he goes back to where he came from, the air. Whether he goes back down, he is finished. But a bad man, a bad man, when he passed away, they dig a hole in the ground and they put him down, face down at that.

But now, it is not too long ago, it is around 1928 or 1929, there was an old man. He was a very old man. He was sick and he was going down. And every time a person visited him, or people that were staying there watched over him, he was just begging them not to bury him. I heard him say it. I was there when he asked the people, he said, "Don't bury me. Don't put me in the ground. I am not a bad man. I never hurt nobody, I never fight nobody, I never steal nobody so why should you put me in the ground where the bad people are going, where you put the bad people. Wrap me up in my blanket or I got a tent here, so wrap me up and put me on a—if you can't put me up on a scaffold, put me up on a hill someplace in the bush and leave me there," he said. My grandfather said when this man died, he was a good man, he wasn't bad you know but he took sick and he was—it seems that he was poisoned so they didn't know what to do, whether to put him up on a scaffold or bury him. Well, they decided, you see, they said, "We are close to the white man's territory. If they see him up on the scaffold they might not like it," so they buried him. That is one death that had a very sad dance. (Robert Goodvoice 3, 1977, 12–17)

The Move to Prince Albert

James McKay, *Húpa Iyáȟpeya* and the 1876–1877
Trek to the Prince Albert District

[RG 1977: Robert Goodvoice gives two slightly differing accounts of the trek, in tape 2 and tape 9. What follows is the tape 2 account supplemented by occasional inserts from the tape 9 account, marked by parentheses.] I am Robert Goodvoice. My age is seventy-six and I am a Dakota.

There is a question that has been asked of me many times. The question is this: How come you Dakota, or the Sioux Indians, are in the Prince Albert district? Well this is what I am going to tell.

Back in 1876 there was a big Indian camp (a huge camp of Dakotas), and in that camp there was a man known as a Medicine Man and his name was *Húpa Iyáȟpeya*.[12] One day a white man visited the camp looking for *Húpa Iyáȟpeya*. When he found him this white man told the Indian Medicine Man that his wife had been sick for quite a while and the doctors had told him that there was no hope for her. And they told him to keep that lady as comfortable as he possibly could for she was not going to live very long. (She is not going to live no more than ten days. Before ten days is up, she will be dead.) So this white man's name was McKay. I don't know his first name or his initials but that's the way the Dakotas call him—McKay. [McKay was Metis; see note.][13] Now Mr. McKay visited the camp looking for *Húpa Iyáȟpeya* and told him of his troubles and *Húpa Iyáȟpeya* in answer said that he would come over and look at Mrs. McKay, which he did.

He went to Mr. McKay's home and this Indian Medicine Man performed over this sick woman by praying and singing some sacred songs. (He had an extra power to heal the sick. He got this power from a power that moved through the air, a power from above, as he always said. Now, he had to pray to that and tell him what he is up against and recite certain prayers, and he also had to sing some sacred songs, which he did. And in his vision he saw this, he saw through this sick woman's body, and he knows what was wrong with her. And there was four roots that were shown to him. And he knows what to do then. So he went home and dug up these roots and boiled them and took the juice to this sick white woman.)

That evening he went back to McKay's place and the woman was lying in bed, very sick. Again he prayed over her and sang some sacred songs as he had done before and then gave her a drink of what he had boiled up, which we call medicine. He brought a pot full. By midnight this lady drank every bit of it. This Indian Medicine Man went home and said he would come again tomorrow, which he did, with another pot. When he got there the next day the sick woman was sitting up in bed. She drank what he brought to her for her to drink.

He did this day after day and on the fourth day when he went to this sick woman, the sick woman was out of the bed sitting on a chair. On the sixth day she was sitting outside the house. On the eighth day she was walking back and forth outside her home. On the tenth day he went back and she was standing beside her husband, who was working in the garden. From there on her health improved and he didn't go back to that home until he was called by Mr. McKay. (Mr. McKay told him to bring two or three of his relations or a man with him.)

Húpa Iyáȟpeya took his cousin with him. (And when he got there, when the Indians got to Mr. McKay's home, he invited them into his house and into the room, and then Mr. McKay said to *Húpa Iyáȟpeya*, "Now,"—they had a halfbreed as an interpreter—"now," he said), "You have done me a great favor. . . . My wife is well, my wife has gained her health and she is happy and I am happy, but I can't pay you too much. (I am a very, very poor man and I can't give you very much but I will give you what I could spare." And he gave him some blankets and some clothing and some pots and pans and a few dollars and then he told him, "Now, I am going to tell you something *Húpa Iyáȟpeya*, but don't tell anybody, especially a white man, don't tell them what I am going to tell you. This is what I am going to tell you.")

He told him, "You Dakota or Sioux Indians fought the United States, fought the *Isáŋ Ťáŋka*." (That means the United States—Americans. *Isáŋ Ťáŋka* means the Big Knife, and that's the way the Dakotas used to call the Americans, *Isáŋ Ťáŋka*.) "Anyway, you fought them and you caused a lot of damage. You killed the horses and cattle, whatever was alive in your path you killed it and you've got to pay [for] this some way. Now the United States government is going to build houses for your people some place and they are going to feed you and they are going to treat you real well and every Dakota or Sioux would be asked to go there and live in that community. When everybody is there, they will all have a house. There will be things there to entertain them and when they are all gathered at this one spot some morning you are going to wake up and you will be surrounded by American soldiers. They are going to take the best of you, maybe every one of you and you are going to go through some torture of some kind. They are going to hang you, they are going to kill most of you, maybe all of you."

Now this is what McKay told *Húpa Iyáȟpeya*. "Now *Húpa Iyáȟpeya*, I want you to escape this persecution. You go straight north from here, keep going. There is a town over there and I have a friend there." This is Mr. McKay's conversation. He is telling this to *Húpa Iyáȟpeya*. ("I got a friend straight north from here, across the line." That means McKay's friend is across the line in Canada, a place called Portage.) "You go north to this town (and take your friends, all your relations, all those that want to live, take them and go straight north from here.) I've got a friend there, I'll write a letter and you give him this letter when you arrive at that town. From there he will direct you to another town farther north and when you get to that town away north (it's a long way) but when you get there you will be safe. (There are two rivers there and north of these two rivers there is lots of land there. Nobody is there). There is lots of game there and there are lots of fur bearing animals there. Your living is there. There are lots of lakes and it is all timber. You won't suffer. There is a big store there, everything you want is there. He will direct you from there on. So you do that and get all your friends, your relatives, your close relations and anybody that wants to go. "Go, you will be safe."

So *Húpa Iyáȟpeya* and his cousin went home and told the people what he heard. He didn't say McKay told him that, but he said that he heard that when he was in the village, in the white village. So he told them he was going to journey northward to that safety, to that safe place where he was told to go. This he did. About thirty or forty families moved northward. They moved straight north until they came to a town. That town is known as Portage la Prairie (that's today). That's the name of the town today and they landed there and *Húpa Iyáȟpeya* showed this letter to a person and this person saw the name on the envelope and told him to go to a certain place. He went there but the man wasn't home. He waited there until he came home. When he came home the Medicine Man gave him the letter and he read it. They could see in his face that he was accepting these visitors and he sent a man to show the group of Indians where to camp, to make their home for the winter.

They stayed there that winter. They say they spent a good winter. They made baskets and they made rugs, mats, quilts. They tanned hides and made moccasins and they sold whatever they made to this man in Portage. They didn't know his name. They never knew his name. They called him "That White Man," *Wašíču He*, which means that white man. This referred to this man who told them to camp at this certain place.

They stayed there all winter and they made baskets, as I have said. They were busy all winter. When the crows arrived from the south, that means it is spring. (In the spring of 1876, in the month of March, they started moving). Then they packed up and they headed for the north. This man in Portage told them, in the evening he called them, and told them in the northwestward from where Portage was, "You see that star over there (in the northwest), right under there is where that town is. So go to that star, that is your guide. Every evening get a stick or something pointing to that star and in the morning follow that until you come to that town. It is a long, long way." He said, "There are two rivers, one in the south and the other north. One is called the South Saskatchewan and the other is called the North Saskatchewan. He told him of these two rivers. These two rivers, they join and from there, there is only one river.

You cross the first one, but don't cross the second one. Follow the second river toward the west and you will come to that town.

So they started off in March to come to Prince Albert. Their children, some of them four years old, some of them six years old, some of them ten years old, but they walked every step from Portage la Prairie to Prince Albert.[14]

On their way they came to a lake, a body of water where you can't see the shore [Lake Manitoba? DB]. Looking toward the east they say you can't see the shore. Looking toward the northeast you can't see the shore. They figured they had come to the ocean. If possible they would go around it by going westward, which they did. They kept going and finally the shoreline commenced to turn northward and they followed it until they were just straight across from where they started going west and then they hit north from there. They walked on and on and on and wherever they came to a slough if there were muskrat houses they trapped them all and they caught minks, raccoons, muskrats, foxes and other fur-bearing animals. They skinned them and dried the pelts and they carried them. If they shot two or three jumpers and if they had two or three, maybe four, hides then they stopped and they tanned them and they wear that, that's their footwear. They travelled northwest from Portage and they carried all the dried pelts that they have trapped on the way.

One day they came to a road, straight across from east to west.[15] They made camp a little way from that road. Pretty soon somebody said that something appeared in the east and it was something very strange. They watched it and they watched it and that's the freighters or settlers going from someplace down east and going west. This is, I would say, a wagon train, horses and mules and oxen or whatever can pull a wagon. They had them loaded and they were going west. They said there was at least fifty of them, maybe more. There was an odd [rider on] horseback among them. As they camped there a man rode toward them. He came to this camp and he was what they call a halfbreed. Nowadays they call them Metis. He is a halfbreed, a French halfbreed. But this halfbreed could talk the Dakota language, not too well, but he could master it enough that he could make them understand what he wanted. He wanted some *wahánuŋ* which means pelts, fur-bearing animals. That's what he wanted and he made them understand that. So they sold all their furs to this man, to the people who were travelling west. Oh yes, this man on horseback, he went back to the wagon train and a man drove up in the wagon and they loaded all the fur that they had for sale and he gave them money. He gave them lots of money, everybody had money.

Now they kept on coming north. They camped here for two days and then they kept going for two or three days without [stopping?]. They travelled every day, all day, and then they had a rest for two or three days, then they kept going. They left Portage la Prairie in March and they landed in Prince Albert in August. Since then they have stayed around Prince Albert.

Oh yes, one evening they made camp on a high hill and in the evening toward when it is getting dark they could see fog rising. It was in the low place and the fog was rising, so they knew there was a river or a lake. So in the morning they sent four men to go to see if it was a lake or a river. In the morning the fog was still hanging over the low land. These four men went there and sure enough it was the river. Two went upstream and two went downstream looking for the place where these two rivers joined. (I think they call that Colt Falls today [La Colle Falls. DB]. From there, there is only one river. It is the Saskatchewan River from there. I believe that is what they call that river now, the North Saskatchewan River.) There they found a place where they could cross. The river was wide and it looked as if it were shallow there. They got down and they crossed it, and sure enough there was only one place where the water came above their knees and the rest of it was below their knees. So they crossed it and they put a sign there and they went back. They crossed back to where they started.

The other two boys who went upstream [*sic* downstream?], they came back and they told them that they found a place where the two rivers joined. They went to the camp and they told the people. They went down to the river and that's where they crossed, still going north, until they came to the second river. That's the North Saskatchewan River. Then they followed it upstream until they came to a place which is called the Miller's Hill nowadays. When they came there they could see the village below. Anyway, they made camp there and the next day the men took that letter and the leader *Húpa Iyáȟpeya* and they went to this village and they looked for this man. And they saw him and he read the letter. He was glad and he received them. He told them to camp in a certain place, which they did, and they stayed around there and they started working for this man, doing odd jobs, and in the wintertime they cut cord wood for a living all winter. Whatever they caught trapping they sold it to the store. That store is known as the Hudson's Bay Company.

The Dakotas made a deal with the Hudson's Bay Company that whatever they catch when the trapping season is open, whatever fur they catch they will sell to the Hudson's Bay Company, no other buyer. So they made his agreement and then the Hudson's Bay Company told them that they could live on the Hudson's Bay land. Wherever there is Hudson's Bay land they can live there, which they did. Since that time the Dakotas that came from Portage la Prairie, they lived independently on Hudson's Bay lands up until 1918. [The Little Red River site, Indian Reserve 94B, northeast of Prince Albert; see map 5. DB] Then they moved into what is known as Round Plain Reserve. [Indian Reserve 94A, northwest of Prince Albert. Now both sites are called Wahpeton Dakota Nation. DB] This Reserve was surveyed in 1893 and the people, the Wahpatons, Wahpetona. Wahpatons is what they call them today. They didn't pronounce the word right, but it is known better by Wahpaton than Wahpetona.

The first teacher and missionary who was here was Miss Lucy Baker.[16] At that time the Reserve was only three and three-quarter sections, but there were lots of sloughs, lots of timber and lots of game, fish and ducks. The [Shell] river ran through the Reserve so there was fish there, which was a good place for them. When they moved here the Indian Department helped them by giving them ploughs and oxen, hoes and rakes and binders and showed them how to run the ploughs and they started farming. And they gave them cattle. That farming has improved a lot since then. All that land that I just mentioned it is all under cultivation and the people are all doing well, some have high school education. They have improved a lot since then and we still intend to improve some more, especially this year.

Since Lucy Baker, there was a fellow by the name of Johnny Beverley who was a teacher and Reverend J. G. Meek, a minister and teacher; Mrs. Mary Hilliard; Mr. Charlie Fetch. Just a few of the teachers.

Now I am telling this story as my grandparents told me. There are a few things that I have forgotten that I would now like to mention.

Now the first thing that I would like to mention is Mr. McKay, the man who told them to come here, said he would be travelling this way the following year, which he did. The Dakotas were in Prince Albert and not the following year but the second year Mr. McKay introduced them to his relatives. There were lots of McKays in the Prince Albert district at that time. So they were really, really happy and they felt very safe from there on until about 1885, that's the year the Northwest Rebellion broke out.

There were at least 350 families of Dakotas living in Prince Albert district, living on the Hudson's Bay lands. When the war [the North-West Rebellion/Resistance of 1885. DB] broke out most of them went back and there was only about thirty-five or forty families left. Some of them came back after and some left and that's the way it has been going since until the Indian Department registered the Indians and their names were written in what they call a band list and wherever their name is, that is where they have to stay and they don't travel back and forth as they used to. (Robert Goodvoice 2, 1977, 2–8, with inserts from Robert Goodvoice 9, 1977, 2–5)

The Wahpeton Chiefs; *Ahíyaŋke* Obtains Land for Round Plain Reserve in 1893

[RG 1977] Now as I said, [long, long ago] the people used to live in four big circles. There was one big circle inside of another one. They divided and it came to a time when there were too many in one place so they had to divide, which they did. Then that's the time when the people moved in every direction. A group moved northeast and that's where my grandparents and their parents, way back, were in that bunch that moved northeast. [Note similarity with Sam's account near the end of part 2, in The Dakota Turning Point. DB]

They had a man there who was a real good man in every way. So they had him as their leader. He finished one season and then they had to try him out for another season and he did good, another one and another one and that's a year. Then he was still young and strong and able, so they gave him another try for another season. This carries on for four years. He led the people out of trouble and he always led them to where there was food and in the wintertime where there was lots of wood and shelter. He was a good leader in every way. At the end of four years they got together, the older people got together and they selected him. They went through a ceremony and he was pronounced the leader of that tribe. They say there were over two hundred families. I have forgotten his name. I heard his name many times but I have forgotten. He has an Indian name and I forgot it. But anyway, this is the first chief of this *Wahpétuŋwaŋ* and *Isáŋti* and *Bdewákaŋtuŋwaŋ* people. This is their first chief.

This chief had a son, his oldest son was alive and this oldest son they told him to stay with his father and learn his habits and learn his good works and learn everything that his father did to gain that position as the main leader of the old tribe. This young boy stayed with his father for many years. By that time this boy got married and he had a young son. Now the chief had his son there and his oldest grandchild. He had these two with him all the time and he would speak to them and teach them whatever he knew that was good for himself and good for the people. He led the people in a way that they all remained in good faith with one another. There was no fighting or nothing. Everybody helped each other, especially the young people. He taught them that they should respect the old people and help them. The young boys stayed with the old chief and they learned all they could, the experiences of the old chief. They were two good boys. They say they were kind and they were obedient and they worked for the old chief until he died. Then his son took over and he took over and as long as he was alive he was a chief. By that time he was getting old and then his oldest boy still remained with his dad, and he learned from his dad and his grandfather how to be a good leader and what he did and what they did, the three of them, to satisfy the people. They have to carry this out as their duty. (Robert Goodvoice 1, 1977, 11–12)

[RG 1977] Now I will [tell of] 1851, when the 1851 treaty was signed. A chief by the name of *Śákpe*, he is my grandmother's uncle and chief. *Śákpe* had four councilors. I only remember the names of two of them, *Íŋyaŋgmani* and *Ištáhba*. The other two, I have forgotten their names. But anyway, *Śákpe* didn't have a family and he died. Also all of his councilors died before 1862 when the Minnesota Massacre occurred, so *Śákpe's* chieftainship ended. None of his councilors or himself came to Canada.

On the other hand, there is a chief by the name of *Upí Iyahdéya*. He was a chief in the United States. I am not sure whether he was one who signed the treaty or not. I can't say. I have never heard anybody say that he did. *Upí Iyahdéya's* nephew was *Ahíyaŋke*. And *Ahíyaŋke's* nephew was *Íto Imáza*. He became a chief after his uncle *Ahíyaŋke* died. This *Ahíyaŋke* is a man who asked for a piece of land which is the Round Plain Reserve, also called Wahpeton.

Now, *Ahíyaŋke* worked for two people in Prince Albert. One of them was a rancher. His name was Ed McKennon. The other was a farmer by the name of Dick Pigeon. Now these two men knew how *Ahíyaŋke* fitted. He inherited a chieftainship from way back in the United States. So they suggested he try to restore that chieftainship by asking the Dominion Government for a piece of land and he would be a chief there. So Ed McKennon and Dick Pigeon wrote a letter for him. Sure enough, they got an answer in favor of *Ahíyaŋke*'s request. So he picked this land here. This Reserve was surveyed in 1893 by a surveyor. The surveyor's name was Clark. I don't know his initials, but I am sure that his name was Clark. It was in 1893 and they moved him here in 1894 and they named this Reserve *Tíŋtaŋ Mibéna. Tíŋtaŋ Mibéna* means Round Plain. That's what it was called to start with. The tribe who lived here are Wahpeton. *Ahíyaŋke*, that's the chief. He died around 1902, maybe 1903. He died somewhere around there. Then his nephew *Íto Imáza* took over the same year. I am not sure of the year, but then it was on May 24 when *Íto Imáza* was pronounced chief. He took his uncle's name *Ahíyaŋke*. They used to call him *Ahíyaŋke* the Second. He remained as a chief of the Round Plain Reserve until late September 1936 and then he died. So *Upí Iyahdéya*'s [hereditary line of] chieftainship ended then.

If it was in the old system, that chieftainship of *Upí Iyahdéya* would be in existence yet because of *Ahíyaŋke*'s nephew Herbert Buffalo. His Indian name was *Ṫawáduta Óta* and he died around 1971. His son, Herbert Buffalo's only son, alive today, is Sammy Buffalo. If they followed the old system he would be the chief, but due to the Indian Department's ruling, the people have to nominate a person and then vote him in to be the chief of a tribe of the reserve. (Robert Goodvoice 1, 1977, 10–11)[17]

How My Grandfather Was Lost and Received Guidance from a Poplar Tree

[RG 1977] First of all, I am going to tell a story that my grandfather had experienced himself. He was lost. And what he went through and what he heard and how he got home and what brought him home. This is the experience that he had and it is a good experience and he often told this to people.

Now, one day he went, it was a nice and bright morning so he went out hunting. From where they camped, he went southwest. And before midday, the day was cloudy. Pretty soon, you can't see the sun and there was very, very little wind. And he was hunting, he was hunting this way and that way and pretty soon it started to rain. Just a very fine rain. You can't see anything. The sun was out of sight. There was no wind and there was a very, very fine rain. It was just a heavy fog. That is what it is he said.

Anyway, he figured toward evening, he sat down and come to a slough where there is water and he boiled a pot of tea and had lunch and then he started out for home. He said he didn't know which way he was going but he was going anyway. He walked and walked and walked and pretty soon it got dark. Still he was walking. He thought he was—he thought his home was that direction and that is the way he was going. And he walked and walked the biggest part of the night. He sat down, he come to a bush. So he went into the bush and sat down, lay down and went to sleep.

He woke up, it was daylight. So he started. And the day was just the same as it was yesterday, a heavy fog. And in the low places you can't see nothing. A little rain, everything was wet. And he was walking all day, couldn't find no place that he knew or where he has been before but anyway he kept on walking. He couldn't see no game. He scared up some game but he couldn't see them. He come to a slough but he can't see if there are any ducks or anything in the slough for him to shoot at and have something to eat because he can't see them. And then he stopped and boiled up what little tea he had left and what little lunch he had. He had that. And then he walked, walked all day. There was a river running east and west. This was—this place where he got lost is between Regina and along south of Moose Jaw and up toward the border. Up in there someplace, toward Wood Mountain. So he kept on walking, then he changed his direction. He turned right around and walked the other way, backtracked himself. Well, he thought he did. Of course, this was in the fall of the year, it wasn't too cold yet. And he walked, walked all day. Evening came, nothing to eat, no more tea left. He had a kettle all right now. He was going to make fire and all the matches that he had were wet, no good. And he walked all night, the biggest part of the night, searching for his home.

He noticed that the formation of the land was different. Hills, small hills and lots of them. He was climbing one or going down one, that is just how close these hills were. And he couldn't make out where that land is of that shape. Small little hills and lots of them. He couldn't remember knowing any [such] place, but he figures he must be southwest, a long way from home. And then he walked and it was the third night. He was getting weak, sleepy, tired, worried, and the sun didn't shine. He couldn't make out where he was and the wind was blowing but what direction was it coming from? He didn't know whether it was blowing from the north, east, south, or west. When he looks up, he can't see the stars, he can't see the sun. The third night, by this time he was weak, hungry, tired and he was—he commenced to worry very much. So he started praying. He prayed to the *Wakáŋ Taŋká*, the most holy, and he prayed. And while he was praying, the tears would come in his eyes. And he was wet and feeling cold so he stopped, if he would climb a hill, he gets on top of the hill, he knows he was on top of a little hill, he would stand there and look toward the heavens and pray toward the *Wakáŋ Taŋká*, to God, the most holy. And walk on, keep on walking, and he don't know whether he is going straight or in circles. He don't know what. He couldn't see far enough ahead to tell whether he is going straight or walking in circles. When he goes walking down the hill, he makes sure he gets right to the bottom to see if he could find some water. But no, by this time, where he was, the ground is very light, it is sandy.

Then he kept on walking and that night he said, if he stopped for a short time, he would fall asleep. And he was walking and he commenced to go downhill. So he walked downhill and by gosh, that is a little bluff. He walked down and he felt some trees, pretty fair sized trees. Now, he knows that he is a long, long way from home. So he made up his mind he is going to stay there and hope [that] tomorrow morning he would see the sun. Or tonight he can see the stars and the dipper, what they call the dipper in the sky and the north star. He knows his directions, he can get home even if it is in the dark. The stars, he can't see not even one. The moon—if there is one, he can't see it. The same complete darkness. He walked into this bush and he felt his way and by gosh, he come to a poplar tree. It is about the size of a stove pipe, he says. He stood there and he hung onto that. And by gosh, he said he felt kind of safe and relaxed when he come into that bush. Just a little bit thicker than the other bush he had come through. So he sat up against this poplar tree, his head against it, and sat there and prayed and cried, cried and prayed.

Finally he fell asleep. He said he don't know how long he slept. All at once he was awakened by somebody talking to him. So he opened his eyes, it is still dark but there is somebody talking to him. His head was against this white poplar tree that is about the size of a stove pipe. And he says, "You are crying, your voice is heard and I am sent here to show you the direction to go so that you will get home. Your people in your home are waiting for you. So when you get up, you go this way, this way, not that way but right straight this way and keep going straight ahead, keep going, you will get home. Your people are waiting for you. They are asking for help for you to return home safely so you do that." And he felt where this voice was coming from. That's the poplar tree right where his head was against the tree, that is where the voice was coming from. So he got up and he put his hands on this tree in return of thanks for what he heard.

He was expected to go a certain way to get home so he started that way. He didn't know which way that was, but he . . . followed it. He went that way. He kept going, kept going, kept going, he can't stop. Pretty soon daylight, daybreak. He kept on walking, he didn't feel tired, he wasn't hungry and he wasn't worried. He knew he was going home and he was happy so he kept going. And he never stopped, never looked around but he just looked straight ahead and kept going. And the sun was between the sunrise and midday, between there. That would be about nine, ten o'clock. Finally he could see, the day was getting brighter, the sun was shining through the clouds once in a while, and he knew which way he was going. He was going straight east. So all the time he was lost, he was travelling toward the west all the time. He kept going, kept going, pretty soon he come home.

When he got home he told them what an experience he had when he was lost. He couldn't find his way home so he prayed and he cried and he sat up against a poplar tree, a white poplar tree and went to sleep. And during that sleep, that tree woke him up by talking to him. That tree guided him, give him the direction to follow. And he said he followed it and then he said he came home. If it wasn't for that tree he said he could have been out someplace for another day or so. And from that time, from that time my grandfather used to say, he told me very many, many times, he said, "Don't ever cut a poplar tree, don't ever bruise a poplar tree that big. That is a living thing. It might be one of us." He said, "For sure he is one of us because he spoke to me in my language, in the language that I understood every word he said. So never cut a poplar tree that big. Never cut it down. That is a living thing. Only it is in one place, it is a person. So never, never bruise a white poplar in any way. You can cut a smaller one or bigger one but that size of poplar tree, it is a living thing. If you ever get lost or get hurt while you are in the bush, if you can get up to a poplar tree that big, put your hand on it, both hands and ask for his help. Ask him to help you to get home. To guide you to your home. He will." This is what my grandfather used to say. Many, many times. He used to tell me that and I heard him tell my brother that. And he never cut a poplar tree that is about the size of—the same as—about six or seven inches in diameter. He said, "That is a living thing, they can talk. If you are going to respect anything in the forest," he always told me, "that poplar tree, that white poplar tree. If you go beside a poplar tree just put your hand on it, touch it. And think, you don't have to say, just think, you are touching a friend, you are touching a living thing. Bear it in mind and do that. Even if you have to touch one every ten, fifteen yards, do so. You are touching a living thing. The *Wakáŋ Taŋká* put that there and gave it that language for us Dakotas or Indians to depend on. And if it wasn't for that poplar tree, I could have been, I could have played out and dropped someplace among them little hills. I could have been fox meat or coyote meat if it wasn't for that white poplar. I was lost, I couldn't find my way and that is how I come home to them. By the guidance of that white poplar. He spoke to me, told me which way to go and I followed it and I came home." This is what he said. That is my grandfather. He was lost for three days and the fourth day, he came home. He spent two nights and the third night, part of the night, he started walking home. That is that. (Robert Goodvoice 4, 1977, 1–5)

People with the Power to Find Things

[RG 1977. This is one of the half-dozen stories Robert tells of Indigenous people he knows of with the special power to find people or lost things (a cow, horse, keys, etc.) DB] And then another one. This is a white boy. This is blueberry time. This happened between Round Plain and Prince Albert. He was a white boy. He was about four years old. His parents were picking blueberries and he was playing around the trees, running around here and there and when it was time to come home, he was gone. And they yelled and called him and run in circles here this way and that way and all the blueberry pickers who heard this yelled and cried with this lady. They all come there. And little—what was his name now?— anyway his last name is Cook, he was lost. Nobody knows where he is. They searched and searched in the dark and the night came, they made a fire then and some people stayed there. They thought he might see the fire through the bushes and come back to the fire.

The next morning there was a bunch of Mounties there and lots of people from Prince Albert went out there to look for this little lost boy.

They walked and they covered every square yard of that bush only within about a mile radius. And an old Indian woman, she had this extra power for finding things and she happened to be there. And one white man. He was our minister on the Round Plain Reserve, he was there. He joined the search party. Just then this old lady and her husband were both going to town with a team of horses. So he stopped her and he told her that there was a little boy lost yesterday. Last night, he is out in the bush some-place, and all day today. And this is getting toward evening again. About mid-afternoon. So they asked her if she can help. She said she would try.

So she got up out of the wagon onto the ground. "And where was he last seen?" "Over there on that place there." And they took her there and the little boy's tracks were there. So this is where she stood and she prayed, sang, and prayed and this and that. "By gosh," she said, "That lit-tle boy is lying down. He is not dead but he is lying down. He can't get up. Straight over here," she said, northeast from where she stood. "Straight over here," she said, "there is a lake, a good sized lake, and on the west side of it, the west side of that lake, he is lying among the tall grass, bul-rushes. He is laying there.

He is not dead but he is pretty sick, pretty weak." So they all rushed that way. They didn't look for that little boy but they looked for that lake. Somebody found that lake and then he followed. On the west side of the lake, walking toward the north and sure enough, there he was, lying in the tall grass, bulrushes, he was lying there. The little boy went to the slough and took a drink of water and then coming back, he lay down and he couldn't get up. So that is how they found this little boy, that lost boy. . . .

There are lots of people like that. They have kind of the ability of find-ing things. . . . But it all amounted to the same thing of this here power and coming right down to brass tacks about where this power comes from. It seems to me that—I'll ask the few people, two people who have that power, I said, "How do you get this power?" Well they spend a night or a day someplace fasting and asking for power, the ability to see things that nobody else can through the power of him that created human life and the giver of wisdom and all that. They say they pray to the most holy, the *Wakáŋ Táŋka*. But they don't think he is the one that appeared to them. They figure it is this here, what we call *Uŋktómi*. He is the one that appears to them and he is the one that talks to them. But when they are in that position of communicating with some spirit power, they don't see things, they don't see but they hear the voice. That is the only thing they hear is the voice. And they all seem to—when they hear the voice, the first thought that comes into their mind is *Uŋktómi*. With the Crees they call this being *Wičaȟkečaȟ*. We call—we have one too among us and we call him *Uŋktómi*. It seems to me that the Crees, they wrestle with him and they run races with him and he takes the girls away and this and that, but our *Uŋktómi* doesn't do that. Nobody touches him. Nobody ever touched this *Uŋktómi* of ours. So I often wonder if that could be the same—what do you call it?—the same person or same being or same power. We had one here on this reserve. He passed away about seven, eight years ago. (Robert Goodvoice 4, 1977, 8–9)

Part 4

The *Wakáŋ Waćípi* Songs and Song Stick of Henry Two Bear and the Pictographic Notebooks of James Black (Jim Sapa)

Introduction

DANIEL M. BEVERIDGE

Although much of this book has been concerned with traditional ceremonies that were considered sacred by participants, part 4 deals with these ceremonial subjects in a more direct way. Although our main purpose is to pass on traditional knowledge so that others can understand and appreciate it, we must remember to treat our subjects with proper respect.

Part 4 brings us into the twentieth century and to the final expressions of what Sam called the *Wakáŋ Waćípi* religion. It features mainly the contributions of two men. The voice of James Black (Jim Sapa), member of and participant in the *Wakáŋ Waćípi*, is featured in two ways: in his interviews with Sam regarding the very last *Wakáŋ Waćípi* ceremony, in 1934; and in the two pictographic notebooks of which he was the keeper and which were used in the *Wakáŋ Waćípi* ceremony. He may have been the artist who created the forty-five images in those notebooks. Included too is commentary on the Cree syllabics that appear on several pages of one pictographic notebook.

Henry Two Bear was the transcriber of the actual songs used in the *Wakáŋ Waćípi* ceremonies: these may be the oldest known Dakota texts. He also was keeper of the song stick that guided the singers of the songs.

Part 4 begins with an article I wrote in 1987. This is followed by four more segments: what Sam and I said in 1985 about Henry Two Bear, the transcriber of the songs; Jurgita Antoine's full retranslation into English of the Dakota songs transcribed by Henry Two Bear in his diary and initially translated by Sam; Sam's 1985 account of his earlier discussion with James Black, the keeper of the picture notebooks, about the last ever *Wakáŋ Waćípi* complete ceremony and the last ever *Wakáŋ Waćípi* feast; and selected photographs from the pictographic notebooks.

Discovering the *Wakáŋ Waćípi* Dakota Song Stick

DANIEL M. BEVERIDGE

In October 1987 the *Indian Record* published my article "A Prairie Puzzle: The *Wakan-Wacipi* Dakota Song Stick." I described four items: a song stick or song board, a diary-notebook with Dakota songs, and two picture-book notebooks containing hand-drawn pictures and Cree syllabic writing. As noted in that article, Samuel Mniyo states that not only the song stick and the Dakota songs but also the two notebooks were used in the *Wakáŋ Waćípi*; Sam translates several lines of the songs here. That article is reproduced here, but without the two black and white photos (one of the song stick and one of a sample page from one of the two picture-books showing both pictures and Cree syllabics). My scale drawing of Henry Two Bear's song stick is retained.

The reference to Nakota as the Yankton Dakota dialect (in 2. Diary-notebook) is incorrect and should be deleted. Instead it should read Western Dakota or Yankton-Yanktonai dialect. Also, the "puzzle" of the Cree syllabics presented in this article is no longer a puzzle and is explained later in part 4. The Beveridge and Mniyo item cited in the references as being "in progress" (in 1987) has finally reached the stage of publication in the present volume, over thirty years later.

A Prairie Puzzle: The *Wakan-Wacipi* Dakota Song Stick

(Originally published in the *Indian Record* 50, no. 4 [October 1987]: 11–12.)

About 1967 I located four items: a "song stick" or mnemonic song board and a diary-notebook with several pages of songs hand-written in the Dakota language,[1] which had both belonged to Mr. Henry Two Bear of the Round Plain (Wahpeton Dakota) reserve near Prince Albert, Saskatchewan, and which I purchased after his death; and two illustrated notebooks which contained numerous pages of picture writing and Cree syllabics, and which belonged to a man from Moose Woods (Whitecap) reserve near Saskatoon, who lent them to me in 1968 to photograph page by page.[2]

1. The song stick is a dark brown wooden board over a foot long with simple line drawings of persons, teepees, and animals incised onto both obverse and reverse faces, as shown in the figure [scale drawing/tracing].

Mr. Samuel Mniyo of Saskatoon (formerly Samuel Buffalo of Round Plain) states that this "song stick" was used to guide the singers in the Holy Dance *(wakan wacipi)* ceremony. The Two Bear song stick may resemble a Yankto-

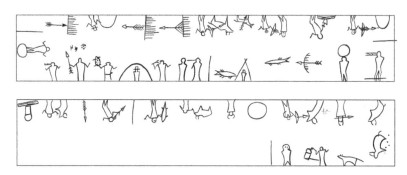

FIGURE 9. Scale drawing/tracing of Henry Two Bear's "song stick" for the Santee Dakota *Wakáŋ Waćípi* showing incised pictures on both faces. Drawn by Daniel M. Beveridge.

nai Dakota *wakan wacipi* song board shown in Howard (1952, p. 135), and six such Wahpeton Dakota song boards shown in photographs and drawings in Skinner (1920, pp. 268–273). The *wakan wacipi* itself resembles the *midewiwin* or medicine ceremony of the Ojibwa, who passed it to both the Dakota (Howard, 1984; Skinner, 1920) and the Cree (Mandelbaum, 1979).[3]

2. Diary-notebook with Dakota songs. With the song stick Two Bear kept a small notebook which has nine pages of songs, written in 1911 or later, in Dakota script handwriting (strictly speaking, Nakota, the Yankton Dakota dialect) [sic]. It is arranged in short numbered verses ending in lines with ha, he ho, Wi Wi Wi, Mi Mi Mi, etc. The complete text with literal translation by Mr. Mniyo appears elsewhere (Beveridge and Mniyo, in progress); Mniyo says these verses are *wakan wacipi* songs written down by Henry Two Bear.

Several translated lines (with Dakota original) which somewhat resemble those reported years ago (Neill, 1872, cited in Wallis, 1947, p. 76) are:

Mystery / *wakan, iwakan*
Within-water medicine / *nide pejihuta*

This mystery I made / *Wakan de wakage*
This mystery, I saw, I swear / *De wakan de wanbdake do he*
In the water, I saw, I swear / *Mniyata wanbdake do he* . . .
Arrow soaring in the air / *Wan kinyan hiyaye* . . .
I shot you, so it be, so it be / *Cio nunwe, dowan nunwe*
My people are co-believers/ *Koda mitaoyate wasicu*

3 and 4. Picture-Books "A" and "B" with pictures and Cree syllabics once belonged to Jim Sapa (James Black) who was a principal member of the Holy Dance society (Mniyo in Goodvoice, 1977) and who used these books in the *wakan wacipi*, perhaps as song books.[4] In Book "A," written in 1905 or later, appear the names of Jim Sapa, Dan Melvin, and J. S. McKay, and 33 pictures. Each picture occupies one page and several also extend onto the facing page. In 13 of these pictures Cree syllabics occupy the facing page, as shown in figure _ [not shown here. DB]. Book "B" has 14 pictures, most similar to "A," one with Cree syllabics.

The Cree syllabics were examined by three Cree clergymen.[5] Rev. Dr. Adam Cuthand, an Anglican priest in Regina, translates the syllabics in photos 10A and 11A as follows:

> 10A: Jesus rose up to heaven. Jesus rose from the dead. Jesus died for us. Jesus at the end of time will come down to judge all people.
>
> 11A: Jesus met his mother. Jesus will have joy. Jesus has been allowed to die.

Cuthand goes on to suggest that these two books may have been used as instructional material to explain the Christian faith.[6]

A Dilemma? The puzzle these two pictures present to me is this: Why would Dakota people in southern Saskatchewan use books in their traditional *wakan wacipi* feasts which were not only written in unfamiliar syllabic characters and Cree dialects from northern regions, but were presenting themes from the Christian religion? When confronted with this (to me) apparent contradiction, Mniyo suggested that the Dakota then may have been struggling for their physical survival and therefore willing to turn to any source of supernatural assistance, and could have blended aspects or themes of the Christian religion into their traditional practice. Thus Ojibwa, Dakota, and Christian elements appear to have blended together in the religious life of this Dakota group.

I would welcome any assistance in further pursuing these questions.

References

Beveridge, Daniel, and Samuel Mniyo. "The *Wakan Wacipi* of the Dakota." In progress.

Goodvoice, Robert (Collector). Oral History of the Wahpeton Dakota. 1977. 3 informants. 17 tapes. 16 hours. Accession nos. R78–14, R80–611. In Saskatchewan Archives. Regina, SK.

Howard, James H. *The Canadian Sioux*. Lincoln: University of Nebraska Press, 1984.

———. "A Yanktonai Dakota Mide Bundle." *North Dakota History* 19 (1952): 133–39.

Mandelbaum, David G. *The Plains Cree*. Regina, SK: Canadian Plains Research Center, University of Regina. 1979, pp. 212, 313.

Skinner, Alanson B. *Medicine Ceremony of the Menomini, Iowa, and Wahpeton Dakota, with Notes on the Ceremony among the Ponca, Bungi Ojibwa, and Potawatomi Indians*. Indian Notes and Monographs. Vol. 4. New York: Museum of the American Indian, Heye Foundation, 1920.

Wallis, Wilson D. *The Canadian Dakota*. New York: American Museum of Natural History, 1947 (Anthropological Papers of the American Museum of Natural History, vol. 41, part 1; first published 1912).

Henry Two Bear: Transcriber of the Songs and Keeper of the Song Stick

COMMENTS BY SAMUEL MNIYO

[SM 1985] Henry Two Bear wrote this, it's in his writing! Two Bear was writing in the Yankton Sioux dialect, not in the *Isáŋti* Sioux dialect. . . . The songs he heard were in *Isáŋti*, but he wrote them in his dialect. [Sam is referring to the *Wakáŋ Waćípi* songs Henry had heard and written down, on nine pages in a notebook. Sam may have been referring to the orthographies or spelling systems of the two dialects. DB]

Henry Two Bear was born in Standing Rock, South Dakota. His mother was Yankton [*sic*] and his father was Teton [*sic*: see following]. His mother moved to Fort Totten, North Dakota, and he became a member of the Devil's Lake reservation. His name in the U.S.A. was Henry *Padána*. He went to Griswold, Manitoba [the Sioux Valley reserve], where he was a lay catechist in the Anglican Church.

He left there when he was discovered by two visitors from the U.S.A. [probably scouts for the U.S. government]—James *Kiŋyéwakaŋ* [of Sioux Valley] told me about this—and went to Round Plain reserve near Prince Albert.[7] He did not approach our reserve as being with the church, but brought two medicine bags and said, "My grandma and grandpa were members of the *Wakáŋ Waćípi*: I keep these." So he became an orphan of the *Wakáŋ Waćípi* society, and the members of the *Wakáŋ Waćípi* society accepted him: James Black, Chief *Tamah*, Baptiste, Iron Buffalo, John *Wadítaka*'s mother, Grey Horse, Spoon Maker, Willy Gunn, his mom and dad, John Sioux, and *Tahasota* (James Black's father-in-law), all the older people.[8] Henry Two Bear saw the feasts and singing connected with the *Wakáŋ Waćípi*, but not the complete ceremony itself, which involves the coughing up of shells or other small objects by those who are genuine members.

He died in March 1966 [at about age eighty-eight] at Round Plain. His daughter Florence was married to Joe Duquette from Sandy Lake reserve.

There were no members at Moose Woods (Whitecap reserve), since that reserve is mostly Sisseton Sioux. (Mniyo April 30, 1985)

[SM 1985. Sam talks about Henry Two Bear:] When people he was afraid of died, he, caught between two beliefs, Dakota and Christian, professed Christianity. He became an evangelist [for the Anglican Church]. He claims he was authorized to preach. Before Rev. Meek came [to Round Plain] he [Henry] held church for children (the adults ignored him). He was active in community work. Every spring and fall he held a *Wakáŋ Waćípi* feast. After 1957 when the Presbyterian Church was reestablished on Round Plain by Rev. W. W. Moore, Henry Two Bear was a regular attender of church. He never missed! (even if Anglican). He made parties in the winter (playing cards, singing songs, [relating] his experience. He was a real story teller. He never did religious education, preaching. (Mniyo July 29, 1985)

COMMENTS BY DANIEL M. BEVERIDGE

Robert Goodvoice says Henry Two Bear was born in 1878 and died on March 5 or 6, 1966, at age eighty-seven, but some other aspects of Henry Two Bear's background are difficult to verify. (Robert Goodvoice 3, 1977, 9)

Leo Omani claims, based on an archival document in Ottawa, that Henry Two Bear was Wahpeton, originally from Upper Sioux, Minnesota, who then moved with his family to the Wahpeton-Sisseton Reservation [North and South Dakota], where he received a land allotment in the 1880s, and who then moved to Fort Totten [Devil's Lake Reservation, North Dakota] and later to Wahpeton in Saskatchewan as a lay missionary (Omani, e-mail to DB, May 31, 2007).

Louis Garcia, honorary tribal historian for the Devil's Lake Sioux Tribe, asserts that Henry Two Bear (also named *Padáni Kúwapi*, Chase the Ree) was a member of the Devil's Lake Sioux Tribe, as were his parents. His father was *Mato Núŋpa* (Two Bear) and his mother was *Oyéhotewin* (Grey Track Woman). His paternal grandfather was *Mato Núŋpa* (Two Bear), the famous Yanktonai chief of the 1863 battle of Whitestone Hill (Garcia June 12, 1988, unpublished letter in bibliography). So almost certainly Henry's father was Yanktonai (living on the Yanktonai side of the Dev-

PHOTO 10. Henry Two Bear (left) and Herbert Buffalo in about 1964. Photo by Daniel M. Beveridge.

il's Lake reservation) and very probably Henry's mother was Wahpeton (coming from Granite Falls, Minnesota, the Upper Sioux reservation), but Garcia cautions that tribal affiliation may not be possible to ascertain (Garcia, e-mail to DB, June 2017).

My conclusion is that Henry Two Bear's father was Yanktonai and his mother was Wahpeton. Henry's grandpa and grandma, to whom Sam refers as members of the *Wakáŋ Waćípi* and from whom he received the two medicine bags including the song stick, were certainly his maternal grandparents and very likely Wahpetons from the Upper Sioux reservation. Henry stored the song stick wrapped in a reddish cloth in one of the bags.

The Henry Two Bear Song Stick or Song Board (*Wakáŋ Dowáŋpi*)

DANIEL M. BEVERIDGE

As mentioned in part 1, these song sticks or song boards were memory aids, inscribed not with words but with symbols or mnemonic representations of animals, people, arrows, etc. referring to the various songs, "which assisted the singer to remember the correct sequence of songs in the medicine dance. The picture merely suggested the subject matter of the song" (James Howard, letter to DB, April 19, 1967) to those particular singers. The singers would sing the songs on one side of the board, then the songs on the other side.

The figures or symbols on the Henry Two Bear song stick are arranged in a linear fashion along the edge or circumference of the board. I assume that singers would start at one end of the board at an incised line, work their way along the "bottom" edge, around the end, and back along the "top" to stop at another incised line.

I suspect that the songs in the following section may be the same songs that are indicated on the song stick featuring drawings of arrows flying in the air, buffalo/bison, and perhaps otter skin medicine bags, for example.

Another question is: where did this song board come from? The most likely answer is the Upper Sioux reservation. Although there were some Wahpeton living in the Upper Sioux area in the early 1800s, many more were moved there from villages along the lower Minnesota River after the 1851 Treaty of Traverse des Sioux. So it is possible that the song board came from *Mazámani* (Walking Iron) who was a Wahpeton chief and *Wakáŋ Waćípi* leader at Little Rapids (now Carver Rapids, a Wahpeton summer village on the lower Minnesota River near present-day Shakopee) and after 1851 at the *Mazámani* village near Lac qui Parle in the Upper Sioux Agency.[9]

The Songs of the *Wakáŋ Waćípi*

Introduction

DANIEL M. BEVERIDGE AND JURGITA ANTOINE

Here are the *Wakáŋ Waćípi* songs that were written down by Henry Two Bear and later typed and translated word-for-word by Samuel Mniyo. Recently, in preparation for this book, the Two Bear handwritten texts were reviewed and retranslated by Jurgita Antoine, resulting in some changes and more accurate interpretation.

Henry Two Bear, along with the *Wakáŋ Waćípi* song stick in his possession, kept a small notebook in which he wrote down nine pages of songs in 1911 or later. Mniyo says these were *Wakáŋ Waćípi* songs that Two Bear observed being used in the *Wakáŋ Waćípi* ceremonies held at Round Plain/Wahpeton, or at least those portions which he was permitted to observe, since he was not a full member. Two Bear used Riggs's orthography (1890). This notebook is now in the Henry Two Bear Papers, Provincial Archives of Saskatchewan, Regina. Selected scanned images of four of those nine pages are presented here, following the translation.

I assume that the main purpose of the songs was to guide the *Wakáŋ Waćípi* ceremony. In these songs we see references to the mystery of the rib (which relates to the origin myth and the *Uŋktéhi*), to the shooting of arrows (which relates to the "shooting" ceremony), and to the stone (a key element of Dakota creation stories).[10]

Mniyo viewed five black and white photographic prints of the nine pages, translated them into English, and typed them in April 1985. I, and later Louie Garcia, attempted to add a free translation of Mniyo's literal word-for-word translation into common English usage (word order in the Dakota language differs from that in English). More recently, in preparation for this book, Jurgita Antoine reviewed five newly scanned images of the original nine pages of handwritten texts, which at times are hard to read, and found inaccuracies that changed the meaning in places. The text that follows is her reading of them, transcribed using the modern orthography that is used throughout this manuscript. Her English translations, completed in consultation with elders, were kept as close as possible to the original Dakota expression and are interpreted in the context of traditional thought and philosophy.

We refer to the five scanned images as Songs image 1, 2, 3, etc. Following the translations we present Songs image 2, showing pages 2 and 3, and Songs image 4, showing pages 6 and 7.

Dakota songs are not descriptive, and therefore even fluent speakers find them hard to translate. The texts are stories condensed to a few details, which help the audience reconstruct the entire story. Since in small societies stories or community happenings are common knowledge to everyone, there was no need to tell the entire story every time: mentioning a few details was sufficient to bring out the memory of a certain event. This way the information also was protected from outsiders. Stories and teachings in their full form, however, were presented by the leaders or knowledge-keepers to members of societies such as *Wakáŋ Waćípi*, who had to go through a process to gain access to such information and who also accepted a responsibility to pass it down in the same way.

When we started working on the project, we did not know what those songs were, besides the fact that they were somehow connected to the *Wakáŋ Waćípi* society. Due to the method of composition described earlier, songs are best interpreted by the people who use them. In this case, since the ceremony has not been performed for a century, research was the main tool. Translation and analysis in the light of what we know about *Wakáŋ Waćípi* revealed that these songs are *Wakáŋ Waćípi* songs, directly referencing and empowering the actions performed by the participants of the ceremony. As such, they are the oldest known Dakota texts. Although their exact age still remains to be established, they must come from before the 1800s.

Dakota grammatical structures and punctuation present another challenge to translators. In Dakota sentences the object precedes the subject, and the adjective describing a noun follows that noun. Markers of evidentiality (e.g., *-do*, meaning an emphatic statement made by the speaker), or reportative action (*héya, keyé*, meaning that the information was passed on by another speaker) sometimes do not have any lexical meaning in English. Since the Dakota language developed as an oral language, these markers serve as punctuation marks.

Two Bear arranged the songs as short numbered verses. Most lines are repeated at least twice, which is indicated by the first letter of the line to be repeated. Thus, for example *W. W.* after the line means that the previous line in which the first word started with a *W* is repeated two more times. Also, some lines end (or reframe) with vocables that have no lexical meaning (e.g., *ha, he, ho*), which are not to be confused with the words *héya, keyé* or *eyá*, which mean "he said that" or "he said" and are common attributes to indicate reported speech in Dakota storytelling and songs. The last two pages of Two Bear's handwritten notes (Songs image 5) contain numbered Dakota phrases that seem to lack arrangement into song text units.[11] This transcription follows the line arrangement in the handwritten manuscript so as not to affect the structure of the songs.

In each song that follows, the translation is presented in a set of three lines for each verse, using different print styles or fonts:

first line: Henry Two Bear's Dakota text in modern transcription in italic font thus;
> second line: a word-for-word translation
> third line: a free translation into English

The Songs of the *Wakáŋ Waćípi* (*Wakaŋ Waćipi Odowaŋ*)

AS WRITTEN DOWN BY HENRY TWO BEAR AND
TRANSLATED BY JURGITA ANTOINE

Songs image 1 (page 1)

Waskuyeća wohaŋpi ća de ahiyayapi kta.
    Fruit / feast / when / this / they.sing / will /
    This will be sung at the Fruit Feast.

1

Maka amanimaye. M. M. M.
    Earth / I.walk /
    On this earth, I am walking.

Ṫataŋka maka oićaǵe ćiŋ he. M. M.
    Buffalo / earth / creature / the / that /
    The buffalo is the creature of the earth.

2

Ṫuŋkaŋ niye he? T.
    Stone / you / that /
    Stone, is that you?

Ṫuŋkaŋ wakuŋza niye he?
    Stone / cause / you / that /
    Are you stone, the cause of life?

T. T. He he he he heyahe.
    / that / he.said.that /
    He said that.

Ṫuŋkaŋ wakuŋza heyahe.
    Stone / cause / he.said.that /
    Stone, the cause of life, he said that.

T. T. he heya, eye.
    / that / he.said.that / he.said /
    He said that, he said.

3

Ṫuŋkaŋ uŋśimadaye. T.
  Stone / take.pity.on.me /
  Stone, take pity on me.

Ṫuŋkaŋ ċeĥpi maza eċeċa yuŋke ċik'uŋ. T. T.
  Stone / flesh / iron / like / lie / that-past t. /
  Stone with flesh like iron lay there.

Keya ċe. T. T. Keya ċe. T.
  He.said / so / he.said / so /
  He said so. T. T. He said so. T.

Ṫuŋkaŋ ċeĥpi maza eċeċa yuŋke ċik'uŋ.
  Stone / flesh / iron / like / lie / that—past t.
  Stone with flesh like iron lay there. T. T.

T. T. Keya ċe. T. T. Keya ċe. T.
  / he.said / so / he.said / so /
  He said so. He said so.

Songs image 2 (pages 2 and 3)

4

Tuwa niye he? T.
  Who / you / that /
  Who are you?

Ċeĥpi pejiĥuta niye he? T. T.
  Flesh / medicine / you / that /
  Is your flesh medicine?

Yani kta ċe.
  You.live / will / so /
  You will live.

Ċeĥpi pejiĥuta niye he?
  Flesh / medicine / you / that /
  Is your flesh medicine?

T. T. T. Yani kta će.
  / You.live / will / so /
  You will live.

5

Miye će. M.
  Me / that.is /
  That is me.

Wašićuŋ kiŋ ite waŋmayaŋka. M. M. M.
  Spirit / the / face / see.me /
  The spirit saw my face.

W. M. W. M. M. M. ha he he.

6

Wakaŋ W.
  Sacred /
  Sacred.

Ćuwi kiŋ dehaŋna mawakaŋye.
  Rib / the / now / me.sacred.became
  The rib now made me sacred.

Ć. Ć.

Ć. Ć. he heye.
  / that / he.said /
  He said that.

5, 6

Hena oya waskuyeća ćaŋpa k'a wajušteća ohaŋpi.
  Those / verse / fruit /chokecherry / and / strawberry / feast.
  Those verses (are for) the chokecherry and strawberry fruit feast.

7

Wiŋyaŋ peta wašićuŋ waŋ takuwaye.
  Woman / fire / spirit / a / I.am.related.to
  I am related to a fire spirit woman.

Waŋ kiŋ de waśteya ewakiyo ċe. W. W. W. W.
  Arrow / the / this / good / I.said / that /
  I said this arrow is good.

Waŋ kiŋ de waśteya ewakiyo ċe. W. W. W. W.
  Arrow / the / this / good / I.said / that /
  I said this arrow is good.

8
Kaŋ nu he. K.
  There / let.it.be.so / that /
  Right now!

Winyan de waduta waśteyada. K. K. K.
  Woman / this / scarlet / like /
  The woman likes scarlet.

W. K. K. K.

Songs image 3 (pages 4 and 5)

1
Wakaŋ wakaġe. W. W. W.
  Sacred / I.made /
  I made it sacred.

Nide pejiḣuta. W. W. W.
  Water / medicine /
  Water is medicine.

2
Wakaŋ de wakaġe. W. W. W. W. W.
  Sacred / this / I.made /
  I made this sacred.

Ṫa upi hotuŋ waŋ de wakaġe. W. W. W. W.
  Its / tail / roar / arrow / this / I made
  I made this arrow's tail feathers roar through the air.

3

De wakaŋ de waŋbdakedo he. D. D. D. D.
   This / sacred / this / I.saw / that /
   This is sacred, I saw that.

Mniyata waŋbdakedo he. D. D. D. D.
   Water.at / I.saw / that /
   I saw it in the water.

4

Den muŋkedo. Waŋmadake. D. D.
   Here / I.lie / saw.me.you /
   Here I lie. You saw me.

Pejiȟuta wakaŋ muŋkedo.
   Medicine / sacred / I.lie /
   Medicine is sacred. I lie.

D. D. ha he ha he ho.

5

Yuha imuŋke. Y. Y. Y. Y. Y. Y. Y.
   With / I.lay.down /
   I lay down with that.

Nide pejiȟuta. Y. Y. Y. Y. Y.
   Water / medicine /
   Water is medicine.

6

Eya namaȟ'uŋwo he. E. E. E. E. E. E.
   Also / hear.me / that /
   Hear me also.

Ṫuŋkaŋ de ṫataŋka eċeċa. E. E. E.
   Stone / this / buffalo / like /
   This stone is like buffalo.

7

De weċaġe, pejiḣuta de weċaġe. D. D. D.
   This / I.made.for.him / medicine / this / I.made.for.him /
   I made this for him, I made this medicine for him.

D. ha he ho.

8

Waŋ de weċaġe. W.
   Arrow / this / I.made.for.him /
   I made this arrow for him.

Haŋyetu weċaġe.
   Darkness / I.made.for.him /
   I made darkness for him.

W. W. W. Wakaŋ de weċaġe.
   / Sacred / this / I.made.for.him /
   I made this sacredness for him.

W. W. W. W. Wakaŋ de weċaġe.
   / Sacred / this / I.made.for.him /
   I made this sacredness for him.

Songs image 4 (pages 6 and 7)

9

Maka tiyopa M. oniye he mitawa.
   Earth / door / / life.breath / that / mine /
   The earth door, the breath of life is mine.

M. Mm. Mm. M.
M. Mm. ha he ho.

10

Maka tiyopa koda waowedo.
   Earth / door / friend / I.marked /
   Friend, I overcame the earth door.

M. M. heya, heyahe.
   / he.said / he.said.that /
   He said, he said that.

Ḱoda waowedo.
   Friend / I.marked /
   Friend, I overcame.

He taku iataŋka eċeċa waowedo.
   That / thing / buffalo / like / I.marked /
   I defeated the Buffalo-like being.

M. he he.

11
Wakaŋ yewaya nuŋwe. W.
   Sacred / I.send / so.it.be /
   I send this sacredness.

Waŋbdi śake maḣpiya okiŋ yewaya nuŋwe.
   Eagle / claw / sky / fly / I.send / so.it.be /
   I send the eagle claw flying across the sky.

Waŋbdi—
   / Eagle /
   Eagle—

W. W. W. W.

12
Waŋ de yewaye, heya.
   Arrow / this / I.send / he.said /
   I send this arrow, he said.

Waŋ de yewaye, heye.
   Arrow / this / I.send / he.said /
   I send this arrow, he said.

Waŋ de yewaye maḣpiya iataŋka heċekċeċa itoheya yewaye eyahe he.
   Arrow / this / I.send / sky / buffalo / that.like / toward / I.send /
   he.said.that / that /
   I send this arrow toward the one who is like buffalo through the
   sky, he said that.

Waŋ de yewaye, heya.
   Arrow / this / I.project / he.said
   I send this arrow, he said.

Waŋ de yewaye, maȟpiya, heye eye.
Arrow / this / I send / sky / he.said.that / he.said.
I send this arrow to the sky, he said that, he said.

Songs image 5 (pages 8 and 9)

1 *Waŋ kiŋyaŋ hiyaye.*
Arrow / flying / comes /
The arrow comes flying.

2 *Itazipa duta*
Bow / scarlet /
A scarlet bow.

3 *De kiŋyaŋ hiyaye.*
This / flying / comes /
This comes flying.

4 *Naǧi de howayuniye.*
Spirit / the / voice.I.send /
I'm sending the voice of my spirit.

5 *Waŋ de topakiya.*
Arrow / this / four.ways /
This arrow has four wings.

6 *Waŋ de kičamu wanuhe.*
Arrow / this / with.I.did / shell /
I countered the arrow with a shell.

1 *Ḱoda hečehna ešta nuŋwe.*
Friend / so / that.is.all / so.it.be /
Friend, so that's all, so be it.

2 *Eya de inaṗedo.*
Also / this / appeared /
He came back, too.

3 *Maḱa wečuŋ.*
Dirt / I.put.on /
I put on dirt.

4 *Ċio nuŋwe, dowaŋ nuŋwe.*
   I.shot.you / so.it.be / sing / so.it.be /
   I shot you, so be it, singing, so be it.

5 *Eya deċeċa muŋkedo.*
   Also / like.this / I.lay /
   I lay like this, too.

6 *Nide inaṗeya wakaŋhdi.*
   Water / appears / lightning /
   Lightning appears from water.

7 *Tuwe ihanmna?*
   Who / dream /
   Who had a vision?

8 *Wadowaŋ wakaŋye.*
   I.sing/ in.a.sacred.way /
   I sing in a sacred way.

9 *Waŋ de iyaṗaya.*
   Arrow / this / strike /
   The arrow strikes.

1 *Nide omaniyaŋ.*
   Water / he.walks /
   He walks in water.

2 *Tipi de topa hiyaye.*
   Lodge / this / four / it.went.by /
   It went by the lodge four times.

3 *Ḳoda mioyeta waśiċuŋ.*
   Friend / my.people / spirit.beings /
   Friend, the spirits are my people.

4 *E. E. wakaŋ wakaġe.*
   / sacred / I.made
   I made sacred.

5 *Hepaŋ de ċuwi wakanye.*
　　Second-born / this / rib / made.sacred /
　　The otter's rib became sacred.

6 *Ḳoda iyapi miyeċaġe.*
　　Friend / words / made.for.me /
　　My friend made my words.

7 *De waŋyaŋka t'a.*
　　This / see / die /
　　I saw this die.

8 *Ṫate uŋye.*
　　Wind / comes.up
　　The wind comes up.

1 *"Waṡte," eyedo.*
　　Good / he.said /
　　It is good, he said.

2 *Miye wowakaŋ waye.*
　　Me / sacredness / I.make /
　　I have the sacredness.

3 *Ḳoda miṫuŋwaŋ.*
　　Friend / my.sacred.power
　　Friend, my sacred power.

4 *Auŋpa mibeya.*
　　Smoke / encircle /
　　Smoke encircles.

5 *Maċuwi de.*
　　My.rib / this /
　　This is my rib.

The Songs: As written down by Henry Two Bear

Songs images 2 and 4 are shown in Photos 11 and 12.

James Black, Keeper of the Notebooks, and the Last *Wakáŋ Waćípi* Ceremony

SAMUEL MNIYO

[SM 1985] James Black (Jim Sapa) was the owner or custodian of the two song books [notebooks]. He was the maternal grandfather of Harry Buffalo.[12] James Black lived at Round Plain reserve and later at Moose Woods reserve. He was a member of the *Wakáŋ Waćípi*. He showed me the two books and was the last person who told me about the *Wakáŋ Waćípi*. This was in December 1951 when the last *Wakáŋ Waćípi* ceremony was held: it was at Charlie Hawk's at Moose Woods.[13] The ceremony was not a complete *Wakáŋ Waćípi* dance but a *Wakáŋ Waćípi* feast. The reason for it was this: my dad's brother Bill Buffalo had died in March 1950 and had some medicine bags. Dad wanted to throw them away but Bill's son Pete Buffalo wanted to keep them. One *Wakáŋ Waćípi* member was still living who was authorized to open and repack the medicine bags: James Black. It was a day or so before that feast that James Black took out the books and was reading them. "I'd like to learn how you read them," I said. "Okay, later on," he said, but he died and never had a chance to show me.

James Black was a Yankton Sioux [more likely Yanktonai Sioux. DB] He came to Minnesota and grew up there. He moved to the Sioux camp at Little Red River (near Prince Albert) between 1900 and 1910 and became a member of the *Wakáŋ Waćípi* with the Wahpeton Sioux. Before his wife died he had one daughter, Jane, who was born and raised at the Sioux Camp (now I.R. 94B, the Little Red River site). He went on to nearby Round Plain where he was a member of our reserve (I.R. 94A) until 1938. Then he moved to Moose Woods [Whitecap] reserve. [His daughter Jane and grandson Harry moved and settled there also. DB]

When James Black died, about 1954 or 1955, his daughter Jane had the books. She was my mother's maternal cousin. She first married my uncle Fred Buffalo and was the mother of both Harry Buffalo and Annie, who married Bob Royal. [Harry Buffalo's daughter Mavis Olson recalls both her grandmother Jane and her great-grandfather James Black at Moose Woods/Whitecap (Olson, telephone conversation with DB, July 12, 2005). Black lived near her home when she was a child. DB]

The last time the complete ceremony of the *Wakáŋ Waćípi* dance (generally an annual celebration) was held in Saskatchewan was in 1921 (Ernest Goodvoice told me). It was near the Prince Albert Sanatorium, not far from the Little Red River site [the 94B location]. (At a later date the RCMP came early one morning and chased all those still living there outside the reserve to the Round Plain reserve, the 94A location).

The last time the complete *Wakáŋ Waćípi* ceremony was held in North America was in 1934, at the Sioux Village near Portage la Prairie, Manitoba. James Black was there and participated (this was when he was still living at Round Plain).[14] Also from Round Plain were Willie Gunn and his wife, Alex Swifthawk, Littlemoose, Chief Tama, and other members, and Ernie Goodvoice, who was not a member. Henry Two Bear told Ernest Goodvoice that he regretted that he (Henry) did not attend that last complete ceremony. Alex Sutherland of Pipestone, Manitoba, took his mother and father there. Over twenty members of the *Wakáŋ Waćípi* were left, but they knew that would be the last *Wakáŋ Waćípi* because there were no new members.

The same as at Prince Albert they had the *wamnúǵa* (white shell) made of feathered prairie chicken downs, made oblong or egg-shaped, used to prove the members, their identity as *Wakáŋ Waćípi* members year to year. [This was referred to as "*wahmnoo-hah* — shell in the throat" — by Skinner (1920, 291) DB]. From the finest down feathers, take the stem off and roll the feathers into a ball-like bead, put on the tip of the tongue, swallow; come back, must bring it out so people will see it. Alex Sutherland's mother was afraid hers would not come out, since it was before World War I the last time she had brought it out, and [she] had not observed the ceremony every year.

James Black had the same feeling, but he brought it out, then someone put it on his tongue, he took it down, and the next day he coughed it out, I don't know where it goes. In 1951 he told me, '"I went up there [to Portage la Prairie] in 1934, over ten years later, I went with doubt, maybe I'll make a fool of myself! I told my story, testimony, why they joined in, what is their hope, how they're working on their hope. I tried it. Suddenly my whole body felt different, so warm, calm, relaxed. Then I felt something on my tongue, I held that like something dropped it! I was surprised, and so glad. Then those guys took a pan of live coals, incense (like sweetgrass, but powder), put it over it, gave it back to me, and I took

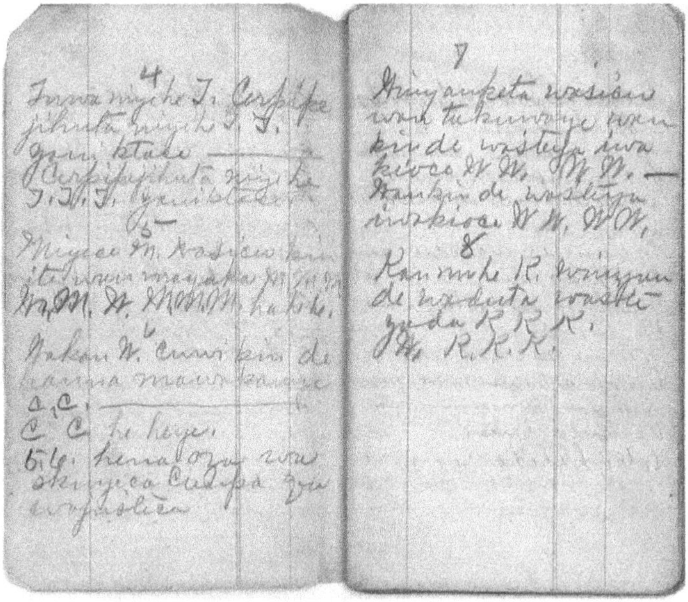

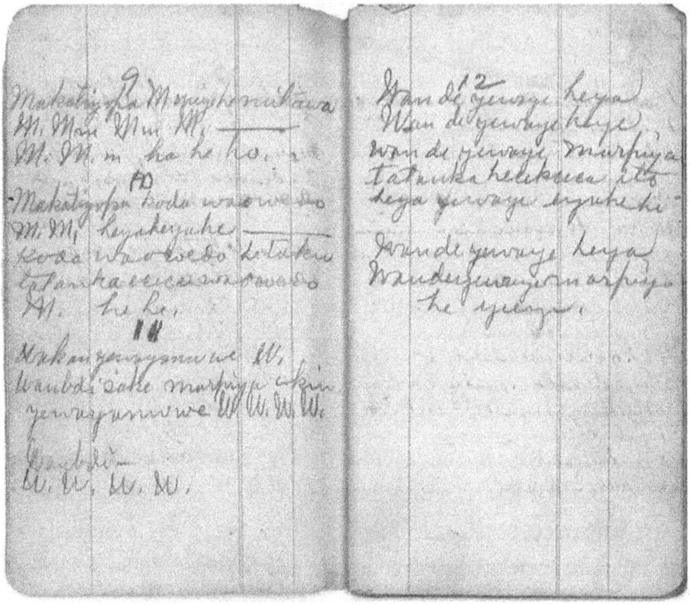

PHOTOS 11 AND 12. Henry Two Bear song book, songs image 2 showing pages 2 and 3 (with songs 4–8 in the first group of songs) and songs image 4 showing pages 6 and 7 (with songs 9–12 in the second group of songs). Courtesy Eric Bird and the Provincial Archives of Saskatchewan, Songs R_625_5.1c.

it back down (swallowed). Since then, 1934, I never had a chance to bring it out again" (Mniyo May 1, 1985).

[James Black is almost certainly the person Sam is referring to in describing the *Wakáŋ Wačípi* to James Howard in 1972:

A man from Round Plain told Sam Buffalo that when he joined the Medicine Dance in 1914 the leaders lectured to him for an entire day about the teachings of the order. Finally, they asked him to swallow the "medicine arrow" in order to protect himself against projectiles shot at him in the ceremony to follow. In this case the medicine arrow was some down from a prairie chicken rolled into a tiny ball. In Santee belief this would gradually change into a shell. (Howard 1984, 135)]

[SM 1987] James Black prayed, lots, coughed, out it came, surprised him, in 1934, what he had swallowed before 1919! "I managed; none of us failed," he said. James Black told me in 1951 about 1934, "Then in the afternoon, had to make the bag come alive, didn't know whether was going to or not! Older men took lead, all came alive, one had bird, was flying, made round. Then my bag came alive! Gives joy of accomplishment which remains with you for whole year, feel proud and strong and connected to some mysterious power. When all finished, they'd start shooting each other."

[The medicine bag], one made out of otter skin, with eyes, with its head and legs stuffed, [would] become alive in the real *Wakáŋ Wačípi* ceremony. In the body were medicine and songs important in the Holy Dance. . . . Up to James Black's time, animal hide [medicine] bags (*juwa čaŋdó*) were used. Every member was supposed to make it come alive, annually. If one couldn't do it, became outcast, expelled. (Mniyo January 1987, edited by DB)[15]

[SM 1985] There were Saulteaux who attended that last ceremony, joined in, and even became members. They taught the Sioux members songs on how to make the ceremony, and the Sioux taught them songs on how to make the ceremony. In the Sioux tradition there are two days ceremony and then two days lectures or teaching to new members. James Black spoke there two days as one of the teachers. He told them the history and how the ancestors prayed to God. Perhaps the Sioux were the only plains Indians whose ancestors prayed to God as *Ajúhowa* (creative voice being). Another teacher spoke also. They exchanged medicines with the lectures. The Saulteaux made a feast (they butchered a steer or cow) and told them this is our prayer meeting so it would be good to put something of theirs into the *Wakáŋ Waćípi* religion. So they taught the songs to the Sioux, put them into song books, and taught them how to read and pronounce.

After at Round Plain Willie Gunn's wife took a black book and sang two songs at the *wakáŋ wóhaŋ* (*wakáŋ* = holy, *wóhaŋ* = feast), the monthly or seasonal feast relating to the *Wakáŋ Waćípi*. The words she sang were Saulteaux words that she learned at Portage la Prairie. . . . A new group needs twelve members, so there must have been more than twelve Saulteaux there. (Mniyo April 30/May 1, 1985)

The Pictographic Notebooks of James Black (Jim Sapa)

DANIEL M. BEVERIDGE

Introduction

Sometime early in the twentieth century an artist drew forty-five vivid colored images in two small notebooks: thirty-three in one and twelve in the other. I refer to them as the Jim Sapa notebooks because Jim Sapa's name is written on the first page of one of the notebooks and because the notebooks were in Jim Sapa's possession until his death about 1953. It is probable that he was the artist of the images in both notebooks. Most of the images include many subjects: persons, mammals, plants, tipis, horned creatures, arrows, guns, wavy lines, and unidentifiable objects. Two other signatures appear later in the same book in which Jim Sapa's name appears: J. A. McKay (or J. S. McKay) and Dan Melvin.

Twelve of the images are accompanied on the same page by statements written in Cree syllabics. Several of the Cree statements refer to Jesus. Dr. Arok Wolvengrey is a Cree scholar and linguist at the First Nations University of Canada in Regina. After translating all these syllabics, his conclusion is that these sentences written in Cree syllabics have nothing to do with the images but appear to have been written later. They are possibly an attempt to practice or repeat a Christian catechism, using any available paper at a time when paper was scarce. He concludes that with the exception of one page, 5A, the first page on which the syllabics appear, which seemed to have words possibly referring to the four drawings, "the rest have nothing to do with the diagrams" (Wolvengrey, e-mail to DB, June 14, 2013).

Although the connection of the two notebooks with this book may not be immediately obvious, we include them here because Sam was certain that they were used, and used by Jim Sapa, in the *Wakáŋ Wačípi* ceremonies in Saskatchewan.

The meaning, purpose, and use of the images and their connection with the *Wakáŋ Wačípi* remain unclear. One possibility is that the images serve as mnemonic aids to the singers, like those on the song stick, although most of the images are more complex scenes, often depicting several humans, creatures, and other objects. Another possibility is that the images depict events in the history of the Dakota people, such as is done in winter counts. But these images are more complex than winter counts, which typically show one simple picture or diagram for each winter or year, with these pictures arranged in a spiral, and where each picture indicates an event widely understood to represent that year. Two examples of Dakota winter counts are those of Lone Dog, a Yanktonai, and Battiste Good, a Sičaŋǧu Lakota who lived in the mid-1800s (Mallery 1972, 266 ff.). Although arrows are shown frequently in winter counts, they are often associated with killing of or by people of neighboring tribes, something not obvious in these Sapa pictographs.

The twelve black and white images that follow are samples of the forty-five color images in the two notebooks. The smaller notebook with the reddish cover (which I refer to as notebook A) has thirty-three images, and the larger notebook with the black cover (which I refer to as notebook B) has twelve images. I placed page markers in the photos: markers 1A, 2A, etc. to indicate pages from book A, while markers 1, 2, etc. indicate pages from book B. Some markers appear to be upside down because they were placed so the syllabics on the facing page would be right side up.

The Images

The twelve images follow in Photos 13, 14, and 15.

Postscript

DANIEL M. BEVERIDGE

Although the celebration of the full *Wakáŋ Wačípi* ceremony came to an end in 1934, and the *Wakáŋ Wačípi* feast in 1951, as Sam has described, another lingering influence was reported in the 1960s at Round Plain: a form of the Ghost Dance called New Tidings. It incorporated aspects of the traditional Dakota *Wakáŋ Wačípi*.[16] This note marks the end of our story of the Red Road and *Wakáŋ Wačípi* of the Dakota.

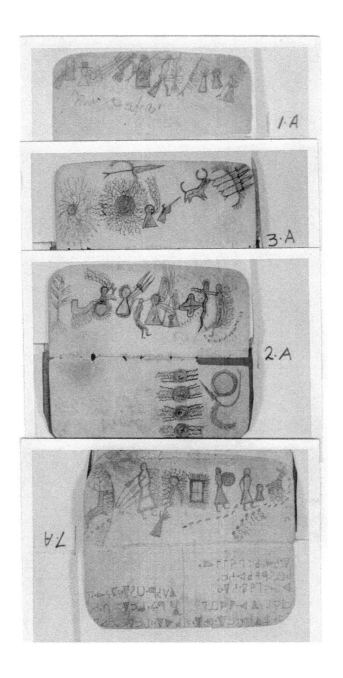

PHOTO 13. Jim Sapa notebook pictographs 1A, 3A, 2A, 7A.
Photos by Daniel M. Beveridge.

PHOTO 14. Jim Sapa notebook pictographs 8A, 11, 13, 14.
Photos by Daniel M. Beveridge.

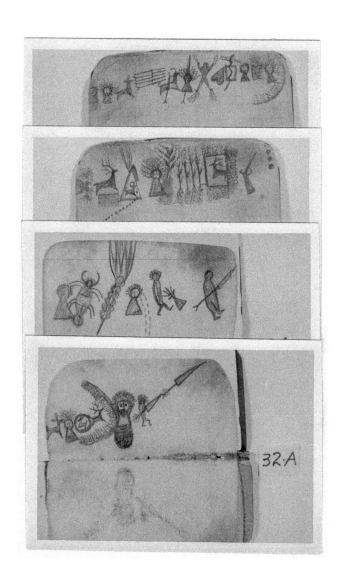

PHOTO 15. Jim Sapa notebook pictographs 10A, 24A, 29A, 32A.
Photos by Daniel M. Beveridge.

Appendix 1

Santee (Eastern Sioux) History Timeline

(Sources: DeMallie 2001b, 718–60; Elias 1988, chapter 1; Danyluk et al. 2016; and others)

Pre-contact Period

Unknown, various theories including origin on Atlantic seaboard and movement westward

Mille Lacs and Upper Mississippi R. Period: 1640 to 1700

1640	First mention of Sioux by Europeans, the French explorer Jean Nicollet and the Jesuit Le Jeune, in the *Jesuit Relations* (cited in McGee 1897, 189–90); for the next century, they lived in an area stretching from Mille Lacs Lake in Minnesota west to Missouri R.
mid-1600s	Ojibwa began moving west from Sault Sainte Marie, transforming into a more tightly structured political system; *Midewiwin* or Medicine Lodge developed and served to integrate Ojibwa bands into a religious and social network
mid-1600s	Easternmost Dakota bands made peace with Ojibwa (who served as trade middlemen with French), in time Sioux adopted Medicine Lodge
1660	Dakota visited by Radisson and Groselliers, Dakota said they wanted to trade for guns, etc.
1670	Hudson's Bay Company receives charter from British crown to trade in Rupert's Land (Hudson's Bay watershed including Red River of the North)
1680	Father Louis Hennepin was captured and taken by the Mdewakanton Dakota to their village near the mouth of the Rum River on Mille Lacs Lake (east of the upper Mississippi R.) in present-day Minnesota; rescued by Duluth (Elias 1988, 5)

| 1686 | Perrot built first French trading post for Dakota at Lake Pepin (on Mississippi R. downstream from present-day Minneapolis); Le Sueur and others continued trade until 1696, Dakota conflict with Ojibwa increased |
| 1697 | Le Sueur counted twenty-two Sioux villages, half on each side of the Mississippi R. |

West of Mississippi R. Period: 1760s to 1851

1700s	All Dakota divisions shifted their territory westward: pushed by better-armed Ojibwa, pulled by westward-receding buffalo herds, pulled by traders
mid-1700s	Santee abandoned Mille Lacs region: Mdewakanton moved villages to Mississippi R. and lower Minnesota R., Wahpekute were south and west (Cannon R. and Traverse des Sioux), most Wahpeton went farther west up the Minnesota R. (until by 1800 most joined Sisseton), Sisseton went farther up Minnesota R. to Big Stone Lake and Lake Traverse and prairies west; locations remained relatively stable from 1760s until 1851 treaties
1736	Most Dakota lived west of Mississippi R.
1742	French Governor Beauharnois pledges support to Dakota Nation
1756–1763	Dakota assist British against French in Seven Years War
1763	British gained control of North America French territories east of the Mississippi by Treaty of Paris; territory west of Mississippi ceded to Spain
1763	Royal Proclamation by King George III protects all First Nations land west of the Appalachian Mountains and east of the Mississippi River from settlement
1764	Council of Niagara: Twenty-four First Nations including Dakota affirm alliance with British Crown through Nation-to-Nation Agreement
1774	Yankton and Teton on prairies had many horses
1775–1783	Dakota Chief Wabasha and others supported British in war against Americans (American War of Independence), received medals; British lost much eastern territory to Americans

1783	Smallpox epidemic in northern plains wipes out over 90 percent of Dakota population
1787	Michilimackinac Treaty of peace and friendship, first written treaty signed between Dakota (all seven groups) and British Crown, renewing bonds of Dakota-Crown alliance
1803	Americans gained much (French) western territory by Louisiana Purchase (Mississippi-Missouri watershed west of Mississippi River)
1812–1813	Santee supported British in War of 1812 against the Americans
1814	Treaty of Ghent ends War of 1812
1815–1816	Treaties of "peace and friendship" were forced upon the Santee by the Americans and signed by the Mdewakanton, Wahpeton, and Wahpekute, providing for the admission of whites to the Dakota lands
1818	The 49th parallel became the southern boundary of Rupert's Land, referred to as the "medicine line," placing most of the Red River watershed (including much of the Dakota traditional territory) in the United States rather than in British North America; Canada-United States boundary marked later, in 1873
1823	Santee still had few horses, some used dogs for transport, horses still remained scarce
1830s	Buffalo herds dwindling, white settlement growing, food resources scarcer
1834	Christian Protestant missionaries began work among Dakota, introducing them to Christianity, focusing on education; they translated Bible, wrote the Dakota language, began schools; Congregational missionaries Samuel W. Pond and Gideon H. Pond devised an orthography for writing the Dakota language; Presbyterians Thomas S. Williamson and Stephen R. Riggs settled at Lac qui Parle on Minnesota R., wrote dictionaries

Treaty and Reservation Period: 1851–1862

1830 Santee signed the Treaty of Prairie du Chien, Treaty of 1837 ceded all their territory east of the Mississippi R.

1830s and 1840s White settlement pressed, wild game became scarce, trade goods prices inflated, much of treaty funding paid to traders, destitution and hunger common, even starvation

1851 Through Treaty of Traverse des Sioux (with the Sisseton and Wahpeton) and Treaty of Mendota (with the Mdewakanton and Wahpekute), Santee ceded all their remaining land in Minnesota and some land in present South Dakota and northern Iowa; were to receive financial compensation and a small, narrow reservation (Lower Sioux Agency near Redwood Falls and Upper Sioux Agency near Granite Falls) along the upper Minnesota R. where they were forced to live while farmers flooded in around them

1858 Reservation conditions worsened; embitterment grew from delays in annuity fund payment and siphoning of these monies to pay traders' debts

Dakota War of 1862 and Aftermath

1862 Frustration and anger drove some Santee (mostly Mdewakanton and Wahpekute) to erupt into violence in western Minnesota, pillage white settlements, and kill hundreds (400–700?); American military forces broke Dakota offensive, retaliated against all Santee; thirty-eight Dakota were hanged at Mankato; many Dakota died from disease and starvation (as prisoners or fleeing to escape capture)

1863 U.S.A. abrogated its treaty obligations to Santee (including reservations), most remaining Santee were exiled and removed from Minnesota to sites in Nebraska and South Dakota (Crow Creek, Santee, and Flandreau reservations)

1867 Some Santee (of the majority of Santee who escaped capture after 1862) signed treaty leading to formation of Devil's Lake (now Spirit Lake) Reservation in North Dakota and Lake Traverse (Sisseton) Reservation in South Dakota

1862–1863	First of several bands of survivors moved across the "medicine line" and arrived at Fort Garry (present-day Winnipeg, Manitoba, Canada)
1862–1864	After spending time at Devil's Lake or on both sides of the boundary, Dakota bands came north, some to Fort Garry, some moved on to Poplar Point, and some went farther west to Portage la Prairie, Turtle Mountain, Fort Ellice (all in present-day Manitoba) and Moose Mountain (in present-day Saskatchewan).
1860s and 1870s	Many Santees fled north to Canada and remained, others stayed close to Canada boundary in present-day North Dakota and Montana while buffalo remained, or in northern Minnesota; all were granted reserves in present-day Manitoba (Sioux Valley/Oak River and Birdtail in 1873; Oak Lake in 1878; Portage la Prairie in 1898) and present-day Saskatchewan (Standing Buffalo in 1877, White Cap/Moose Woods in 1881, and Wahpeton/ Round Plain in 1894)
1867	Dominion of Canada is formed of British North America
1869–1870	Hudson's Bay Company sold Rupert's Land and transferred North-Western Territory to Dominion of Canada without consulting inhabitants (Indians, Metis, and Europeans)
1869–1870	Red River Resistance/Rebellion by Metis of Fort Garry (now Winnipeg), Manitoba
1870	Manitoba and Northwest Territories formed in Canada
1871	Bison (buffalo) begin to disappear, almost all gone by end of 1870s in Canada
1873	Survey of U.S.A.-Canada international boundary (49th parallel); cairn markers
1873	Canada government established Royal North-West Mounted Police
1874	Royal North-West Mounted Police trek from Fort Dufferin, Manitoba, to Fort McLeod (present-day Alberta)
1874	Treaty 4 signed in Canada (Fort Qu'Appelle, Saskatchewan)

1876	Treaty 6 signed in Canada (Fort Carlton and Fort Pitt, Saskatchewan)
1876	Indian Act passed in Canada
1876	Battle of the Little Bighorn and Custer's defeat by the Teton who then fled to Canada, some to Prince Albert, Saskatchewan area
1877–1878	A band of about twenty lodges led by Chief *Húpa Iyáhpeya* (a descendant of Flying Thunder), which had remained near the international boundary on the American side in the woodlands of northern Minnesota and North Dakota until 1877, headed for Portage la Prairie and then moved to Prince Albert upon the advice of James McKay, who had been their trader in the northern states; they were Mdewakanton and Wahpeton
1879	Another band, mainly Sisseton, arrived in the Prince Albert area under the leadership of *Bdo*, who was a headman and a son of Chief Whitecap
1879	Another band, who were Wahpeton, led by the Chief *Ahíyaŋke*, arrived in the Prince Albert area from the Fort Ellice area (near the Saskatchewan-Manitoba border)
1883	The Canadian Pacific Railway reached Regina from Winnipeg and soon became transcontinental
1885	North-West Resistance (or Second Riel Rebellion) in Saskatchewan
1890	Band one, living near the mouth of the Little Red River just northeast of Prince Albert, among whom the Presbyterians had commenced a school, made a request for a reserve
1891	Band two expressed interest in obtaining a reserve near the Shell River northwest of Prince Albert
1894	Reserve I.R. 94A (Round Plain) was granted to band two; additional land was confirmed in 1963.
2018	Framework agreement for a Whitecap Dakota treaty to advance Dakota reconciliation was signed between WDFN and Government of Canada (accessible at http://whitecapdakota.com/wp-content/uploads/2018/01/WDFN-Treaty-Framework-1.pdf, retrieved April 15, 2019)

Appendix 2

Family History and Family Tree of Sam Buffalo

DRAWN BY DANIEL M. AND DANNY BEVERIDGE

This diagrammed family tree of Sam Buffalo/Samuel Mniyo is presented as originally prepared, mainly from information that Sam provided, without the italics and diacritics later applied for Dakota names elsewhere in the book. Most notable, and shown in bolder boxes in the tree, are the close relationships of the four key contributors to this cultural preservation initiative. The notes that follow include more information, including that obtained from Louis Garcia (personal correspondence, July 19, 1987), Leo Omani (personal e-mail correspondence, May 27, 2007), and several other sources, and not confirmed with Sam. With this numbering system each person's number includes the number of one parent (normally the father) and indicates the generation by the number of digits.

Samuel Buffalo Family Tree: Paternal Side

Generation One (Sam's paternal great-grandparents)

1. *Wapáhaska* (Chief Whitecap, Chief White Warbonnet, Sam's father's father's father), son of *Tióde* (who was a blind man who raised fast horses), was a Sisseton born about 1840 and raised in buffalo culture. He left behind his brick house and many horses at Sisseton, South Dakota; became nomadic, ranging near the border between the Souris River and Cypress Hills, his last buffalo hunt in 1879; and secured a reserve for his band at Moose Woods (Whitecap). He died in 1889. Children of *Wapáhaska*:

    1.1 **Bdo**

        1.2 Yankee Whitecap (not to be confused with *Ahíyaŋke*, chief of a Wahpeton band that settled at Prince Albert about 1879)

        1.3 Mary Whitecap

        1.4 Maggie

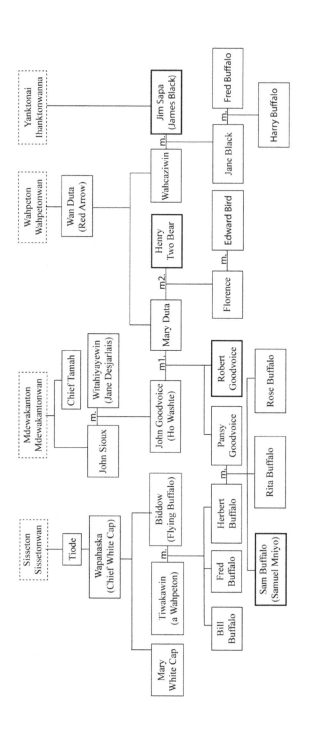

Drawn by Daniel M. Beveridge, Danny Beveridge, and Molly Seaton-Fast.

[1.5 Thomas *Ćapkté* (Beaver Trap, Kills-the-Beaver) youngest brother of *Bdo*? Granduncle of Sam, lived at Devil's Lake, North Dakota]

Generation Two (Sam's paternal grandparents)

1.1 **Bdo** (*Bedow, Biddow* or *Mdo*, potato, Flying Buffalo, Sam's father's father), a Sisseton, was a headman and son of *Wapáhaska*. His first wife was **Tiwakawin**, a Wahpeton of Sioux Valley; his second wife was *Taté Waśté* (Goodwind), a Wahpeton; they lived at Wahpeton I.R. 94A.

Children of *Bdo* and *Tiwákawiŋ*:

    1.11 **Herbert Flying Buffalo**

    1.12 Bill Buffalo

    1.13 Fred Buffalo

    1.14 Maggie Flying Buffalo

    1.15 Eva

    1.16 Agnes

    1.17 Victoria

    1.18 Annie

    1.19 Salome

    1.20 Cathleen?

1.2 Yankee Whitecap (possibly *Ihanki* or *Iyanki*?)

1.3 Mary Whitecap, daughter of *Wapáhaska*, married Charles Red Eagle (a Yankton or Yanktonai). Children:

    1.31 Bill Eagle

    1.32 Archie Eagle

1.4 Maggie, daughter of *Wapáhaska*

2.1 *Tiwákawiŋ* (Wahpeton, wife of *Bdo*; no information on parents or siblings)

Generation Three (Sam's parents)

1.11 **Herbert Flying Buffalo** (Sam's father), born about 1890; married **Ho Waśté** (**Pansy Goodvoice**), a Wahpeton who was sister of Robert Goodvoice; died after 1960s (1971?), lived at Wahpeton. Children:

    1.111 Rose Buffalo

    1.112 **Samuel Buffalo** (later Samuel Mniyo)

1.113 Rita Buffalo

(others died young)

1.12 Bill Buffalo, married Lizzie Hawk

1.13 Fred Buffalo, married Jane Black (daughter of James Black). Children:

> 1.131 Harry Buffalo, born 1918, died after 1970
>
> 1.132 Annie, married Bob Royal, lived at Whitecap

1.14 Maggie Flying Buffalo, married John *Wadítaka*, lived at Wahpeton.

Children:

> 1.141 Ruth (married Lawrence Eyapaise, lived at Beardy's)
>
> 1.142 Archie *Wadítaka* (married Edith Eyapaise, lived at Wahpeton)

1.15 Eva, married Charlie Hawk, lived at Whitecap

1.16 Agnes

1.17 Victoria, married John Royal, lived at Whitecap

1.18 Annie, married William Littlecrow

1.19 Salome (*Maȟpiya Waštéwiŋ*), married Cook Ironsides. Children: Mary, who married Tom Standing

Samuel Buffalo Family Tree: Maternal Side

Generation One (Sam's maternal great-grandparents)

3. *Waŋdúta*/**Red Arrow/Scarlet Arrow** (Wahpeton? of Sioux Valley) married a "Sioux woman" from Louisiana or lower Mississippi River whose mother was a French girl. He had a log house and chickens; nomadic life was over (Sam's mother's mother's parents). Children:

> 3.1 Mary Duta, married (1) *Ho Wašté* (John Goodvoice), (2) Henry Two Bear
>
> 3.2 *Wahčáziwiŋ*, was wife of James Sapa (Black)

4. **John Sioux**/*Aŋpétu Wašíčuŋ* (Sam's mother's father's father), Mdewakanton, oldest brother of seven, with Chief Tama being the youngest. Married **Witahiyayewin/Jane Desjarlais** (Sam's mother's father's mother), Wahpeton. Children:

4.1 *Hupehan*/Willie Gunn

4.2 *Mahpeya* Omani/Walking Cloud/Joe Omani

4.3 *Ho Waśte* (John Goodvoice)

Generation Two (Sam's maternal grandparents)

4.3 **Ho Waśté** (*Máza Ho Waśténa* = Iron Goodvoice, John Goodvoice, Sam's mother's father), married 3.1 **Mary Duta** (also named *Iwakanwin*) (Sam's mother's mother), daughter of *Waŋdúta*/Red Arrow (they later separated and she married Henry Two Bear). Children with *Ho Waśté*:

4.11 *Ho Waśté* (Pansy Goodvoice)

4.12 Robert Goodvoice

4.13 Ernest Goodvoice

4.14 *Wakáŋ Máni Wiŋ Péta Ehuake*

3.1 Mary Duta. Children with Henry Two Bear:

3.11 George

3.12 Florence, who married (1) Edward Bird, and (2) Joe Duquette

3.13 Paul Isaac

3.2 *Wahčáziwiŋ* married James Sapa (Black). Child:

3.21 Jane Black, married Fred Buffalo (see 1.13)

Generation Three (Sam's parents)

4.11 **Pansy Goodvoice** (*Ho Waśté*, also named *Kimámaziwin* = Yellow Butterfly Woman, Sam's mother), married **Herbert Buffalo** (see 1.11)

4.12 Robert Goodvoice. Children:

4.121 Ed Goodvoice

4.122 Leo Goodvoice

4.13 Ernest Goodvoice

4.131 Maurice Goodvoice

Appendix 3

Biographical Sketches

Jurgita Antoine (b. 1975)

A field linguist and anthropologist, Jurgita Antoine has worked with indigenous organizations and educational institutions in the Plains region for twenty years. She holds a PhD in anthropology from the University of Oklahoma. As an ethnographer, she worked in Cultural Resource Management on northern Plains. At Sinte Gleska University, she worked with elders on translations of Lakota songs and on Don Moccasin's oral history collection. She directed the Lakota Documentaries project at Sinte Gleska University for seven years.

She is fluent in three languages and has working knowledge of seven more. She is the recipient of grants and awards from the American Philosophical Society, South Dakota Humanities Council, and Altrusa International, Inc., but her most important award received is the teachings of Lakota elders. Her research focuses on language revitalization, translation, and Siouan languages.

Lucy Baker (1836–1909)

Born in Summertown, Glengarry County, Ontario, Lucy Baker moved to Prince Albert in 1878 as a missionary teacher for the Presbyterian Church in Canada—two years after Custer's battle and the influx of "Sitting Bull Sioux." In 1885 she nursed the wounded from the North-West Rebellion. She relocated as a teacher in 1890 to Round Plain reserve, where she had a school and church built. After she retired she left Prince Albert in 1907 for Montreal, where she died. For more see the Provincial Archives of Saskatchewan (PAS) exhibit Documenting the Dakota (https://www.saskarchives.com/Dakota_Lucy_Baker).

Daniel M. Beveridge (b. 1938)

Dan Beveridge was born and raised in rural Saskatchewan, where his father was a United Church of Canada minister. Dan went to the University of Saskatchewan and studied the four Dakota and Lakota communities in Saskatchewan as part of his MA in sociology (1965). Later he received a PhD at the University of Wisconsin–Madison. His major education was a one-year hitch-hiking trip around the world at age twenty-one.

For two years (1962–1964) Dan served as United Church student lay minister at Moose Woods Indian Reserve (now Whitecap Dakota First Nation). He led Sunday worship, social events, etc., some with Saskatoon youth groups. He engaged with Sam Buffalo in a project (1965–1966) cutting and selling jack pine poles for corral rails in Saskatchewan and Montana.

Dan worked as an educator at a co-operative college, at a community development center in Africa (Congo/Zaire), in university extension, and in university teaching (Faculty of Education). He retired in 2003 after thirty-one years at the University of Regina and is a regular guest lecturer in Dakota history class in the First Nations University of Canada.

His family background is that of a Canadian settler of British ancestry. His grandparents came to present Manitoba and Saskatchewan from Ontario as homesteaders in the 1870s and 1880s, and his parents were born and raised in rural Saskatchewan.

James Black/Jim Sapa (1867–1953)

A Yankton or Yanktonai Dakota, James Black was born in the United States and grew up in Minnesota. He moved to the Little Red River "Sioux Camp" (I.R. 94B) between 1900 and 1910. He married *Wahčaziwiŋ* (daughter of *Waŋdúta*/Red Arrow, and maternal aunt of Sam Mniyo's mother); *Waŋdúta* was also called *Ṫawásuwota* (Mniyo 1985). Their child was Jane Black, who grew up there. Black became a *Čaŋdójuha Yuhá* (principal member) there of the *Wakáŋ Waćípi* society, the Red Path.

He moved to Round Plain (I.R. 94A) and lived there as a member of that reserve until 1938, when he moved to Whitecap (Moose Woods; Mniyo 1985). There he lived there in a small house near Harry Buffalo's; he died there in 1953. Sam Buffalo learned much from Black's traditional teachings.

Black had land or entitlement in the U.S.A. (South Dakota?) through his father *Wasúsnakena*, who had come to Canada earlier, returned to the United States, received a quarter section, and died in 1913 or 1914, leaving the land to his son (see Robert Goodvoice 5, 1977, 4). Black's daughter Jane Black married Fred Buffalo, Sam Mniyo's paternal uncle; their children were Harry Buffalo (1918–1978) and Annie Royal (Mniyo 1985).

Herbert Buffalo (1890–1971)

Herbert Buffalo, Sam's father, was raised on the Wahpeton Dakota Reserve. According to Robert Goodvoice, "His Indian name was *Tawáduta Ota*" (Robert Goodvoice 1, 1977, 11). His gravestone reads: Herbert Flyingbuffalo, *Wanbdiwayagmani*, 1890–1972.

Herbert's father was *Bdo* (*Biddow*, Flying Buffalo = *Tatáŋka Kiŋyéyapi*), a Sisseton who had come from the Moose Woods (Whitecap) Reserve in the 1890s to live at Wahpeton Dakota Reserve. His mother was *Tiwákawiŋ*, a Wahpeton. His brothers and sisters included Fred Buffalo (who married Jane Black), Bill, and Maggie.

Herbert learned to read and write from Lucy Baker, the first Presbyterian missionary teacher in the Prince Albert area, who worked with the Dakota north of the North Saskatchewan River. He was known to be a shaman/medicine man/herbalist: he had knowledge of herbs and plants and how to use them as medicine, Sam said, including to help remedy diabetes. He also had other traditional knowledge and powers, participated in the Ghost Dance, and possessed a Ghost Dance shirt.

In 1963 he had a one and a half-storey log house in the center of the reserve, and a team of horses, and spent time camped in the nearby Nisbet Forest Reserve cutting jack pine rails.

Sam Buffalo/Samuel Mniyo (1929–1999)

Born in Prince Albert on October 29, 1929, Sam Buffalo was raised in the Wahpeton Dakota Reserve no. 94A. His gravestone reads: Samuel Isaac Buffalo, *Mniyódowaŋ* (meaning singing in water, a stone rippling in water, rhythm in motion).

His father was Herbert Buffalo (Herbert Flying Buffalo), half Sisseton, half Wahpeton. His mother was Pansy Goodvoice/Pansy *Ho Wašté*, Wahpeton (gravestone: *Kimama Zikoyakewin*, 1892–1953). Sam was the second child, after Rose and before Rita; many other children died in infancy. Sam suffered from a physical handicap, partial paralysis on his left side, for most of his life.

Robert Goodvoice (1901–1986)

Robert Goodvoice was born in 1901 or 1900. His father was *Ho Wašté*/ John Goodvoice, Mdewakanton; his mother was Mary Duta, Wahpeton, daughter of *Waŋdúta*/Red Arrow; his sister was Pansy Goodvoice, his brother was Ernest Goodvoice, and his paternal grandfather was John Sioux (see biographical sketch). Robert was raised by Henry Two Bear after his mother married Henry. In 1977 he made seventeen tape recordings as the Wahpaton (sic) Oral History Project (see Bibliography), which were used by the PAS in their Documenting the Dakota project (see https://www.saskarchives.com/dakota_Intro_Essay).

James H. Howard (1925–1982)

Born of pioneer Protestant parents, Howard grew up in a small prairie town in South Dakota, had a strong interest in American Indians, and had friends among them. This interest led him into the academic world and continued throughout his career as an archeologist, museum preparator, museum director, consultant on American Indian land claims, and university professor in ethnology and anthropology.

He graduated with MA and PhD degrees and taught at the University of North Dakota, University of South Dakota, and Oklahoma State University. Howard expressed his lifelong interest in Plains Indians through his teaching, research, acquiring an impressive collection of materials, participating in Indian dances and ceremonies, and forming long-lasting friendships with Indian informants.

In 1972 he visited all the Dakota/Lakota reserves in Canada, attempting to record as full a picture as possible of all aspects of traditional culture: this was the first systematic anthropological survey of the Canadian Sioux reserves. He published more than one hundred professional papers and books (Woolworth 1997).

James McKay (1828–1879)

James McKay was a Metis trader, guide, entrepreneur, politician, and interpreter. Facile with many languages, he spoke English, French, Ojibwa, Cree, and Dakota He lived in the Red River district (now Winnipeg), where he was visited often by Dakota chiefs after 1862. In 1876 he advised a group of *Isáŋti* Dakota in the United States under Chief *Húpa Iyáȟpeya* to flee to Prince Albert, which they did (see Turner 2000).

John Sioux/*Aŋpétu Wašíčuŋ*

Born in what is now Minnesota, John Sioux was a Mdewakanton, the eldest of seven brothers, the youngest being *Tamah*. He came to the Prince

Albert area with his brothers and with Chief *Húpa Iyáhpeya* in 1877. He married *Witahiyayewin*/Jane Desjarlais. He was the paternal grandfather of Robert Goodvoice and told Robert about the Red Path and other stories. John Sioux was photographed in the fall of 1912 when aged seventy-one (a photo not included in this book); he died at ninety-five.

Henry Two Bear (1878–1966)

"The grandson of the Hunkpati-Yanktonai Chief [Two Bear] of the battle of Whitestone Hill fame, Henry Two Bear was born in 1878. His father was See Walker or *Matononpa* (Two Bear); his mother *Oyehotewin* or Grey Track Woman" (Louis Garcia, citing Henry Two Bear Papers). His gravestone dates read: 1872–1966. My conclusion is that his father was Yanktonai and his mother was Wahpeton (DB). He married Mary Duta (Mary Red Arrow, Mary Goodvoice, Mary Two Bear, 1868–1940). They had three children: George, Florence (1909–2000), and Paul Isaac.

Appendix 4

Oral History of the Wahpaton Dakota

Summary—Indian History Film Project at Provincial Archives of Saskatchewan, Regina, Saskatchewan

Title: *An Oral History of the Wahpaton [sic] Dakota*
Collector: Robert Goodvoice
Year of Project: 1977
No. of Informants: 3
No. of Tapes: 17
No. of Hours: 16
Accession Nos.: R78–14, R80–611
Call Nos.: R-A1334 to R-A1347, R-5761 to R-5763

[Note 1. The seventeen audiotape cassettes and the printed transcripts made from them are available at PAS, Regina. using the call numbers listed here. The transcripts also are available online in pdf format through the University of Regina Library using the designations Robert Goodvoice 1, 2, etc. and Samuel Buffalo 1, 2, etc., in accordance with the file titles used by the library. In addition to thirteen tapes of Robert Goodvoice (one including Archie Eagle of Whitecap), the collection includes four tapes of Samuel Buffalo. Most of these recordings were done without an interviewer. The transcripts were done by non-speakers of Dakota, consequently most Dakota proper names and other Dakota words are either missing or rendered inadequately.

Note 2: The spelling Wahpaton was used by some until the 1970s but has been replaced with the spelling Wahpeton.

Note on SB and SM citations: For the 1985–97 Samuel Mniyo narrations, see the opening note in the bibliography. DB]

Concerned that the history of the Wahpaton Sioux had not been recorded accurately, Robert Goodvoice, an elder of the Wahpaton Band, began narrating onto tape the stories that had been told to him by his grandfather. Sam Buffalo and Archie Eagle also contributed, relating those stories that they could remember. The tapes deal with historical, cultural, and spiritual topics. A list of these with brief descriptions follows, organized according to tape number. [The tapes and/or transcripts may be searched by the PAS call number (e.g., R-A1334) or the University of Regina Library search term (e.g., Robert Goodvoice 1). DB]

R-A1334 — [Robert Goodvoice 1] The origin of the Dakota tribe, the prophecy of the coming of white civilization, the Dakota people's experience of first contact with white civilization, the Minnesota Massacre in 1862, the flight of the Dakota people to Canada, obtaining land for the Round Plain Reserve from the federal government in 1893, and Wahpaton chiefs both hereditary and elected.

R-A1335 — [Robert Goodvoice 2] How the Dakota came to settle in the Prince Albert district, farming with assistance from the government, the coming of the McKays, the effect of the Riel Rebellion on the Dakota, ownership of Manhattan Island, New York, by Indian people, the traditional structure of a Dakota village, division of the Dakota tribe into smaller groups, how knowledge is passed from one generation to another, observations on animal behavior, premonitions concerning the weather, medicine, and curing and drying of meat.

R-A1336 — [Robert Goodvoice 3] The story of the Dakota alliance in the War of 1812 and the chiefs' awards for aiding the British, how these medals have been passed down to successive Dakota chiefs, how the Dakota in Canada relinquished rights to the goods that were awarded annually by the British as a tribute to their loyalty, how at one time written permission was required for a Dakota to leave the reserve, a story of how two Dakota leaders were kidnapped and sold by white men.

R-A1337 — [Robert Goodvoice 3 ctd.] The story of Red Top, death and burial practices, the dislocation of families during and after the Sioux Uprising in 1862 and the long search for relatives, digging and roasting wild vegetables, and making pemmican from buffalo meat.

R-A1338 — [Robert Goodvoice 4] How his lost grandfather receives divine guidance from a poplar tree, how spiritual powers are invoked to locate a lost child and a horse, a discussion of spiritual powers and how they work, the white man's misunderstanding of the Indians' spiritual powers, a story of finding lost keys and a lost cow.

R-A1339 — [Robert Goodvoice 5] How United States authorities offer bribes to the Dakota to return from Canada to the U.S., how a man is punished for breaking a rule during a buffalo hunt, the kidnapping of a Dakota woman and children, poisoning of the Dakota by a white man, a gift of contaminated underwear causing sickness and death to recipients, a gift of poisoned buns and other poisonous foods, the song of the rabbit hunt and a description of how the rabbit is hunted, the song for gathering wild duck eggs and a description of how they are gathered, the practice of children dancing in front of the chief's lodge in the evening.

R-A1340 — [Robert Goodvoice 6] The origin of the sun dance, how the sun dance is performed today and the function of the sun dance in healing, when and where a sun dance is held, *Uŋktómi*, a spirit who appears in human form to help and guide the people, and the red path.

R-A1341 — [Robert Goodvoice 6 ctd.] The red path and *Ċaŋkú Dúta* (Red Path) society, rejection of a person from the *Ċaŋkú Dúta* society, the demanding role of a society member, a story of raiding for horses, which is the first time the Dakota saw horses.

R-A1342 — [Robert Goodvoice 7] Burning sweet grass to purify water, drying and storing berries and roots, how *Uŋktómi* guides the people and how this belief is dying out, the story of a woman's treachery to her own people and her punishment, the purification rite for a person who has committed a crime.

R-A1343 — [Robert Goodvoice 8] The story of the first shot to be fired in the Minnesota Massacre, the Dakota fight and the division into two groups at the Cypress Hills, how the Dakota reacted to the Northwest Rebellion.

R-A1344 — [Samuel Buffalo 3] Dakota child discipline, the sacred hoop, childhood and adult education, sponsorship of children in their training, how Dakota identity is learned, a children's story about friendship, the Dakota system of counting, how carving is taught to young children.

R-A1345 — [Samuel Buffalo 2] The circle ceremony, the meaning of *tiyóti*, the circle of knowledge, judging women by the expressiveness of their hands, the practice of vegetarianism among the early Dakota, *ċaŋyá* or wood counting—a record keeping of Dakota generations, skills taught by *tiyóti*, Holy Dance ceremonies, the separation of the Dakota nation into four parts, territorial losses at the time of the Minnesota Massacre, the disorganization and confusion caused by reserve life, the Chief White Cap story, hardships, the location of the seven Dakota reserves in Canada.

R-A1346 — [Samuel Buffalo 1] Dakota elders' predictions, a description of early reserve life, the practice of home singing of *tiódowaŋ*, disruptions in the pursuit of traditional practices and their breakdown, the depression of the 1930s and a destructive form of dancing that sprang up, the effects of the introduction of social-welfare assistance on reserve life, the Big Top Celebrations, Dakota language lessons, and the history of the Wahpaton Reserve.

R-A1347 — [Samuel Buffalo 4] The Holy Dance Society and the story of its origin, the red circle, stories of *Uŋktómi*, a story of the first gramophone on a Dakota reserve, *Uŋktómi*'s physical appearance, the spiritual powers of large poplar trees, and *Uŋktómi*'s power to predict.

R-5761 to R-5763 — [Robert Goodvoice 9 and Robert Goodvoice 10] Indian medicines and how the Dakota tribe came to live in the Prince Albert area.

Informant	Address	Tape No. (call number)	Documentation
Buffalo, Sam	Round Plain Reserve	R-A1344 to R-A1347	Transcript
Eagle, Archie	White Cap Reserve	R-5763	Transcript
Goodvoice, Robert	Round Plain Reserve	R-A1334 to R-A1347, R-5761 to R-5763	Transcript

Appendix 5

Etude de cas: Une tradition chez les Dakotas

This case study appeared in a school textbook (or other instructional resource) used in a Grade 8 French Immersion course in Saskatchewan, probably *Sciences humaines*. About 1990 it was brought home from school (Regina Public School Board) by Dan Beveridge's son Danny. It features a translation into French of the first portion of one of Sam Buffalo's 1977 oral history interviews, identified here as Samuel Buffalo 3, 1977, 2. Attempts to locate the French language source of this case study were unsuccessful.

Étude de cas :
UNE TRADITION CHEZ LES DAKOTAS

Le type d'éducation formelle qui existe au sein d'une culture est un aspect important de la structure éducationnelle. Cependant, on doit noter que l'éducation formelle n'est pas nécessairement dispensée entre les murs d'une école. Voici comment Mniyo l'explique :

« Je me présente. Mon nom est Samuel Buffalo et j'ai également un nom dakota, Mniyo. Je suis membre de la réserve Dakota Wahpeton 94A située à dix milles (16,1 km) au nord-ouest de Prince-Albert. Je suis né le 29 octobre 1929. J'ai vécu presque toute ma vie, soit 47 ans, à Wahpeton.

« Nous sommes le mercredi 14 septembre 1977. Je recueille des données en vue de la préparation de livres et de cours sur la langue des Dakotas, parce qu'il se peut que l'on enseigne la langue des Dakotas dans chaque réserve dakota. Je suis très intéressé par ce genre de travail. De plus, je suis handicapé physique et j'ai le temps d'étudier et de me former dans le champ de connaissances que je viens de mentionner...

« Un vieil homme du nom de Ite Wapikida, mon parrain, est celui qui m'a formé selon le vieux système traditionnel des Dakotas, tiyoti owihduhe, qui signifie la maison dans la maison, la vie dans la vie. Pour un enfant dakota, la discipline commence vers l'âge de deux ans. Les parents choisissent un homme âgé et l'invitent à venir chez eux. Après lui avoir offert de la nourriture, des cadeaux et une pipe bourrée à fumer, la mère de l'enfant demande à cette personne de waiyedkiya son enfant, c'est-à-dire de le parrainer. Ce parrainage se poursuit jusqu'à la mort de l'une des deux parties. Ils se rencontrent aussi souvent que possible, et le garçon doit rendre visite à son parrain, ne serait-ce que pour avoir une conversation. Une fois qu'ils se connaissent suffisamment bien, le véritable enseignement commence.

« Dans mon cas, en plus du reste, Ite Wapikida s'assit un jour les jambes croisées. Il était grand, mince et âgé. Ses cheveux étaient blancs et clairsemés, et de courtes tresses pendaient de chaque côté de sa tête. Il tenait dans chaque main plusieurs objets que je ne pouvais pas identifier. Il avait placé devant ses genoux pliés un cerceau qui portait différentes marques.

« Il me dit que ce cerceau était le symbole de la voix mystérieuse qui avait promis à nos ancêtres qu'une nouvelle génération verrait le jour au pays du soleil couchant. Ce cerceau était le tiyoti owihduhe dont nos grands-pères observaient les principes et les règles. Il représentait la durée de vie des Dakotas et leur assurait une bonne santé, un gîte confortable, une chasse fructueuse et de la joie. Ce cerceau était le cerceau sacré qui permettait le développement des croyances, de l'identité, des aptitudes et du sentiment d'estime personnelle des Dakotas. »

Questions
1. La structure éducationnelle des Dakotas décrite par Mniyo repose sur la relation privilégiée d'une personne âgée avec un enfant. Donnez quelques adjectifs qui caractérisent cette relation particulière.
2. Pourquoi Mniyo nous a-t-il donné sa date de naissance lorsqu'il s'est présenté?
3. Mniyo nous mentionne qu'il prépare du matériel pédagogique pour les écoles des Dakotas. Faites un parallèle entre votre vie scolaire et la structure éducationnelle selon laquelle Mniyo a été formé.
4. Ite Wapikida se sert du cerceau comme symbole de la culture des Dakotas. Quel type de connaissances Ite Wapikida allait-il finir par transmettre à Mniyo?

Appendix 6

Guide to Pronunciation and Orthography

PREPARED BY JURGITA ANTOINE

Riggs 1890	LaFontaine and McKay 2004	Ullrich 2008	Beveridge 2019	Description Example
a	a	a	a	as in pasta
aŋ	aŋ	aŋ	aŋ	as in French maman
b	b	b	b	as in bet
ć	c	č	c̄	unaspirated, as in chum, almost like j in job
ć	ҫ	čh	ċ	aspirated, as in chin
ҫ̇	c'	č'	c̓'	a glottal stop, pronounced with a pause between this sound and the following vowel, as in church art
d	d	d	d	as in door
e	e	e	e	as in den
g	g	g	g	used when a final k is contracted, as in dog
g	ġ	ğ	ġ	a voiced glottal h sound
h	h	h	h	as in help
r	ħ	ȟ	ħ	a voiceless glottal h sound, as in German buchen
r	ħ	ȟ'	ħ'	a glottal stop, an ħ sound pronounced with a pause after it and the following vowel
i	i	i	i	as in pizza
iŋ	iŋ	iŋ	iŋ	nasal i as in ink

k	k	k	k	unaspirated, as in skunk
k	ḳ	kh	k	aspirated, as in kite
k	ḳ	kȟ	ḱ	a glottal k
q	k'	k'	k'	a glottal stop, pronounced with a pause after this sound and a following vowel
m	m	m	m	as in mother
n	n	n	n	as in nine
o	o	o	o	as in water
p	p	p	p	unaspirated, as in spin
p	p̣	ph	p	aspirated, as in pen
p	p̣	pȟ	ṗ	a glottal p
p̣	p'	p'	p'	a glottal stop, pronounced with a pause after this sound and a following vowel
s	s	s	s	as in silk
s	s'	s'	s'	a glottal stop, pronounced with a pause after this sound and a following vowel
ś	ṡ	š	ṡ	as in shop
ś	ṡ'	š'	ṡ'	a glottal stop, pronounced with a pause after this sound and a following vowel
t	t	t	t	unaspirated, as in stop
t	ṭ	th	t	aspirated, as in ten
t	ṭ	tȟ	ṫ	a glottal t
ṭ	t'	t'	t'	a glottal stop, pronounced with a pause after this sound and a following vowel
u	u	u	u	as in wood
on	uŋ	uŋ	uŋ	nasal u, sometimes approximates nasal o

w	w	w	w	as in **w**in
y	y	y	y	as in **y**et
z	z	z	z	as in **z**ero
ź	ż	ž	j	as in fu**s**ion

Dakota nasal vowels approximate those in the French language (e. g., *maman*).

Aspirated consonants are pronounced with a slight puff of air. In English, consonants d, k, p, and t are commonly pronounced this way.

Glottal consonants are articulated with a friction in the glottis (e.g., *hoġaŋ*).

Glottal stops in Dakota occur between a vowel and a preceding consonant. There is a pause (or trap of air in the glottis) after such a consonant. Similarly, if two vowels occur next to each other, each one is pronounced separately (e.g., *o-íhduhe*). Sometimes a consonant is inserted between the two vowels to help pronounce them (e.g., *owíhduhe*).

In our orthography for the purposes of this book, we chose not to mark aspirated consonants for several reasons. First, aspiration and glottalization in Dakota are softer than in Lakota, which is probably a consequence of language evolution. In some cases, glottalization is a feature that was perhaps more strongly pronounced in earlier times, but as the Dakota language was receding, it started approximating English sounds; that is, sounds became softened to aspiration. We chose to mark the original feature, as fluent speakers today are still heard making that distinction. Second, with just a handful of first language fluent Dakota speakers remaining, Dakota speakers with the English language background tend to aspirate all their consonants just like in English. Since the original aspiration (unlike glottalization) is not a meaning-changing feature and sometimes even depends on the context of other words or phrase stress, we did not mark it. Glottalization in some words does change meaning (e.g., *wakaŋ* means sacred, but *wakaŋ* means old) and thus has to be marked.

Glossary

COMPILED BY JURGITA ANTOINE

This glossary focuses on the Dakota words found in this volume. It documents the meanings provided by Samuel Mniyo and Robert Goodvoice. In some cases commonly known meanings of Dakota words are used. Some of the words are not in dictionaries. Following the main glossary listing are brief sections giving the objects belonging to a *Wakáŋ Waćípi* member and the Dakota names for months of the year.

Ahíyaŋke: comes and stays

Akíćita: police or guards (in this case, of the *Wakáŋ Waćípi*)

Aŋpétu Wašíćuŋ: Light Spirit

Anúka anapikíćipi: guarding each other

Apá: to strike, shatter

Atúŋwaŋ: to live, stay at a place

Bahá: lit. "curved over"; a term for old people at or beyond eighty-four (twelfth *nióbe*)

Bde Íyedaŋ: Lac qui Parle in Minnesota

Bdo: potato

Bdokétu ćokáŋyaŋ: midsummer

Ċaŋ: timber, wood

Ċaŋdí: tobacco

Ċaŋdójuha Yuhá: a principal member of the Holy Dance Society, lit. bundle owner

Ċaŋhdéśka: hoop

Ċaŋkú Dúta: Red Road

Ċaŋnúŋpa Wašté: Good Pipe

Ċaŋyá: wood counting

Ċaŋyáwa: a wooden generation counter

Ċápa: beaver

Ċaské: the name of the firstborn child, if a son

Ċaoéhde: a step in a *nióbe*

Ċiŋċá: offspring

Ċusdípa Oyáte: people of dew lickers.

Dakóta Ċístina: a small cannon painted yellow given to the Dakota by the British at the conclusion of the 1812 war

Dakóta Oyáte: Dakota Nation, *Oċéti Ṡakówiŋ*, the greater Sioux nation

Dakóta Ṗejí: Grass Dance songs and dancing costumes

Dowáŋpi: a song stick

Dúta: red, scarlet

Eyáŋ: the herald man

Haŋbdé: four-day fasting

Ḣe: a mountain

Heyóka: a clown

Hezá: a vulture

Ho Ṫáŋke: the Winnebago, lit. "Big Voice"

Hokṡín Wamná: the Orphan Boy

Hokṡín Wamnáda: the Respected Boy

Huhú Wakpá: Bone River (Regina, Saskatchewan)

I: a mouth

Iŋhdépi: an altar made of stone, a pile of stones (lit. *Íŋyaŋ hdépi*, "rocks piled up")

Iŋkpadúta: Red Top

Íŋyaŋ Ṡaṡá Pasdátapi: a landmark of red stones known as the boundary between the United States and Canada

Isáŋ: a knife; sharp

Isáŋ Ṫáŋka: a big knife, refers to the U.S. Army

Ité Wapíkida: face appreciation

Itúḣ'aŋ: to donate, from *itúya oḣ'áŋ*, voluntary actions

Iyá: to speak

Iyáḣpeya: to grab

Izó: a peninsula

Iwákċi: a custom of praising a person

Iwósu: the seed or purpose of life

Júhowa or Ajúhowa: Creative Voice Being (*jú* = to decorate or beautify, *ho* = voice, and *wa* = being)

Kahómni: a slow beat dance, lit. "rotate swing"

Kawíŋġa: to turn, turn around, turn back

Kičí: companionship, lit. "with"

Kičíwa: co-worker; husband and wife addressed each other this word

Kičíčuŋza: cursing one another

Kičíȟmuŋġa: killing in a secret way

Kiŋyéwakaŋ: Flies Sacred

Ḳoda: a friend; co-believer in *Wakáŋ Wačípi*; a spirit helper

Maśtíŋgpazi: rabbit-hunting

Maṭó Núŋpa: Two Bears

Máza: iron

Mde: a lake

Mihúŋ: my mother

Mni: water

Mniȟáȟa: water falls

Miníȟaȟa Wakpá: a "river with many falls," known today as the Mississippi River

Mniyódowaŋ: rhythm in motion, or motion like whirlpool ripple within singing or rhythm; lit. "water song"

Nína: very or most

Nióbe: a phase; a seven-year period of the human life span

Očéti: a fireplace; a campsite (camp fireplace representing a campsite)

Očéti Śakówiŋ: seven smokestacks referring to seven boatloads (there was one smokestack on each of seven boats); also, Seven Council Fires

Odákota: a lifestyle, identity, and fellowship through sharing a common Dakota spiritual belief, one god, *Ajúhowa*, and one quest (for the Hill of Truth)

Odówaŋ: a song

Ohóčokaŋyaŋ: the space between the *tiyóti* lodge in the middle and the camp circle; also, the lifestyle of *tiyóti*

Ohítikapi: Dakota heroes

Oíhduhe: related to citizenship, see *Tiyóti oíhduhe*

Okičiyúȟpapi: they pull one another down

Oḳódakičiye: a society

Oḳóta: a fellowship

Ómaka: a season

Omníćiye: a circle ceremony

Opíić'iyapi: attitude

Ośpáye: a band (as a social unit)

Oúŋ: a place or condition where all people will live together, share equally in good health, have similar homes, have work and prosperity, and become a nation; *Oúŋ* means homeland—not land itself but home in the sense of community, people

Oúŋ hdamní: pilgrimage

Owíyahaŋtùkeśni: unpopularity

Oyáte: people, nation

Oyáte anúka: the main structure, of oblong shape, east of the *wópida* lodge, where the other believers gathered for the *Wakáŋ Waćípi*; lit. "people on both sides"

Oyáte ókíju: the annual summer gathering of Dakota people; lit. "people gathered together"

Ozúye: an attack process to strike the target and return without a stop

Páha ićáǧe: Growing Hill (place in Qu'Appelle Valley)

Ṗahíŋ Śaśá: Red Hair, referring to Robert Dickson

Pajódaŋ iyéćetu: the Hill or Knoll of Truth

Ṗaŋǧí: a carrot

Ṗehíŋ Háŋska: Long Hair, referring to General Custer

Píksina: a wild turnip

Psíŋ: wild rice

Psiŋćíŋċa: an egg-shaped root. Also, a name Dakotas gave to the storekeeper who distributed promised goods to them after the War of 1812.

Pśiŋ: onion

Ptaŋ: otter

Sagyé oéhde: lit. "cane markings," the thirteenth and fourteenth *nióbes*

Siŋkpé: muskrat

Siŋtómni: the area as far as you can see around you

Skúye: sweet

Taćúhupa Otúŋwaŋ: Moose Jaw, Saskatchewan

Ṫaŋíŋ: tangible aspects of life

Ṫaíŋśni: intangible aspects of life

Ṫatáŋka Nájiŋ: Standing Buffalo

Ṫaté: wind

Ṫawásu Óta: Many Hailstones

Ṫawíću: a wife, lit. "his take"

Tiŋtáŋ: a prairie

Tíŋtaŋ Mibéna: Round Plain

Tióde: Looks for Home

Tiódowaŋ: home singing

Tiókiti: physically handicapped persons, mostly blind

Típi: lit. "they live," a cone-shaped Dakota lodge

Tiúŋ/tihdé: home or dwelling

Tiwópida: a thanksgiving lodge and prayer refuge; the place of meeting
     to give thanks to God; the tent of the elders in the *Tiwópida Oíh-
     duhe* era; for more detail see *The Wakáŋ Waćípi Practice: Ceremony
     and Physical Layout,* early in part 2

Tiwópida oíhduhe: the lifestyle and social system based on the *tiwópida;* see
     Changing from the *Tiwópida Oíhduhe* to the *Tiyóti Oíhduhe,* in part 2.

Tiyóti: a big tipi in the center of the camp; council tipi or soldiers' lodge;
     it had two literal translations, "home and home" or "life and life,"
     usually described as "home within home" or "life within life"

Tiyóti yaŋká: lit. "*tiyóti* residers," the selected men conducting *tiyóti* duties,
     which included making decisions for the people

Tiyóti oíhduhe: the lifestyle and social system based on the *tiyóti;* see
     Changing from the *Tiwópida Oíhduhe* to the *Tiyóti Oíhduhe,* in part 2.

Ṫoká wićóićaġe: lit. "first generation," the beginning of the human race

Toktópawiŋġe: one thousand

Tu: a time period of twelve moons, especially four seasons (a year)

Ṫuŋkáŋ: a stone

Uŋktómi: a spider; a trickster figure, a human, looks like a person but
     nobody touched him, also a Dakota spirit helper (Lakota, *Iktómi;*
     Cree, *Wićáhkeċah*)

Upí Iyahdéya: Extended Tail Feathers

Wa: a circle of knowledge available for any purpose

Waánataŋ: Charger

Waáyate: a seer or prophet of God

Wahánuŋ: pelts, fur-bearing animals

Wahúwapa or Wamnáheza: corn

Wakté: a victory song

Waŋ: an arrow

Wambdí Iyótake: Sitting Eagle

Wakáŋ: sacred

Wakáŋ Dowáŋpi: Song Stick for the *Wakáŋ Waċípi*

Wakáŋ Ťáŋka: the most holy in the universe

Wakáŋ Waċípi: Medicine Dance

Wakíŋyaŋ: Thunder Beings

Wakpá: a river, stream

Wakpa Ozate: River Fork (forty miles east of Prince Albert, Saskatchewan)

Wanása: the buffalo hunts

Waóbe: a quest

Wapáhaska: White Warbonnet

Wapíkidapi: appreciation

Waśíċu: white people

Waśté: good

Watéśdake ska: a headgear of white, a crown of white

Wazí Pahá: the Cypress Hills; lit. pine hills

Wiċáħċa: lit. "true mature, bloom," a term for man at the age of ninety-eight (fourteenth *nióbe* or full life span)

Wiċáśta wakáŋ: a medicine man; a messenger to people from God

Wiċíoni: skills or career

Wiċíspa: human elbow; Elbow, Saskatchewn (bend in the Saskatchewan River)

Wiċóbe: encampment

Wiċóħtani: everyday living and food gathering and performing work that was part of maintaining life in harmony

Wiċoiċaġe: a generation

Wiċoimaġaġa: social activities

Wiċóuŋ: the work and the relationship between the home encampment and *Tiyóti*, including homecare practices

Wiċóti: community, encampment

Wiċóti akíkta: to be encampment wise

Wičózani: health preserving methods

Wíŋkte: a homosexual man

Winóna or Winúna: the eldest daughter of the family (if firstborn)

Wíŋyaŋ: a woman

Wíta or Wíto Wakáŋ: lit. "holy island," Manhattan Island

Wiyóȟpeyatàkiya: westward

Wizí: old folks, or orphans living with grandparents

Woókiya: peace-making

Wópȟetuŋ Háŋska: Tall Merchant

Wópida or wópide: thanks, thanksgiving, gratitude; tent or place of thanksgiving

Wópida ikíni uŋ: thanks-living; singing, praying, giving of testimonies, and demonstrating gifts such as medicines, all for the purpose of giving thanks or thanks-living

Wópiye: a new medicine bag

Wósu: faith

Wóšiče: lit. "trouble," refers to the 1862 conflict in Minnesota

Wótawa: personal spiritual belongings

Wówičada: belief

Wówiyekiya or wičóiyekiyapi: identity

Wówidake: use, to make use of

Wóyawa táŋka: one million

Objects Belonging to *Wakáŋ Wačípi* Member

Čaŋdójuha: a leather pouch with pictograms and symbols on the outside

Čaŋská: a wooden board about two feet long and decorated

Wakšíča: a bowl, also decorated; most are wood, some are stone or shell, and a very few are made of clay

Wačíŋhe: a plume

Wakáŋ Dowáŋpi: the song stick

Dakota Names for the Months

January: Witéȟi Wi, Hard moon

February: Wičáta Wi, Moon of the raccoon

March: Ištá Wičáyezaŋ Wi, Something in the air gives people sore eyes

April: Maǧá Okáda Wi, Moon when geese come from the south
May: Ṗeji Ićaǧa Wi, Moon when the grass grows
June: Wajuṡteća Ṡa Wi, Moon of strawberries
July: Bdokétu Ćokáŋyaŋ Wi, Midsummer moon
August: Wasútuŋ Wi, Everything is ripe and fully matured
September: Ćaŋwáṗa Ġi Wi, When the leaves are brown
October: Ptaŋyétu Wi, Moon of autumn
November: Takíyuha Wi, Breeding season for jumpers, for that special deer
December: Ṫahéćapṡuŋ Wi, Moon when the animals lose their horns

Notes

Preface and Acknowledgments

1. Some of the most obvious changes since the 1960s and 1970s, which are indicative of other deeper changes, include education levels and names of organizations. When I attended the University of Saskatchewan in Saskatoon there were only three Indigenous students registered in 1962–63 (Indian and Metis) and nine the following year. In 2018 there were 3,100 self-declared Indigenous students registered at that university, and 1,955 at the University of Regina. The Federation of Saskatchewan Indians became the Federation of Saskatchewan Indian Nations and that became the Federation of Sovereign Indigenous Nations. Similarly, the Saskatchewan Indian Federated College, which was created in 1976 at the University of Regina, became the First Nations University of Canada.

Part 1. Editor's Introduction

1. For details on Robert Goodvoice's oral history collection see appendix 4 and see Goodvoice 1977 (unpublished) in the bibliography.

Some writers distinguish between "oral history," which is spoken by persons who themselves experienced the events they speak about, and "oral tradition," which is knowledge passed from prior generations of a group and not necessarily experienced by the narrator (Maroukis 2004). In this book we use the term "oral history" in a more general way but mainly to refer to knowledge passed from prior generations.

2. Hassrick (1964, 6) claims that in early times the Chippewa, threatened on one side by the powerful Iroquois and on the other side by the Sioux, dubbed the Iroquois "the True Adders" and the Sioux "the Lesser Adders." Parks and DeMallie (1992, 234), however, show that the Ojibwa (Chippewa) term *Nadoues-sioux* originally referred to people of an alien tribe and not to a snake or adder.

3. Similar listings of the seven tribes or subdivisions of the Sioux nation are given by Pond (1986, 4–6) and Anderson (1986, 6). The suffix *-tonwan* or *-tunwan* means dwellers at, or campers at, or village.

4. Dorsey states as follows: "They camped in two sets of concentric circles, one of four circles, consisting probably of the Mdewakantonwan, Waqpe-kute, Waqpe-tonwan and Sisitonwan; and the other of three circles, including the Ihanktonwan, Ihanktonwanna, and Titonwan" (1897, 215).

5. See also these three publications: Office of the Treaty Commissioner, *Wahpeton Dakota Nation: The Story of the Dakota Oyate in Canada*, 2015; Danyluk et al., *Wa Pa Ha Ska: Whitecap Dakota First Nation*, 2016; and Office of the Treaty Commissioner,

The Story of the Dakota Oyate and the People of Standing Buffalo, 2015. All were published and/or co-authored by the Office of the Treaty Commissioner (Saskatchewan).

6. The Cree now living along the Churchill River in northern Saskatchewan confirm a long history of Dakota war expeditions to the north (Elias 1988). Cree place names referring to the Dakota include *Puat sipi* (Dakota River, also called Ballantyne River); *Kimoso puatinak* (Home of the Ancient Dakota, now a Cree settlement called Deschambault Lake); and *Opowekustikunik* (Narrows of Fear, named after a Dakota-Woodland Cree encounter, now a settlement called Pelican Narrows) (Elias 1988, 5–6). Another Cree place name is *Pwottah Nootintoonihk*, translated as "Sioux Battle Ground" by the Swampy Cree at this settlement on the Saskatchewan River, Cumberland House (Omani 2010, 228). These raids no doubt were related to the French-British rivalry for the fur trade. "By the late 1720s, the raids of the Sioux were having a serious effect on the trade at York Factory (Ray 1974, 16). Omani also lists place names of towns and villages in southern Saskatchewan and Manitoba—five with Dakota names and three with Lakota names, suggesting considerable Sioux presence—and of numerous lakes and rivers.

7. Acton and the chicken incident (described by Robert in part 3 of the present volume): In July 1862 a soldiers' lodge formed at two Mdewakanton encampments in the Lower Council (Shakopee's village and Rice Creek village), which were in the hands of non-farmers. A few members of the lodge went hunting in the Big Woods to the east. As they were returning, on August 17, 1862, four members left the main party to call on Robinson Jones of Acton, a settler with whom they had traded for whiskey in the past. They were Wahpetons by birth but came from the Rice Creek village, a splinter faction of Shakopee's band and the most militant of the lower reservation. "Near Jones's house, they discovered several chicken eggs and debated whether to take them. The horseplay evolved into a dare as one man taunted another over his unwillingness to kill white settlers. Aroused, they met Jones and quarreled with him, then shot him, his wife, and three others" (Anderson 1997, 252–53). Acton is about twenty-five miles northeast of Rice Creek village in the Lower Council.

8. For details on the medals presented to the Dakota chiefs in recognition for their support for the British in the American War of Independence see endnotes for part 3.

9. Danyluk et al. 2016, 23.

10. If the Dakota received the *Wakáŋ Waćípi* from the Ojibwa, this transfer possibly was after 1680 and thus after contact. The ethno-historian Hickerson (in Dewdney 1975) notes that from 1650 to 1680 the Ojibwa came together and settled around the fisheries at the rapids the French called Sault Sainte Marie. From 1680 to 1736 "a trading and hunting arrangement with the Sioux-speaking Dakota of the south Superior shore, promoted by the French, stimulated westward expansion of Saulteur (people of the rapids) families and bands." From 1736 to 1780 was warfare with the Dakota and further expansion westward. Meanwhile other related bands were moving along the north shore of Lake Superior, migrating into Manitoba and mingling with the southern Ojibwa as early as 1800 (Dewdney 1975, 59). They are commonly known in Saskatchewan as Saulteaux.

11. The account of the "Origin of the Medicine Dance" given by Oneroad and Skinner (2003, 188–89) is very similar. The key elements include the following:

(1) The Great Mysterious One (*Wakáŋ Táŋka*) descended from above in a rainbow upon the deep sea, and said, "I will make two Powers to be leaders of the Medicine Dance and preserve it for mankind" (188), took two of his ribs, sank them into the water from which rose two *uŋktéhi*, and spoke to them. The *uŋktéhi* were powerful water spirits: "Oneroad specified that this [male *uŋktéhi*] was a four-footed, long-tailed monster with shiny horns, somewhat resembling a buffalo, but their heads were white like snow" (Oneroad and Skinner 2003, 188).

(2) The female monster (who seemed to more intelligent than the other) spoke first, saying, "There is no earth, but we shall cause it to appear," the two *uŋktéhi* caused several animals to appear—the loon, otter, grebe and muskrat—and commanded each one in turn to dive in search of black soil; the first three died in the attempt but the muskrat was successful in finding black earth.

(3) The *uŋktéhi* and the animals went west, sighted land, and landed in a large bay, where the *uŋktéhi* took their positions on the shore facing east and called on the animals and birds to participate in the Medicine Dance; the two *uŋktéhi* sang different songs and the animals and birds, changing into human form, began to dance; they used missiles to shoot their magic into each other, first claws but then the carved shell missiles used today. The *uŋktéhi* monsters showed the dancers how to restore those who had been shot, and bring them back to life again, and instructed them in the lore of the roots, the inner bark of trees, the plants and seeds (189).

(4) The two *uŋktéhi* said, "We leaders will lie beneath the ground with our ears spread out wide to hear the prayers and listen to the songs of the ceremonies. From our backs will grow the roots and herbs to heal the wounds and cure the sick." They then sank under the soil and the birds and animals carried their secrets to the Indians, and instructed them in their dreams (189).

12. The only other known photo of a *Wakáŋ Waćípi* was taken at the Oak River Reserve (present Sioux Valley First Nation) in Manitoba in 1929 and is shown in Howard's book, *The Canadian Sioux*, 2014 edition.

13. Hoffman, in his discussion of the *Midewiwin* as practiced by the Ojibway of Minnesota and Wisconsin before 1891, provides a detailed description of the *Mide* songs used in the preparation and initiation of candidates to the first, second, third and fourth degrees of the Grand Medicine Society of the Ojibway. He reproduces the pictographic symbols which serve as mnemonic aids to the singers, which are etched into birchbark scrolls, and which number well over one hundred. He provides each song in Ojibway with the English translation and the musical score for the chants (2005). The *Midewiwin* has been a major influence in the paintings of the notable Canadian Anishinaabe artist Norval Morrisseau, founder of the Woodland school of art (Giese 1997).

14. A note on names: in Dakota the same person could have and be known by several different names. Also the names could have been spelled in different ways. Names,

like songs, are very hard to translate, because they might reference a personal story or an event. Various spelling systems have been used for names through time. Some of the names for which spelling did not follow Dakota sound patterns were left in their original form. When lexical knowledge was insufficient to translate the names, no translation was attempted. Further research on these issues is recommended.

Part 2. The Narratives of Samuel Mniyo (Sam Buffalo)

1. Sam's three versions of the origin of the *Wakáŋ Waćipi* are remarkably similar although they were given over a twenty-year period. To me this indicates an effective method of passing on oral history with a minimum of error. Charles Eastman, a Wahpeton Dakota, describes how this method of training was used to develop oral skills for "preserving and transmitting the legends of his ancestors and his race. Almost every evening a myth, or a true story of some deed done in the past was narrated by one of the parents or grandparents, while the boy listened. . . . On the following evening, he was usually required to repeat it. . . . As a rule, the Indian boy is a good listener and has a good memory, so that the stories were tolerably well mastered. The household became his audience by which he was alternately criticized and applauded" (Eastman 1971, 43). The phrase "Remember this!" used by Eli Taylor of the Sioux Valley First Nation provides another example of this central method in the passing on of oral history (Wilson 2005, 28; 82).

2. With some exceptions, Sam appears to use these terms as follows:

Holy Dance Fellowship (*okóta* = fellowship) in the Red Road Journey or *Tiwópida* era;

Holy Dance Society (*okódakićiye* = society, *okódakićiyepi* = societies) in the Circle Power or *Tiyóti* era; and

Holy Dance Religion (*wóćekiye* = religion) in the Reserve era.

3. It is tempting to speculate that this "unknown point" might be near the mouth of the Santee River on the Atlantic coast of present South Carolina.

4. I believe Sam later refers to these four eras as the Red Road era, turning point era, era of the circle power, and trading and reserve era.

5. I believe Sam means here that some of the songs transcribed by Henry Two Bear had recently been translated by Sam from words in the Dakota language into English. Sam also may assume that these songs are the ones depicted on the song stick kept by Henry Two Bear or in the Jim Sapa pictographs.

6. *Wakáŋ* was a central concept in Sioux culture, religion and belief. In describing traditional Lakota Sioux belief, DeMallie states that humankind and nature were one; humankind existed not outside nature but as part of it; the universe was incomprehensible; and "The incomprehensibility of the universe, in which humankind, through ritual, could share, was called *wakáŋ*" (1987, 28). *Wakáŋ* designated anything that was hard to understand. "It was the animating force of the universe, the common denominator of its oneness. The totality of these life-giving forces was called

Wakáŋ Táŋka, "great incomprehensibility" (1987, 28). Not until Christian influences began to affect Lakota belief did *Wakáŋ Táŋka* become personified as the Great Spirit.

7. Louis Garcia, after talking with Sam in July 1987, suggests that what Sam calls *Juhówa* (creative voice being: *ju* = whistle, *ho* = voice, *wa* = being) may be an alternate name for *Uŋktéhi*, the Water Spirit: the water spirit has a whistle as loud as a train locomotive (Louis Garcia, personal correspondence, July 19, 1987). Mniyo also gave the name of God as *Ajúhowa*. He doubtless knew of Jehovah as a name for God in the Hebrew scriptures.

8. Mniyo's folk etymology is highly idiosyncratic but reflective of his thoughtful approach to explaining Dakota linguistic forms.

9. One of several suggestions regarding the origin of the term *Isáŋati*: the sharp-edged peninsula jutting into the Atlantic Ocean; also Knife Lake in Minnesota, named because of sharp-edged stones.

10. Regarding *Ćaské*, Mniyo did not specify "if a firstborn" here, perhaps assuming it was understood. See for example Oneroad and Skinner 2003, 88.

11. After describing the origin of the Red Road and the *Wakáŋ Waćípi*, Mniyo continues with his account of the Red Road Journey westward. He refers not only to going westward along the Mississippi River, which is puzzling—could he mean southward?—but he also makes four references to the ocean, including one reference to the point where the Mississippi River drains into the ocean.

12. Mniyo uses *hezá* as the word for vulture, but the usual pronunciation is *hećá*. The word for corn or maize is *wamnáheza* (Riggs 1992, 518).

13. Sam was not satisfied with my initial transcription of this story of corn as a human-animal partnership. Already suffering considerably from pain and weakness, he insisted that I make the connection with the God *Ajúhowa* more obvious, showing corn as a gift to humans from God, living with thanksgiving to God, extending peace to other nations while trading with them, and continuing the Red Road Journey in search for the Hill of Truth, and making this story a God-animal-human partnership.

14. This legend of corn, expressing the partnership relationship among humans, animals and plants, and what Sam calls the heavenly god, *Ajúhowa*, or what Robert calls the most holy, the *Wakáŋ Táŋka*, also resonates with one theme in the Dakota *Wakáŋ Waćípi* and the Ojibwe *mide* origin myths described by Skinner and by Angel, namely, the key role of animals in passing knowledge about plants to humans. This also resonates with another theme connecting to the *Wakáŋ Waćípi* and Red Road narratives, which is the giving of 150 plants by the *Wakáŋ Táŋka* or other supernatural or spirit being(s) to humans for their use, health and long life. The *Wakáŋ Waćípi* ritual features use of the sacred bundle, which includes skin of different types of animals as well as four species of *wakáŋ* medicines representing quadrupeds, fowls, medicinal herbs, and medicinal trees (Wallis 1947, 74).

15. If we assume forty years to each generation, Sam's great-grandmother would have been born about 1810, and grown up at *Isáŋ ta mde*, which may refer to Knife Lake, not far from Mille Lacs Lake, east of the Mississippi; then they were moved, so his grandmother Mary Duta grew up at Lac qui Parle, much farther west, on the upper

Minnesota River. DeMallie maintains, however, that "by 1736 most of the Sioux lived west of the Mississippi" (2001b, 722), and that the Santee abandoned the Mille Lacs region in the mid-eighteenth century, or the 1700s (727). By the time of the 1851 treaties the Sisseton and Wahpeton were already living on lands that would be included in the Upper Sioux reservation on the upper Minnesota River, but the Mdewakanton and Wahpekute had to move from where they had made a significant start at farming along the lower Minnesota River (Elias 1988, 16).

16. *Wazí Pahá* means Pine Hills, named after the dominant tree species, lodgepole pine, which the French mistakenly named cypress. Locations: Cypress Hills — southern Saskatchewan and Alberta; Fort Qu'Appelle — southern Saskatchewan; Griswold and Turtle Mountain — southern Manitoba.

17. His name was *Bdo*, which means potato; Biddow is an anglicized form.

18. Black Elk, the Oglala Sioux [Lakota] holy man, also speaks about the power of circles and cycles as manifested in both space and time. In 1931 he says:

"You have noticed that everything an Indian does is in a circle, and that is because the Power of the World always works in circles, and everything tries to be round. In the old days when we were a strong and happy people, all our power came to us through the sacred hoop of the nation, and so long as the hoop was unbroken, the people flourished. The flowering tree was the living centre of the hoop, and the circle of the four quarters nourished it. . . . Everything the Power of the World does is done in a circle. The sky is round, and I have heard that the earth is round like a ball, and so are all the stars. The wind, in its greatest power, whirls. Birds make their nests in circles, for theirs is the same religion as ours. The sum comes forth and goes down in a circle. The moon does the same, and both are round. Even the seasons form a great circle in their changing, and always come back again to where they were. The life of a man is a circle from childhood to childhood, and so it is with everything where power moves. Our tepees were round like the nests of birds, and these were always set in a circle, the nation's hoop, a nest of many nests, where the Great Spirit meant for us to hatch our children. "But the Wasichus [whites] have put us in these square boxes [log houses]. Our power is gone and we are dying, for the power is not in us any more. . . .

"Well, it is as it is. We are prisoners of war while we are waiting here. But there is another world." (Neihardt 1972, 164–66).

19. For Sam, the term *services* refers to training areas for the mastery of developmental tasks at different stages of human development. Sam is outlining a theory somewhat comparable to the well-known model of eight stages of psychosocial development developed by Erikson (1950).

20. Sam also refers to homosexual men. "There were some *wíŋkte* or practicing homosexual men in every Dakota community. . . . Some boys, according to their dreams and development, will tell their parents they will become a homosexual. They had a dream of sexual offer with a man, and their body and mind was developing toward being a woman. They were born that way. By the age of 8 to 10 or 14 they'd know and tell their

parents about the dreams. The parents would accept that, but they know he'll be an outcast of the community, and accepted only in the war party. One of the duties of the akíčitas (police, guards) was to guard, to keep the wíŋktes away from the encampment. The wíŋkte would camp here and there and make their own shelter. If someone had three or four wives, they'll show up there and become the fifth wife. Some, another class, only go four years as wíŋkte; others go a lifetime. But their life was very short . . . . The wíŋkte come into our names and language development" (Mniyo, September 30, 1987).

21. G. C. Anderson, Introduction, in S. W. Pond 1986, xiii. Dr. Thomas S. Williamson was sent by the American Board of Commissioners for Foreign Missions in Boston.

22. About this time, 1997 and later, Sam expressed to me his conviction that the Dakota people needed to turn to God and find salvation in Jesus Christ. He told me that he became a Christian in 1981. He was often visited at the Sherbrooke Community Centre by one or more persons who presented an evangelical view of Christianity. While living at Round Plain/Wahpeton, Sam was at least a nominal Presbyterian. Rev. W. W. Moore was the Presbyterian missionary responsible for serving Round Plain. He lived in Prince Albert. Sam and others frequently asked him for rides to and from the reserve. Sam also no doubt was acquainted with Bill Isnana of the Standing Buffalo (Dakota) reserve near Fort Qu'Appelle and others who were active in an aboriginal Christian revival movement, of which members often had been nominal Roman Catholics or Protestants.

23. "The French intermarried with Dakota at many places on the Mississippi: Minneapolis–St. Paul (Fort Snelling), also Mankato, Lac Qui Parle, etc." (Louis Garcia, personal correspondence, October 5, 1987). I assume such intermarriage was mainly before the Louisiana Purchase of 1803, when the French lost control of the Mississippi and territory west of it to the U.S.A. As Sam says, "That's how my maternal grandmother's grandmother or great-grandmother was a French girl from France." If we assume one generation to be forty years, going back five generations (to Sam's grandmother's great-grandmother) would place the year of birth of the "French girl" at about 1730. Sam told me his grandmother said, "My great-grandmother was a full-blooded French woman." Sam's maternal grandmother was Mary Duta. But Sam also said, "My great-grandmother was French and my great-grandfather was Sioux. She had light brown, curly hair, brown eyes, a black birth-mark on her cheek" (Mniyo, August 1996). He continued: "Fifty Dakota boys were taken for training (building houses, farming, etc.) for 10 years, each returning with a French girl, from the Mississippi River. [They're] supposed to return five years later to the fort, but only a ruin left; the French people left[,] said they were in hiding, said U.S. soldiers raided, burnt down, so survivors returned with Indians to Minnesota or Illinois." So there was definitely some French in Sam's ancestry.

24. The time and place of Wapáhaska's flight from his brick house and the American militia to take up a nomadic life is puzzling to me. Since the Sisseton Indian Reserve in South Dakota was not established until 1867, well after the 1862 war, could there have been a serious threat from a U.S. militia at that time? Sam's later reference to

the U.S. Army and General Custer would place *Wapáhaska* in western North Dakota or eastern Montana in 1876 when Custer was heading west to attack the Lakota and Cheyenne (an expedition that ended badly for him at the Battle of the Little Big Horn), but *Wapáhaska* was in Canada: the day after the signing of Treaty Four at Fort Qu'Appelle in 1874 he and Chief Standing Buffalo met Alexander Morris, Canada's minister of the interior, about obtaining land to live on (McCrady 2006, 44).

25. In 1873 the International Boundary Commission laid out the western portion of the U.S.A.-Canada boundary along the 49th parallel, as agreed to in the Convention of 1818 after the War of 1812 between Britain and the U.S.A. It was called the Medicine Line because it had appeared to have the magical powers of keeping the American troops from crossing it.

26. Sam may be referring to Assiniboia Territory Governor A. G. Dallas, Hudson's Bay Company Governor William McTavish, or more probably the Roman Catholic Bishop of Fort Garry (later Archbishop of St. Boniface) Alexandre Taché.

27. This trek to Prince Albert was 1876–77 (see part 3). Treaties 4 and 6 with the Cree and Saulteaux were made in 1874 and 1876. I believe that Sam may have confused two McKay families, which I discovered were separate families.

28. *Bdo/Biddow* also went by the name Flying Buffalo, as did his son Herbert (Leo Omani, e-mail to DB, May 21, 2007). Mniyo says that *Bdo* got a job at Emmanuel College in Prince Albert (because at Fort Garry he was trained to be a maintenance man) and lived west of the Prince Albert penitentiary site until 1898, when he moved to the new reserve 94A. When he married a Wahpeton, they told him to stay! He married again, his wife's sister. So he married two sisters, both Wahpetons (Mniyo, August 1996).

29. The people lived at the Sioux Camp or Wahpeton Indian Reserve 94B site "until the flu epidemic of 1917 wiped out 20 of the 25 families. The remaining five families . . . kept using 94B in the summer through the 1930s and 1940s" (Leo Omani, interview with DB, September 13, 2007).

30. By Dakota minority movement I believe Sam refers to a sense of Dakota identity and destiny, stronger at some times than others, through Dakota history. He may also mean a type of nationalism movement including movement toward greater self-awareness as a Dakota nation or even a Great Sioux Nation (*Dakóta Oyáte*).

31. In my view the central difference between the two periods Sam describes — the short-lived initial period of "living well" on the Indian Reserve and the ensuing period of "we live disorderly" — is the degree of autonomy, power or control the people had over their own affairs. This was associated also with retention of their Dakota identity. The initial period had high autonomy and minimal interference from government officials and others. But as Rupert Ross, when an assistant crown attorney at Kenora, Ontario, states in his insightful description of disempowerment in the context of colonization, residential schools, and criminal behavior, the second period was marked with several types of interference: with physical movement (the pass system, whereby aboriginal people were not permitted to leave their home reserve unless specifically permitted by the Indian agent); with selling farm products; and with cultural practices (traditional language and ceremonies, "making it punishable

by jail for aboriginal people to participate in certain traditional ceremonies" (Ross 2009, 6). The community thus was subjected to two major tools of colonization of aboriginal people: disempowerment and disconnection.

In the earlier period, although the Dakota who came to Canada after 1862 had been granted reserves, they had not entered into treaties. Many had been farming since the early 1800s in Minnesota, were skilled farm workers whose labor was in demand in the new settlements, did not require much assistance from the Dominion of Canada authorities, and were largely economically autonomous. For a time they were almost ignored and relatively free of the oppressive management of the Department of Indian Affairs. This was in contrast to the plight of the overwhelming majority of First Nations (Cree, Saulteaux and Assiniboine) who had signed treaties (Treaty Four in 1874 and Treaty Six in 1876) and who had depended wholly on the bison herds. When the herds collapsed suddenly and finally in the late 1870s, this provoked a regionwide famine, malnutrition if not outright starvation, and widespread emergence of tuberculosis in the indigenous population. They were dependent on the federal government, which used food aid policy as a tool for their subjugation and control (Daschuk 2013, 125–26).

32. "And he made from one every nation of men to live on the all the face of the earth, having determined allotted periods and the boundaries of their habitation, that they should seek God, in the hope that they might feel after him and find him. Yet he is not far from each one of us" (Acts 17: 26–27, *Holy Bible*, Revised Standard Version, 1946).

Part 3. The Narratives of Robert Goodvoice

1. Robert Dickson was a British trader ("a red-headed Scotch trader") who married the sister of the great hereditary Sisseton-Yanktonai Dakota chief Red Thunder. He became the leading trader in the "northwest" and had extensive influence with the Dakota. After being appointed a colonel in the British Army, "Dickson enlisted Red Thunder and a number of other Dakota leaders in the British cause during the war of 1812 against the Americans" (Diedrich 1987, 30).

Diedrich says that *Waneta* (the Charger), born about 1795, a Yanktonai chief, was the son of Chief Red Thunder, with whom he served in the 1813 campaign against American-held forts in the Ohio country. Although he was quite young, the British recognized his valor and rewarded him with a captain's commission and various medals. "Two of his sons, Black Catfish and *Waanatan* (or Little Charger) became chiefs" (Diedrich 1987, 31). I believe that this *Waneta* is the young chief whom Robert Goodvoice refers to as *Waánataŋ*, because *Waneta*'s son *Waánataŋ* II would be too young to be considered.

2. Regarding the photos of the King George III medal: on the obverse side (left) of this medal is a bust of King George III facing right. The inscription, written in Latin, reads: "GEORGIUS III DEI GRATIA" (By the grace of God, George III). On the reverse side appear in high relief the royal arms, surrounded by a ribbon with motto in French, "HONI SOIT QUI MAL Y PENSE" (Spurned be the one who thinks evil),

surmounted by a crown, supported by the lion and the unicorn; at the bottom is a ribbon with motto in French, "DIEU ET MON DROIT" (God and my right, meaning my divine right to govern). The medal is silver, 3 inches (7.5 cm.) in diameter, with loop for suspension.

3. King George III medals were given to Dakota and other Indian allies for their support for the British in two wars: the War of 1812 and the earlier American War of Independence (1775–83). Although at the close of the war of 1812 the British government did produce and present silver medals to chiefs "marking its appreciation of the services rendered by its Indian allies," this particular medal [held at the Prince Albert Historical Museum] does not match their description. Of about a dozen different medals issued by the government in the 1700s and 1800s, this medal matches most closely those presented in 1778, when "A large body of Indians assembled in general council in Montreal, Aug. 17, 1778, representing the Sioux, Sauk, Foxes, Menominee, Winnebago, Ottawa, Potawatomi, and Chippewa." This was "in consideration of the assistance rendered the British in the campaigns of Kentucky and Illinois and during the war of the Revolution" (*Handbook of Indians in Canada* 1974 [1913], 281–85).

"The Canadian Dakota oral tradition retains the names of eleven Santee chiefs who received George III medals on August 17, 1778, in recognition of the assistance given during the War of Independence: *Wabasha* (Red-standard) of the Mdewakantons; *Hin-ton-kasa-wakan* (Sacred-weasel) of the Mdewakantons; *Wakan-to* (Blue-above) of the Wahpekutes; *Wakinyan-duta* (Red-thunder) a Sisseton; *Hupa-duta* (Red-wing), a Sisseton; *Inyang-mani* (Runs-walking), a Wahpeton; *Wambdi-hoton-mani* (Eagle-cries-walks), a Wahpeton; *Ta-cante* (His-heart), a Wahpeton; *Waanatan* (Charges-at), a Yanktonai; *Wamaza* (Maize), a Yankton; and *Ta-wahukeza-nonpa* (His-two-lances), a Teton" (Laviolette 1991, 101).

4. Lieutenant-Colonel Robert McDowall, British commander at Fort Michilimackinac, "reported that he gave the Dakotas a three-pound cannon from York Factory which they called the 'Little Dakota'" (Laviolette 1991, 108).

5. Both Robert Goodvoice and Sam Buffalo clearly do not agree with the common translation of *Oćéti Śakówiŋ* as Seven Council Fires.

6. I was told by authorities at the Glenbow Museum in Calgary that no items from Round Plain/Wahpeton Dakota First Nation were there.

7. This must refer to the cairns marking the Canada-U.S.A. boundary along the 49th parallel between present Minnesota and Manitoba and west to the Rocky Mountains. These cairns were placed by the International Boundary Commission in 1873. Following the War of 1812 the Convention of 1818 established the 49th parallel north latitude as the southern boundary of Rupert's Land, initially the Hudson Bay watershed, which was controlled by the British (Brown 2001, 300) and became Canada.

8. Anderson describes the Acton incident, causes of the Dakota War, and the war itself, which began in the Redwood Lower Sioux Agency on August 18, 1862 (Anderson 1986, 116 ff., 133 ff.; see my summary in note 7 to part 1, this volume).

9. "Where the man had fired the first shot, his name is Ṫawásu Óta. He came to Prince Albert in 1876 and stayed in Prince Albert district and died about 1909 or 1910. He died a natural death and is buried among the other Dakotas in the Prince Albert district" (Robert Goodvoice 8, 1977, 3).

10. Laviolette (1991) describes the kidnapping of two Mdewakanton chiefs, Little-Six (*Shakopee*), who was a half-brother of Little Crow, and Medicine-Bottle (*Tate-icasn-mani*); their transport by dog sled from Fort Garry to Pembina (in the United States); and their trial and execution for murder (151–53). Elias (1988) also describes the kidnapping of the Dakota chiefs *Shak'pay* and *Wakanozhan* by the Americans. In his daring raid on January 17 or 18, 1864, Lieutenant Cochrane of the Pembina garrison had them drugged with opium and chloroform, tied to a sled, and quickly hauled across the boundary to Pembina. They were taken to Fort Snelling in Minnesota and hanged on November 11, 1865 (23). These must be the men whom Goodvoice is referring to as *Iátokča* and *Ṫaté Icásna Máni*.

11. *Iŋkpadúta*: is this the same man as the Wahpekute war chief notorious for the 1857 Spirit Lake Massacre (Iowa), who was active in the 1876 Battle of the Little Bighorn and who fled to Canada where he died, but apparently in Manitoba in 1881? (Beck 2008). Goodvoice does not say.

12. The camp of *Húpa Iyáȟpeya* presumably was close to the Canadian-U.S. boundary but west of the Red River and south of Portage la Prairie.

13. Almost certainly this is James McKay, 1827–79, the influential Metis guide, interpreter, trader and politician. James McKay had been a freighter transporting goods from Minneapolis–St. Paul to Fort Garry (Winnipeg) across northwestern Minnesota, so he would have known the country well and he knew the Dakota language well. His wife was Marguerite Rowand, a wealthy Metis. They built a large home on the Assiniboine River just west of Fort Garry. Dakota chiefs considered him a friend and called at his house when passing by.

When the new (1867) Dominion of Canada took over ownership of the settlement, the French-speaking Metis (then called half-breeds) protested that they were not consulted. Like many other "English-speaking half-breeds," McKay did not actively join Louis Riel and his supporters when the unrest grew, although he helped with the early negotiations as they were drawing up the list of rights they wanted respected. He had a trusted position with both groups in the conflict but did not wish to take sides. When the Red River Resistance/Rebellion broke out in 1869 McKay and his wife left their home temporarily and went to the United States but only until the unrest was over (Grant 1994, 50–51). When the Province of Manitoba was established in 1870, he was appointed president of the Executive Council (Grant 1994, 84–85). James McKay was a treaty commissioner for Treaty 6 which was made in August and September 1876 in Fort Carlton, Northwest Territories (now Saskatchewan).

In 1915 he requested the government of Canada to allow the Dakota at the Wahpeton reserve to purchase adjacent land (rather than have it held in trust by the Crown), but this request was not accepted (see https://www.saskarchives.com/Dakota_Land, retrieved April 29, 2019). Thus the Dakota were denied both the advantages of Treaty Indian status and the Homestead Act privileges of non-Indigenous settlers.

It was in 1877 that my own grandfather Daniel Beveridge with his parents and family arrived in Winnipeg from Ontario and settled just west of the new city of three thousand inhabitants, not far from the McKay home.

14. A similar but brief account of this trek led by Chief *Húpa Iyáȟpeya* to the Prince Albert area, also referring to Hon. James McKay and to being guided by a star, is given by Laviolette (1991, 259).

Another account, probably written by Henry Two Bear, reports that ninety-seven families of Sioux Indians travelled on foot with travois ("two poles tied to a dog to transport their goods"). They left Portage la Prairie in March 1876, passed by Fort Qu'Appelle in June, and in October 1876 came to Prince Albert, which then had only three stores (Henry Two Bear, Records of Henry Two Bear, Provincial Archives of Saskatchewan, Regina SK, call no. R-625, file 5.4).

15. Probably the Carlton Trail, the important ox-cart trail from Winnipeg to Fort Carlton, used until the completion of the Canadian Pacific Railway westward about 1883.

16. Lucy Baker (1836–1909) came to Prince Albert in 1878 as a missionary teacher for the Presbyterian Church in Canada. She established the day school and church at the new Round Plain Reserve and remained until her retirement in 1905 (or 1907); Herbert Buffalo was one of her pupils. See MacEwan (1975) for a chapter on her life, and Provincial Archives of Saskatchewan (PAS) for a documentary exhibit at https://www.saskarchives.com/dakota_Intro_Essay.

17. My summary of Robert's listing of Wahpeton hereditary chiefs:

First chief (soon after move to northeast in present-day Minnesota)

Son of first chief

Son of second chief

Šákpe (1851 to 1862)

Upí Iyahdéya (chief in the United States)

Ahíyaŋke (Round Plain 1893 to 1902)

Íto Imáza (Ahíyaŋke II) (Round Plain 1902 to 1936)

Part 4. Henry Two Bear and James Black (Jim Sapa)

1. Size of items is song stick 34.6 cm x 1.6 cm; diary notebook 13.5 cm long x 15.5 cm wide when open; picture book "A" 13.6 cm long; picture book "B" 16.5 cm long. Pages, some smudged or stained, have very rounded corners, probably cut to remove worn edges, and are held together with hand-stitched linen thread. My photographs of the two picture books consist of 48 color prints with two pages in each photo.

2. This book, diaries for the period 1911–29, and other items from the estate are held at the Saskatchewan Archives in Regina.

3. Mniyo discusses the *Wakáŋ Waćípi* in interviews with Howard (1984), in oral history recordings (Goodvoice 1977), and in interviews with me. Skinner (1920) indicates that the *Mide* ceremony serves to repeat the origin myth. It may also serve as

a reenactment of the migration from the East. Skinner (281–83) lists "The Ten Rules of Life" associated with the Wahpeton rite of *mide*, including: "Love your neighbors. . . . Respect the fellow members of the *Wakanwacipi*. . . . The members of the *Wakanwacipi* are as one and should regard each other equal." Some members were women (Mniyo, interview).

4. Mniyo says he observed James Black reading these books at a *Wakáŋ Waćípi* feast at Moose Wood reserve in 1951, which he claims was the last *Wakáŋ Waćípi* feast ever held. He says the last complete ceremony was held at the Sioux Village near Portage la Prairie, Manitoba, in 1934.

5. The syllabic alphabet developed by Rev. James Evans is used by the Cree in northern Saskatchewan and Manitoba and by the eastern Inuit.

6. Rev. Dr. Ahab Spence, linguistics professor at Saskatchewan Indian Federated College, Regina, agrees with Cuthand that the syllabics are written mostly in the Woods Cree or "N" dialect now spoken around Cumberland House and The Pas, with some Swampy Cree (a northern Manitoba dialect) mixed in. The translation by Rev. Nelson Hart of Nelson House, Manitoba, is similar to Cuthand's. Hart also finds some syllabics difficult to decipher because they are in a different dialect.

7. Sam says that Henry was afraid of the U.S. scouts looking for Sioux in Canada. Sam says James *Kiŋyéwakaŋ* (of Sioux Valley near Griswold, Manitoba) told him that Henry Two Bear left Griswold when he was discovered by two visitors from the United States, presumably scouts for the U.S. government. Sam also spoke of one white scout working for the U.S. government, but claiming to represent a church, who came to the Prince Albert area and poisoned one hundred people one winter. He spoke fluently. He had a long house on the airport road (near Prince Albert) with tables; he called them in and gave them food, all one winter; in the spring he packed up and left, and soon after, the Indians died. Why? To wipe out the Dakotas, like Custer wanted to wipe out all the Sioux (Mniyo April 30, 1985).

Robert Goodvoice tells four similar stories of treachery by Americans against the Dakota who had fled to the Prince Albert area, including distribution of disease-infested clothing and poisoned food, which killed many families (Robert Goodvoice 5, 1977, 11).

8. Leo Omani, a great-grandchild of John Sioux, recalls, "When I was 12 years of age, my late mother, *Mahpeya Ku Winyan* (Edith Omani), having me bury the 'Medicine Bundle' of my late grandfather, *Maypeya Omani* (Joe Omani), the son of *Aŋpétu Waśíćuŋ* /John Sioux, which contained all the 'Medicine Bowls' for the Dakota '*Wakáŋ Waćípi*,' meaning the 'Dakota Medicine Lodge'" . . . . (Leo Omani, e-mail to DB, September 6, 2007).

9. The first *Mazámani* died of smallpox in 1838. His son *Mazámani*, who signed the Treaty of Traverse des Sioux on behalf of the Wahpetons in 1851 and also the 1858 treaty, died in 1862 in the Dakota War of 1862 (near present Montevideo on the upper Minnesota River) while carrying a white flag of truce. Both were *Wakáŋ Waćípi* leaders.

10. See White Hat (2012, 122 ff.) regarding the key role of the stone in creation and the Lakota origin story.

11. Further research is needed to determine the place of these phrases in the ceremony or the context in which they were written down.

12. It was Harry Buffalo at Moose Woods (Whitecap Dakota) Reserve who lent me the two notebooks in or about 1968, at which time I had them photographed.

13. Charlie Hawk's wife Eva was a sister of Herbert, Sam's father. Charlie Hawk taught at the on-reserve day school at Whitecap, the first Whitecap member to do so, in the early 1900s. The Charles Red Hawk Elementary School there is named after him.

14. In 1914 the *wakan a tci'pi* (*Wakáŋ Waćípi*) at Portage la Prairie had a membership of seven men and six women (Wallis 1947, 71). In 1920 Skinner noted that the Medicine Dance ceremony was still performed by "Eastern Dakota refugees near Portage La Prairie, Manitoba." Among other Siouan tribes, he claimed that it still survived among some bands of Winnebago in the United States and among some non-Siouan tribes: the Menomini, Ojibwa, Potawatomi, and Sauk (Skinner 1920, 10).

15. Sam says that after James Black died, some of his *Wakáŋ Waćípi* items, an otter skin medicine bag and contents, may have been sold, perhaps to the Glenbow Museum in Calgary (Mniyo May 1985). My inquiry at Glenbow Museum in Calgary in May 1988, however, did not turn up material from any Canadian Sioux Indian Reserve. Likewise, my inquiry to Glenbow in November 2010 and subsequent search of their collection did not locate any medicine bag nor any material from the Whitecap or Wahpeton Dakota First Nations (Conaty 2010).

16. The Ghost Dance was a revitalization movement that originated in the United States and reached the Dakota in Saskatchewan in modified form around 1900. As Sam Buffalo and Robert Goodvoice told James Howard, the version called New Tidings (*Wóyaka Ťeċa*) was brought by Fred Robinson, a *Hóhe* (Assiniboine) from Wolf Point, Montana, and persisted in Round Plain and Whitecap as late as 1950 (Howard 1984, 175). Herbert Buffalo, Sam's father, was an active member and had a Ghost Dance shirt. I mention this here because in his description of the Ghost Dance to Howard Sam refers to the *Ċaŋkú Dúta*, thus indicating a remarkable continuing influence of that tradition. Sam says that in the typical ceremony, the group would meet at someone's house and sit on the floor in a circle: "In the middle of the floor was a small mound of earth. Going from east to west across this circle was a trail of red paint [*wasé*]. This symbolized the *ċaŋkú dúta* or good red path" (Howard 1984, 176). As Howard concludes, "it is apparent that the earlier Medicine Dance and its ancillary rite, the Medicine Feast, had a strong influence on the . . . (Prayer Feast) and the *Wóyaka Ťeċa* (New Tidings) Ghost Dance derivatives (178).

Alice Kehoe, an American anthropologist who visited Wahpeton, states that Henry Two Bear was the leader of a New Tidings Ghost Dance congregation at Round Plain, which she claims gathered regularly for many years. In 1961 Two Bear recited to Kehoe the lengthy origin story of "New Tidings" in Dakota, which Two Bear's stepson Robert Goodvoice translated into English for her. For Kehoe, New Tidings at Round Plain was an example of revitalization of traditional Dakota beliefs and ceremonies (Kehoe 1989, 47–48). But New Tidings came to an end and with it came the end of this story of the Red Road and the *Wakáŋ Waćípi* of the Dakota.

Bibliography

The narration sessions of Samuel Buffalo/Samuel Mniyo are listed here as unpublished items. Several of these were recorded. The recordings were transcribed and edited by Daniel M. Beveridge. The Provincial Archives of Saskatchewan (PAS) has a copy of any tapes made and has completed cataloguing. They may be accessed as sound recordings by date and author. PAS is in the process of making these available online.

Unpublished

Buffalo, Samuel (see also Mniyo, Samuel). May 30, 1965. Speech at Wahpeton Reserve cemetery. Tape and transcript.

———. December 27, 1966. Song stick. Letter to Dan Beveridge.

———. January 1, 1967. Telephone interview with Dan Beveridge.

———. 1967 (date unknown). Narration session with Dan Beveridge.

———. 1977. Four tapes. In Goodvoice, Robert (Collector). Oral History of the Wahpaton Dakota (Saskatchewan Sound Archives Program), in Provincial Archives of Saskatchewan, Regina SK. Accessible online at www.uregina.ca/library as Samuel Buffalo 1, 2, etc. See also appendix 4, this volume.

Buffalo, Samuel I., and Daniel M. Beveridge. January 3, 1967. Draft research proposal regarding the Wakan Wacipi (Holy Dance) of the Dakota, and its significance in Dakota society.

Conaty, Gerald. 2010, December 13. Personal communication (telephone), reply to my e-mail letter of November 22, 2010.

Garcia, Louis. 1988, June 12. Covering Letter. Henry Two Bear, Records of. Call no. R-625, Provincial Archives of Saskatchewan, Regina SK.

Goodvoice, Robert (Collector). Oral History of the Wahpaton Dakota (Saskatchewan Sound Archives Program). 1977. 3 informants, 17 cassette tapes, 16 hours, with transcripts. In Provincial Archives of Saskatchewan, Regina SK [transcripts only also in First Nations University Library, Regina SK]. Includes Samuel Buffalo, Informant: four cassette tapes, call nos. R-A1344 to R-A1347. See appendix 4, this volume, for summary of contents, with key to reference interviews with Samuel Buffalo and Robert Goodvoice. Accessible online at www.uregina.ca/library: Robert Goodvoice 1, 2, etc., and Samuel Buffalo 1, 2, etc.

Mniyo, Samuel (see also Buffalo, Samuel). April 30 and May 1, 1985. Narration session with Dan Beveridge. Tape #1.

———. January 26, 1986. Personal correspondence to Dan Beveridge

———. April 12, 1986. Narration session with Dan Beveridge. No tape record.

———. April 28, 1986. Narration session with Dan Beveridge. No tape record.

———. January 1987. Narration session with Dan Beveridge. No tape record.

———. September 30, 1987. Narration session with Dan Beveridge. No tape record.

———. June 13, 1988. Narration session with Dan Beveridge. No tape record.

———. March 20, 1990. Narration session with Dan Beveridge. No tape record.

———. August 1996. Narration session with Dan Beveridge. No tape record.

———. May 10, 1997. Narration session with Dan Beveridge. Tape #2.

———. May 31, 1997. Narration session with Dan Beveridge. Tapes #3 and #4.

Omani, Leo J. 2011. "Aboriginal Diplomacy—Saskatchewan Dakota/Lakota Elders Perspectives: The Original Concepts of Dakota *Oyate* Treaty-Making, as Well as the Canadian Treaty Process." Unpublished paper.

Provincial Archives of Saskatchewan. "Documenting the Dakota" exhibit. Accessible at https://www.saskarchives.com/dakota_Intro_Essay. Retrieved April 29, 2019.

Two Bear, Henry. No date. *Waskuyeca wohampi* (Songs for *Wakan Wacipi*). File 5.2, (Notebooks ca 1943–1945), Call no. R-625, Records of Henry Two Bear. Provincial Archives of Saskatchewan, Regina SK.

Two Bear, Henry. Papers (see Henry Two Bear, Records of; see also Guide to Records of Henry Two Bear, SAFA 70, Provincial Archives of Saskatchewan, Regina, SK).

Two Bear, Henry. Records of Henry Two Bear. Call no. R-625. Provincial Archives of Saskatchewan, Regina SK.

Whitecap Dakota First Nation. January 22, 2018. Framework Agreement for a Whitecap Dakota Treaty to Advance Dakota Reconciliation. Accessible at http://whitecapdakota.com/wp-content/uploads/2018/01/WDFN-Treaty-Framework-1.pdf. Retrieved April 20, 2019.

Whitecap Dakota First Nation Signs Framework Agreement for Treaty. January 22, 2018. Accessible at https://www.cbc.ca/news/ . . . /whitecap-dakota-nation-treaty-framework-1.4502549. Retrieved April 20, 2019.

Whitecap Dakota First Nation. 2019. "Whitecap Dakota Lessons: Exploring Dakota History, Language and Culture." Accessible at http://dakotalessons.ca. Retrieved May 1, 2019.

Published

Albers, Patricia C. 2001. "Santee." In *Handbook of North American Indians*, vol. 13: *Plains*, ed. Raymond J. DeMallie, pt. 2 of 2, 761–76. William C. Sturtevant, gen. ed. Washington DC: Smithsonian Institution.

Anderson, Gary Clayton. 1986. *Little Crow: Spokesman for the Sioux*. St. Paul: Minnesota Historical Society Press.

———. 1997. *Kinsmen of Another Kind: Dakota-White Relations in the Upper Mississippi Valley, 1650–1862*. St. Paul: Minnesota Historical Society Press (originally published Lincoln: University of Nebraska Press, 1984).

Angel, Michael. 2002. *Preserving the Sacred: Historical Perspectives on the Ojibwa Midewiwin*. Winnipeg: University of Manitoba Press.

Beck, Paul N. 2008. *Inkpaduta: Dakota Leader.* Norman: University of Oklahoma Press.

Beveridge, Daniel M. 1964. *The Socio-Ecological Correlates of Economic Dependence in Four Dakota (Sioux) Communities in Saskatchewan.* Unpublished M.A. thesis, University of Saskatchewan, Saskatoon.

———. 1987. "A Prairie Puzzle: The *Wakan-Wacipi* Dakota Song Stick." *Indian Record* (Winnipeg MB), vol. 50, no. 4 (October), 11–12.

Beveridge, Thomas M. 1992. *A Beveridge-McLeish Family History.* Regina SK: D. M. Beveridge, 3619 Van Horne Ave., S4S 1M5 (self-published).

Brown, Jennifer S. H. 2001. "History of the Canadian Plains until 1870." In *Handbook of North American Indians,* vol. 13: *Plains,* ed. Raymond J. DeMallie, pt. 1 of 2, 300–12. William C. Sturtevant, gen. ed. Washington DC: Smithsonian Institution.

Cadotte, Marcel. 1985. "Epidemic." In *The Canadian Encyclopedia,* vol. 1, 557. Edmonton AB: Hurtig Publishers.

Cajete, Gregory. 2000. *Native Science: Natural Laws of Interdependence.* Santa Fe NM: Clear Light Publishers.

Danyluk, Stephanie. 2014. "'Recollecting Sovereignty': First Nations–Crown Alliance and the Legacy of the War of 1812." In *Canada and the Crown: Essays in Constitutional Monarchy,* ed. D. Michael Jackson and Philippe Lagassé, 239–53. Montreal: McGill-Queen's University Press.

Danyluk, Stephanie, Max Faille, Jarita Greyeyes, and George Rathwell. 2016. *Wa Pa Ha Ska: Whitecap Dakota First Nation.* Saskatoon SK: Whitecap Dakota First Nation and Office of the Treaty Commissioner.

Daschuk, James. 2013. *Clearing the Plains: Disease, Politics of Starvation, and the Loss of Aboriginal Life.* Regina SK: University of Regina Press.

Deloria, Ella. 1998. *Speaking of Indians.* Lincoln: University of Nebraska Press (originally published New York: Friendship Press, 1944).

DeMallie, Raymond J. 1987. "Lakota Belief and Ritual in the Nineteenth Century." In *Sioux Indian Religion: Tradition and Innovation,* ed. Raymond J. DeMallie and Douglas R. Parks, 25–44. Norman: University of Oklahoma Press.

———. 2001b. "Sioux Until 1850." In *Handbook of North American Indians,* vol. 13: *Plains,* ed. Raymond J. DeMallie, pt. 2 of 2, 718–60. William C. Sturtevant, gen. ed. Washington DC: Smithsonian Institution.

———. 2001c. "Yankton and Yanktonai." In *Handbook of North American Indians,* vol. 13: *Plains,* ed. Raymond J. DeMallie, pt. 2 of 2, 777–93. William C. Sturtevant, gen. ed. Washington DC: Smithsonian Institution.

Densmore, Frances. 1929. *Chippewa Customs.* Bureau of American Ethnology Bulletin 86. Washington DC: Smithsonian Institution.

Dewdney, Selwyn. 1975. *The Sacred Scrolls of the Southern Ojibway.* Toronto: University of Toronto Press, for the Glenbow-Alberta Institute, Calgary AB.

Diedrich, Mark. 1987. *Famous Chiefs of the Eastern Sioux.* Minneapolis MN: Coyote Books.

Dorsey, James O. 1897. "Siouan Sociology." In *Fifteenth Annual Report of the Bureau of Ethnology to the Secretary of the Smithsonian Institution 1893-94,* ed. J. W. Powell, 213–44. Washington DC: Government Printing Office.

Eastman, Charles A. 1971. *Indian Boyhood*. New York: Dover (originally published 1902).

Elias, Peter Douglas. 1988. *The Dakota of the Canadian Northwest: Lessons for Survival*. Winnipeg: University of Manitoba Press.

———. 1999. "Dakota." In *The Canadian Encyclopedia*. 618–19. Toronto: McClelland and Stewart.

Erikson, Erik H. 1950. *Childhood and Society*. New York: Norton.

Ferguson, Mary M. 1972. *The Honourable James McKay of Deer Lodge*. Winnipeg, MB: M. M. Ferguson, 62 Deer Lodge Place.

Giese, Paula. 1997. "Norval Morrisseau and Medicine Painting." Native American Indian Resources. Accessible at http://www.kstrom.net/isk/art/morriss/art_morr.html. Retrieved April 26, 2019.

Gillette, G. M. 1906. "The Medicine Society of the Dakota Indians." *Collections of the Historical Society of North Dakota* 1: 459–74.

Goddard, I. 2001. "The Languages of the Plains: Introduction." In *Handbook of North American Indians*, vol. 13: *Plains*, ed. Raymond J. DeMallie, pt. 1 of 2, 61–70. William C. Sturtevant, gen. ed. Washington DC: Smithsonian Institution.

Grant, Agnes. 1994. *James McKay: A Metis Builder of Canada*. Winnipeg, MB: Pemmican Publications.

Handbook of Indians in Canada. 1974. Toronto: Coles Canadiana Edition (originally published Ottawa: Geographic Board of Canada, C. H. Parmalee, 1913).

Hassrick, Royal B. 1964. *The Sioux: Life and Customs of a Warrior Society*. Norman: University of Oklahoma Press.

Hoffman, Walter James. 2005. *The Mide'wiwin: "Grand Medicine Society" of the Ojibway*. Honolulu, Hawaii: University Press of the Pacific (reprinted from 1891 edition).

Holy Bible, Revised Standard Version. 1946. New York: Thomas Nelson and Sons.

Howard, James H. 1952. "A Yanktonai Dakota Mide Bundle." *North Dakota History* 19, no. 1: 132–39.

———. 1953. "Notes on Two Dakota 'Holy Dance' Medicines and Their Uses." *American Anthropologist* 55: 608–9.

———. 1966. *The Dakota or Sioux Indians: A Study in Human Ecology*. Anthropological Papers no. 2. Vermillion: Dakota Museum, University of South Dakota.

———. 1984. *The Canadian Sioux*. Lincoln: University of Nebraska Press.

———. 2014. *The Canadian Sioux*. 2nd ed. Lincoln: University of Nebraska Press.

Kehoe, Alice B. 1989. *The Ghost Dance: Ethnohistory and Revitalization*. Chicago: Holt, Rinehart and Winston.

LaFontaine, Harlan, and Neil McKay. 2004. *550 Dakota Verbs*. St. Paul: Minnesota Historical Society Press.

Landes, Ruth. 1968a. *The Mystic Lake Sioux: Sociology of the Mdewakantonwan Santee*. Madison: University of Wisconsin Press.

———. 1968b. *Ojibwa Religion and the Midewiwin*. Madison: University of Wisconsin Press.

Laviolette, Gontran. 1991. *The Dakota Sioux in Canada*. Winnipeg MB: DLM Publications.

MacEwan, Grant. 1975. "Lucy Margaret Baker: With the Brave Heart of a Bullfighter." In *And Mighty Women Too: Stories of Notable Western Canadian Women*, 76–83. Saskatoon SK: Western Producer Prairie Books.

Mallery, Garrick. 1972. *Picture-Writing of the American Indians*. 2 vols. New York: Dover Publications.

Marino, Mary C. 2002. "Siouans." In *Aboriginal Peoples of Canada.*, ed. P. R. Magocsi, 251–63. Toronto: University of Toronto Press.

Maroukis, Thomas C. 2004. *Peyote and the Yankton Sioux: The Life and Times of Sam Necklace*. Norman: University of Oklahoma Press.

Martin, J. B. 2004. "Languages." In *Handbook of North American Indians*, vol. 14: *Southeast*, ed. R. D. Fogelson, 68–86. William C. Sturtevant, gen. ed. Washington DC: Smithsonian Institution.

McCrady, David G. 2006. *Living with Strangers: The Nineteenth-Century Sioux and the Canadian-American Borderlands*. Lincoln: University of Nebraska Press.

McGee, W. J. 1897. "The Siouan Indians: A Preliminary Sketch." In J. W. Powell, *Fifteenth Annual Report of the Bureau of Ethnology to the Secretary of the Smithsonian Institution 1893-94*, 157–204. Washington DC: Government Printing Office.

Neihardt, John D. 1972. *Black Elk Speaks: Being the Life Story of a Holy Man of the Oglala Sioux*. New York: Pocket Books (originally published 1932).

Office of the Treaty Commissioner (Saskatchewan). 2015. *The Story of the Dakota Oyate and the People of Standing Buffalo*. *Saskatoon* SK: Office of the Treaty Commissioner (Saskatchewan).

———. 2015. *Wahpeton Dakota Nation: The Story of the Dakota Oyate in Canada*. Saskatoon SK: Office of the Treaty Commissioner (Saskatchewan).

Omani, Leo J. 2010. "Perspectives of Saskatchewan Dakota/Lakota Elders on the Treaty Process within Canada." Unpublished doctoral dissertation, University of Saskatchewan, Saskatoon.

Oneroad, Amos E., and Alanson B. Skinner. 2003. *Being Dakota: Tales and Traditions of the Sisseton and Wahpeton*. Ed. L. Anderson. St. Paul: Minnesota Historical Society Press.

Parks, Douglas R., and Raymond J. DeMallie. 1992. "Sioux, Assiniboine, and Stoney Dialects: A Classification." *Anthropological Linguistics* 34, nos. 1–4: 233–55.

Parks, Douglas R., and Robert L. Rankin. 2001. "Siouan Languages." In *Handbook of North American Indians*, vol. 13: *Plains*, ed. Raymond J. DeMallie, pt. 1 of 2, 94–114. William C. Sturtevant, gen. ed. Washington DC: Smithsonian Institution.

Pond, Samuel W. 1986. *The Dakota or Sioux as They Were in 1834*. St. Paul: Minnesota Historical Society Press (originally published in *Minnesota Historical Collections*, vol. 12, 1908).

Ray, Arthur J. 1974. *Indians in the Fur Trade*. Toronto: University of Toronto Press.

Riggs, Stephen R. 1992. *A Dakota-English Dictionary*. St. Paul: Minnesota Historical Society Press (originally published Washington DC: Government Printing Office, 1890).

Ross, Rupert. 2009. "Criminal Conduct and Colonization: Exploring the Link." Accessible at http://www.wabano.com/wp-content/uploads/2015/03/Criminal-Conduct-And-Colonization-Rupert-Ross.pdf. Retrieved May 22, 2019.

Rudes, Blair A., Thomas J. Blumer, and J. Alan May. 2004. "Catawba and Neighboring Groups." In *Handbook of North American Indians*, vol. 14: *Southeast*, ed. R. D. Fogelson, 301–18. William C. Sturtevant, gen. ed. Washington DC: Smithsonian Institution.

Skinner, Alanson. 1920. *Medicine Ceremony of the Menomini, Iowa, and Wahpeton Dakota, With Notes on the Ceremony Among the Ponca, Bungi Ojibwa, and Potawatomi*. Indian Notes and Monographs 4. New York: Museum of the American Indian, Heye Foundation.

Spector, Janet D. 1993. *What This Awl Means: Feminist Archaeology at a Wahpeton Dakota Village*. St. Paul: Minnesota Historical Society Press.

Stonechild, Blair. 2016. *The Knowledge Seeker: Embracing Indigenous Spirituality*. Regina: University of Regina Press.

Turner, Allan R. 2000. "James McKay." *Dictionary of Canadian Biography Online*, vol. X. University of Toronto and Universite Laval. Accessible at http://www.biographi.ca. Retrieved December 23, 2010.

Ullrich, Jan F. 2008. *The New Lakhota Dictionary: Lakhotiyapi-English/English-Lakhotiyapi and Incorporating the Dakota Dialects of Yankton-Yanktonai and Santee-Sisseton*. Bloomington IN: Lakota Language Consortium.

Walker, James R. 1980. *Lakota Belief and Ritual*. Ed. Raymond J. DeMallie, and Elaine A. Jahner. Lincoln: University of Nebraska Press.

Wahpeton Dakota Nation Community History. 2012. Wahpeton Dakota Nation SK.

Wallis, Wilson D. 1947. *The Canadian Dakota*. Anthropological Papers 41, part 1. New York: American Museum of Natural History.

Westerman, Gwen, and Bruce White. 2012. *Mni Sota Macoce: The Land of the Dakota*. St. Paul: Minnesota Historical Society Press.

White Hat, Albert. 1999. *Reading and Writing the Lakota Language*. Salt Lake City: University of Utah Press.

———. 2012. *Life's Journey—Zuya: Oral Teachings from Rosebud*. Salt Lake City: University of Utah Press.

Williamson, John P. 1902. *An English-Dakota Dictionary*. New York: American Tract Society.

Wilson, Waziyatawin Angela. 2005. *Remember This! Dakota Decolonization and the Eli Taylor Narratives*. Lincoln: University of Nebraska Press.

Woolworth, Alan R. 1997. "James H. Howard, Ethnographer (1925–1982) Observations and Recollections of a Friend." *Kansas Anthropologist* 18, no. 2: 59–70.

Powhatan's World and Colonial Virginia: A Conflict of Cultures
By Frederic W. Gleach

Native Languages and Language Families of North America
(folded study map and wall display map)
Compiled by Ives Goddard

Native Languages of the Southeastern United States
Edited by Heather K. Hardy and Janine Scancarelli

The Heiltsuks: Dialogues of Culture and History on the Northwest Coast
By Michael E. Harkin

Prophecy and Power among the Dogrib Indians
By June Helm

A Totem Pole History: The Work of Lummi Carver Joe Hillaire
By Pauline Hillaire
Edited by Gregory P. Fields

Corbett Mack: The Life of a Northern Paiute
As told by Michael Hittman

The Spirit and the Sky: Lakota Visions of the Cosmos
By Mark Hollabaugh

The Canadian Sioux
By James H. Howard

The Canadian Sioux, Second Edition
By James H. Howard, with a new foreword by Raymond J. DeMallie and
Douglas R. Parks

*Yuchi Ceremonial Life: Performance, Meaning, and Tradition in a Contemporary
American Indian Community*
By Jason Baird Jackson

*Comanche Ethnography: Field Notes of E. Adamson Hoebel, Waldo R. Wedel,
Gustav G. Carlson, and Robert H. Lowie*
Compiled and edited by Thomas W. Kavanagh

The Comanches: A History, 1706–1875
By Thomas W. Kavanagh

Koasati Dictionary
By Geoffrey D. Kimball with the assistance of Bel Abbey, Martha John, and
Ruth Poncho

Koasati Grammar
By Geoffrey D. Kimball with the assistance of Bel Abbey, Nora Abbey,
Martha John, Ed John, and Ruth Poncho

Koasati Traditional Narratives
By Geoffrey D. Kimball

Kiowa Belief and Ritual
By Benjamin Kracht

The Salish Language Family: Reconstructing Syntax
By Paul D. Kroeber

Tales from Maliseet Country: The Maliseet Texts of Karl V. Teeter
Translated and edited by Philip S. LeSourd

The Medicine Men: Oglala Sioux Ceremony and Healing
By Thomas H. Lewis

A Grammar of Creek (Muskogee)
By Jack B. Martin

A Dictionary of Creek/Muskogee
By Jack B. Martin and Margaret McKane Mauldin

The Red Road and Other Narratives of the Dakota Sioux
Samuel Minyo and Robert Goodvoice
Edited by Daniel M. Beveridge

Wolverine Myths and Visions: Dene Traditions from Northern Alberta
Edited by Patrick Moore and Angela Wheelock

Ceremonies of the Pawnee
By James R. Murie
Edited by Douglas R. Parks

Households and Families of the Longhouse Iroquois at Six Nations Reserve
By Merlin G. Myers
Foreword by Fred Eggan
Afterword by M. Sam Cronk

Archaeology and Ethnohistory of the Omaha Indians: The Big Village Site
By John M. O'Shea and John Ludwickson

Traditional Narratives of the Arikara Indians (4 vols.)
By Douglas R. Parks

A Dictionary of Skiri Pawnee
By Douglas R. Parks and Lula Nora Pratt

Osage Grammar
By Carolyn Quintero

*A Fur Trader on the Upper Missouri: The Journal and Description of Jean-Baptiste Tru-
teau, 1794–1796*
By Jean-Baptiste Truteau
Edited by Raymond J. DeMallie, Douglas R. Parks, and Robert Vézina
Translated by Mildred Mott Wedel, Raymond J. DeMallie, and Robert Vézina

They Treated Us Just Like Indians: The Worlds of Bennett County, South Dakota
By Paula L. Wagoner

A Grammar of Kiowa
By Laurel J. Watkins with the assistance of Parker McKenzie

To order or obtain more information on these or other University of Nebraska Press titles,
visit nebraskapress.unl.edu.